THE LIFE AND LETTERS OF
BENJAMIN FRANKLIN

THE LIFE AND LETTERS OF BENJAMIN FRANKLIN

E. M. HALE & COMPANY

Eau Claire, Wisconsin

PRINTED IN THE UNITED STATES OF AMERICA
AMERICAN BOOK—STRATFORD PRESS, INC., NEW YORK

CONTENTS

LIFE AND LETTERS
OF
BENJAMIN FRANKLIN

The Autobiography.

TWYFORD, *at the Bishop of St. Asaph's, 1771.*

DEAR SON: I have ever had pleasure in obtaining any little anecdotes of my ancestors. You may remember the inquiries I made among the remains of my relations when you were with me in England, and the journey I undertook for that purpose. Imagining it may be equally agreeable to you to know the circumstances of my life, many of which you are yet unacquainted with, and expecting the enjoyment of a week's uninterrupted leisure in my present country retirement, I sit down to write them for you. To which I have besides some other inducements. Having emerged from the poverty and obscurity in which I was born and bred, to a state of affluence and some degree of reputation in the world, and having gone so far through life with a considerable share of felicity, the conducing means I made use of, which with the blessing of God so well succeeded, my posterity may like to know, as they may find some of them suitable to their own situations, and therefore fit to be imitated.

That felicity, when I reflected on it, has induced me sometimes to say, that were it offered to my choice, I should have no objection to a repetition of the same life from its beginning, only asking the advantages authors have in a second edition to correct some faults of the first. So I might, besides correcting the faults, change some sinister accidents and events of it for others more favorable. But though this were denied, I should still accept the offer. Since such a repetition is not to be expected, the next thing most like living one's life over again seems to be a recollection of that life, and to make that recollection as durable as possible by putting it down in writing.

Hereby, too, I shall indulge the inclination so natural in old men, to be talking of themselves and their own past actions; and I shall indulge it without being tiresome to others, who, through respect to age, might conceive themselves obliged to give me a hearing, since this may be read or not as any one pleases. And, lastly (I may as well confess it, since my denial of it will be believed by nobody), perhaps I shall a good deal gratify my own *vanity*. Indeed, I scarce ever heard or saw the introductory words, "*Without vanity I may say*," &c., but some vain thing immediately followed. Most people dislike vanity in others, whatever share they have of it themselves; but I give it fair quarter wherever I meet with it, being persuaded that it is often productive of good to the possessor, and to others that are within his sphere of action; and therefore, in many cases, it would not be altogether absurd if a man were to thank God for his vanity among the other comforts of life.

And now I speak of thanking God, I desire with all humility to acknowledge that I owe the mentioned happiness of my past life to His kind providence, which led me to the means I used and gave them success. My belief of this induces me to *hope*, though I must not *presume*, that the same goodness will still be exercised toward me, in continuing that happiness, or enabling me to bear a fatal reverse, which I may experience as others have done; the complexion of my future fortune being known to Him only in whose power it is to bless to us even our afflictions.

The notes one of my uncles (who had the same kind of curiosity in collecting family anecdotes) once put into my hands, furnished me with several particulars relating to our ancestors. From these notes I learned that the family had lived in the same village, Ecton, in Northamptonshire, for three hundred years, and how much longer he knew not (perhaps from the time when the name of Franklin, that before was the name of an order of people, was assumed by them as a surname when others took surnames all over the kingdom), on a freehold of about thirty acres, aided by the smith's business, which had continued in the family till his time, the eldest son being always bred to that business; a custom which he and my father followed as to their eldest sons. When I searched the registers at Ecton, I found an account of their births, marriages and burials from the year 1555 only, there being no registers kept in that parish at any time preceding. By that register I perceived that I was the youngest son of the youngest son for five generations back. My grandfather Thomas, who was born in 1598, lived at Ecton till he grew too old to follow business longer, when he went to live with his son John, a dyer at Banbury, in Oxfordshire, with whom my father served an apprenticeship. There my grandfather died and lies buried. We saw his gravestone in 1758. His eldest son Thomas lived in the house at Ecton, and left it with the land to his only child, a daughter, who, with her husband, one Fisher, of Wellingborough, sold it to Mr. Isted, now lord of the manor there. My grandfather had four sons that grew up, viz.: Thomas, John, Benjamin and Josiah. I will give you what account I can of them, at this distance from my papers, and if these are not lost in my absence, you will among them find many more particulars.

Thomas was bred a smith under his father; but, being ingenious, and encouraged in learning (as all my brothers were) by an Esquire Palmer, then the principal gentleman in that parish, he qualified himself for the business of scrivener; became a considerable man in the county; was a chief mover of all public-spirited undertakings for the county or town of Northampton, and his own village, of which many instances were related of him; and much taken notice of and patronized by the then Lord Halifax. He died in 1702, January 6, old style, just four years to a day before I was born. The account we received of his life and character from some old people at Ecton, I remember, struck you as something extraordinary, from its similarity to what you knew of mine. "Had he died on the same day," you said, "one might have supposed a transmigration."

John was bred a dyer, I believe of woolens. Benjamin was bred a silk dyer, serving an apprenticeship at London. He was an ingenious man. I remember him well, for when I was a boy he came over to my father in Boston, and lived in the house with us some years. He lived to a great age. His grandson, Samuel Franklin, now lives in Boston. He left behind him two quarto volumes, MS., of his own poetry, consisting of little occasional pieces addressed to his friends and relations, of which the following, sent to me, is a specimen. He had formed a short-hand of his own, which he taught me, but, never practising it, I have now forgot it. I was named after this uncle, there being a particular affection between him and my father. He was very pious, a great attender of sermons of the best preachers, which he took down in his short-hand, and had with him many volumes of them. He was also much of a politician; too much, perhaps, for his station. There fell lately into my hands, in London, a collection he had made of all the principal pamphlets relating to public affairs, from 1641 to 1717; many of the volumes are wanting as appears by the numbering, but there still remain eight volumes in folio, and twenty-four in quarto and in octavo. A dealer in old books met with them, and knowing me by my sometimes buying of him, he brought them to me. It seems my uncle must have left them here when he went to America, which was above fifty years since. There are many of his notes in the margins.

This obscure family of ours was early in the Reformation, and continued Protestants through the reign of Queen Mary, when they were sometimes in danger of trouble on account of their zeal against popery. They had got an English Bible, and to conceal and secure it, it was fastened open with tapes under and within the cover of a joint-stool. When my great-great-grandfather read it to his family, he turned up the joint-stool upon his knees, turning over the leaves then under the tapes. One of the children stood at the door to give notice if he saw the apparitor coming, who was an officer of the spiritual court. In that case the stool was turned down again upon its feet, when the Bible remained concealed under it as before. This anecdote I had from my uncle Benjamin. The family continued all of the Church of England till about the end of Charles the Second's reign, when some of the ministers that had been outed for non-conformity holding conventicles in Northamptonshire, Benjamin and Josiah adhered to them, and so continued all their lives: the rest of the family remained with the Episcopal Church.

Josiah, my father, married young, and carried his wife with three children into New England, about 1682. The conventicles having been forbidden by law, and frequently disturbed, induced some considerable men of his acquaintance to remove to that country, and he was prevailed with to accompany them thither, where they expected to enjoy their mode of religion with freedom. By the same wife he had four children more born there, and by a second wife ten more, in all seventeen; of which I remember thirteen sitting at one time at his table, who all grew up to be men and women, and married; I was the youngest son, and the youngest child but two, and was born in Boston, New England. My mother, the second wife, was Abiah Folger, daughter of Peter Folger, one of the first settlers of New England, of whom honorable mention is made by Cotton Mather, in his church history of that country, entitled Magnalia Christi Americana, as "*a godly, learned Englishman,*" if I remember the words rightly. I have heard that he wrote sundry small occasional pieces, but only one of them was printed, which I saw now many years since. It was written in 1675, in the home-spun verse of that time and people, and addressed to those then concerned in the government there. It was in favor of liberty of conscience, and in behalf of the Baptists, Quakers, and other sectaries that had been under persecution, ascribing the Indian wars, and other distresses that had befallen the country, to that persecution, as so many judgments of God to punish so heinous an offense, and exhorting a repeal of those uncharitable laws. The whole appeared to me as written with a good deal of decent plainness and manly freedom. The six concluding lines I remember, though I have forgotten the two first of the stanza; but the purport of them was, that his censures proceeded from good-will, and, therefore he would be known to be the author.

> "Because to be a libeller (says he)
>   I hate it with my heart;
> From Sherburne town, where now I dwell
>   My name I do put here;
> Without offense your real friend,
>   It is Peter Folgier."

My elder brothers were all put apprentices to different trades. I was put to the grammar-school at eight years of age, my father intending to devote me, as the tithe of his sons, to the service of the Church. My early readiness in learning to read (which must have been very early, as I do not remember when I could not read), and the opinion of all his friends, that I should certainly make a good scholar, encouraged him in this purpose of his. My uncle Benjamin, too, approved of it, and proposed to give me all his shorthand volumes of sermons, I suppose as a stock to set up with, if I would learn his character. I continued, however, at the grammar-school not quite one year, though in that time I had risen gradually from the middle of the class of that year to be the head of it, and farther was removed into the next class above it, in order to go with that into the third at the end of the year. But my father, in the mean time, from a view of the expense of a college education, which having so large a family he could not well afford, and the mean living many so educated were afterwards able to obtain—reasons that he gave to his friends in my hearing—altered his first intention, took me from the grammar-school, and sent me to a school for writing and arithmetic, kept by a then famous man, Mr. George Brownell, very successful in his profession generally, and that by mild, encouraging methods. Under him I acquired fair writing pretty soon, but I failed in the arithmetic, and made no progress in it. At ten years old I was taken home to assist my father in his business, which was that of a tallow-chandler and sope-boiler; a business he was not bred to, but had assumed on his arrival in New England, and on finding his dying trade would not maintain his family, being in little request. Accordingly, I was employed in cutting wick for the candles, filling the dipping mold and the molds for cast candles, attending the shop, going of errands, etc.

I disliked the trade, and had a strong inclination for the sea, but my father declared against it; however, living near the water, I was much in and about it, learnt early to swim well, and to manage boats; and when in a boat or canoe with other boys, I was commonly allowed to govern, especially in any case of difficulty; and upon other occasions I was generally a leader among the boys, and sometimes led them into scrapes, of which I will mention one instance, as it shows an early projecting public spirit, tho' not then justly conducted.

There was a salt-marsh that bounded part of the mill-pond, on the edge of which, at high water, we used to stand to fish for minnows. By much trampling, we had made it a mere quagmire. My proposal was to build a wharff there fit for us to stand upon, and I showed my comrades a large heap of stones, which were intended for a new house near the marsh, and which would very well suit our purpose. Accordingly, in the evening, when the workmen were gone, I assembled a number of my play-fellows, and working with them diligently like so many emmets, sometimes two or three to a stone, we brought them all away and built our little wharff. The next morning the workmen were surprised at missing the stones, which were found in our wharff. Inquiry was made after the removers; we were discovered and complained of; several of us were corrected by our fathers; and, though I pleaded the usefulness of the work, mine convinced me that nothing was useful which was not honest.

I think you may like to know something of his person and character. He had an excellent constitution of body, was of middle stature, but well set, and very strong; he was ingenious, could draw prettily, was skilled a little in music, and had a clear pleasing voice, so that when he played psalm tunes on his violin and sung withal, as he sometimes did in an evening after the business of the day was over, it was extremely agreeable to hear. He had a mechanical genius too, and, on occasion, was very handy in the use of other tradesmen's tools; but his great excellence lay in a sound understanding and solid judgment in prudential matters, both in private and publick affairs. In the latter, indeed, he was never employed, the numerous family he had to educate and the straitness of his circumstances keeping him close to his trade; but I remember well his being frequently visited by leading people, who consulted him for his opinion in affairs of the town or of the church he belonged to, and showed a good deal of respect for his judgment and advice: he was also much consulted by private persons about their affairs when any difficulty occurred, and frequently chosen an arbitrator between contending parties. At his table he liked to have, as often as he could, some sensible friend or neighbor to converse with, and always took care to start some ingenious or useful topic for discourse, which might tend to improve the minds of his children. By this means he turned our attention to what was good, just, and prudent in the conduct of life; and little or no notice was ever taken of what related to the victuals on the table, whether it was well or ill dressed, in or out of season, of good or bad flavor, preferable or inferior to this or that other thing of the kind, so that I was bro't up in such a perfect inattention to those matters as to be quite indifferent what kind of food was set before me, and so unobservant of it, that to this day if I am asked I can scarce tell a few hours after dinner what I dined upon. This has been a convenience to me in travelling, where my companions have been sometimes very unhappy for want of a suitable gratification of their more delicate, because better instructed, tastes and appetites.

My mother had likewise an excellent constitution: she suckled all her ten children. I never knew either my father or mother to have any sickness but that of which they dy'd, he at 89, and she at 85 years of age. They lie buried together at Boston, where I some years since placed a marble over their grave, with this inscription:

> JOSIAH FRANKLIN,
> and
> ABIAH his wife,
> lie here interred.
> They lived lovingly together in wedlock
> fifty-five years.
> Without an estate, or any gainful employment,
> By constant labor and industry,
> with God's blessing,
> They maintained a large family
> comfortably,
> and brought up thirteen children
> and seven grandchildren
> reputably.
> From this instance, reader,
> Be encouraged to diligence in thy calling,
> And distrust not Providence.
> He was a pious and prudent man;
> She, a discreet and virtuous woman.
> Their youngest son,
> In filial regard to their memory,
> Places this stone.
> J. F. born 1655, died 1744, Ætat 89.
> A. F. born 1667, died 1752, ——85.

By my rambling digressions I perceive myself to be grown old. I us'd to write more methodically. But one does not dress for private company as for a publick ball. 'Tis perhaps only negligence.

To return: I continued thus employed in my father's business for two years, that is, till I was twelve years old; and my brother John, who was bred to that business, having left my father, married, and set up for himself at Rhode Island, there was all appearance that I was destined to supply his place, and become a tallow-chandler. But my dislike to the trade continuing, my father was under apprehensions that if he did not find one for me more agreeable, I should break away and get to sea, as his son Josiah had done, to his great vexation. He therefore sometimes took me to walk with him, and see joiners, bricklayers, turners, braziers, etc., at their work, that he might observe my inclination, and endeavor to fix it on some trade or other on land. It has ever since been a pleasure to me to see good workmen handle their tools; and it has been useful to me, having learnt so much by it as to be able to do little jobs myself in my house when a workman could not readily be got, and to construct little machines for my experiments, while the intention of making the experiment was fresh and warm in my mind. My father at last fixed upon the cutler's trade, and my uncle Benjamin's son Samuel, who was bred to that business in London, being about that time established in Boston, I was sent to be with him some time on liking. But his expectations of a fee with me displeasing my father, I was taken home again.

From a child I was fond of reading, and all the little money that came into my hands was ever laid out in books. Pleased with the Pilgrim's Progress, my first collection was of John Bunyan's works in separate little volumes. I afterward sold them to enable me to buy R. Burton's Historical Collections; they were small chapmen's books, and cheap, 40 or 50 in all. My father's little library consisted chiefly of books in polemic divinity, most of which I read, and have since often regretted that, at a time when I had such a thirst for knowledge, more proper books had not fallen in my way, since it was now resolved I should not be a clergyman. Plutarch's Lives there was in which I read abundantly, and I still think that time spent to great advantage. There was also a book of De Foe's, called an Essay on Projects, and another of Dr. Mather's, called Essays to do Good, which perhaps gave me a turn of thinking that had an influence on some of the principal future events of my life.

This bookish inclination at length determined my father to make me a printer, though he had already one son (James) of that profession. In 1717 my brother James returned from England with a press and letters to set up his business in Boston. I liked it much better than that of my father, but still had a hankering for the sea. To prevent the apprehended effect of such an inclination, my father was impatient to have me bound to my brother. I stood out some time, but at last was persuaded, and signed the indentures when I was yet but twelve years old. I was to serve as an apprentice till I was twenty-one years of age, only I was to be allowed journeyman's wages during the last year. In a little time I made great proficiency in the business, and became a useful hand to my brother. I now had access to better books. An acquaintance with the apprentices of booksellers enabled me sometimes to borrow a small one, which I was careful to return soon and clean. Often I sat up in my room reading the greatest part of the night, when the book was borrowed in the evening and to be returned early in the morning, lest it should be missed or wanted.

And after some time an ingenious tradesman, Mr. Matthew Adams, who had a pretty collection of books, and who frequented our printing-house, took notice of me, invited me to his library, and very kindly lent me such books as I chose to read. I now took a fancy to poetry, and made some little pieces; my brother, thinking it might turn to account, encouraged me, and put me on composing occasional ballads. One was called *The Lighthouse Tragedy*, and contained an account of the drowning of Captain Worthilake, with his two daughters: the other was a sailor's song, on the taking of *Teach* (or Blackbeard) the pirate. They were wretched stuff, in the Grub-street-ballad style; and when they were printed he sent me about the town to sell them. The first sold wonderfully, the event being recent, having made a great noise. This flattered my vanity; but my father discouraged me by ridiculing my performances, and telling me verse-makers were generally beggars. So I escaped being a poet, most probably a very bad one; but as prose writing has been of great use to me in the course of my life, and was a principal means of my advancement, I shall tell you how, in such a situation, I acquired what little ability I have in that way.

There was another bookish lad in the town, John Collins by name, with whom I was intimately acquainted. We sometimes disputed, and very fond we were of argument, and very desirous of confuting one another, which disputatious turn, by the way, is apt to become a very bad habit, making people often extremely disagreeable in company by the contradiction that is necessary to bring it into practice; and thence, besides souring and spoiling the conversation, is productive of disgusts and, perhaps enmities where you may have occasion for friendship. I had caught it by reading my father's books of dispute about religion. Persons of good sense, I have since observed, seldom fall into it, except lawyers, university men, and men of all sorts that have been bred at Edinborough.

A question was once, somehow or other, started between Collins and me, of the propriety of educating the female sex in learning, and their abilities for study. He was of opinion that it was improper, and that they were naturally unequal to it. I took the contrary side, perhaps a little for dispute's sake. He was naturally more eloquent, had a ready plenty of words; and sometimes, as I thought, bore me down more by his fluency than by the strength of his reasons. As we parted without settling the point, and were not to see one another again for some time, I sat down to put my arguments in writing, which I copied fair and sent to him. He answered, and I replied. Three or four letters of a side had passed, when my father happened to find my papers and read them. Without entering into the discussion, he took occasion to talk to me about the manner of my writing; observed that, though I had the advantage of my antagonist in correct spelling and pointing (which I ow'd to the printing-house), I fell far short in elegance of expression, in method and in perspicuity, of which he convinced me by several instances. I saw the justice of his remarks, and thence grew more attentive to the manner in writing, and determined to endeavor at improvement.

About this time I met with an odd volume of the *Spectator*. It was the third. I had never before seen any of them. I bought it, read it over and over, and was much delighted with it. I thought the writing excellent, and wished, if possible, to imitate it. With this view I took some of the papers, and, making short hints of the sentiment in each sentence, laid them by a few days, and then, without looking at the book, try'd to compleat the papers again, by expressing each hinted sentiment at length, and as fully as it had been expressed before, in any suitable words that should come to hand. Then I compared my *Spectator* with the original, discovered some of my faults, and corrected them. But I found I wanted a stock of words, or a readiness in recollecting and using them, which I thought I should have acquired before that time if I had gone on making verses; since the continual occasion for words of the same import, but of different length, to suit the measure, or of different sound for the rhyme, would have laid me under a constant necessity of searching for variety, and also have tended to fix that variety in my mind, and make me master of it. Therefore I took some of the tales and turned them into verse; and, after a time, when I had pretty well forgotten the prose, turned them back again. I also sometimes jumbled my collections of hints into confusion, and after some weeks endeavored to reduce them into the best order, before I began to form the full sentences and compleat the paper. This was to teach me method in the arrangement of thoughts. By comparing my work afterwards with the original, I discovered many faults and amended them; but I sometimes had the pleasure of fancying that, in certain particulars of small import, I had been lucky enough to improve the method or the language, and this encouraged me to think I might possibly in time come to be a tolerable English writer, of which I was extreamly ambitious. My time for these exercises and for reading was at night, after work or before it began in the morning, or on Sundays, when I contrived to be in the printing-house alone, evading as much as I could the common attendance on public worship which my father used to exact of me when I was under his care, and which indeed I still thought a duty, though I could not, as it seemed to me, afford time to practise it.

When about 16 years of age I happened to meet with a book, written by one Tryon, recommending a vegetable diet. I determined to go into it. My brother, being yet unmarried, did not keep house, but boarded himself and his apprentices in another family. My refusing to eat flesh occasioned an inconveniency, and I was frequently chid for my singularity. I made myself acquainted with Tryon's manner of preparing some of his dishes, such as boiling potatoes or rice, making hasty pudding, and a few others, and then proposed to my brother, that if he would give me, weekly, half the money he paid for my board, I would board myself. He instantly agreed to it, and I presently found that I could save half what he paid me. This was an additional fund for buying books. But I had another advantage in it. My brother and the rest going from the printing-house to their meals, I remained there alone, and, despatching presently my light repast, which often was no more than a bisket or a slice of bread, a handful of raisins or a tart from the pastry-cook's, and a glass of water, had the rest of the time till their return for study, in which I made the greater progress, from that greater clearness of head and quicker apprehension which usually attend temperance in eating and drinking.

And now it was that, being on some occasion made asham'd of my ignorance in figures, which I had twice failed in learning when at school, I took Cocker's book of Arithmetik, and went through the whole by myself with great ease. I also read Seller's and Shermy's books of Navigation, and became acquainted with the little geometry they contain; but never proceeded far in that science. And I read about this time Locke *on Human Understanding,* and the *Art of Thinking,* by Messrs. du Port Royal.

While I was intent on improving my language, I met with an English grammar (I think it was Greenwood's), at the end of which there were two little sketches of the arts of rhetoric and logic, the latter finishing with a specimen of a dispute in the Socratic method; and soon after I procur'd Xenophon's Memorable Things of Socrates, wherein there are many instances of the same method. I was charm'd with it, adopted it, dropt my abrupt contradiction and positive argumentation, and put on the humble inquirer and doubter. And being then, from reading Shaftesbury and Collins, become a real doubter in many points of our religious doctrine, I found this method safest for myself and very embarrassing to those against whom I used it; therefore I took a delight in it, practis'd it continually, and grew very artful and expert in drawing people, even of superior knowledge, into concessions, the consequences of which they did not foresee, entangling them in difficulties out of which they could not extricate themselves, and so obtaining victories that neither myself nor my cause always deserved. I continu'd this method some few years, but gradually left it, retaining only the habit of expressing myself in terms of modest diffidence; never using, when I advanced any thing that may possibly be disputed, the words *certainly, undoubtedly,* or any others that give the air of positiveness to an opinion; but rather say, I conceive or apprehend a thing to be so and so; it appears to me, or *I should think it so or so,* for such and such reasons; or *I imagine it to be so;* or *it is so, if I am not mistaken.* This habit, I believe, has been of great advantage to me when I have had occasion to inculcate my opinions, and persuade men into measures that I have been from time to time engag'd in promoting; and, as the chief ends of conversation are to *inform* or to be *informed,* to *please* or to *persuade,* I wish well-meaning, sensible men would not lessen their power of doing good by a positive, assuming manner, that seldom fails to disgust, tends to create opposition, and to defeat every one of those purposes for which speech was given to us, to wit, giving or receiving information or pleasure. For, if you would inform, a positive and dogmatical manner in advancing your sentiments may provoke contradiction and prevent a candid attention. If you wish information and improvement from the knowledge of others, and yet at the same time express yourself as firmly fix'd in your present opinions, modest, sensible men, who do not love disputation, will probably leave you undisturbed in the possession of your error. And by such a manner, you can seldom hope to recommend yourself in *pleasing* your hearers, or to persuade those whose concurrence you desire. Pope says, judiciously:

> "*Men should be taught as if you taught them not,
> And things unknown propos'd as things forgot*";

farther recommending to us

> "To speak, tho' sure, with seeming diffidence."

And he might have coupled with this line that which he has coupled with another, I think, less properly,

> "For want of modesty is want of sense."

If you ask, Why less properly? I must repeat the lines,

> "Immodest words admit of no defense,
> For want of modesty is want of sense."

Now, is not *want of sense* (where a man is so unfortunate as to want it) some apology for his *want of modesty?* and would not the lines stand more justly thus?

> "Immodest words admit *but* this defense,
> That want of modesty is want of sense."

This, however, I should submit to better judgments.

My brother had, in 1720 or 1721, begun to print a newspaper. It was the second that appeared in America, and was called the New England Courant. The only one before it was the Boston News-Letter. I remember his being dissuaded by some of his friends from the undertaking, as not likely to succeed, one newspaper being, in their judgment, enough for America. At this time (1771) there are not less than five-and-twenty. He went on, however, with the undertaking, and after having worked in composing the types and printing off the sheets, I was employed to carry the papers thro' the streets to the customers.

He had some ingenious men among his friends, who amus'd themselves by writing little pieces for this paper, which gain'd it credit and made it more in demand, and these gentlemen often visited us. Hearing their conversations, and their accounts of the approbation their papers were received with, I was excited to try my hand among them; but, being still a boy, and suspecting that my brother would object to printing anything of mine in his paper if he knew it to be mine, I contrived to disguise my hand, and, writing an anonymous paper, I put it in at night under the door of the printing-house. It was found in the morning, and communicated to his writing friends when they call'd in as usual. They read it, commented on it in my hearing, and I had the exquisite pleasure of finding it met with their approbation, and that, in their different guesses at the author, none were named but men of some character among us for learning and ingenuity. I suppose now that I was rather lucky in my judges, and that perhaps they were not really so very good ones as I then esteem'd them.

Encourag'd, however, by this, I wrote and convey'd in the same way to the press several more papers which were equally approv'd; and I kept my secret till my small fund of sense for such performances was pretty well exhausted, and then I discovered it, when I began to be considered a little more by my brother's acquaintance, and in a manner that did not quite please him, as he thought, probably with reason, that it tended to make me too vain. And, perhaps, this might be one occasion of the differences that we began to have about this time. Though a brother, he considered himself as my master, and me as his apprentice, and, accordingly, expected the same services from me as he would from another, while I thought he demean'd me too much in some he requir'd of me, who from a brother expected more indulgence. Our disputes were often brought before our father, and I fancy I was either generally in the right, or else a better pleader, because the judgment was generally in my favor. But my brother was passionate, and had often beaten me, which I took extreamly amiss; and, thinking my apprenticeship very tedious, I was continually wishing for some opportunity of shortening it, which at length offered in a manner unexpected.

One of the pieces in our newspaper on some political point, which I have now forgotten, gave offense to the Assembly. He was taken up, censur'd, and imprison'd for a month, by the speaker's warrant, I suppose, because he would not discover his author. I too was taken up and examin'd before the council; but, tho' I did not give them any satisfaction, they content'd themselves with admonishing me, and dismissed me, considering me, perhaps, as an apprentice, who was bound to keep his master's secrets.

During my brother's confinement, which I resented a good deal, notwithstanding our private differences, I had the management of the paper; and I made bold to give our rulers some rubs in it, which my brother took very kindly, while others began to consider me in an unfavorable light, as a young genius that had a turn for libelling and satyr. My brother's discharge was accompany'd with an order of the House (a very odd one), that *"James Franklin should no longer print the paper called the New England Courant."*

There was a consultation held in our printing-house among his friends, what he should do in this case. Some proposed to evade the order by changing the name of the paper; but my brother, seeing inconveniences in that, it was finally concluded on as a better way, to let it be printed for the future under the name of BENJAMIN FRANKLIN; and to avoid the censure of the Assembly, that might fall on him as still printing it by his apprentice, the contrivance was that my old indenture should be return'd to me, with a full discharge on the back of it, to be shown on occasion, but to secure to him the benefit of my service, I was to sign new indentures for the remainder of the term, which were to be kept private. A very flimsy scheme it was; however, it was immediately executed, and the paper went on accordingly, under my name for several months.

At length, a fresh difference arising between my brother and me, I took upon me to assert my freedom, presuming that he would not venture to produce the new indentures. It was not fair in me to take this advantage, and this I therefore reckon one of the first errata of my life; but the unfairness of it weighed little with me, when under the impressions of resentment for the blows his passion too often urged him to bestow upon me, though he was otherwise not an ill-natur'd man: perhaps I was too saucy and provoking.

When he found I would leave him, he took care to prevent my getting employment in any other printing-house of the town, by going round and speaking to every master, who accordingly refus'd to give me work. I then thought of going to New York, as the nearest place where there was a printer; and I was rather inclin'd to leave Boston when I reflected that I had already made myself a little obnoxious to the governing party, and, from the arbitrary proceedings of the Assembly in my brother's case, it was likely I might, if I stay'd, soon bring myself into scrapes; and farther, that my indiscrete disputations about religion began to make me pointed at with horror by good people as an infidel or atheist. I determin'd on the point, but my father now siding with my brother, I was sensible that, if I attempted to go openly, means would be used to prevent me. My friend Collins, therefore, undertook to manage a little for me. He agreed with the captain of a New York sloop for my passage, under the notion of my being a young acquaintance of his, that had got a naughty girl with child, whose friends would compel me to marry her, and therefore I could not appear or come away publicly. So I sold some of my books to raise a little money, was taken on board privately, and as we had a fair wind, in three days I found myself in New York, near 300 miles from home, a boy of but 17, without the least recommendation to, or knowledge of any person in the place, and with very little money in my pocket.

My inclinations for the sea were by this time worne out, or I might now have gratify'd them. But, having a trade, and supposing myself a pretty good workman, I offer'd my service to the printer in the place, old Mr. William Bradford, who had been the first printer in Pennsylvania, but removed from thence upon the quarrel of George Keith. He could give me no employment, having little to do, and help enough already; but says he, "My son at Philadelphia has lately lost his principal hand, Aquila Rose, by death; if you go thither, I believe he may employ you." Philadelphia was a hundred miles further; I set out, however, in a boat for Amboy, leaving my chest and things to follow me round by sea.

In crossing the bay, we met with a squall that tore our rotten sails to pieces, prevented our getting into the Kill, and drove us upon Long Island. In our way, a drunken Dutchman, who was a passenger too, fell overboard;

when he was sinking, I reached through the water to his shock pate, and drew him up, so that we got him in again. His ducking sobered him a little, and he went to sleep, taking first out of his pocket a book, which he desir'd I would dry for him. It proved to be my old favorite author, Bunyan's Pilgrim's Progress, in Dutch, finely printed on good paper, with copper cuts, a dress better than I had ever seen it wear in its own language. I have since found that it has been translated into most of the languages of Europe, and suppose it has been more generally read than any other book, except perhaps the Bible. Honest John was the first that I know of who mix'd narration and dialogue; a method of writing very engaging to the reader, who in the most interesting parts finds himself, as it were, brought into the company and present at the discourse. De Foe in his Cruso, his Moll Flanders, Religious Courtship, Family Instructor, and other pieces, has imitated it with success; and Richardson has done the same in his Pamela, etc.

When we drew near the island, we found it was at a place where there could be no landing, there being a great surff on the stony beach. So we dropt anchor, and swung round towards the shore. Some people came down to the water edge and hallow'd to us, as we did to them; but the wind was so high, and the surff so loud, that we could not hear so as to understand each other. There were canoes on the shore, and we made signs, and hallow'd that they should fetch us; but they either did not understand us, or thought it impracticable, so they went away, and night coming on, we had no remedy but to wait till the wind should abate; and, in the mean time, the boatman and I concluded to sleep, if we could; and so crowded into the scuttle, with the Dutchman, who was still wet, and the spray beating over the head of our boat, leak'd thro' to us, so that we were soon almost as wet as he. In this manner we lay all night, with very little rest; but, the wind abating the next day, we made a shift to reach Amboy before night, having been thirty hours on the water, without victuals, or any drink but a bottle of filthy rum, the water we sail'd on being salt.

In the evening I found myself very feverish, and went in to bed; but, having read somewhere that cold water drank plentifully was good for a fever, I follow'd the prescription, sweat plentifully most of the night, my fever left me, and in the morning, crossing the ferry, I proceeded on my journey on foot, having fifty miles to Burlington, where I was told I should find boats that would carry me the rest of the way to Philadelphia.

It rained very hard all the day; I was thoroughly soak'd, and by noon a good deal tired; so I stopt at a poor inn, where I staid all night, beginning now to wish that I had never left home. I cut so miserable a figure, too, that I found, by the questions ask'd me, I was suspected to be some runaway servant, and in danger of being taken up on that suspicion. However, I proceeded the next day, and got in the evening to an inn, within eight or ten miles of Burlington, kept by one Dr. Brown. He entered into conversation with me while I took some refreshment, and, finding I had read a little, became very sociable and friendly. Our acquaintance continu'd as long as he liv'd. He had been, I imagine, an itinerant doctor, for there was no town in England, or country in Europe, of which he could not give a very particular account. He had some letters, and was ingenious, but much of an unbeliever, and wickedly undertook, some years after, to travestie the Bible in doggrel verse, as Cotton had done Virgil. By this means he set many of the facts in a very ridiculous light, and might have hurt weak minds if his work had been published; but it never was.

At his house I lay that night, and the next morning reach'd Burlington, but had the mortification to find that the regular boats were gone a little before my coming, and no other expected to go before Tuesday, this being Saturday; wherefore I returned to an old woman in the town, of whom I had bought gingerbread to eat on the water, and ask'd her advice. She invited me to lodge at her house till a passage by water should offer; and being tired with my foot travelling, I accepted the invitation. She understanding I was a printer, would have had me stay at that town and follow my business, being ignorant of the stock necessary to begin with. She was very hospitable, gave me a dinner of ox-cheek with great good will, accepting only of a pot of ale in return; and I thought myself fixed till Tuesday should come. However, walking in the evening by the side of the river, a boat came by, which I found was going towards Philadelphia, with several people in her. They took me in, and, as there was no wind, we row'd all the way; and about midnight, not having yet seen the city, some of the company were confident we must have passed it, and would row no farther; the others knew not where we were; so we put toward the shore, got into a creek, landed near an old fence, with the rails of which we made a fire, the night being cold, in October, and there we remained till daylight. Then one of the company knew the place to be Cooper's Creek, a little above Philadelphia, which we saw as soon as we got out of the creek, and arriv'd there about eight or nine o'clock on the Sunday morning, and landed at the Market-street wharf.

I have been the more particular in this description of my journey, and shall be so of my first entry into that city, that you may in your mind compare such unlikely beginnings with the figure I have since made there. I was in my working dress, my best cloaths being to come round by sea. I was dirty from my journey; my pockets were stuff'd out with shirts and stockings, and I knew no soul nor where to look for lodging. I was fatigued with travelling, rowing and want of rest, I was very hungry; and my whole stock of cash consisted of a Dutch dollar, and about a shilling in copper. The latter I gave the people of the boat for my passage, who at first refus'd it, on account of my rowing; but I insisted on their taking it. A man being sometimes more generous when he has but a little money than when he has plenty, perhaps thro' fear of being thought to have but little.

Then I walked up the street, gazing about till near the market-house I met a boy with bread. I had made many a meal on bread, and, inquiring where he got it, I went immediately to the baker's he directed me to, in Second-street, and ask'd for bisket, intending such as we had in Boston; but they, it seems, were not made in Philadelphia. Then I asked for a three-penny loaf, and was told they had none such. So not considering or knowing the difference of money, and the greater cheapness nor the names of his bread, I bad him give me three-penny worth of any sort. He gave me, accordingly, three great puffy rolls. I was surpriz'd at the quantity, but took it, and, having no room in my pockets, walk'd off with a roll under each arm, and eating the other. Thus I went up Market-street as far as Fourth-street, passing by the door of Mr. Read, my future wife's father; when she, standing at the door, saw me, and thought I made, as I certainly did, a most awkward, ridiculous appearance. Then I turned and went down Chestnut-street and part of Walnut-street, eating my roll all the way, and, coming round, found myself again at Market-street wharf, near the boat I came in, to which I went for a draught of the river water; and, being filled with one of my rolls, gave the other two to a woman and her child that came down the river in the boat with us, and were waiting to go farther.

Thus refreshed, I walked again up the street, which by this time had many clean-dressed people in it, who were all walking the same way. I joined them, and thereby was led into the great meeting-house of the Quakers near the market. I sat down among them, and, after looking round awhile and hearing nothing said, being very drowsy thro' labor and want of rest the preceding night, I fell fast asleep, and continu'd so till the meeting broke up, when one was kind enough to rouse me. This was, therefore, the first house I was in, or slept in, in Philadelphia.

Walking down again toward the river, and, looking in the faces of people, I met a young Quaker man, whose countenance I lik'd, and, accosting him, requested he would tell me where a stranger could get lodging. We were then near the sign of the Three Mariners. "Here," says he, "is one place that entertains strangers, but it is not a reputable house; if thee wilt walk with me, I'll show thee a better." He brought me to the Crooked Billet in Water-street. Here I got a dinner; and, while I was eating it, several sly questions were asked me, as it seemed to be suspected from my youth and appearance, that I might be some runaway.

After dinner, my sleepiness return'd, and being shown to a bed, I lay down without undressing, and slept till six in the evening, was call'd to supper, went to bed again very early, and slept soundly till next morning. Then I made myself as tidy as I could, and went to Andrew Bradford the printer's. I found in the shop the old man his father, whom I had seen at New York, and who, travelling on horseback, had got to Philadelphia before me. He introduc'd me to his son, who receiv'd me civilly, gave me a breakfast, but told me he did not at present want a hand, being lately suppli'd with one; but there was another printer in town, lately set up, one Keimer, who, perhaps, might employ me; if not, I should be welcome to lodge at his house, and he would give me a little work to do now and then till fuller business should offer.

The old gentleman said he would go with me to the new printer; and when we found him, "Neighbor," says Bradford, "I have brought to see you a young man of your business; perhaps you may want such a one." He ask'd me a few questions, put a composing stick in my hand to see how I work'd, and then said he would employ me soon, though he had just then nothing for me to do; and, taking old Bradford, whom he had never seen before, to be one of the town's people that had a good will for him, enter'd into a conversation on his present undertaking and prospects; while Bradford, not discovering that he was the other printer's father, on Keimer's saying he expected soon to get the greatest part of the business into his own hands, drew him on by artful questions, and starting little doubts, to explain all his views, what interest he reli'd on, and in what manner he intended to proceed. I, who stood by and heard all, saw immediately that one of them was a crafty old sophister, and the other a mere novice. Bradford left me with Keimer, who was greatly surpris'd when I told him who the old man was.

Keimer's printing-house, I found, consisted of an old shatter'd press, and one small, worn-out font of English, which he was then using himself, composing an Elegy on Aquila Rose, before mentioned, an ingenious young man, of excellent character, much respected in the town, clerk of the Assembly, and a pretty poet. Keimer made verses too, but very indifferently. He could not be said to write them, for his manner was to compose them in the types directly out of his head. So there being no copy, but one pair of cases, and the Elegy likely to require all the letter, no one could help him. I endeavor'd to put his press (which he had not yet us'd, and of which he understood nothing) into order fit to be work'd with; and, promising to come and print off his Elegy as soon as he should have got it ready, I return'd to Bradford's, who gave me a little job to do for the present, and there I lodged and dieted. A few days after, Keimer sent for me to print off the Elegy. And now he had got another pair of cases, and a pamphlet to reprint, on which he set me to work.

These two printers I found poorly qualified for their business. Bradford had not been bred to it, and was very illiterate; and Keimer, tho' something of a scholar, was a mere compositor, knowing nothing of presswork. He had been one of the French prophets, and could act their enthusiastic agitations. At this time he did not profess any particular religion, but something of all on occasion; was very ignorant of the world, and had, as I afterward found, a good deal of the knave in his composition. He did not like my lodging at Bradford's while I work'd with him. He had a house, indeed, but without furniture, so he could not lodge me; but he got me a lodging at Mr. Read's, before mentioned, who was the owner of his house; and, my chest and clothes being come by this time, I made rather a more respectable appearance in the eyes of Miss Read than I had done when she first happen'd to see me eating my roll in the street.

I began now to have some acquaintance among the young people of the town, that were lovers of reading, with whom I spent my evenings very pleasantly; and gaining money by my industry and frugality, I lived very agreeably, forgetting Boston as much as I could, and not desiring that any there should know where I resided, except my friend Collins, who was in my secret, and kept it when I wrote to him. At length, an incident happened that sent me back again much sooner than I had intended. I had a brother-in-law, Robert Holmes, master of a sloop that traded between Boston and Delaware.

He being at Newcastle, forty miles below Philadelphia, heard there of me, and wrote me a letter mentioning the concern of my friends in Boston at my abrupt departure, assuring me of their good will to me, and that every thing would be accommodated to my mind if I would return, to which he exhorted me very earnestly. I wrote an answer to his letter, thank'd him for his advice, but stated my reasons for quitting Boston fully and in such a light as to convince him I was not so wrong as he had apprehended.

Sir William Keith, governor of the province, was then at Newcastle, and Captain Holmes, happening to be in company with him when my letter came to hand, spoke to him of me, and show'd him the letter. The governor read it, and seem'd surpris'd when he was told my age. He said I appear'd a young man of promising parts, and therefore should be encouraged; the printers at Philadelphia were wretched ones; and, if I would set up there, he made no doubt I should succeed; for his part, he would procure me the public business, and do me every other service in his power. This my brother-in-law afterwards told me in Boston, but I knew as yet nothing of it; when, one day, Keimer and I being at work together near the window, we saw the governor and another gentleman (which proved to be Colonel French, of Newcastle), finely dress'd, come directly across the street to our house, and heard them at the door.

Keimer ran down immediately, thinking it a visit to him; but the governor inquir'd for me, came up, and with a condescension and politeness I had been quite unus'd to, made me many compliments, desired to be acquainted with me, blam'd me kindly for not having made myself known to him when I first came to the place, and would have me away with him to the tavern, where he was going with Colonel French to taste, as he said, some excellent Madeira. I was not a little surprised, and Keimer star'd like a pig poison'd. I went, however, with the governor and Colonel French to a tavern, at the corner of Third-street, and over the Madeira he propos'd my setting up my business, laid before me the probabilities of success, and both he and Colonel French assur'd me I should have their interest and influence in procuring the public business of both governments. On my doubting whether my father would assist me in it, Sir William said he would give me a letter to him, in which he would state the advantages, and he did not doubt of prevailing with him. So it was concluded I should return to Boston in the first vessel, with the governor's letter recommending me to my father. In the mean time the intention was to be kept a secret, and I went on working with Keimer as usual, the governor sending for me now and then to dine with him, a very great honor I thought it, and conversing with me in the most affable, familiar, and friendly manner imaginable.

About the end of April, 1724, a little vessel offer'd for Boston. I took leave of Keimer as going to see my friends. The governor gave me an ample letter, saying many flattering things of me to my father, and strongly recommending the project of my setting up at Philadelphia as a thing that must make my fortune. We struck on a shoal in going down the bay, and sprung a leak; we had a blustering time at sea, and were oblig'd to pump almost continually, at which I took my turn. We arriv'd safe, however, at Boston in about a fortnight. I had been absent seven months, and my friends had heard nothing of me; for my br. Holmes was not yet return'd, and had not written about me. My unexpected appearance surpriz'd the family; all were, however, very glad to see me, and made me welcome, except my brother. I went to see him at his printing-house. I was better dress'd than ever while in his service, having a genteel new suit from head to foot, a watch, and my pockets lin'd with near five pounds sterling in silver. He receiv'd me not very frankly, look'd me all over, and turn'd to his work again.

The journeymen were inquisitive where I had been, what sort of a country it was, and how I lik'd it. I prais'd it much, and the happy life I led in it, expressing strongly my intention of returning to it; and, one of them asking what kind of money we had there, I produc'd a handful of silver, and spread it before them, which was a kind of raree-show they had not been us'd to, paper being the money of Boston. Then I took an opportunity of letting them see my watch; and, lastly (my brother still grum and sullen), I gave them a piece of eight to drink, and took my leave. This visit of mine offended him extreamly; for, when my mother some time after spoke to him of a reconciliation, and of her wishes to see us on good terms together, and that we might live for the future as brothers, he said I had insulted him in such a manner before his people that he could never forget or forgive it. In this, however, he was mistaken.

My father received the governor's letter with some apparent surprise, but said little of it to me for some days, when Capt. Holmes returning he show'd it to him, ask'd him if he knew Keith, and what kind of man he was; adding his opinion that he must be of small discretion to think of setting a boy up in business who wanted yet three years of being at man's estate. Holmes said what he could in favor of the project, but my father was clear in the impropriety of it, and at last gave a flat denial to it. Then he wrote a civil letter to Sir William, thanking him for the patronage he had so kindly offered me, but declining to assist me as yet in setting up, I being, in his opinion, too young to be trusted with the management of a business so important, and for which the preparation must be so expensive.

My friend and companion Collins, who was a clerk in the post-office, pleas'd with the account I gave him of my new country, determined to go thither also; and, while I waited for my father's determination, he set out before me by land to Rhode Island, leaving his books, which were a pretty collection of mathematicks and natural philosophy, to come with mine and me to New York, where he propos'd to wait for me.

My father, tho' he did not approve Sir William's proposition, was yet pleas'd that I had been able to obtain so advantageous a character from a person of such note where I had resided, and that I had been so industrious and careful as to equip myself so handsomely in so short a time; therefore, seeing no prospect of an accommodation between my brother and me, he gave his consent to my returning again to Philadelphia, advis'd me to behave respectfully to the people there, endeavor to obtain the general esteem, and avoid lampooning and libeling, to which he thought I had too much inclination; telling me, that by steady industry and a prudent parsimony I might save enough by the time I was one-and-twenty to set me up; and that, if I came near the matter, he would help me out with the rest. This was all I could obtain, except some small gifts as tokens of his and my mother's love, when I embark'd again for New York, now with their approbation and their blessing.

The sloop putting in at Newport, Rhode Island, I visited my brother John, who had been married and settled there some years. He received me very affectionately, for he always lov'd me. A friend of his, one Vernon, having some money due to him in Pensilvania, about thirty-five pounds currency, desired I would receive it for him, and keep it till I had his directions what to remit it in. Accordingly, he gave me an order. This afterwards occasion'd me a good deal of uneasiness.

At Newport we took in a number of passengers for New York, among which were two young women, companions, and a grave, sensible, matronlike Quaker woman, with her attendants. I had shown an obliging readiness to do her some little services, which impress'd her I suppose with a degree of good will toward me; therefore, when she saw a daily growing familiarity between me and the two young women, which they appear'd to encourage, she took me aside, and said, "Young man, I am concern'd for thee, as thou has no friend with thee, and seems not to know much of the world, or of the snares youth is expos'd to; depend upon it, those are very bad women; I can see it in all their actions; and if thee art not upon thy guard, they will draw thee into some danger; they are strangers to thee, and I advise thee, in a friendly concern for thy welfare, to have no acquaintance with them." As I seem'd at first not to think so ill of them as she did, she mentioned some things she had observ'd and heard that had escap'd my notice, but now convinc'd me she was right. I thank'd her for her kind advice, and promis'd to follow it. When we arriv'd at New York, they told me where they liv'd, and invited me to come and see them; but I avoided it, and it was well I did; for the next day the captain miss'd a silver spoon and some other things, that had been taken out of his cabbin, and, knowing that these were a couple of strumpets, he got a warrant to search their lodgings, found the stolen goods, and had the thieves punish'd. So, tho' we had escap'd a sunken rock, which we scrap'd upon in the passage, I thought this escape of rather more importance to me.

At New York I found my friend Collins, who had arriv'd there some time before me. We had been intimate from children, and had read the same books together; but he had the advantage of more time for reading and studying, and a wonderful genius for mathematical learning, in which he far outstript me. While I liv'd in Boston, most of my hours of leisure for conversation were spent with him, and he continu'd a sober as well as an industrious lad; was much respected for his learning by several of the clergy and other gentlemen, and seemed to promise making a good figure in life. But, during my absence, he had acquir'd a habit of sotting with brandy; and I found by his own account, and what I heard from others, that he had been drunk every day since his arrival at New York, and behav'd very oddly. He had gam'd, too, and lost his money, so that I was oblig'd to discharge his lodgings, and defray his expenses to and at Philadelphia, which prov'd extremely inconvenient to me.

The then governor of New York, Burnet (son of Bishop Burnet), hearing from the captain that a young man, one of his passengers, had a great many books, desir'd he would bring me to see him. I waited upon him accordingly, and should have taken Collins with me but that he was not sober. The gov'r. treated me with great civility, show'd me his library, which was a very large one, and we had a good deal of conversation about books and authors. This was the second governor who had done me the honor to take notice of me; which, to a poor boy like me, was very pleasing.

We proceeded to Philadelphia. I received on the way Vernon's money, without which we could hardly have finish'd our journey. Collins wished to be employ'd in some counting-house; but, whether they discover'd his dramming by his breath, or by his behaviour, tho' he had some recommendations, he met with no success in any application, and continu'd lodging and boarding at the same house with me, and at my expense. Knowing I had that money of Vernon's, he was continually borrowing of me, still promising repayment as soon as he should be in business. At length he had got so much of it that I was distress'd to think what I should do in case of being call'd on to remit it.

His drinking continu'd, about which we sometimes quarrel'd; for, when a little intoxicated, he was very fractious. Once, in a boat on the Delaware with some other young men, he refused to row in his turn. "I will be row'd home," says he. "We will not row you," says I. "You must, or stay all night on the water," says he, "just as you please." The others said, "Let us row; what signifies it?" But, my mind being soured with his other conduct, I continu'd to refuse. So he swore he would make me row, or throw me overboard; and coming along, stepping on the thwarts, toward me, when he came up and struck at me, I clapped my hand under his crutch, and, rising, pitched him head-foremost into the river. I knew he was a good swimmer, and so was under little concern about him; but before he could get round to lay hold of the boat, we had with a few strokes pull'd her out of his reach; and ever when he drew near the boat, we ask'd if he would row, striking a few strokes to slide her away from him. He was ready to die with vexation, and obstinately would not promise to row. However, seeing him at last beginning to tire, we lifted him in and brought him home dripping wet in the evening. We hardly exchang'd a civil word afterwards, and a West India captain, who had a commission to procure a tutor for the sons of a gentleman at Barbadoes, happening to meet with him, agreed to carry him thither. He left me then, promising to remit me the first money he should receive in order to discharge the debt; but I never heard of him after.

The breaking into this money of Vernon's was one of the first great errata of my life; and this affair show'd that my father was not much out in his judgment when he suppos'd me too young to manage business of importance. But Sir William, on reading his letter, said he was too prudent. There was great difference in persons; and discretion did not always accompany years, nor was youth always without it. "And since he will not set you up," says he, "I will do it myself. Give me an inventory of the things necessary to be had from England, and I will send for them. You shall repay me when you are able; I am resolv'd to have a good printer here, and I am sure you must succeed." This was spoken with such an appearance of cordiality, that I had not the least doubt of his meaning what he said. I had hitherto kept the proposition of my setting up, a secret in Philadelphia, and I still kept it. Had it been known that I depended on the governor, probably some friend, that knew him better, would have advis'd me not to rely on him, as I afterwards heard it as his known character to be liberal of promises which he never meant to keep. Yet, unsolicited as he was by me, how could I think his generous offers insincere? I believ'd him one of the best men in the world.

I presented him an inventory of a little print'g-house, amounting by my computation to about one hundred pounds sterling. He lik'd it, but ask'd me if my being on the spot in England to chuse the types, and see that every thing was good of the kind, might not be of some advantage. "Then," says he, "when there, you may make acquaintances, and establish correspondences in the book-selling and stationery way." I agreed that this might be advantageous. "Then," says he, "get yourself ready to go with Annis"; which was the annual ship, and the only one at that time usually passing between London and Philadelphia. But it would be some months before Annis sail'd, so I continu'd working with Keimer, fretting about the money Collins had got from me, and in daily apprehensions of being call'd upon by Vernon, which, however, did not happen for some years after.

I believe I have omitted mentioning that, in my first voyage from Boston, being becalm'd off Block Island, our people set about catching cod, and hauled up a great many. Hitherto I had stuck to my resolution of not eating animal food, and on this occasion I consider'd, with my master Tryon, the taking every fish as a kind of unprovok'd murder, since none of them had, or ever could do us any injury that might justify the slaughter. All this seemed very reasonable. But I had formerly been a great lover of fish, and, when this came hot out of the frying-pan, it smelt admirably well. I balanc'd some time between principle and inclination, till I recollected that, when the fish were opened, I saw smaller fish taken out of their stomachs; then thought I, "If you eat one another, I don't see why we mayn't eat you." So I din'd upon cod very heartily, and continued to eat with other people, returning only now and then occasionally to a vegetable diet. So convenient a thing it is to be a *reasonable creature*, since it enables one to find or make a reason for every thing one has a mind to do.

Keimer and I liv'd on a pretty good familiar footing, and agreed tolerably well, for he suspected nothing of my setting up. He retained a great deal of his old enthusiasms and lov'd argumentation. We therefore had many disputations. I used to work him so with my Socratic method, and had trepann'd him so often by questions apparently so distant from any point we had in hand, and yet by degrees lead to the point, and brought him into difficulties and contradictions, that at last he grew ridiculously cautious, and would hardly answer me the most common question, without asking first, "*What do you intend to infer from that?*" However, it gave him so high an opinion of my abilities in the confuting way, that he seriously proposed my being his colleague in a project he had of setting up a new sect. He was to preach the doctrines, and I was to confound all opponents. When he came to explain with me upon the doctrines, I found several conundrums which I objected to, unless I might have my way a little too, and introduce some of mine.

Keimer wore his beard at full length, because somewhere in the Mosaic law it is said, "*Thou shalt not mar the corners of thy beard.*" He likewise kept the seventh day, Sabbath; and these two points were essentials with him. I dislik'd both; but agreed to admit them upon condition of his adopting the doctrine of using no animal food. "I doubt," said he, "my constitution will not bear that." I assur'd him it would, and that he would be the better for it. He was usually a great glutton, and I promised myself some diversion in half starving him. He agreed to try the practice, if I would keep him company. I did so, and we held it for three months. We had our victuals dress'd, and brought to us regularly by a woman in the neighborhood, who had from me a list of forty dishes, to be prepar'd for us at different times, in all which there was neither fish, flesh, nor fowl, and the whim suited me the better at this time from the cheapness of it, not costing us above eighteen pence sterling each per week. I have since kept several Lents most strictly, leaving the common diet for that, and that for the common, abruptly, without the least inconvenience, so that I think there is little in the advice of making those changes by easy gradations. I went on pleasantly, but poor Keimer suffered grievously, tired of the project, long'd for the flesh-pots of Egypt, and order'd a roast pig. He invited me and two women friends to dine with him; but, it being brought too soon upon table, he could not resist the temptation, and ate the whole before we came.

I had made some courtship during this time to Miss Read. I had a great respect and affection for her, and had some reason to believe she had the same for me; but, as I was about to take a long voyage, and we were both very young, only a little above eighteen, it was thought most prudent by her mother to prevent our going too far at present, as a marriage, if it was to take place, would be more convenient after my return, when I should be, as I expected, set up in my business. Perhaps, too, she thought my expectations not so well founded as I imagined them to be.

My chief acquaintances at this time were Charles Osborne, Joseph Watson, and James Ralph, all lovers of reading. The two first were clerks to an eminent scrivener or conveyancer in the town, Charles Brogden; the other was clerk to a merchant. Watson was a pious, sensible young man, of great integrity; the others rather more lax in their principles of religion, particularly Ralph, who, as well as Collins, had been unsettled by me, for which they both made me suffer. Osborne was sensible, candid, frank; sincere and affectionate to his friends; but, in literary matters, too fond of criticising. Ralph was ingenious, genteel in his manners, and extremely eloquent; I think I never knew a prettier talker. Both of them great admirers of poetry, and began to try their hands in little pieces. Many pleasant walks we four had together on Sundays into the woods, near Schuylkill, where we read to one another, and conferr'd on what we read.

Ralph was inclin'd to pursue the study of poetry, not doubting but he might become eminent in it, and make his fortune by it, alleging that the best poets must, when they first began to write, make as many faults as he did. Osborne dissuaded him, assur'd him he had no genius for poetry, and advis'd him to think of nothing beyond the business he was bred to; that, in the mercantile way, tho' he had no stock, he might, by his diligence and punctuality, recommend himself to employment as a factor, and in time acquire wherewith to trade on his own account. I approv'd the amusing one's self with poetry now and then, so far as to improve one's language, but no farther.

On this it was propos'd that we should each of us, at our next meeting, produce a piece of our own composing, in order to improve by our mutual observations, criticisms, and corrections. As language and expression were what we had in view, we excluded all considerations of invention by agreeing that the task should be a version of the eighteenth Psalm, which describes the descent of a Deity. When the time of our meeting drew nigh, Ralph called on me first, and let me know his piece was ready. I told him I had been busy, and, having little inclination, had done nothing. He then show'd me his piece for my opinion, and I much approv'd it, as it appear'd to me to have great merit. "Now," says he, "Osborne never will allow the least merit in any thing of mine, but makes 1000 criticisms out of mere envy. He is not so jealous of you; I wish, therefore, you would take this piece, and produce it as yours; I will pretend not to have had time, and so produce nothing. We shall then see what he will say to it." It was agreed, and I immediately transcrib'd it, that it might appear in my own hand.

We met; Watson's performance was read; there were some beauties in it, but many defects. Osborne's was read; it was much better; Ralph did it justice; remarked some faults, but applauded the beauties. He himself had nothing to produce. I was backward; seemed desirous of being excused;

had not had sufficient time to correct, etc.; but no excuse could be admitted; produce I must. It was read and repeated; Watson and Osborne gave up the contest, and join'd in applauding it. Ralph only made some criticisms, and propos'd some amendments; but I defended my text. Osborne was against Ralph, and told him he was no better a critic than poet, so he dropt the argument. As they two went home together, Osborne expressed himself still more strongly in favor of what he thought my production; having restrain'd himself before, as he said, lest I should think it flattery. "But who would have imagin'd," said he, "that Franklin had been capable of such a performance; such painting, such force, such fire! He has even improv'd the original. In his common conversation he seems to have no choice of words; he hesitates and blunders; and yet, good God! how he writes!" When we next met, Ralph discovered the trick we had plaid him, and Osborne was a little laught at.

This transaction fixed Ralph in his resolution of becoming a poet. I did all I could to dissuade him from it, but he continued scribbling verses till *Pope* cured him. He became, however, a pretty good prose writer. More of him hereafter. But, as I may not have occasion again to mention the other two, I shall just remark here, that Watson died in my arms a few years after, much lamented, being the best of our set. Osborne went to the West Indies, where he became an eminent lawyer and made money, but died young. He and I had made a serious agreement, that the one who happen'd first to die should, if possible, make a friendly visit to the other, and acquaint him how he found things in that separate state. But he never fulfill'd his promise.

The governor, seeming to like my company, had me frequently to his house, and his setting me up was always mention'd as a fixed thing. I was to take with me letters recommendatory to a number of his friends, besides the letter of credit to furnish me with the necessary money for purchasing the press and types, paper, etc. For these letters I was appointed to call at different times, when they were to be ready; but a future time was still named. Thus he went on till the ship, whose departure too had been several times postponed, was on the point of sailing. Then, when I call'd to take my leave and receive the letters, his secretary, Dr. Bard, came out to me and said the governor was extremely busy in writing, but would be down at Newcastle before the ship, and there the letters would be delivered to me.

Ralph, though married, and having one child, had determined to accompany me in this voyage. It was thought he intended to establish a correspondence, and obtain goods to sell on commission; but I found afterwards, that, thro' some discontent with his wife's relations, he purposed to leave her on their hands, and never return again. Having taken leave of my friends, and interchang'd some promises with Miss Read, I left Philadelphia in the ship, which anchor'd at Newcastle. The governor was there; but when I went to his lodging, the secretary came to me from him with the civillest message in the world, that he could not then see me, being engaged in business of the utmost importance, but should send the letters to me on board, wish'd me heartily a good voyage and a speedy return, etc. I returned on board a little puzzled, but still not doubting.

Mr. Andrew Hamilton, a famous lawyer of Philadelphia, had taken passage in the same ship for himself and son, and with Mr. Denham, a Quaker merchant, and Messrs. Onion and Russel, masters of an iron work in Maryland, had engag'd the great cabin; so that Ralph and I were forced to take up with a berth in the steerage, and none on board knowing us, were considered as ordinary persons. But Mr. Hamilton and his son (it was James, since governor) return'd from Newcastle to Philadelphia, the father being recall'd by a great fee to plead for a seized ship; and, just before we sail'd, Colonel French coming on board, and showing me great respect, I was more taken notice of, and, with my friend Ralph, invited by the other gentlemen to come into the cabin, there being now room. Accordingly, we remov'd thither.

Understanding that Colonel French had brought on board the governor's despatches, I ask'd the captain for those letters that were to be under my care. He said all were put into the bag together and he could not then come at them; but, before we landed in England, I should have an opportunity of picking them out; so I was satisfied for the present, and we proceeded on our voyage. We had a sociable company in the cabin, and lived uncommonly well, having the addition of all Mr. Hamilton's stores, who had laid in plentifully. In this passage Mr. Denham contracted a friendship for me that continued during his life. The voyage was otherwise not a pleasant one, as we had a great deal of bad weather.

When we came into the Channel, the captain kept his word with me, and gave me an opportunity of examining the bag for the governor's letters. I found none upon which my name was put as under my care. I picked out six or seven, that, by the handwriting, I thought might be the promised letters, especially as one of them was directed to Basket, the king's printer, and another to some stationer. We arriv'd in London the 24th of December, 1724. I waited upon the stationer, who came first in my way, delivering the letter as from Governor Keith. "I don't know such a person," says he; but, opening the letter, "O! this is from Riddlesden. I have lately found him to be a compleat rascal, and I will have nothing to do with him, nor receive any letters from him." So, putting the letter into my hand, he turn'd on his heel and left me to serve some customer. I was surprized to find these were not the governor's letters; and, after recollecting and comparing circumstances, I began to doubt his sincerity. I found my friend Denham, and opened the whole affair to him. He let me into Keith's character; told me there was not the least probability that he had written any letters for me; that no one, who knew him, had the smallest dependence on him; and he laught at the notion of the governor's giving me a letter of credit, having, as he said, no credit to give. On my expressing some concern about what I should do, he advised me to endeavor getting some employment in the way of my business. "Among the printers here," said he, "you will improve yourself, and when you return to America, you will set up to greater advantage."

We both of us happen'd to know, as well as the stationer, that Riddlesden, the attorney, was a very knave. He had half ruin'd Miss Read's father by persuading him to be bound for him. By this letter it appear'd there was a secret scheme on foot to the prejudice of Hamilton (suppos'd to be then coming over with us); and that Keith was concerned in it with Riddlesden. Denham, who was a friend of Hamilton's, thought he ought to be acquainted with it; so, when he arriv'd in England, which was soon after, partly from resentment and ill-will to Keith and Riddlesden, and partly from good-will to him, I waited on him, and gave him the letter. He thank'd me cordially, the information being of importance to him; and from that time he became my friend, greatly to my advantage afterwards on many occasions.

But what shall we think of a governor's playing such pitiful tricks, and imposing so grossly on a poor ignorant boy! It was a habit he had acquired. He wish'd to please everybody; and, having little to give, he gave expectations. He was otherwise an ingenious, sensible man, a pretty good writer, and a good governor for the people, tho' not for his constituents, the proprietaries, whose instructions he sometimes disregarded. Several of our best laws were of his planning and passed during his administration.

Ralph and I were inseparable companions. We took lodgings together in Little Britain at three shillings and sixpence a week—as much as we could then afford. He found some relations, but they were poor, and unable to assist him. He now let me know his intentions of remaining in London, and that he never meant to return to Philadelphia. He had brought no money with him, the whole he could muster having been expended in paying his passage. I had fifteen pistoles; so he borrowed occasionally of me to subsist, while he was looking out for business. He first endeavored to get into the playhouse, believing himself qualify'd for an actor; but Wilkes, to whom he apply'd, advis'd him candidly not to think of that employment, as it was impossible he should succeed in it. Then he propos'd to Roberts, a publisher in Paternoster Row, to write for him a weekly paper like the *Spectator*, on certain conditions, which Roberts did not approve. Then he endeavored to get employment as a hackney writer, to copy for the stationers and lawyers about the Temple, but could find no vacancy.

I immediately got into work at Palmer's, then a famous printing-house in Bartholomew Close, and here I continu'd near a year. I was pretty diligent, but spent with Ralph a good deal of my earnings in going to plays and other places of amusement. We had together consumed all my pistoles, and now just rubbed on from hand to mouth. He seem'd quite to forget his wife and child, and I, by degrees, my engagements with Miss Read, to whom I never wrote more than one letter, and that was to let her know I was not likely soon to return. This was another of the great errata of my life, which I should wish to correct if I were to live it over again. In fact, by our expenses, I was constantly kept unable to pay my passage.

At Palmer's I was employed in composing for the second edition of Wollaston's "Religion of Nature." Some of his reasonings not appearing to me well founded, I wrote a little metaphysical piece in which I made remarks on them. It was entitled "A Dissertation on Liberty and Necessity, Pleasure and Pain." I inscribed it to my friend Ralph; I printed a small number. It occasion'd my being more consider'd by Mr. Palmer as a young man of some ingenuity, tho' he seriously expostulated with me upon the principles of my pamphlet, which to him appear'd abominable. My printing this pamphlet was another erratum. While I lodg'd in Little Britain, I made an acquaintance with one Wilcox, a bookseller, whose shop was at the next door. He had an immense collection of second-hand books. Circulating libraries were not then in use; but we agreed that, on certain reasonable terms, which I have now forgotten, I might take, read, and return any of his books. This I esteem'd a great advantage, and I made as much use of it as I could.

My pamphlet by some means falling into the hands of one Lyons, a surgeon, author of a book entitled "The Infallibility of Human Judgment," it occasioned an acquaintance between us. He took great notice of me, called on me often to converse on those subjects, carried me to the Horns, a pale alehouse in —— Lane, Cheapside, and introduced me to Dr. Mandeville, author of the "Fable of the Bees," who had a club there, of which he was the soul, being a most facetious, entertaining companion. Lyons, too, introduced me to Dr. Pemberton, at Batson's Coffee-house, who promis'd to give me an opportunity, some time or other, of seeing Sir Isaac Newton, of which I was extreamely desirous; but this never happened.

I had brought over a few curiosities, among which the principal was a purse made of the asbestos, which purifies by fire. Sir Hans Sloane heard of it, came to see me, and invited me to his house in Bloomsbury Square, where he show'd me all his curiosities, and persuaded me to let him add that to the number, for which he paid me handsomely.

In our house there lodg'd a young woman, a milliner, who, I think, had a shop in the Cloisters. She had been genteelly bred, was sensible and lively, and of most pleasing conversation. Ralph read plays to her in the evenings, they grew intimate, she took another lodging, and he followed her. They liv'd together some time; but, he being still out of business, and her income not sufficient to maintain them with her child, he took a resolution of going from London, to try for a country school, which he thought himself well qualified to undertake, as he wrote an excellent hand, and was a master of arithmetic and accounts. This, however, he deemed a business below him, and confident of future better fortune, when he should be unwilling to have it known that he once was so meanly employed, he changed his name, and did me the honor to assume mine; for I soon after had a letter from him, acquainting me that he was settled in a small village (in Berkshire, I think it was, where he taught reading and writing to ten or a dozen boys, at sixpence each per week), recommending Mrs. T—— to my care, and desiring me to write to him, directing for Mr. Franklin, schoolmaster, at such a place.

He continued to write frequently, sending me large specimens of an epic poem which he was then composing, and desiring my remarks and corrections. These I gave him from time to time, but endeavor'd rather to discourage his proceeding. One of Young's Satires was then just published. I copy'd and sent him a great part of it, which set in a strong light the folly of pursuing the Muses with any hope of advancement by them. All was in vain; sheets of the poem continued to come by every post. In the mean time, Mrs. T ——, having on his account lost her friends and business, was often in distresses, and us'd to send for me, and borrow what I could spare to help her out of them. I grew fond of her company, and, being at that time under no religious restraint, and presuming upon my importance to her, I attempted familiarities (another erratum) which she repuls'd with a proper resentment, and acquainted him with my behaviour. This made a breach between us; and, when he returned again to London, he let me know he thought I had cancell'd all the obligations he had been under to me. So I found I was never to expect his repaying me what I lent to him, or advanc'd for him. This, however, was not then of much consequence, as he was totally unable; and in the loss of his friendship I found myself relieved from a burthen. I now began to think of getting a little money beforehand, and, expecting better work, I left Palmer's to work at Watts's, near Lincoln's Inn Fields, a still greater printing-house. Here I continued all the rest of my stay in London.

At my first admission into this printing-house I took to working at press, imagining I felt a want of the bodily exercise I had been us'd to in America, where presswork is mix'd with composing. I drank only water; the other workmen, near fifty in number, were great guzzlers of beer. On occasion, I carried up and down stairs a large form of types in each hand, when others carried but one in both hands. They wondered to see, from this and several instances, that the *Water-American*, as they called me, was *stronger* than themselves, who drank *strong* beer! We had an alehouse boy who attended always in the house to supply the workmen. My companion at the press drank every day a pint before breakfast, a pint at breakfast with his bread and cheese, a pint between breakfast and dinner, a pint at dinner, a pint in the afternoon about six o'clock, and another when he had done his day's work. I thought it a detestable custom; but it was necessary, he suppos'd, to drink *strong* beer, that he might be *strong* to labor. I endeavored to convince him that the bodily strength afforded by beer could only be in proportion to the grain or flour of the barley dissolved in the water of which it was made; that there was more flour in a pennyworth of bread; and therefore, if he would eat that with a pint of water, it would give him more strength than a quart of beer. He drank on, however, and had four or five shillings to pay out of his wages every Saturday night for that muddling liquor; an expense I was free from. And thus these poor devils keep themselves always under.

Watts, after some weeks, desiring to have me in the composing-room, I left the pressmen; a new bien venu or sum for drink, being five shillings, was demanded of me by the compositors. I thought it an imposition, as I had paid below; the master thought so too, and forbad my paying it. I stood out two or three weeks, was accordingly considered as an excommunicate, and had so many little pieces of private mischief done me, by mixing my sorts, transposing my pages, breaking my matter, etc., etc., if I were ever so little out of the room, and all ascribed to the chappel ghost, which they said ever haunted those not regularly admitted, that, notwithstanding the master's protection, I found myself oblig'd to comply and pay the money, convinc'd of the folly of being on ill terms with those one is to live with continually.

I was now on a fair footing with them, and soon acquir'd considerable influence. I propos'd some reasonable alterations in their chappel laws, and carried them against all opposition. From my example, a great part of them left their muddling breakfast of beer, and bread, and cheese, finding they could with me be supply'd from a neighboring house with a large por- ringer of hot water-gruel, sprinkled with pepper, crumb'd with bread, and a bit of butter in it, for the price of a pint of beer, viz., three half-pence. This was a more comfortable as well as cheaper breakfast, and kept their heads clearer. Those who continued sotting with beer all day, were often, by not paying, out of credit at the alehouse, and us'd to make interest with me to get beer; their *light*, as they phrased it, *being out*. I watch'd the pay- table on Saturday night, and collected what I stood engag'd for them, having to pay sometimes near thirty shillings a week on their accounts. This, and my being esteem'd a pretty good *riggite*, that is, a jocular verbal satirist, supported my consequence in the society. My constant attendance (I never making a St. Monday) recommended me to the master; and my uncommon quickness at composing occasioned my being put upon all work of dispatch, which was generally better paid. So I went on now very agree- ably.

My lodging in Little Britain being too remote, I found another in Duke- street, opposite to the Romish Chapel. It was two pair of stairs backwards, at an Italian warehouse. A widow lady kept the house; she had a daughter, and a maid servant, and a journeyman who attended the warehouse, but lodg'd abroad. After sending to inquire my character at the house where I last lodg'd, she agreed to take me in at the same rate, 3s. 6d. per week; cheaper, as she said, from the protection she expected in having a man lodge in the house. She was a widow, an elderly woman; had been bred a Protestant, being a clergyman's daughter, but was converted to the Cath- olic religion by her husband, whose memory she much revered; had lived much among people of distinction, and knew a thousand anecdotes of them as far back as the times of Charles the Second. She was lame in her knees with the gout, and, therefore, seldom stirred out of her room, so sometimes wanted company; and hers was so highly amusing to me, that I was sure to spend an evening with her whenever she desired it. Our supper was only half an anchovy each, on a very little strip of bread and butter, and half a pint of ale between us; but the entertainment was in her conversation. My always keeping good hours, and giving little trouble in the family, made her unwilling to part with me; so that, when I talk'd of a lodging I had heard of, nearer my business, for two shillings a week, which, intent as I now was on saving money, made some difference, she bid me not think of it, for she would abate me two shillings a week for the future; so I remained with her at one shilling and sixpence as long as I staid in London.

In a garret of her house there lived a maiden lady of seventy, in the most retired manner, of whom my landlady gave me this account: that she was a Roman Catholic, had been sent abroad when young, and lodg'd in a nunnery with an intent of becoming a nun; but, the country not agreeing with her, she returned to England, where, there being no nunnery, she had vow'd to lead the life of a nun, as near as might be done in those circumstances. Accordingly, she had given all her estate to charitable uses, reserving only twelve pounds a year to live on, and out of this sum she still gave a great deal in charity, living herself on water-gruel only, and using no fire but to boil it. She had lived many years in that garret, being permitted to remain there gratis by successive Catholic tenants of the house below, as they deemed it a blessing to have her there. A priest visited her to confess her every day. "I have ask'd her," says my landlady, "how she, as she liv'd, could possibly find so much employment for a confessor?" "Oh," said she, "it is impossible to avoid *vain thoughts*." I was permitted once to visit her. She was chearful and polite, and convers'd pleasantly. The room was clean, but had no other furniture than a matras, a table with a crucifix and book, a stool which she gave me to sit on, and a picture over the chimney of Saint Veronica displaying her handkerchief, with the miraculous figure of Christ's bleeding face on it, which she explained to me with great seriousness. She look'd pale, but was never sick; and I give it as another instance on how small an income, life and health may be supported.

At Watts's printing-house I contracted an acquaintance with an ingenious young man, one Wygate, who, having wealthy relations, had been better educated than most printers; was a tolerable Latinist, spoke French, and lov'd reading. I taught him and a friend of his to swim at twice going into the river, and they soon became good swimmers. They introduc'd me to some gentlemen from the country, who went to Chelsea by water to see the College and Don Saltero's curiosities. In our return, at the request of the company, whose curiosity Wygate had excited, I stripped and leaped into the river, and swam from near Chelsea to Blackfryar's, performing on the way many feats of activity, both upon and under water, that surpris'd and pleas'd those to whom they were novelties.

I had from a child been ever delighted with this exercise, had studied and practis'd all Thevenot's motions and positions, added some of my own, aiming at the graceful and easy as well as the useful. All these I took this occasion of exhibiting to the company, and was much flatter'd by their admiration; and Wygate, who was desirous of becoming a master, grew more and more attach'd to me on that account, as well as from the similarity of our studies. He at length proposed to me travelling all over Europe together, supporting ourselves everywhere by working at our business. I was once inclined to it; but, mentioning it to my good friend Mr. Denham, with whom I often spent an hour when I had leisure, he dissuaded me from it, advising me to think only of returning to Pennsilvania, which he was now about to do.

I must record one trait of this good man's character. He had formerly been in business at Bristol, but failed in debt to a number of people, compounded and went to America. There, by a close application to business as a merchant, he acquir'd a plentiful fortune in a few years. Returning to England in the ship with me, he invited his old creditors to an entertainment, at which he thank'd them for the easy composition they had favored him with, and, when they expected nothing but the treat, every man at the first remove found under his plate an order on a banker for the full amount of the unpaid remainder with interest.

He now told me he was about to return to Philadelphia, and should carry over a great quantity of goods in order to open a store there. He propos'd to take me over as his clerk, to keep his books, in which he would instruct me, copy his letters, and attend the store. He added, that, as soon as I should be acquainted with mercantile business, he would promote me by sending me with a cargo of flour and bread, etc., to the West Indies, and procure me commissions from others which would be profitable; and, if I manag'd well, would establish me handsomely. The thing pleas'd me; for I was grown tired of London, remembered with pleasure the happy months I had spent in Pennsylvania, and wish'd again to see it; therefore I immediately agreed on the terms of fifty pounds a year, Pennsylvania money; less, indeed, than my present gettings as a compositor, but affording a better prospect.

I now took leave of printing, as I thought, for ever, and was daily employ'd in my new business, going about with Mr. Denham among the tradesmen to purchase various articles, and seeing them pack'd up, doing errands, calling upon workmen to dispatch, etc.; and, when all was on board, I had a few days' leisure. On one of these days, I was, to my surprise, sent for by a great man I knew only by name, a Sir William Wyndham, and I waited upon him. He had heard by some means or other of my swimming from Chelsea to Blackfriar's, and of my teaching Wygate and another young man to swim in a few hours. He had two sons, about to set out on their travels; he wish'd to have them first taught swimming, and proposed to gratify me handsomely if I would teach them. They were not yet come to town, and my stay was uncertain, so I could not undertake it; but, from this incident, I thought it likely that, if I were to remain in England and open a swimming-school, I might get a good deal of money; and it struck me so strongly, that, had the overture been sooner made me, probably I should not so soon have returned to America. After many years, you and I had something of more importance to do with one of these sons of Sir William Wyndham, become Earl of Egremont, which I shall mention in its place.

Thus I spent about eighteen months in London; most part of the time I work'd hard at my business, and spent but little upon myself except in seeing plays and in books. My friend Ralph had kept me poor; he owed me about twenty-seven pounds, which I was now never likely to receive; a great sum out of my small earnings! I lov'd him, notwithstanding, for he had many amiable qualities. I had by no means improv'd my fortune; but I had picked up some very ingenious acquaintance, whose conversation was of great advantage to me; and I had read considerably.

We sail'd from Gravesend on the 23d of July, 1726. For the incidents of the voyage, I refer you to my Journal, where you will find them all minutely related. Perhaps the most important part of that journal is the *plan* to be found in it, which I formed at sea, for regulating my future conduct in life. It is the more remarkable, as being formed when I was so young, and yet being pretty faithfully adhered to quite thro' to old age.

We landed in Philadelphia on the 11th of October, where I found sundry alterations. Keith was no longer governor, being superseded by Major Gordon. I met him walking the streets as a common citizen. He seem'd a little asham'd at seeing me, but pass'd without saying any thing. I should have been as much asham'd at seeing Miss Read, had not her friends, despairing with reason of my return after the receipt of my letter, persuaded her to marry another, one Rogers, a potter, which was done in my absence. With him, however, she was never happy, and soon parted from him, refusing to cohabit with him or bear his name, it being now said that he had another wife. He was a worthless fellow, tho' an excellent workman, which was the temptation to her friends. He got into debt, ran away in 1727 or 1728, went to the West Indies, and died there. Keimer had got a better house, a shop well supply'd with stationery, plenty of new types, a number of hands, tho' none good, and seem'd to have a great deal of business.

Mr. Denham took a store in Water-street, where we open'd our goods; I attended the business diligently, studied accounts, and grew, in a little time, expert at selling. We lodg'd and boarded together; he counsell'd me as a father, having a sincere regard for me. I respected and lov'd him, and we might have gone on together very happy; but, in the beginning of February, 1727, when I had just pass'd my twenty-first year, we both were taken ill. My distemper was a pleurisy, which very nearly carried me off. I suffered a good deal, gave up the point in my own mind, and was rather disappointed when I found myself recovering, regretting, in some degree, that I must now, some time or other, have all that disagreeable work to do over again. I forget what his distemper was; it held him a long time, and at length carried him off. He left me a small legacy in a nuncupative will, as a token of his kindness for me, and he left me once more to the wide world; for the store was taken into the care of his executors, and my employment under him ended.

My brother-in-law, Holmes, being now at Philadelphia, advised my return to my business; and Keimer tempted me, with an offer of large wages by the year, to come and take the management of his printing-house, that he might better attend his stationer's shop. I had heard a bad character of him in London from his wife and her friends, and was not fond of having any more to do with him. I tri'd for farther employment as a merchant's clerk; but, not readily meeting with any, I clos'd again with Keimer. I found in his house these hands: Hugh Meredith, a Welsh Pensilvanian, thirty years of age, bred to country work; honest, sensible, had a great deal of solid observation, was something of a reader, but given to drink. Stephen Potts, a young countryman of full age, bred to the same, of uncommon natural parts, and great wit and humor, but a little idle. These he had agreed with at extream low wages per week, to be rais'd a shilling every three months, as they would deserve by improving in their business; and the expectation of these high wages, to come on hereafter, was what he had drawn them in with. Meredith was to work at press, Potts at book-binding, which he, by agreement, was to teach them, though he knew neither one nor t'other. John ——, a wild Irishman, brought up to no business, whose service, for four years, Keimer had purchased from the captain of a ship; he, too, was to be made a pressman. George Webb, an Oxford scholar, whose time for four years he had likewise bought, intending him for a compositor, of whom more presently; and David Harry, a country boy, whom he had taken apprentice.

I soon perceiv'd that the intention of engaging me at wages so much higher than he had been us'd to give, was, to have these raw, cheap hands form'd thro' me; and, as soon as I had instructed them, then they being all articled to him, he should be able to do without me. I went on, however, very cheerfully, put his printing-house in order, which had been in great confusion, and brought his hands by degrees to mind their business and to do it better.

It was an odd thing to find an Oxford scholar in the situation of a bought servant. He was not more than eighteen years of age, and gave me this account of himself; that he was born in Gloucester, educated at a grammar-school there, had been distinguish'd among the scholars for some apparent superiority in performing his part, when they exhibited plays; belong'd to the Witty Club there, and had written some pieces in prose and verse, which were printed in the Gloucester newspapers; thence he was sent to Oxford; where he continued about a year, but not well satisfi'd, wishing of all things to see London, and become a player. At length, receiving his quarterly allowance of fifteen guineas, instead of discharging his debts he walk'd out of town, hid his gown in a furze bush, and footed it to London, where, having no friend to advise him, he fell into bad company, soon spent his guineas, found no means of being introduc'd among the players, grew necessitous, pawn'd his cloaths, and wanted bread. Walking the street very hungry, and not knowing what to do with himself, a crimp's bill was put into his hand, offering immediate entertainment and encouragement to such as would bind themselves to serve in America. He went directly, sign'd the indentures, was put into the ship, and came over, never writing a line to acquaint his friends what was become of him. He was lively, witty, good-natur'd, and a pleasant companion, but idle, thoughtless, and imprudent to the last degree.

John, the Irishman, soon ran away; with the rest I began to live very agreeably, for they all respected me the more, as they found Keimer incapable of instructing them, and that from me they learned something daily. We never worked on Saturday, that being Keimer's Sabbath, so I had two days for reading. My acquaintance with ingenious people in the town increased. Keimer himself treated me with great civility and apparent regard, and nothing now made me uneasy but my debt to Vernon, which I was yet unable to pay, being hitherto but a poor œconomist. He, however, kindly made no demand of it.

Our printing-house often wanted sorts, and there was no letter-founder in America; I had seen types cast at James's in London, but without much attention to the manner; however, I now contrived a mould, made use of the letters we had as puncheons, struck the matrices in lead, and thus supply'd in a pretty tolerable way all deficiencies. I also engrav'd several things on occasion; I made the ink; I was warehouseman, and everything, and, in short, quite a fac-totum.

But, however serviceable I might be, I found that my services became every day of less importance, as the other hands improv'd in the business; and, when Keimer paid my second quarter's wages, he let me know that he felt them too heavy, and thought I should make an abatement. He grew by degrees less civil, put on more of the master, frequently found fault, was captious, and seem'd ready for an outbreaking. I went on, nevertheless, with a good deal of patience, thinking that his encumber'd circumstances were partly the cause. At length a trifle snapt our connections; for, a great noise happening near the court-house, I put my head out of the window to see what was the matter. Keimer, being in the street, look'd up and saw me, call'd out to me in a loud voice and angry tone to mind my business, adding some reproachful words, that nettled me the more for their publicity, all the neighbors who were looking out on the same occasion, being witnesses how I was treated. He came up immediately into the printing-house, continu'd the quarrel, high words pass'd on both sides, he gave me the quarter's warning we had stipulated, expressing a wish that he had not been oblig'd to so long a warning. I told him his wish was unnecessary, for I would leave him that instant; and so, taking my hat, walk'd out of doors, desiring Meredith, whom I saw below, to take care of some things I left, and bring them to my lodgings.

Meredith came accordingly in the evening, when we talked my affair over. He had conceiv'd a great regard for me, and was very unwilling that I should leave the house while he remain'd in it. He dissuaded me from returning to my native country, which I began to think of; he reminded me that Keimer was in debt for all he possess'd; that his creditors began to be uneasy; that he kept his shop miserably, sold often without profit for ready money, and often trusted without keeping accounts; that he must therefore fail, which would make a vacancy I might profit of. I objected my want of money. He then let me know that his father had a high opinion of me, and, from some discourse that had pass'd between them, he was sure would advance money to set us up, if I would enter into partnership with him. "My time," says he, "will be out with Keimer in the spring; by that time we may have our press and types in from London. I am sensible I am no workman; if you like it, your skill in the business shall be set against the stock I furnish, and we will share the profits equally."

The proposal was agreeable, and I consented; his father was in town and approv'd of it; the more as he saw I had great influence with his son, had prevail'd on him to abstain long from dram-drinking, and he hop'd might break him of that wretched habit entirely, when we came to be so closely connected. I gave an inventory to the father, who carry'd it to a merchant; the things were sent for, the secret was to be kept till they should arrive, and in the mean time I was to get work, if I could, at the other printing-house. But I found no vacancy there, and so remain'd idle a few days, when Keimer, on a prospect of being employ'd to print some paper money in New Jersey, which would require cuts and various types that I only could supply, and apprehending Bradford might engage me and get the jobb from him, sent me a very civil message, that old friends should not part for a few words, the effect of sudden passion, and wishing me to return. Meredith persuaded me to comply, as it would give more opportunity for his improvement under my daily instructions; so I return'd, and we went on more smoothly than for some time before. The New Jersey jobb was obtain'd, I contriv'd a copper-plate press for it, the first that had been seen in the country; I cut several ornaments and checks for the bills. We went together to Burlington, where I executed the whole to satisfaction; and he received so large a sum for the work as to be enabled thereby to keep his head much longer above water.

At Burlington I made an acquaintance with many principal people of the province. Several of them had been appointed by the Assembly a committee to attend the press, and take care that no more bills were printed than the law directed. They were therefore, by turns, constantly with us, and generally he who attended, brought with him a friend or two for company. My mind having been much more improv'd by reading than Keimer's, I suppose it was for that reason my conversation seem'd to be more valu'd. They had me to their houses, introduced me to their friends, and show'd me much civility; while he, tho' the master, was a little neglected. In truth, he was an odd fish; ignorant of common life, fond of rudely opposing receiv'd opinions, slovenly to extream dirtiness, enthusiastic in some points of religion, and a little knavish withal.

We continu'd there near three months; and by that time I could reckon among my acquired friends, Judge Allen, Samuel Bustill, the secretary of the Province, Isaac Pearson, Joseph Cooper, and several of the Smiths, members of Assembly, and Isaac Decow, the surveyor-general. The latter was a shrewd, sagacious old man, who told me that he began for himself, when young, by wheeling clay for the brickmakers, learned to write after he was of age, carri'd the chain for surveyors, who taught him surveying, and he had now by his industry, acquir'd a good estate; and says he, "I foresee that you will soon work this man out of his business, and make a fortune in it at Philadelphia." He had not then the least intimation of my intention to set up there or anywhere. These friends were afterwards of great use to me, as I occasionally was to some of them. They all continued their regard for me as long as they lived.

Before I enter upon my public appearance in business, it may be well to let you know the then state of my mind with regard to my principles and morals, that you may see how far those influenc'd the future events of my life. My parents had early given me religious impressions, and brought me through my childhood piously in the Dissenting way. But I was scarce fifteen, when, after doubting by turns of several points, as I found them disputed in the different books I read, I began to doubt of Revelation itself. Some books against Deism fell into my hands; they were said to be the substance of sermons preached at Boyle's Lectures. It happened that they wrought an effect on me quite contrary to what was intended by them; for the arguments of the Deists, which were quoted to be refuted, appeared to me much stronger than the refutations; in short, I soon became a thorough Deist. My arguments perverted some others, particularly Collins and Ralph; but, each of them having afterwards wrong'd me greatly without the least compunction, and recollecting Keith's conduct towards me (who was another freethinker), and my own towards Vernon and Miss Read, which at times gave me great trouble, I began to suspect that this doctrine, tho' it might be true, was not very useful. My London pamphlet, which had for its motto these lines of Dryden:

> "Whatever is, is right. Though purblind man
> Sees but a part o' the chain, the nearest link:
> His eyes not carrying to the equal beam,
> That poises all above";

and from the attributes of God, his infinite wisdom, goodness and power, concluded that nothing could possibly be wrong in the world, and that vice and virtue were empty distinctions, no such things existing, appear'd now not so clever a performance as I once thought it; and I doubted whether some error had not insinuated itself unperceiv'd into my argument, so as to infect all that follow'd, as is common in metaphysical reasonings.

I grew convinc'd that *truth*, *sincerity* and *integrity* in dealings between man and man were of the utmost importance to the felicity of life; and I form'd written resolutions, which still remain in my journal book, to practice them ever while I lived. Revelation had indeed no weight with me, as such; but I entertain'd an opinion that, though certain actions might not be bad *because* they were forbidden by it, or good *because* it commanded them, yet probably those actions might be forbidden *because* they were bad for us, or commanded *because* they were beneficial to us, in their own natures, all the circumstances of things considered. And this persuasion, with the kind hand of Providence, or some guardian angel, or accidental favorable circumstances and situations, or all together, preserved me, thro' this dangerous time of youth, and the hazardous situations I was sometimes in among strangers, remote from the eye and advice of my father,

without any willful gross immorality or injustice, that might have been
expected from my want of religion. I say willful, because the instances I
have mentioned had something of *necessity* in them, from my youth, inex-
perience, and the knavery of others. I had therefore a tolerable character
to begin the world with; I valued it properly, and determin'd to preserve it.

We had not been long return'd to Philadelphia before the new types
arriv'd from London. We settled with Keimer, and left him by his consent
before he heard of it. We found a house to hire near the market, and took
it. To lessen the rent, which was then but twenty-four pounds a year, tho'
I have since known it to let for seventy, we took in Thomas Godfrey, a
glazier, and his family, who were to pay a considerable part of it to us,
and we to board with them. We had scarce opened our letters and put our
press in order, before George House, an acquaintance of mine, brought a
countryman to us, whom he had met in the street inquiring for a printer.
All our cash was now expended in the variety of particulars we had been
obliged to procure, and this countryman's five shillings, being our first-
fruits, and coming so seasonably, gave me more pleasure than any crown
I have since earned; and the gratitude I felt toward House has made me
often more ready than perhaps I should otherwise have been to assist young
beginners.

There are croakers in every country, always boding its ruin. Such a one
then lived in Philadelphia; a person of note, an elderly man, with a wise
look and a very grave manner of speaking; his name was Samuel Mickle.
This gentleman, a stranger to me, stopt one day at my door, and asked me
if I was the young man who had lately opened a new printing-house. Being
answered in the affirmative, he said he was sorry for me, because it was an
expensive undertaking, and the expense would be lost; for Philadelphia
was a sinking place, the people already half bankrupts, or near being so; all
appearances to the contrary, such as new buildings and the rise of rents,
being to his certain knowledge fallacious; for they were, in fact, among the
things that would soon ruin us. And he gave me such a detail of misfortunes now existing, or that were soon to exist, that he left me half melancholy. Had I known him before I engaged in this business, probably I never
should have done it. This man continued to live in this decaying place, and
to declaim in the same strain, refusing for many years to buy a house there,
because all was going to destruction; and at last I had the pleasure of seeing
him give five times as much for one as he might have bought it for when
he first began his croaking.

I should have mentioned before, that, in the autumn of the preceding
year, I had form'd most of my ingenious acquaintance into a club of mutual
improvement, which we called the JUNTO; we met on Friday evenings. The
rules that I drew up required that every member, in his turn, should produce
one or more queries on any point of Morals, Politics, or Natural Philosophy,
to be discuss'd by the company; and once in three months produce and read
an essay of his own writing, on any subject he pleased. Our debates were
to be under the direction of a president, and to be conducted in the sincere

spirit of inquiry after truth, without fondness for dispute, or desire of victory; and, to prevent warmth, all expressions of positiveness in opinions, or direct contradiction, were after some time made contraband, and prohibited under small pecuniary penalties.

The first members were Joseph Breintnal, a copyer of deeds for the scriveners, a good-natur'd, friendly, middle-ag'd man, a great lover of poetry, reading all he could meet with, and writing some that was tolerable; very ingenious in many little Nicknackeries, and of sensible conversation.

Thomas Godfrey, a self-taught mathematician, great in his way, and afterward inventor of what is now called Hadley's Quadrant. But he knew little out of his way, and was not a pleasing companion; as, like most great mathematicians I have met with, he expected universal precision in every thing said, or was for ever denying or distinguishing upon trifles, to the disturbance of all conversation. He soon left us.

Nicholas Scull, a surveyor, afterward surveyor-general, who lov'd books, and sometimes made a few verses.

William Parsons, bred a shoemaker, but, loving reading, had acquir'd a considerable share of mathematics, which he first studied with a view to astrology, that he afterwards laught at it. He also became surveyor-general.

William Maugridge, a joiner, a most exquisite mechanic, and a solid, sensible man.

Hugh Meredith, Stephen Potts, and George Webb I have characteriz'd before.

Robert Grace, a young gentleman of some fortune, generous, lively, and witty; a lover of punning and of his friends.

And William Coleman, then a merchant's clerk, about my age, who had the coolest, clearest head, the best heart, and the exactest morals of almost any man I ever met with. He became afterwards a merchant of great note, and one of our provincial judges. Our friendship continued without interruption to his death, upward of forty years; and the club continued almost as long, and was the best school of philosophy, morality, and politics that then existed in the province; for our queries, which were read the week preceding their discussion, put us upon reading with attention upon the several subjects, that we might speak more to the purpose; and here, too, we acquired better habits of conversation, every thing being studied in our rules which might prevent our disgusting each other. From hence the long continuance of the club, which I shall have frequent occasion to speak further of hereafter.

But my giving this account of it here is to show something of the interest I had, every one of these exerting themselves in recommending business to us. Breintnal particularly procur'd us from the Quakers the printing forty sheets of their history, the rest being to be done by Keimer; and upon this we work'd exceedingly hard, for the price was low. It was a folio, pro patria size, in pica, with long primer notes. I compos'd of it a sheet a day, and Meredith worked it off at press; it was often eleven at night, and sometimes later, before I had finished my distribution for the next day's work, for the little jobbs sent in by our other friends now and then put us back. But so determin'd I was to continue doing a sheet a day of the folio, that one night, when, having impos'd my forms, I thought my day's work over, one of them by accident was broken, and two pages reduced to pi, I immediately distributed and compos'd it over again before I went to bed; and this industry, visible to our neighbors, began to give us character and credit; particularly, I was told, that mention being made of the new printing-office at the merchants' Every-night club, the general opinion was that it must fail, there being already two printers in the place, Keimer and Bradford; but Dr. Baird (whom you and I saw many years after at his native place, St. Andrew's in Scotland) gave a contrary opinion: "For the industry of that Franklin," says he, "is superior to any thing I ever saw of the kind; I see him still at work when I go home from club, and he is at work again before his neighbors are out of bed." This struck the rest, and we soon after had offers from one of them to supply us with stationery; but as yet we did not chuse to engage in shop business.

I mention this industry the more particularly and the more freely, tho' it seems to be talking in my own praise, that those of my posterity, who shall read it, may know the use of that virtue, when they see its effects in my favour throughout this relation.

George Webb, who had found a female friend that lent him wherewith to purchase his time of Keimer, now came to offer himself as a journeyman to us. We could not then imploy him; but I foolishly let him know as a secret that I soon intended to begin a newspaper, and might then have work for him. My hopes of success, as I told him, were founded on this, that the then only newspaper, printed by Bradford, was a paltry thing, wretchedly manag'd, no way entertaining, and yet was profitable to him; I therefore thought a good paper would scarcely fail of good encouragement. I requested Webb not to mention it; but he told it to Keimer, who immediately, to be beforehand with me, published proposals for printing one himself, on which Webb was to be employ'd. I resented this; and, to counteract them, as I could not yet begin our paper, I wrote several pieces of entertainment for Bradford's paper, under the title of the Busy Body, which Breintnal continu'd some months. By this means the attention of the publick was fixed on that paper, and Keimer's proposals, which we burlesqu'd and ridicul'd, were disregarded. He began his paper, however, and, after carrying it on three quarters of a year, with at most only ninety subscribers, he offer'd it to me for a trifle; and I, having been ready some time to go on with it, took it in hand directly; and it prov'd in a few years extremely profitable to me.

I perceive that I am apt to speak in the singular number, though our partnership still continu'd; the reason may be that, in fact, the whole management of the business lay upon me. Meredith was no compositor, a poor pressman, and seldom sober. My friends lamented my connection with him, but I was to make the best of it.

Our first papers made a quite different appearance from any before in the province; a better type, and better printed; but some spirited remarks of my writing, on the dispute then going on between Governor Burnet and the Massachusetts Assembly, struck the principal people, occasioned the paper and the manager of it to be much talk'd of, and in a few weeks brought them all to be our subscribers.

Their example was follow'd by many, and our number went on growing continually. This was one of the first good effects of my having learnt a little to scribble; another was, that the leading men, seeing a newspaper now in the hands of one who could also handle a pen, thought it convenient to oblige and encourage me. Bradford still printed the votes, and laws, and other publick business. He had printed an address of the House to the governor, in a coarse, blundering manner; we reprinted it elegantly and correctly, and sent one to every member. They were sensible of the difference: it strengthened the hands of our friends in the House, and they voted us their printers for the year ensuing.

Among my friends in the House I must not forget Mr. Hamilton, before mentioned, who was then returned from England, and had a seat in it. He interested himself for me strongly in that instance, as he did in many others afterward, continuing his patronage till his death.

Mr. Vernon, about this time, put me in mind of the debt I ow'd him, but did not press me. I wrote him an ingenuous letter of acknowledgment, crav'd his forbearance a little longer, which he allow'd me, and as soon as I was able, I paid the principal with interest, and many thanks; so that erratum was in some degree corrected.

But now another difficulty came upon me which I had never the least reason to expect. Mr. Meredith's father, who was to have paid for our printing-house, according to the expectations given me, was able to advance only one hundred pounds currency, which had been paid; and a hundred more was due to the merchant, who grew impatient, and su'd us all. We gave bail, but saw that, if the money could not be rais'd in time, the suit must soon come to a judgment and execution, and our hopeful prospects must, with us, be ruined, as the press and letters must be sold for payment, perhaps at half price.

In this distress two true friends, whose kindness I have never forgotten, nor ever shall forget while I can remember any thing, came to me separately, unknown to each other, and, without any application from me, offering each of them to advance me all the money that should be necessary to enable me to take the whole business upon myself, if that should be practicable; but they did not like my continuing the partnership with Meredith, who, as they said, was often seen drunk in the streets, and playing at low games in alehouses, much to our discredit. These two friends were William Coleman and Robert Grace. I told them I could not propose a separation while any prospect remain'd of the Merediths' fulfilling their part of our agreement, because I thought myself under great obligations to them for what they had done, and would do if they could; but, if they finally fail'd in their performance, and our partnership must be dissolv'd, I should then think myself at liberty to accept the assistance of my friends.

Thus the matter rested for some time, when I said to my partner, "Perhaps your father is dissatisfied at the part you have undertaken in this affair of ours, and is unwilling to advance for you and me what he would for you alone. If that is the case, tell me, and I will resign the whole to you, and go about my business." "No," said he, "my father has really been disappointed, and is really unable; and I am unwilling to distress him farther. I see this is a business I am not fit for. I was bred a farmer, and it was a folly in me to come to town, and put myself, at thirty years of age, an apprentice to learn a new trade. Many of our Welsh people are going to settle in North Carolina, where land is cheap. I am inclin'd to go with them, and follow my old employment. You may find friends to assist you. If you will take the debts of the company upon you; return to my father the hundred pound he has advanced; pay my little personal debts, and give me thirty pounds and a new saddle, I will relinquish the partnership, and leave the whole in your hands." I agreed to this proposal; it was drawn up in writing, sign'd, and seal'd immediately. I gave him what he demanded, and he went soon after to Carolina, from whence he sent me next year two long letters, containing the best account that had been given of that country, the climate, the soil, husbandry, etc., for in those matters he was very judicious. I printed them in the papers, and they gave great satisfaction to the publick.

As soon as he was gone, I recurr'd to my two friends; and because I would not give an unkind preference to either, I took half of what each had offered and I wanted of one, and half of the other; paid off the company's debts, and went on with the business in my own name, advertising that the partnership was dissolved. I think this was in or about the year 1729.

About this time there was a cry among the people for more paper money, only fifteen thousand pounds being extant in the province, and that soon to be sunk. The wealthy inhabitants oppos'd any addition, being against all paper currency, from an apprehension that it would depreciate, as it had done in New England, to the prejudice of all creditors. We had discuss'd this point in our Junto, where I was on the side of an addition, being persuaded that the first small sum struck in 1723 had done much good by increasing the trade, employment, and number of inhabitants in the province, since I now saw all the old houses inhabited, and many new ones building: whereas I remembered well, that when I first walk'd about the streets of Philadelphia, eating my roll, I saw most of the houses in Walnut-street, between Second and Front streets, with bills on their doors, "To be let"; and many likewise in Chestnut-street and other streets, which made me then think the inhabitants of the city were deserting it one after another.

Our debates possess'd me so fully of the subject, that I wrote and printed an anonymous pamphlet on it, entitled "*The Nature and Necessity of a Paper Currency.*" It was well receiv'd by the common people in general; but the rich men dislik'd it, for it increas'd and strengthen'd the clamor for more money, and they happening to have no writers among them that were able to answer it, their opposition slacken'd, and the point was carried by a majority in the House. My friends there, who conceiv'd I had been of some service, thought fit to reward me by employing me in printing the money; a very profitable jobb and a great help to me. This was another advantage gain'd by my being able to write.

The utility of this currency became by time and experience so evident as never afterwards to be much disputed; so that it grew soon to fifty-five thousand pounds, and in 1739 to eighty thousand pounds, since which it arose during war to upwards of three hundred and fifty thousand pounds, trade, building, and inhabitants all the while increasing, tho' I now think there are limits beyond which the quantity may be hurtful.

I soon after obtain'd, thro' my friend Hamilton, the printing of the New-castle paper money, another profitable jobb as I then thought it; small things appearing great to those in small circumstances; and these, to me, were really great advantages, as they were great encouragements. He procured for me, also, the printing of the laws and votes of that government, which continu'd in my hands as long as I follow'd the business.

I now open'd a little stationer's shop. I had in it blanks of all sorts, the correctest that ever appear'd among us, being assisted in that by my friend Breintnal. I had also paper, parchment, chapmen's books, etc. One White-mash, a compositor I had known in London, an excellent workman, now came to me, and work'd with me constantly and diligently; and I took an apprentice, the son of Aquila Rose.

I began now gradually to pay off the debt I was under for the printing-house. In order to secure my credit and character as a tradesman, I took care not only to be in *reality* industrious and frugal, but to avoid all appearances to the contrary. I drest plainly; I was seen at no places of idle diversion. I never went out a fishing or shooting; a book, indeed, sometimes debauch'd me from my work, but that was seldom, snug, and gave no scandal; and, to show that I was not above my business, I sometimes brought home the paper I purchas'd at the stores thro' the streets on a wheelbarrow. Thus being esteem'd an industrious, thriving young man, and paying duly for what I bought, the merchants who imported stationery solicited my custom; others proposed supplying me with books, and I went on swimmingly. In the mean time, Keimer's credit and business declining daily, he was at last forc'd to sell his printing-house to satisfy his creditors. He went to Barbadoes, and there lived some years in very poor circumstances.

His apprentice, David Harry, whom I had instructed while I work'd with him, set up in his place at Philadelphia, having bought his materials. I was at first apprehensive of a powerful rival in Harry, as his friends were very able, and had a good deal of interest. I therefore propos'd a partnership to him, which he, fortunately for me, rejected with scorn. He was very proud, dress'd like a gentleman, liv'd expensively, took much diversion and pleasure abroad, ran in debt, and neglected his business; upon which, all business left him; and, finding nothing to do, he follow'd Keimer to Barbadoes, taking the printing-house with him. There this apprentice employ'd his former master as a journeyman; they quarrel'd often; Harry went continually be-hindhand, and at length was forc'd to sell his types and return to his country work in Pensilvania. The person that bought them employ'd Keimer to use them, but in a few years he died.

There remained now no competitor with me at Philadelphia but the old one, Bradford; who was rich and easy, did a little printing now and then by straggling hands, but was not very anxious about the business. However, as he kept the post-office, it was imagined he had better opportunities of obtaining news; his paper was thought a better distributer of advertisements than mine, and therefore had many more, which was a profitable thing to him, and a disadvantage to me; for, tho' I did indeed receive and send papers by the post, yet the publick opinion was otherwise, for what I did send was by bribing the riders, who took them privately, Bradford being unkind enough to forbid it, which occasion'd some resentment on my part; and I thought so meanly of him for it, that, when I afterward came into his situation, I took care never to imitate it.

I had hitherto continu'd to board with Godfrey, who lived in part of my house with his wife and children, and had one side of the shop for his glazier's business, tho' he worked little, being always absorbed in his mathematics. Mrs. Godfrey projected a match for me with a relation's daughter, took opportunities of bringing us often together, till a serious courtship on my part ensu'd, the girl being in herself very deserving. The old folks encourag'd me by continual invitations to supper, and by leaving us together, till at length it was time to explain. Mrs. Godfrey manag'd our little treaty. I let her know that I expected as much money with their daughter as would pay off my remaining debt for the printing-house, which I believe was not then above a hundred pounds. She brought me word they had no such sum to spare; I said they might mortgage their house in the loan-office. The answer to this, after some days, was, that they did not approve the match; that, on inquiry of Bradford, they had been inform'd the printing business was not a profitable one; the types would soon be worn out, and more wanted; that S. Keimer and D. Harry had failed one after the other, and I should probably soon follow them; and, therefore, I was forbidden the house, and the daughter shut up.

Whether this was a real change of sentiment or only artifice, on a supposition of our being too far engaged in affection to retract, and therefore that we should steal a marriage, which would leave them at liberty to give or withhold what they pleas'd, I know not; but I suspected the latter, resented it, and went no more. Mrs. Godfrey brought me afterward some more favorable accounts of their disposition, and would have drawn me on again; but I declared absolutely my resolution to have nothing more to do with that family. This was resented by the Godfreys; we differ'd, and they removed, leaving me the whole house, and I resolved to take no more inmates.

But this affair having turned my thoughts to marriage, I look'd round me and made overtures of acquaintance in other places; but soon found that, the business of a printer being generally thought a poor one, I was not to expect money with a wife, unless with such a one as I should not otherwise think agreeable. In the mean time, that hard-to-be-governed passion of youth hurried me frequently into intrigues with low women that fell in my way, which were attended with some expense and great inconvenience, besides a continual risque to my health by a distemper which of all things I dreaded, though by great good luck I escaped it. A friendly correspondence as neighbors and old acquaintances had continued between me and Mrs. Read's family, who all had a regard for me from the time of my first lodging in their house. I was often invited there and consulted in their affairs, wherein I sometimes was of service. I piti'd poor Miss Read's unfortunate situation, who was generally dejected, seldom cheerful, and avoided company. I considered my giddiness and inconstancy when in London as in a great degree the cause of her unhappiness, tho' the mother was good enough to think the fault more her own than mine, as she had prevented our marrying before I went thither, and persuaded the other match in my absence. Our mutual affection was revived, but there were now great objections to our union. The match was indeed looked upon as invalid, a preceding wife being said to be living in England; but this could not easily be prov'd, because of the distance; and, tho' there was a report of his death, it was not certain. Then, tho' it should be true, he had left many debts, which his successor might be call'd upon to pay. We ventured, however, over all these difficulties, and I took her to wife, September 1st, 1730. None of the inconveniences happened that we had apprehended; she proved a good and faithful helpmate, assisted me much by attending the shop; we throve together, and have ever mutually endeavor'd to make each other happy. Thus I corrected that great *erratum* as well as I could.

About this time, our club meeting, not at a tavern, but in a little room of Mr. Grace's, set apart for that purpose, a proposition was made by me, that, since our books were often referr'd to in our disquisitions upon the queries, it might be convenient to us to have them altogether where we met, that upon occasion they might be consulted; and by thus clubbing our books to a common library, we should, while we lik'd to keep them together, have each of us the advantage of using the books of all the other members, which would be nearly as beneficial as if each owned the whole. It was lik'd and agreed to, and we fill'd one end of the room with such books as we could best spare. The number was not so great as we expected; and tho' they had been of great use, yet some inconveniences occurring for want of due care of them, the collection, after about a year, was separated, and each took his books home again.

And now I set on foot my first project of a public nature, that for a subscription library. I drew up the proposals, got them put into form by our great scrivener, Brockden, and, by the help of my friends in the Junto, procured fifty subscribers of forty shillings each to begin with, and ten shillings a year for fifty years, the term our company was to continue. We afterwards obtain'd a charter, the company being increased to one hundred: this was the mother of all the North American subscription libraries, now so numerous. It is become a great thing itself, and continually increasing.

These libraries have improved the general conversation of the Americans, made the common tradesmen and farmers as intelligent as most gentlemen from other countries, and perhaps have contributed in some degree to the stand, so generally made throughout the colonies in defence of their privileges.

Mem°. Thus far was written with the intention express'd in the beginning and therefore contains several little family anecdotes of no importance to others. What follows was written many years after in compliance with the advice contain'd in these letters, and accordingly intended for the public. The affairs of the Revolution occasion'd the interruption.

Letter from Mr. Abel James, with Notes of my Life (received in Paris).

"MY DEAR AND HONORED FRIEND: I have often been desirous of writing to thee, but could not be reconciled to the thought, that the letter might fall into the hands of the British, lest some printer or busy-body should publish some part of the contents, and give our friend pain, and myself censure.

"Some time since there fell into my hands, to my great joy, about twenty-three sheets in thy own handwriting, containing an account of the parentage and life of thyself, directed to thy son, ending in the year 1730, with which there were notes, likewise in thy writing; a copy of which I inclose, in hopes it may be a means, if thou continued it up to a later period, that the first and latter part may be put together; and if it is not yet continued, I hope thee will not delay it. Life is uncertain, as the preacher tells us; and what will the world say if kind, humane, and benevolent Ben. Franklin should leave his friends and the world deprived of so pleasing and profitable a work; a work which would be useful and entertaining not only to a few, but to millions? The influence writings under that class have on the minds of youth is very great, and has nowhere appeared to me so plain, as in our public friend's journals. It almost insensibly leads the youth into the resolution of endeavoring to become as good and eminent as the journalist. Should thine, for instance, when published (and I think it could not fail of it), lead the youth to equal the industry and temperance of thy early youth, what a blessing with that class would such a work be! I know of no character living, nor many of them put together, who has so much in his power as thyself to promote a greater spirit of industry and early attention to business, frugality, and temperance with the American youth. Not that I think the work would have no other merit and use in the world, far from it; but the first is of such vast importance that I know nothing that can equal it."

The foregoing letter and the minutes accompanying it being shown to a friend, I received from him the following:

Letter from Mr. Benjamin Vaughan. "Paris, January 31, 1783.

"MY DEAREST SIR: When I had read over your sheets of minutes of the principal incidents of your life, recovered for you by your Quaker acquaintance, I told you I would send you a letter expressing my reasons why I thought it would be useful to complete and publish it as he desired. Various concerns have for some time past prevented this letter being written, and I do not know whether it was worth any expectation; happening to be at leisure, however, at present, I shall by writing, at least, interest and instruct myself; but as the terms I am inclined to use may tend to offend a person of your manners, I shall only tell you how I would address any other person, who was as good and as great as yourself, but less diffident. I would say to him, Sir, I solicit the history of your life from the following motives: Your history is so remarkable, that if you do not give it, somebody else will certainly give it; and perhaps so as nearly to do as much harm, as your own management of the thing might do good. It will moreover present a table of the internal circumstances of your country, which will very much tend to invite to it settlers of virtuous and manly minds. And considering the eagerness with which such information is sought by them, and the extent of your reputation, I do not know of a more efficacious advertisement than your biography would give. All that has happened to you is also connected with the detail of the manners and situation of a rising people; and in this respect I do not think that the writings of Cæsar and Tacitus can be more interesting to a true judge of human nature and society. But these, sir, are small reasons, in my opinion, compared with the chance which your life will give for the forming of future great men; and in conjunction with your Art of Virtue (which you design to publish) of improving the features of private character, and consequently of aiding all happiness, both public and domestic. The two works I allude to, sir, will in particular give a noble rule and example of self-education. School and other education constantly proceed upon false principles, and show a clumsy apparatus pointed at a false mark; but your apparatus is simple, and the mark a true one; and while parents and young persons are left destitute of other just means of estimating and becoming prepared for a reasonable course in life, your discovery that the thing is in many a man's private power, will be invaluable! Influence upon the private character, late in life, is not only an influence late in life, but a weak influence. It is in youth that we plant our chief habits and prejudices; it is in youth that we take our party as to profession, pursuits and matrimony. In youth, therefore, the turn is given; in youth the education even of the next generation is given; in youth the private and public character is determined; and the term of life extending but from youth to age, life ought to begin well from youth, and more especially before we take our party as to our principal objects. But your biography will not merely teach self-education, but the education of a wise man; and the wisest man will receive lights and improve his progress, by seeing detailed the conduct of another wise man. And why are weaker men to be deprived of such helps, when we see our race has been blundering on in the dark, almost without a guide in this particular, from the farthest trace of time? Show then, sir, how much is to be done, both to sons and fathers; and invite all wise men to become like yourself, and other men to become wise. When we see how cruel statesmen and warriors can be to the human race, and how absurd distinguished men can be to their acquaintance, it will be instructive to observe the instances multiply of pacific, acquiescing manners; and to find how compatible it is to be great and domestic, enviable and yet good-humored.

"The little private incidents which you will also have to relate, will have considerable use, as we want, above all things, rules of prudence in ordinary affairs; and it will be curious to see how you have acted in these. It will be so far a sort of key to life, and explain many things that all men ought to have once explained to them, to give them a chance of becoming wise by foresight. The nearest thing to having experience of one's own, is to have other people's affairs brought before us in a shape that is interesting; this is sure to happen from your pen; our affairs and management will have an air of simplicity or importance that will not fail to strike; and I am convinced you have conducted them with as much originality as if you had been conducting discussions in politics or philosophy; and what more worthy of experiments and system (its importance and its errors considered) than human life?

"Some men have been virtuous blindly, others have speculated fantastically, and others have been shrewd to bad purposes; but you, sir, I am sure, will give under your hand, nothing but what is at the same moment, wise, practical and good. Your account of yourself (for I suppose the parallel I am drawing for Dr. Franklin, will hold not only in point of character, but of private history) will show that you are ashamed of no origin; a thing the more important, as you prove how little necessary all origin is to happiness, virtue, or greatness. As no end likewise happens without a means, so we shall find, sir, that even you yourself framed a plan by which you became considerable; but at the same time we may see that though the event is flattering, the means are as simple as wisdom could make them; that is, depending upon nature, virtue, thought and habit. Another thing demonstrated will be the propriety of every man's waiting for his time for appearing upon the stage of the world. Our sensations being very much fixed to the moment, we are apt to forget that more moments are to follow the first, and consequently that man should arrange his conduct so as to suit the whole of a life. Your attribution appears to have been applied to your life, and the passing moments of it have been enlivened with content and enjoyment, instead of being tormented with foolish impatience or regrets. Such a conduct is easy for those who make virtue and themselves in countenance by examples of other truly great men, of whom patience is so often the characteristic. Your Quaker correspondent, sir (for here again I will suppose the subject of my letter resembling Dr. Franklin), praised your frugality, diligence and temperance, which he considered as a pattern for all youth; but it is singular that he should have forgotten your modesty and your disinterestedness, without which you never could have waited for your advancement, or found your situation in the mean time comfortable; which is a strong lesson to show the poverty of glory and the importance of regulating our minds. If this correspondent had known the nature of your reputation as well as I do, he would have said, Your former writings and measures would secure attention to your Biography, and Art of Virtue; and your Biography and Art of Virtue, in return, would secure attention to them. This is an advantage attendant upon a various character, and which brings all that belongs to it into greater play; and it is the more useful, as perhaps more persons are at a loss for the means of improving their minds and characters, than they are for the time or the inclination to do it. But there is one concluding reflection, sir, that will shew the use of your life as a mere piece of biography. This style of writing seems a little gone out of vogue, and yet it is a very useful one; and your specimen of it may be particularly serviceable, as it will make a subject of comparison with the lives of various public cut-throats and intriguers, and with absurd monastic self-tormentors or vain literary triflers. If it encourages more writings of the same kind with your own, and induces more men to spend lives fit to be written, it will be worth all Plutarch's Lives put together. But being tired of figuring to myself a character of which every feature suits only one man in the world, without giving him the praise of it, I shall end my letter, my dear Dr. Franklin, with a personal application to your proper self. I am earnestly desirous, then, my dear sir, that you should let the world into the traits of your genuine character, as civil broils may otherwise tend to disguise or traduce it. Considering your great age, the caution of your character, and your peculiar style of thinking, it is not likely that any one besides yourself can be sufficiently master of the facts of your life, or the intentions of your mind. Besides all this, the immense revolution of the present period, will necessarily turn our attention towards the author of it, and when virtuous principles have been pretended in it, it will be highly important to shew that such have really influenced; and, as your own character will be the principal one to receive a scrutiny, it is proper (even for its effects upon your vast and rising country, as well as upon England and upon Europe) that it should stand respectable and eternal. For the furtherance of human happiness, I have always maintained that it is necessary to prove that man is not even at present a vicious and detestable animal; and still more to prove that good management may greatly amend him; and it is for much the same reason, that I am anxious to see the opinion established, that there are fair characters existing among the individuals of the race; for the moment that all men, without exception, shall be conceived abandoned, good people will cease efforts deemed to be hopeless, and perhaps think of taking their share in the scramble of life, or at least of making it comfortable principally for themselves. Take then, my dear sir, this work most speedily into hand: shew yourself good as you are good; temperate as you are temperate; and above all things, prove yourself as one, who from your infancy have loved justice, liberty and concord, in a way that has made it natural and consistent for you to have acted, as we have seen you act in the last seventeen years of your life. Let Englishmen be made not only to respect, but even to love you. When they think well of individuals in your native country, they will go nearer to thinking well of your country; and when your countrymen see themselves well thought of by Englishmen, they will go nearer to thinking well of England. Extend your views even further; do not stop at those who speak the English tongue, but after having settled so many points in nature and politics, think of bettering the whole race of men. As I have not read any part of the life in question, but know only the character that lived it, I write somewhat at hazard. I am sure, however, that the life and the treatise I allude to (on the Art of Virtue) will necessarily fulfil the chief of my expectations; and still more so if you take up the measure of suiting these performances to the several views above stated. Should they even prove unsuccessful in all that a sanguine admirer of yours hopes from them, you will at least have framed pieces to interest the human mind; and whoever gives a feeling of pleasure that is innocent to man, has added so much to the fair side of a life otherwise too much darkened by anxiety and too much injured by pain. In the hope, therefore, that you will listen to the prayer addressed to you in this letter, I beg to subscribe myself, my dearest sir, etc., etc.,

"Signed,   BENJ. VAUGHAN."

Continuation of the Account of my Life, begun at Passy, near Paris, 1784.

It is some time since I receiv'd the above letters, but I have been too busy till now to think of complying with the request they contain. It might, too, be much better done if I were at home among my papers, which would aid my memory, and help to ascertain dates; but my return being uncertain, and having just now a little leisure, I will endeavor to recollect and write what I can; if I live to get home, it may there be corrected and improv'd.

Not having any copy here of what is already written, I know not whether an account is given of the means I used to establish the Philadelphia public library, which, from a small beginning, is now become so considerable, though I remember to have come down to near the time of that transaction (1730). I will therefore begin here with an account of it, which may be struck out if found to have been already given.

At the time I establish'd myself in Pennsylvania, there was not a good bookseller's shop in any of the colonies to the southward of Boston. In New York and Philad'a the printers were indeed stationers; they sold only paper, etc., almanacs, ballads, and a few common school-books. Those who lov'd reading were oblig'd to send for their books from England; the members of the Junto had each a few. We had left the alehouse, where we first met, and hired a room to hold our club in. I propos'd that we should all of us bring our books to that room, where they would not only be ready to consult in our conferences, but become a common benefit, each of us being at liberty to borrow such as he wish'd to read at home. This was accordingly done, and for some time contented us.

Finding the advantage of this little collection, I propos'd to render the benefit from books more common, by commencing a public subscription library. I drew a sketch of the plan and rules that would be necessary, and got a skilful conveyancer, Mr. Charles Brockden, to put the whole in form of articles of agreement to be subscribed, by which each subscriber engag'd to pay a certain sum down for the first purchase of books, and an annual contribution for increasing them. So few were the readers at that time in Philadelphia, and the majority of us so poor, that I was not able, with great industry, to find more than fifty persons, mostly young tradesmen, willing to pay down for this purpose forty shillings each, and ten shillings per annum. On this little fund we began. The books were imported; the library was opened one day in the week for lending to the subscribers, on their promissory notes to pay double the value if not duly returned. The institution soon manifested its utility, was imitated by other towns, and in other provinces. The libraries were augmented by donations; reading became fashionable; and our people, having no publick amusements to divert their attention from study, became better acquainted with books, and in a few years were observ'd by strangers to be better instructed and more intelligent than people of the same rank generally are in other countries.

When we were about to sign the above-mentioned articles, which were to be binding on us, our heirs, etc., for fifty years, Mr. Brockden, the scrivener, said to us, "You are young men, but it is scarcely probable that any of you will live to see the expiration of the term fix'd in the instrument." A number of us, however, are yet living; but the instrument was after a few years rendered null by a charter that incorporated and gave perpetuity to the company.

The objections and reluctances I met with in soliciting the subscriptions, made me soon feel the impropriety of presenting one's self as the proposer of any useful project, that might be suppos'd to raise one's reputation in the smallest degree above that of one's neighbors, when one has need of their assistance to accomplish that project. I therefore put myself as much as I could out of sight, and stated it as a scheme of a *number of friends*, who had requested me to go about and propose it to such as they thought lovers of reading. In this way my affair went on more smoothly, and I ever after practis'd it on such occasions; and, from my frequent successes, can heartily recommend it. The present little sacrifice of your vanity will afterwards be amply repaid. If it remains a while uncertain to whom the merit belongs, some one more vain than yourself will be encouraged to claim it, and then even envy will be disposed to do you justice by plucking those assumed feathers, and restoring them to their right owner.

This library afforded me the means of improvement by constant study, for which I set apart an hour or two each day, and thus repair'd in some degree the loss of the learned education my father once intended for me. Reading was the only amusement I allow'd myself. I spent no time in taverns, games, or frolicks of any kind; and my industry in my business continu'd as indefatigable as it was necessary. I was indebted for my printing-house; I had a young family coming on to be educated, and I had to contend with for business two printers, who were established in the place before me. My circumstances, however, grew daily easier. My original habits of frugality continuing, and my father having, among his instructions to me when a boy, frequently repeated a proverb of Solomon, "Seest thou a man diligent in his calling, he shall stand before kings, he shall not stand before mean men," I from thence considered industry as a means of obtaining wealth and distinction, which encourag'd me, tho' I did not think that I should ever literally *stand before kings*, which, however, has since happened; for I have stood before *five*, and even had the honor of sitting down with one, the King of Denmark, to dinner.

We have an English proverb that says, "*He that would thrive, must ask his wife.*" It was lucky for me that I had one as much dispos'd to industry and frugality as myself. She assisted me cheerfully in my business, folding and stitching pamphlets, tending shop, purchasing old linen rags for the papermakers, etc., etc. We kept no idle servants, our table was plain and simple, our furniture of the cheapest. For instance, my breakfast was a long time bread and milk (no tea), and I ate it out of a twopenny earthen porringer, with a pewter spoon. But mark how luxury will enter families, and make a progress, in spite of principle: being call'd one morning to breakfast, I found it in a China bowl, with a spoon of silver! They had been bought for me without my knowledge by my wife, and had cost her the enormous sum of three-and-twenty shillings, for which she had no other excuse or apology to make, but that she thought *her* husband deserv'd a silver spoon and China bowl as well as any of his neighbors. This was the first appearance of plate and China in our house, which afterward, in a course of years, as our wealth increas'd, augmented gradually to several hundred pounds in value.

I had been religiously educated as a Presbyterian; and tho' some of the dogmas of that persuasion, such as *the eternal decrees of God, election, reprobation, etc.*, appeared to me unintelligible, others doubtful, and I early absented myself from the public assemblies of the sect, Sunday being my studying day, I never was without some religious principles. I never doubted, for instance, the existence of the Deity; that he made the world, and govern'd it by his Providence; that the most acceptable service of God was the doing good to man; that our souls are immortal; and that all crime will be punished, and virtue rewarded, either here or hereafter. These I esteem'd the essentials of every religion; and, being to be found in all the religions we had in our country, I respected them all, tho' with different degrees of respect, as I found them more or less mix'd with other articles, which, without any tendency to inspire, promote, or confirm morality, serv'd principally to divide us, and make us unfriendly to one another. This respect to all, with an opinion that the worst had some good effects, induc'd me to avoid all discourse that might tend to lessen the good opinion another might have of his own religion; and as our province increas'd in people, and new places of worship were continually wanted, and generally erected by voluntary contribution, my mite for such purpose, whatever might be the sect, was never refused.

Tho' I seldom attended any public worship, I had still an opinion of its propriety, and of its utility when rightly conducted, and I regularly paid my annual subscription for the support of the only Presbyterian minister or meeting we had in Philadelphia. He us'd to visit me sometimes as a friend, and admonish me to attend his administrations, and I was now and then prevail'd on to do so, once for five Sundays successively. Had he been in my opinion a good preacher, perhaps I might have continued, notwithstanding the occasion I had for the Sunday's leisure in my course of study; but his discourses were chiefly either polemic arguments, or explications of the peculiar doctrines of our sect, and were all to me very dry, uninteresting, and unedifying, since not a single moral principle was inculcated or enforc'd, their aim seeming to be rather to make us Presbyterians than good citizens.

At length he took for his text that verse of the fourth chapter of Philippians, *"Finally, brethren, whatsoever things are true, honest, just, pure, lovely, or of good report, if there be any virtue, or any praise, think on these things."* And I imagin'd, in a sermon on such a text, we could not miss of having some morality. But he confin'd himself to five points only, as meant by the apostle, viz. : 1. Keeping holy the Sabbath day. 2. Being diligent in reading the holy Scriptures. 3. Attending duly the publick worship. 4. Partaking of the Sacrament. 5. Paying a due respect to God's ministers. These might be all good things; but, as they were not the kind of good things that I expected from that text, I despaired of ever meeting with them from any other, was disgusted, and attended his preaching no more. I had some years before compos'd a little Liturgy, or form of prayer, for my own private use (viz., in 1728), entitled, *Articles of Belief and Acts of Religion.* I return'd to the use of this, and went no more to the public assemblies. My conduct might be blameable, but I leave it, without attempting further to excuse it; my present purpose being to relate facts, and not to make apologies for them.

It was about this time I conceiv'd the bold and arduous project of arriving at moral perfection. I wish'd to live without committing any fault at any time; I would conquer all that either natural inclination, custom, or company might lead me into. As I knew, or thought I knew, what was right and wrong, I did not see why I might not always do the one and avoid the other. But I soon found I had undertaken a task of more difficulty than I had imagined. While my care was employ'd in guarding against one fault, I was often surprised by another; habit took the advantage of inattention; inclination was sometimes too strong for reason. I concluded, at length, that the mere speculative conviction that it was our interest to be completely virtuous, was not sufficient to prevent our slipping; and that the contrary habits must be broken, and good ones acquired and established, before we can have any dependence on a steady, uniform rectitude of conduct. For this purpose I therefore contrived the following method.

In the various enumerations of the moral virtues I had met with in my reading, I found the catalogue more or less numerous, as different writers included more or fewer ideas under the same name. Temperance, for example, was by some confined to eating and drinking, while by others it was extended to mean the moderating every other pleasure, appetite, inclination, or passion, bodily or mental, even to our avarice and ambition. I propos'd to myself, for the sake of clearness, to use rather more names, with fewer ideas annex'd to each, than a few names with more ideas; and I included under thirteen names of virtues all that at that time occurr'd to me as necessary or desirable, and annexed to each a short precept, which fully express'd the extent I gave to its meaning.

These names of virtues, with their precepts were:

1. TEMPERANCE.

Eat not to dullness; drink not to elevation.

2. SILENCE.

Speak not but what may benefit others or yourself; avoid trifling conversation.

3. ORDER.

Let all your things have their places; let each part of your business have its time.

4. RESOLUTION.

Resolve to perform what you ought; perform without fail what you resolve.

5. FRUGALITY.

Make no expense but to do good to others or yourself; *i.e.*, waste nothing.

6. INDUSTRY.

Lose no time; be always employ'd in something useful; cut off all unnecessary actions.

7. SINCERITY.

Use no hurtful deceit; think innocently and justly and, if you speak, speak accordingly.

8. JUSTICE.

Wrong none by doing injuries, or omitting the benefits that are your duty.

9. MODERATION.

Avoid extreams; forbear resenting injuries so much as you think they deserve.

10. CLEANLINESS

Tolerate no uncleanliness in body, cloaths, or habitation.

11. TRANQUILLITY.

Be not disturbed at trifles, or at accidents common or unavoidable.

12. CHASTITY.

Rarely use venery but for health or offspring, never to dulness, weakness, or the injury of your own or another's peace or reputation.

13. HUMILITY.

Imitate Jesus and Socrates.

My intention being to acquire the *habitude* of all these virtues, I judg'd it would be well not to distract my attention by attempting the whole at once, but to fix it on one of them at a time; and, when I should be master of that, then to proceed to another, and so on, till I should have gone thro' the thirteen; and, as the previous acquisition of some might facilitate the acquisition of certain others, I arrang'd them with that view, as they stand above. Temperance first, as it tends to procure that coolness and clearness of head, which is so necessary where constant vigilance was to be kept up, and guard maintained against the unremitting attraction of ancient habits, and the force of perpetual temptations. This being acquir'd and establish'd, Silence would be more easy; and my desire being to gain knowledge at the same time that I improv'd in virtue, and considering that in conversation it was obtain'd rather by the use of the ears than of the tongue, and therefore wishing to break a habit I was getting into of prattling, punning, and joking, which only made me acceptable to trifling company, I gave *Silence* the second place. This and the next, *Order,* I expected would allow me more time for attending to my project and my studies. *Resolution,* once become habitual, would keep me firm in my endeavors to obtain all the subsequent virtues; *Frugality* and Industry freeing me from my remaining debt, and producing affluence and independence, would make more easy the practice of Sincerity and Justice, etc., etc. Conceiving then, that, agreeably to the advice of Pythagoras in his Golden Verses, daily examination would be necessary, I contrived the following method for conducting that examination.

I made a little book, in which I allotted a page for each of the virtues. I rul'd each page with red ink, so as to have seven columns, one for each day of the week, marking each column with a letter for the day. I cross'd these columns with thirteen red lines, marking the beginning of each line with the first letter of one of the virtues, on which line, and in its proper column, I might mark, by a little black spot, every fault I found upon examination to have been committed respecting that virtue upon that day.

Form of the pages.

TEMPERANCE.							
EAT NOT TO DULNESS; DRINK NOT TO ELEVATION.							
	S.	M.	T.	W.	T.	F.	S.
T.							
S.	*	*		*		*	
O.	* *	*	*		*	*	*
R.			*			*	
F.		*		*			
I.			*				
S.							
J.							
M.							
C.							
T.							
C.							
H.							

I determined to give a week's strict attention to each of the virtues successively. Thus, in the first week, my great guard was to avoid even the least offence against *Temperance*, leaving the other virtues to their ordinary chance, only marking every evening the faults of the day. Thus, if in the first week I could keep my first line, marked T, clear of spots, I suppos'd the habit of that virtue so much strengthen'd, and its opposite weaken'd, that I might venture extending my attention to include the next, and for the following week keep both lines clear of spots. Proceeding thus to the last, I could go thro' a course compleat in thirteen weeks, and four courses in a year. And like him who, having a garden to weed, does not attempt to eradicate all the bad herbs at once, which would exceed his reach and his strength, but works on one of the beds at a time, and, having accomplish'd the first, proceeds to a second, so I should have, I hoped, the encouraging pleasure of seeing on my pages the progress I made in virtue, by clearing successively my lines of their spots, till in the end, by a number of courses, I should be happy in viewing a clean book, after a thirteen weeks' daily examination.

Thus my little book had for its motto these lines from Addison's *Cato:*

> "Here will I hold. If there's a power above us
> (And that there is, all nature cries aloud
> Thro' all her works), He must delight in virtue;
> And that which he delights in must be happy."

Another from Cicero,

"O vitæ Philosophia dux! O virtutum indagatrix expultrixque vitiorum! Unus dies, bene et ex præceptis tuis actus, peccanti immortalitati est anteponendus."

Another from the Proverbs of Solomon, speaking of wisdom or virtue:

"Length of days is in her right hand, and in her left hand riches and honour. Her ways are ways of pleasantness, and all her paths are peace." iii. 16, 17.

And conceiving God to be the fountain of wisdom, I thought it right and necessary to solicit his assistance for obtaining it; to this end I formed the following little prayer, which was prefix'd to my tables of examination, for daily use.

"O powerful Goodness! bountiful Father! merciful Guide! Increase in me that wisdom which discovers my truest interest. Strengthen my resolutions to perform what that wisdom dictates. Accept my kind offices to thy other children as the only return in my power for thy continual favours to me."

I used also sometimes a little prayer which I took from Thomson's Poems, viz. :

> "Father of light and life, thou Good Supreme!
> O teach me what is good; teach me Thyself!
> Save me from folly, vanity, and vice,
> From every low pursuit; and fill my soul
> With knowledge, conscious peace, and virtue pure;
> Sacred, substantial, never-fading bliss!"

The precept of *Order* requiring that *every part of my business should have its allotted time*, one page in my little book contain'd the following scheme of employment for the twenty-four hours of a natural day.

THE MORNING.	5	Rise, wash, and address *Powerful Goodness!* Contrive day's business, and take the resolution of the day; prosecute the present study, and breakfast.	
Question. What good shall I do this day?	6		
	7		
	8		
	9	Work.	
	10		
	11		
NOON.	12	Read, or overlook my accounts, and dine.	
	1		
	2		
	3	Work.	
	4		
	5		

EVENING.		6		Put things in their places. Supper.
Question. What good have I done to-day?		7		Music or diversion, or conversation.
		8		Examination of the day.
		9		
		10		
		11		
		12		
NIGHT.		1		Sleep.
		2		
		3		
		4		

I enter'd upon the execution of this plan for self-examination, and continu'd it with occasional intermissions for some time. I was surpris'd to find myself so much fuller of faults than I had imagined; but I had the satisfaction of seeing them diminish. To avoid the trouble of renewing now and then my little book, which, by scraping out the marks on the paper of old faults to make room for new ones in a new course, became full of holes, I transferr'd my tables and precepts to the ivory leaves of a memorandum book, on which the lines were drawn with red ink, that made a durable stain, and on those lines I mark'd my faults with a black-lead pencil, which marks I could easily wipe out with a wet sponge. After a while I went thro' one course only in a year, and afterwards only one in several years, till at length I omitted them entirely, being employ'd in voyages and business abroad, with a multiplicity of affairs that interferred; but I always carried my little book with me.

My scheme of ORDER gave me the most trouble; and I found that, tho' it might be practicable where a man's business was such as to leave him the disposition of his time, that of a journeyman printer, for instance, it was not possible to be exactly observed by a master, who must mix with the world, and often receive people of business at their own hours. *Order,* too, with regard to places for things, papers, etc., I found extreamly difficult to acquire. I had not been early accustomed to it, and, having an exceeding good memory, I was not so sensible of the inconvenience attending want of method. This article, therefore, cost me so much painful attention, and my faults in it vexed me so much, and I made so little progress in amendment, and had such frequent relapses, that I was almost ready to give up the attempt, and content myself with a faulty character in that respect, like the man who, in buying an ax of a smith, my neighbour, desired to have the whole of its surface as bright as the edge. The smith consented to grind it bright for him if he would turn the wheel; he turn'd, while the smith press'd the broad face of the ax hard and heavily on the stone, which made the turning of it very fatiguing. The man came every now and then from the wheel to see how the work went on, and at length would take his ax as it was, without farther grinding. "No," said the smith, "turn on, turn on; we shall have it bright by-and-by; as yet, it is only speckled." "Yes," says the man, "*but I think I like a speckled ax best.*" And I believe this may have been the case with many, who, having, for want of some such means as I employ'd, found the difficulty of obtaining good and breaking bad habits in other points of vice and virtue, have given up the struggle, and concluded that "*a speckled ax was best*"; for something, that pretended to be reason, was every now and then suggesting to me that such extream nicety as I exacted of myself might be a kind of foppery in morals, which, if it were known, would make me ridiculous; that a perfect character might be attended with the inconvenience of being envied and hated; and that a benevolent man should allow a few faults in himself, to keep his friends in countenance.

In truth, I found myself incorrigible with respect to Order; and now I am grown old, and my memory bad, I feel very sensibly the want of it. But, on the whole, tho' I never arrived at the perfection I had been so ambitious of obtaining, but fell far short of it, yet I was, by the endeavour, a better and a happier man than I otherwise should have been if I had not attempted it; as those who aim at perfect writing by imitating the engraved copies, tho' they never reach the wish'd-for excellence of those copies, their hand is mended by the endeavor, and is tolerable while it continues fair and legible.

It may be well my posterity should be informed that to this little artifice, with the blessing of God, their ancestor ow'd the constant felicity of his life, down to his 79th year, in which this is written. What reverses may attend the remainder is in the hand of Providence; but, if they arrive, the reflection on past happiness enjoy'd ought to help his bearing them with more resignation. To Temperance he ascribes his long-continued health, and what is still left to him of a good constitution; to Industry and Frugality, the early easiness of his circumstances and acquisition of his fortune, with all that knowledge that enabled him to be a useful citizen, and obtained for him some degree of reputation among the learned; to Sincerity and Justice, the confidence of his country, and the honorable employs it conferred upon him; and to the joint influence of the whole mass of the virtues, even in the imperfect state he was able to acquire them, all that evenness of temper, and that cheerfulness in conversation, which makes his company still sought for, and agreeable even to his younger acquaintance. I hope, therefore, that some of my descendants may follow the example and reap the benefit.

It will be remark'd that, tho' my scheme was not wholly without religion, there was in it no mark of any of the distinguishing tenets of any particular sect. I had purposely avoided them; for, being fully persuaded of the utility and excellency of my method, and that it might be serviceable to people in all religions, and intending some time or other to publish it, I would not have anything in it that should prejudice any one, of any sect, against it. I purposed writing a little comment on each virtue, in which I would have shown the advantages of possessing it, and the mischiefs attending its opposite vice; and I should have called my book THE ART OF VIRTUE, because it would have shown the means and manner of obtaining virtue, which would have distinguished it from the mere exhortation to be good, that does not instruct and indicate the means, but is like the apostle's man of verbal charity, who only without showing to the naked and hungry how or where they might get clothes or victuals, exhorted them to be fed and clothed.

But it so happened that my intention of writing and publishing this comment was never fulfilled. I did, indeed, from time to time, put down short hints of the sentiments, reasonings, etc., to be made use of in it, some of which I have still by me; but the necessary close attention to private business in the earlier part of my life, and public business since, have occasioned my postponing it; for, it being connected in my mind with a *great and extensive project*, that required the whole man to execute, and which an unforeseen succession of employs prevented my attending to, it has hitherto remain'd unfinish'd.

In this piece it was my design to explain and enforce this doctrine, that vicious actions are not hurtful because they are forbidden, but forbidden because they are hurtful, the nature of man alone considered; that it was, therefore, every one's interest to be virtuous who wish'd to be happy even in this world; and I should, from this circumstance (there being always in the world a number of rich merchants, nobility, states, and princes, who have need of honest instruments for the management of their affairs, and such being so rare), have endeavored to convince young persons that no qualities were so likely to make a poor man's fortune as those of probity and integrity.

My list of virtues contain'd at first but twelve; but a Quaker friend having kindly informed me that I was generally thought proud; that my pride show'd itself frequently in conversation; that I was not content with being in the right when discussing any point, but was overbearing, and rather insolent, of which he convinc'd me by mentioning several instances; I determined endeavouring to cure myself, if I could, of this vice or folly among the rest, and I added *Humility* to my list, giving an extensive meaning to the word.

I cannot boast of much success in acquiring the *reality* of this virtue, but I had a good deal with regard to the *appearance* of it. I made it a rule to forbear all direct contradiction to the sentiments of others, and all positive assertion of my own. I even forbid myself, agreeably to the old laws of our Junto, the use of every word or expression in the language that imported a fix'd opinion, such as *certainly, undoubtedly*, etc., and I adopted, instead of them, *I conceive, I apprehend*, or *I imagine* a thing to be so or so; or it *so appears to me at present*. When another asserted something that I thought an error, I deny'd myself the pleasure of contradicting him abruptly, and of showing immediately some absurdity in his proposition; and in answering I began by observing that in certain cases or circumstances his opinion would be right, but in the present case there *appear'd* or *seem'd* to me some difference, etc. I soon found the advantage of this change in my manner; the conversations I engag'd in went on more pleasantly. The modest way in which I propos'd my opinions procur'd them a readier reception and less contradiction; I had less mortification when I was found to be in the wrong, and I more easily prevail'd with others to give up their mistakes and join with me when I happened to be in the right.

And this mode, which I at first put on with some violence to natural inclination, became at length so easy, and so habitual to me, that perhaps for these fifty years past no one has ever heard a dogmatical expression escape me. And to this habit (after my character of integrity) I think it principally owing that I had early so much weight with my fellow-citizens when I proposed new institutions, or alterations in the old, and so much influence in public councils when I became a member; for I was but a bad speaker, never eloquent, subject to much hesitation in my choice of words, hardly correct in language, and yet I generally carried my points.

In reality, there is, perhaps, no one of our natural passions so hard to subdue as *pride*. Disguise it, struggle with it, beat it down, stifle it, mortify it as much as one pleases, it is still alive, and will every now and then peep out and show itself; you will see it, perhaps, often in this history; for, even if I could conceive that I had compleatly overcome it, I should probably be proud of my humility.

[Thus far written at Passy, 1784.]

[*"I am now about to write at home, August, 1788, but can not have the help expected from my papers, many of them being lost in the war. I have, however, found the following."*]

HAVING mentioned *a great and extensive project* which I had conceiv'd, it seems proper that some account should be here given of that project and its object. Its first rise in my mind appears in the following little paper, accidentally preserv'd, viz.:

Observations on my reading history, in Library, May 19th, 1731.

"That the great affairs of the world, the wars, revolutions, etc., are carried on and effected by parties.

"That the view of these parties is their present general interest, or what they take to be such.

"That the different views of these different parties occasion all confusion.

"That while a party is carrying on a general design, each man has his particular private interest in view.

"That as soon as a party has gain'd its general point, each member becomes intent upon his particular interest; which, thwarting others, breaks that party into divisions, and occasions more confusion.

"That few in public affairs act from a meer view of the good of their country, whatever they may pretend; and, tho' their actings bring real good to their country, yet men primarily considered that their own and their country's interest was united, and did not act from a principle of benevolence.

"That fewer still, in public affairs, act with a view to the good of mankind.

"There seems to me at present to be great occasion for raising a United Party for Virtue, by forming the virtuous and good men of all nations into a regular body, to be govern'd by suitable good and wise rules, which good and wise men may probably be more unanimous in their obedience to, than common people are to common laws.

"I at present think that whoever attempts this aright, and is well qualified, can not fail of pleasing God, and of meeting with success.   B. F."

Revolving this project in my mind, as to be undertaken hereafter, when my circumstances should afford me the necessary leisure, I put down from time to time, on pieces of paper, such thoughts as occurr'd to me respecting it. Most of these are lost; but I find one purporting to be the substance of an intended creed, containing, as I thought, the essentials of every known religion, and being free of every thing that might shock the professors of any religion. It is express'd in these words, viz.:

"That there is one God, who made all things.

"That he governs the world by his providence.

"That he ought to be worshiped by adoration, prayer, and thanksgiving.

"But that the most acceptable service of God is doing good to man.

"That the soul is immortal.

"And that God will certainly reward virtue and punish vice, either here or hereafter."

My ideas at that time were, that the sect should be begun and spread at first among young and single men only; that each person to be initiated should not only declare his assent to such creed, but should have exercised himself with the thirteen weeks' examination and practice of the virtues, as in the before-mention'd model; that the existence of such a society should be kept a secret, till it was become considerable, to prevent solicitations for the admission of improper persons, but that the members should each of them search among his acquaintance for ingenuous, well-disposed youths, to whom, with prudent caution, the scheme should be gradually communicated; that the members should engage to afford their advice, assistance, and support to each other in promoting one another's interests, business, and advancement in life; that, for distinction, we should be call'd *The Society of the Free and Easy:* free, as being, by the general practice and habit of the virtues, free from the dominion of vice; and particularly by the practice of industry and frugality, free from debt, which exposes a man to confinement, and a species of slavery to his creditors.

This is as much as I can now recollect of the project, except that I communicated it in part to two young men, who adopted it with some enthusiasm; but my then narrow circumstances, and the necessity I was under of sticking close to my business, occasion'd my postponing the further prosecution of it at that time; and my multifarious occupations, public and private, induc'd me to continue postponing, so that it has been omitted till I have no longer strength or activity left sufficient for such an enterprise; tho' I am still of opinion that it was a practicable scheme, and might have been very useful, by forming a great number of good citizens; and I was not discourag'd by the seeming magnitude of the undertaking, as I have always thought that one man of tolerable abilities may work great changes, and accomplish great affairs among mankind, if he first forms a good plan, and, cutting off all amusements or other employments that would divert his attention, makes the execution of that same plan his sole study and business.

In 1732 I first publish'd my Almanack, under the name of *Richard Saunders;* it was continu'd by me about twenty-five years, commonly call'd *Poor Richard's Almanac.* I endeavor'd to make it both entertaining and useful, and it accordingly came to be in such demand, that I reap'd considerable profit from it, vending annually near ten thousand. And observing that it was generally read, scarce any neighborhood in the province being without it, I consider'd it as a proper vehicle for conveying instruction among the common people, who bought scarcely any other books; I therefore filled all the little spaces that occurr'd between the remarkable days in the calendar with proverbial sentences, chiefly such as inculcated industry and frugality, as the means of procuring wealth, and thereby securing virtue; it being more difficult for a man in want, to act always honestly, as, to use here one of those proverbs, *it is hard for an empty sack to stand upright.*

These proverbs, which contained the wisdom of many ages and nations, I assembled and form'd into a connected discourse prefix'd to the Almanack of 1757, as the harangue of a wise old man to the people attending an auction. The bringing all these scatter'd counsels thus into a focus enabled them to make greater impression. The piece, being universally approved, was copied in all the newspapers of the Continent; reprinted in Britain on a broad side, to be stuck up in houses; two translations were made of it in French, and great numbers bought by the clergy and gentry, to distribute gratis among their poor parishioners and tenants. In Pennsylvania, as it discouraged useless expense in foreign superfluities, some thought it had its share of influence in producing that growing plenty of money which was observable for several years after its publication.

I considered my newspaper, also, as another means of communicating instruction, and in that view frequently reprinted in it extracts from the Spectator, and other moral writers; and sometimes publish'd little pieces of my own, which had been first compos'd for reading in our Junto. Of these are a Socratic dialogue, tending to prove that, whatever might be his parts and abilities, a vicious man could not properly be called a man of sense; and a discourse on self-denial, showing that virtue was not secure till its practice became a habitude, and was free from the opposition of contrary inclinations. These may be found in the papers about the beginning of 1735.

In the conduct of my newspaper, I carefully excluded all libelling and personal abuse, which is of late years become so disgraceful to our country. Whenever I was solicited to insert any thing of that kind, and the writers pleaded, as they generally did, the liberty of the press, and that a newspaper was like a stage-coach, in which any one who would pay had a right to a place, my answer was, that I would print the piece separately if desired, and the author might have as many copies as he pleased to distribute himself, but that I would not take upon me to spread his detraction; and that, having contracted with my subscribers to furnish them with what might be either useful or entertaining, I could not fill their papers with private altercation, in which they had no concern, without doing them manifest injustice. Now, many of our printers make no scruple of gratifying the malice of individuals by false accusations of the fairest characters among ourselves, augmenting animosity even to the producing of duels; and are, moreover, so indiscreet as to print scurrilous reflections on the government of neighboring states, and even on the conduct of our best national allies, which may be attended with the most pernicious consequences. These things I mention as a caution to young printers, and that they may be encouraged not to pollute their presses and disgrace their profession by such infamous practices, but refuse steadily, as they may see by my example that such a course of conduct will not, on the whole, be injurious to their interests.

In 1733 I sent one of my journeymen to Charleston, South Carolina, where a printer was wanting. I furnish'd him with a press and letters, on an agreement of partnership, by which I was to receive one-third of the profits of the business, paying one-third of the expense. He was a man of learning, and honest but ignorant in matters of account; and, tho' he sometimes made me remittances, I could get no account from him, nor any satisfactory state of our partnership while he lived. On his decease, the business was continued by his widow, who, being born and bred in Holland, where, as I have been inform'd, the knowledge of accounts makes a part of female education, she not only sent me as clear a state as she could find of the transactions past, but continued to account with the greatest regularity and exactness every quarter afterwards, and managed the business with such success, that she not only brought up reputably a family of children, but, at the expiration of the term, was able to purchase of me the printing-house, and establish her son in it.

I mention this affair chiefly for the sake of recommending that branch of education for our young females, as likely to be of more use to them and their children, in case of widowhood, than either music or dancing, by preserving them from losses by imposition of crafty men, and enabling them to continue, perhaps, a profitable mercantile house, with establish'd correspondence, till a son is grown up fit to undertake and go on with it, to the lasting advantage and enriching of the family.

About the year 1734 there arrived among us from Ireland a young Presbyterian preacher, named Hemphill, who delivered with a good voice, and apparently extempore, most excellent discourses, which drew together considerable numbers of different persuasions, who join'd in admiring them. Among the rest, I became one of his constant hearers, his sermons pleasing me, as they had little of the dogmatical kind, but inculcated strongly the practice of virtue, or what in the religious stile are called good works. Those, however, of our congregation, who considered themselves as orthodox Presbyterians, disapprov'd his doctrine, and were join'd by most of the old clergy, who arraign'd him of heterodoxy before the synod, in order to have him silenc'd. I became his zealous partisan, and contributed all I could to raise a party in his favour, and we combated for him a while with some hopes of success. There was much scribbling pro and con upon the occasion; and finding that, tho' an elegant preacher, he was but a poor writer, I lent him my pen and wrote for him two or three pamphlets, and one piece in the Gazette of April, 1735. Those pamphlets, as is generally the case with controversial writings, tho' eagerly read at the time, were soon out of vogue, and I question whether a single copy of them now exists.

During the contest an unlucky occurrence hurt his cause exceedingly. One of our adversaries having heard him preach a sermon that was much admired, thought he had somewhere read the sermon before, or at least a part of it. On search, he found that part quoted at length, in one of the British Reviews, from a discourse of Dr. Foster's. This detection gave many of our party disgust, who accordingly abandoned his cause, and occasion'd our more speedy discomfiture in the synod. I stuck by him, however, as I rather approv'd his giving us good sermons compos'd by others, than bad ones of his own manufacture, tho' the latter was the practice of our common teachers. He afterward acknowledg'd to me that none of those he preach'd were his own; adding, that his memory was such as enabled him to retain and repeat any sermon after one reading only. On our defeat, he left us in search elsewhere of better fortune, and I quitted the congregation, never joining it after, tho' I continu'd many years my subscription for the support of its ministers.

I had begun in 1733 to study languages; I soon made myself so much a master of the French as to be able to read the books with ease. I then undertook the Italian. An acquaintance, who was also learning it, us'd often to tempt me to play chess with him. Finding this took up too much of the time I had to spare for study, I at length refus'd to play any more, unless on this condition, that the victor in every game should have a right to impose a task, either in parts of the grammar to be got by heart, or in translations, etc., which tasks the vanquish'd was to perform upon honour, before our next meeting. As we play'd pretty equally, we thus beat one another into that language. I afterwards with a little painstaking, acquir'd as much of the Spanish as to read their books also.

I have already mention'd that I had only one year's instruction in a Latin school, and that when very young, after which I neglected that language entirely. But, when I had attained an acquaintance with the French, Italian, and Spanish, I was surpriz'd to find, on looking over a Latin Testament, that I understood so much more of that language than I had imagined, which encouraged me to apply myself again to the study of it, and I met with more success, as those preceding languages had greatly smooth'd my way.

From these circumstances, I have thought that there is some inconsistency in our common mode of teaching languages. We are told that it is proper to begin first with the Latin, and, having acquir'd that, it will be more easy to attain those modern languages which are deriv'd from it; and yet we do not begin with the Greek, in order more easily to acquire the Latin. It is true that, if you can clamber and get to the top of a staircase without using the steps, you will more easily gain them in descending; but certainly, if you begin with the lowest you will with more ease ascend to the top; and I would therefore offer it to the consideration of those who superintend the education of our youth, whether, since many of those who begin with the Latin quit the same after spending some years without having made any great proficiency, and what they have learnt becomes almost useless, so that their time has been lost, it would not have been better to have begun with the French, proceeding to the Italian, etc.; for, tho', after spending the same time, they should quit the study of languages and never arrive at the Latin, they would, however, have acquired another tongue or two, that, being in modern use, might be serviceable to them in common life.

After ten years' absence from Boston, and having become easy in my circumstances, I made a journey thither to visit my relations, which I could not sooner well afford. In returning, I call'd at Newport to see my brother, then settled there with his printing-house. Our former differences were forgotten, and our meeting was very cordial and affectionate. He was fast declining in his health, and requested of me that, in case of his death, which he apprehended not far distant, I would take home his son, then but ten years of age, and bring him up to the printing business. This I accordingly perform'd, sending him a few years to school before I took him into the office. His mother carried on the business till he was grown up, when I assisted him with an assortment of new types, those of his father being in a manner worn out. Thus it was that I made my brother ample amends for the service I had depriv'd him of by leaving him so early.

In 1736 I lost one of my sons, a fine boy of four years old, by the small-pox, taken in the common way. I long regretted bitterly, and still regret that I had not given it to him by inoculation. This I mention for the sake of parents who omit that operation, on the supposition that they should never forgive themselves if a child died under it; my example showing that the regret may be the same either way, and that, therefore, the safer should be chosen.

Our club, the Junto, was found so useful, and afforded such satisfaction to the members, that several were desirous of introducing their friends, which could not well be done without exceeding what we had settled as a convenient number, viz., twelve. We had from the beginning made it a rule to keep our institution a secret, which was pretty well observ'd; the intention was to avoid applications of improper persons for admittance, some of whom, perhaps, we might find it difficult to refuse. I was one of those who were against any addition to our number, but, instead of it, made in writing a proposal, that every member separately should endeavor to form a subordinate club, with the same rules respecting queries, etc., and without informing them of the connection with the Junto. The advantages proposed were, the improvement of so many more young citizens by the use of our institutions; our better acquaintance with the general sentiments of the inhabitants on any occasion, as the Junto member might propose what queries we should desire, and was to report to the Junto what pass'd in his separate club; the promotion of our particular interests in business by more extensive recommendation, and the increase of our influence in public affairs, and our power of doing good by spreading thro' the several clubs the sentiments of the Junto.

The project was approv'd, and every member undertook to form his club, but they did not all succeed. Five or six only were compleated, which were called by different names, as the Vine, the Union, the Band, etc. They were useful to themselves, and afforded us a good deal of amusement, information, and instruction, besides answering, in some considerable degree, our views of influencing the public opinion on particular occasions, of which I shall give some instances in course of time as they happened.

My first promotion was my being chosen, in 1736, clerk of the General Assembly. The choice was made that year without opposition; but the year following, when I was again propos'd (the choice, like that of the members, being annual), a new member made a long speech against me, in order to favour some other candidate. I was, however, chosen, which was the more agreeable to me, as, besides the pay for the immediate service as clerk, the place gave me a better opportunity of keeping up an interest among the members, which secur'd to me the business of printing the votes, laws, paper money, and other occasional jobbs for the public, that, on the whole, were very profitable.

I therefore did not like the opposition of this new member, who was a gentleman of fortune and education, with talents that were likely to give him, in time, great influence in the House, which, indeed, afterwards happened. I did not, however, aim at gaining his favour by paying any servile respect to him, but, after some time, took this other method. Having heard that he had in his library a certain very scarce and curious book, I wrote a note to him, expressing my desire of perusing that book, and requesting he would do me the favour of lending it to me for a few days. He sent it immediately, and I return'd it in about a week with another note, expressing strongly my sense of the favour. When we next met in the House, he spoke to me (which he had never done before), and with great civility; and he ever after manifested a readiness to serve me on all occasions, so that we became great friends, and our friendship continued to his death. This is another instance of the truth of an old maxim I had learned, which says, *'He that has once done you a kindness will be more ready to do you an-*

other, than he whom you yourself have obliged." And it shows how much more profitable it is prudently to remove, than to resent, return, and continue inimical proceedings.

In 1737, Colonel Spotswood, late governor of Virginia, and then postmaster-general, being dissatisfied with the conduct of his deputy at Philadelphia, respecting some negligence in rendering, and inexactitude of his accounts, took from him the commission and offered it to me. I accepted it readily, and found it of great advantage; for, tho' the salary was small, it facilitated the correspondence that improv'd my newspaper, increas'd the number demanded, as well as the advertisements to be inserted, so that it came to afford me a considerable income. My old competitor's newspaper declin'd proportionably, and I was satisfy'd without retaliating his refusal, while postmaster, to permit my papers being carried by the riders. Thus he suffer'd greatly from his neglect in due accounting; and I mention it as a lesson to those young men who may be employ'd in managing affairs for others, that they should always render accounts, and make remittances, with great clearness and punctuality. The character of observing such a conduct is the most powerful of all recommendations to new employments and increase of business.

I began now to turn my thoughts a little to public affairs, beginning, however, with small matters. The city watch was one of the first things that I conceiv'd to want regulation. It was managed by the constables of the respective wards in turn; the constable warned a number of housekeepers to attend him for the night. Those who chose never to attend, paid him six shillings a year to be excus'd, which was suppos'd to be for hiring substitutes, but was, in reality, much more than was necessary for that purpose, and made the constableship a place of profit; and the constable, for a little drink, often got such ragamuffins about him as a watch, that respectable housekeepers did not choose to mix with. Walking the rounds, too, was often neglected, and most of the nights spent in tippling. I thereupon wrote a paper to be read in Junto, representing these irregularities, but insisting more particularly on the inequality of this six-shilling tax of the constables, respecting the circumstances of those who paid it, since a poor widow housekeeper, all whose property to be guarded by the watch did not perhaps exceed the value of fifty pounds, paid as much as the wealthiest merchant, who had thousands of pounds' worth of goods in his stores.

On the whole, I proposed as a more effectual watch, the hiring of proper men to serve constantly in that business; and as a more equitable way of supporting the charge, the levying a tax that should be proportion'd to the property. This idea, being approv'd by the Junto, was communicated to the other clubs, but as arising in each of them; and though the plan was not immediately carried into execution, yet, by preparing the minds of people for the change, it paved the way for the law obtained a few years after, when the members of our clubs were grown into more influence.

About this time I wrote a paper (first to be read in Junto, but it was afterward publish'd) on the different accidents and carelessnesses by which houses were set on fire, with cautions against them, and means proposed of avoiding them. This was much spoken of as a useful piece, and gave rise to a project, which soon followed it, of forming a company for the more ready extinguishing of fires, and mutual assistance in removing and securing of goods when in danger. Associates in this scheme were presently found, amounting to thirty. Our articles of agreement oblig'd every member to keep always in good order, and fit for use, a certain number of leather buckets, with strong bags and baskets (for packing and transporting of goods), which were to be brought to every fire; and we agreed to meet once a month and spend a social evening together, in discoursing and communicating such ideas as occurred to us upon the subject of fires, as might be useful in our conduct on such occasions.

The utility of this institution soon appeared, and many more desiring to be admitted than we thought convenient for one company, they were advised to form another, which was accordingly done; and this went on, one new company being formed after another, till they became so numerous as to include most of the inhabitants who were men of property; and now, at the time of my writing this, tho' upward of fifty years since its establishment, that which I first formed, called the Union Fire Company, still subsists and flourishes, tho' the first members are all deceas'd but myself and one, who is older by a year than I am. The small fines that have been paid by members for absence at the monthly meetings have been apply'd to the purchase of fire-engines, ladders, fire-hooks, and other useful implements for each company, so that I question whether there is a city in the world better provided with the means of putting a stop to beginning conflagrations; and, in fact, since these institutions, the city has never lost by fire more than one or two houses at a time, and the flames have often been extinguished before the house in which they began has been half consumed.

In 1739 arrived among us from Ireland the Reverend Mr. Whitefield, who had made himself remarkable there as an itinerant preacher. He was at first permitted to preach in some of our churches; but the clergy, taking a dislike to him, soon refus'd him their pulpits, and he was oblig'd to preach in the fields. The multitudes of all sects and denominations that attended his sermons were enormous, and it was matter of speculation to me, who was one of the number, to observe the extraordinary influence of his oratory on his hearers, and how much they admir'd and respected him, notwithstanding his common abuse of them, by assuring them they were naturally *half beasts and half devils*. It was wonderful to see the change soon made in the manners of our inhabitants. From being thoughtless or indifferent about religion, it seem'd as if all the world were growing religious, so that one could not walk thro' the town in an evening without hearing psalms sung in different families of every street.

And it being found inconvenient to assemble in the open air, subject to its inclemencies, the building of a house to meet in was no sooner propos'd, and persons appointed to receive contributions, but sufficient sums were soon receiv'd to procure the ground and erect the building, which was one hundred feet long and seventy broad, about the size of Westminster Hall; and the work was carried on with such spirit as to be finished in a much shorter time than could have been expected. Both house and ground were vested in trustees, expressly for the use of any preacher of any religious persuasion who might desire to say something to the people at Philadelphia; the design in building not being to accommodate any particular sect, but the inhabitants in general; so that even if the Mufti of Constantinople were to send a missionary to preach Mohammedanism to us, he would find a pulpit at his service.

Mr. Whitefield, in leaving us, went preaching all the way thro' the colonies to Georgia. The settlement of that province had lately been begun, but, instead of being made with hardy, industrious husbandmen, accustomed to labor, the only people fit for such an enterprise, it was with families of broken shop-keepers and other insolvent debtors, many of indolent and idle habits, taken out of the jails, who, being set down in the woods, unqualified for clearing land, and unable to endure the hardships of a new settlement, perished in numbers, leaving many helpless children unprovided for. The sight of their miserable situation inspir'd the benevolent heart of Mr. Whitefield with the idea of building an Orphan House there, in which they might be supported and educated. Returning northward, he preach'd up this charity, and made large collections, for his eloquence had a wonderful power over the hearts and purses of his hearers, of which I myself was an instance.

I did not disapprove of the design, but, as Georgia was then destitute of materials and workmen, and it was proposed to send them from Philadelphia at a great expense, I thought it would have been better to have built the house here, and brought the children to it. This I advis'd; but he was resolute in his first project, rejected my counsel, and I therefore refus'd to contribute. I happened soon after to attend one of his sermons, in the course of which I perceived he intended to finish with a collection, and I silently resolved he should get nothing from me. I had in my pocket a handful of copper money, three or four silver dollars, and five pistoles in gold. As he proceeded I began to soften, and concluded to give the coppers. Another stroke of his oratory made me asham'd of that, and determin'd me to give the silver; and he finish'd so admirably, that I empty'd my pocket wholly into the collector's dish, gold and all. At this sermon there was also one of our club, who, being of my sentiments respecting the building in Georgia, and suspecting a collection might be intended, had, by precaution, emptied his pockets before he came from home. Towards the conclusion of the discourse, however, he felt a strong desire to give, and apply'd to a neighbour, who stood near him, to borrow some money for the purpose. The application was unfortunately [made] to perhaps the only man in the company who had the firmness not to be affected by the preacher. His answer was, *"At any other time, Friend Hopkinson, I would lend to thee freely; but not now, for thee seems to be out of thy right senses."*

Some of Mr. Whitefield's enemies affected to suppose that he would apply these collections to his own private emolument; but I, who was intimately acquainted with him (being employed in printing his Sermons and Journals, etc.), never had the least suspicion of his integrity, but am to this day decidedly of opinion that he was in all his conduct a perfectly *honest man;* and methinks my testimony in his favour ought to have the more weight, as we had no religious connection. He us'd, indeed, sometimes to pray for my conversion, but never had the satisfaction of believing that his prayers were heard. Ours was a mere civil friendship, sincere on both sides, and lasted to his death.

The following instance will show something of the terms on which we stood. Upon one of his arrivals from England at Boston, he wrote to me that he should come soon to Philadelphia, but knew not where he could lodge when there, as he understood his old friend and host, Mr. Benezet, was removed to Germantown. My answer was, "You know my house; if you can make shift with its scanty accommodations, you will be most heartily welcome." He reply'd, that if I made that kind offer for Christ's sake, I should not miss of a reward. And I returned, *"Don't let me be mistaken; it was not for Christ's sake, but for your sake."* One of our common acquaintance jocosely remark'd, that, knowing it to be the custom of the saints, when they received any favour, to shift the burden of the obligation from off their own shoulders, and place it in heaven, I had contriv'd to fix it on earth.

The last time I saw Mr. Whitefield was in London, when he consulted me about his Orphan House concern, and his purpose of appropriating it to the establishment of a college.

He had a loud and clear voice, and articulated his words and sentences so perfectly, that he might be heard and understood at a great distance, especially as his auditories, however numerous, observ'd the most exact silence. He preach'd one evening from the top of the Court-house steps, which are in the middle of Market-street, and on the west side of Second-street, which crosses it at right angles. Both streets were fill'd with his hearers to a considerable distance. Being among the hindmost in Market-street, I had the curiosity to learn how far he could be heard, by retiring backwards down the street towards the river; and I found his voice distinct till I came near Front-street, when some noise in that street obscur'd it. Imagining then a semicircle, of which my distance should be the radius, and that it were fill'd with auditors, to each of whom I allow'd two square feet, I computed that he might well be heard by more than thirty thousand. This reconcil'd me to the newspaper accounts of his having preach'd to twenty-five thousand people in the fields, and to the antient histories of generals haranguing whole armies, of which I had sometimes doubted.

By hearing him often, I came to distinguish easily between sermons newly compos'd, and those which he had often preach'd in the course of his travels. His delivery of the latter was so improv'd by frequent repetitions that every accent, every emphasis, every modulation of voice, was so perfectly well turn'd and well plac'd, that, without being interested in the subject, one could not help being pleas'd with the discourse; a pleasure of much the same kind with that receiv'd from an excellent piece of musick. This is an advantage itinerant preachers have over those who are stationary, as the latter can not well improve their delivery of a sermon by so many rehearsals.

His writing and printing from time to time gave great advantage to his enemies; unguarded expressions, and even erroneous opinions, delivered in preaching, might have been afterwards explain'd or qualifi'd by supposing others that might have accompani'd them, or they might have been deny'd; but *litera scripta manet*. Critics attack'd his writings violently, and with so much appearance of reason as to diminish the number of his votaries and prevent their encrease; so that I am of opinion if he had never written any thing, he would have left behind him a much more numerous and important sect, and his reputation might in that case have been still growing, even after his death, as there being nothing of his writing on which to found a censure and give him a lower character, his proselytes would be left at liberty to feign for him as great a variety of excellences as their enthusiastic admiration might wish him to have possessed.

My business was now continually augmenting, and my circumstances growing daily easier, my newspaper having become very profitable, as being for a time almost the only one in this and the neighbouring provinces. I experienced, too, the truth of the observation, *"that after getting the first hundred pound, it is more easy to get the second,"* money itself being of a prolific nature.

The partnership at Carolina having succeeded, I was encourag'd to engage in others, and to promote several of my workmen, who had behaved well, by establishing them with printing-houses in different colonies, on the same terms with that in Carolina. Most of them did well, being enabled at the end of our term, six years, to purchase the types of me and go on working for themselves, by which means several families were raised. Partnerships often finish in quarrels; but I was happy in this, that mine were all carried on and ended amicably, owing, I think, a good deal to the precaution of having very explicitly settled, in our articles, every thing to be done by or expected from each partner, so that there was nothing to dispute, which precaution I would therefore recommend to all who enter into partnerships; for, whatever esteem partners may have for, and confidence in each other at the time of the contract, little jealousies and disgusts may arise, with ideas of inequality in the care and burden of the business, etc., which are attended often with breach of friendship and of the connection, perhaps with lawsuits and other disagreeable consequences.

I had, on the whole, abundant reason to be satisfied with my being established in Pennsylvania. There were, however, two things that I regretted, there being no provision for defense, nor for a compleat education of youth; no militia, nor any college. I therefore, in 1743, drew up a proposal for establishing an academy; and at that time, thinking the Reverend Mr. Peters, who was out of employ, a fit person to superintend such an institution, I communicated the project to him; but he, having more profitable views in the service of the proprietaries, which succeeded, declin'd the under-taking; and, not knowing another at that time suitable for such a trust, I let the scheme lie a while dormant. I succeeded better the next year, 1744, in proposing and establishing a Philosophical Society. The paper I wrote for that purpose will be found among my writings, when collected.

With respect to defense, Spain having been several years at war against Great Britain, and being at length join'd by France, which brought us into great danger; and the laboured and long-continued endeavour of our gov-ernor, Thomas, to prevail with our Quaker Assembly to pass a militia law, and make other provisions for the security of the province, having proved abortive, I determined to try what might be done by a voluntary association of the people. To promote this, I first wrote and published a pamphlet, entitled PLAIN TRUTH, in which I stated our defenseless situation in strong lights, with the necessity of union and discipline for our defense, and prom-is'd to propose in a few days an association, to be generally signed for that purpose. The pamphlet had a sudden and surprising effect. I was call'd upon for the instrument of association, and having settled the draft of it with a few friends, I appointed a meeting of the citizens in the large building be-fore mentioned. The house was pretty full; I had prepared a number of printed copies, and provided pens and ink dispers'd all over the room. I harangued them a little on the subject, read the paper, and explained it, and then distributed the copies, which were eagerly signed, not the least objec-tion being made.

When the company separated, and the papers were collected, we found above twelve hundred hands; and, other copies being dispersed in the coun-try, the subscribers amounted at length to upward of ten thousand. These all furnished themselves as soon as they could with arms, formed themselves into companies and regiments, chose their own officers, and met every week to be instructed in the manual exercise, and other parts of military discipline. The women, by subscriptions among themselves, provided silk colors, which they presented to the companies, painted with different de-vices and mottos, which I supplied.

The officers of the companies composing the Philadelphia regiment, being met, chose me for their colonel; but, conceiving myself unfit, I declin'd that station, and recommended Mr. Lawrence, a fine person, and man of influence, who was accordingly appointed. I then propos'd a lottery to de-fray the expense of building a battery below the town, and furnishing it with cannon. It filled expeditiously, and the battery was soon erected, the merlons being fram'd of logs and fill'd with earth. We bought some old cannon from Boston, but, these not being sufficient, we wrote to England for more, soliciting, at the same time, our proprietaries for some assistance, tho' without much expectation of obtaining it.

Meanwhile, Colonel Lawrence, William Allen, Abram Taylor, Esqr., and myself were sent to New York by the associators, commission'd to borrow some cannon of Governor Clinton. He at first refus'd us peremptorily; but at dinner with his council, where there was great drinking of Madeira wine as the custom of that place then was, he softened by degrees, and said he would lend us six. After a few more bumpers he advanc'd to ten; and at length he very good-naturedly conceded eighteen. They were fine cannon, eighteen-pounders, with their carriages, which we soon transported and mounted on our battery, where the associators kept a nightly guard while the war lasted, and among the rest I regularly took my turn of duty there as a common soldier.

My activity in these operations was agreeable to the governor and council; they took me into confidence, and I was consulted by them in every measure wherein their concurrence was thought useful to the association. Calling in the aid of religion, I propos'd to them the proclaiming a fast, to promote reformation, and implore the blessing of Heaven on our undertaking. They embrac'd the motion; but, as it was the first fast ever thought of in the province, the secretary had no precedent from which to draw the proclamation. My education in New England, where a fast is proclaimed every year, was here of some advantage: I drew it in the accustomed stile, it was translated into German, printed in both languages, and divulg'd thro' the province. This gave the clergy of the different sects an opportunity of influencing their congregations to join in the association, and it would probably have been general among all but Quakers if the peace had not soon interven'd.

It was thought by some of my friends that, by my activity in these affairs, I should offend that sect, and thereby lose my interest in the Assembly of the province, where they formed a great majority. A young gentleman who had likewise some friends in the House, and wished to succeed me a, their clerk, acquainted me that it was decided to displace me at the nex, election; and he, therefore, in good will, advis'd me to resign, as more consistent with my honour than being turn'd out. My answer to him was, that I had read or heard of some public man who made it a rule never to ask for an office, and never to refuse one when offer'd to him. "I approve," says I, "of his rule, and will practice it with a small addition; I shall never *ask*, never *refuse*, nor ever *resign* an office. If they will have my office of clerk to dispose of to another, they shall take it from me. I will not, by giving it up, lose my right of some time or other making reprisals on my adversaries." I heard, however, no more of this; I was chosen again unanimously as usual at the next election. Possibly, as they dislik'd my late intimacy with the members of council, who had join'd the governors in all the disputes about military preparations, with which the House had long been harass'd, they might have been pleas'd if I would voluntarily have left them; but they did not care to displace me on account merely of my zeal for the association, and they could not well give another reason.

Indeed I had some cause to believe that the defense of the country was not disagreeable to any of them, provided they were not requir'd to assist in it. And I found that a much greater number of them than I could have imagined, tho' against offensive war, were clearly for the defensive. Many pamphlets *pro* and *con* were publish'd on the subject, and some by good

Quakers, in favour of defense, which I believe convinc'd most of their younger people.

A transaction in our fire company gave me some insight into their prevailing sentiments. It had been propos'd that we should encourage the scheme for building a battery by laying out the present stock, then about sixty pounds, in tickets of the lottery. By our rules, no money could be dispos'd of till the next meeting after the proposal. The company consisted of thirty members, of which twenty-two were Quakers, and eight only of other persuasions. We eight punctually attended the meeting; but, tho' we thought that some of the Quakers would join us, we were by no means sure of a majority. Only one Quaker, Mr. James Morris, appear'd to oppose the measure. He expressed much sorrow that it had ever been propos'd, as he said *Friends* were all against it, and it would create such discord as might break up the company. We told him that we saw no reason for that; we were the minority, and if *Friends* were against the measure, and outvoted us, we must and should, agreeably to the usage of all societies, submit. When the hour for business arriv'd it was mov'd to put the vote; he allow'd we might then do it by the rules, but, as he could assure us that a number of members intended to be present for the purpose of opposing it, it would be but candid to allow a little time for their appearing.

While we were disputing this, a waiter came to tell me two gentlemen below desir'd to speak with me. I went down, and found they were two of our Quaker members. They told me there were eight of them assembled at a tavern just by; that they were determin'd to come and vote with us if there should be occasion, which they hop'd would not be the case, and desir'd we would not call for their assistance if we could do without it, as their voting for such a measure might embroil them with their elders and friends. Being thus secure of a majority, I went up, and after a little seeming hesitation, agreed to a delay of another hour. This Mr. Morris allow'd to be extreamly fair. Not one of his opposing friends appear'd, at which he express'd great surprise; and, at the expiration of the hour, we carry'd the resolution eight to one; and as, of the twenty-two Quakers, eight were ready to vote with us, and thirteen, by their absence, manifested that they were not inclin'd to oppose the measure, I afterward estimated the proportion of Quakers sincerely against defense as one to twenty-one only; for these were all regular members of that society, and in good reputation among them, and had due notice of what was propos'd at that meeting.

The honorable and learned Mr. Logan, who had always been of that sect, was one who wrote an address to them, declaring his approbation of defensive war, and supporting his opinion by many strong arguments. He put into my hands sixty pounds to be laid out in lottery tickets for the battery, with directions to apply what prizes might be drawn wholly to that service. He told me the following anecdote of his old master, William Penn, respecting defense. He came over from England, when a young man, with that proprietary, and as his secretary. It was war-time, and their ship was chas'd by an armed vessel, suppos'd to be an enemy. Their captain prepar'd for defense; but told William Penn, and his company of Quakers, that he did not expect their assistance, and they might retire into the cabin, which they did, except James Logan, who chose to stay upon deck, and was quarter'd to a gun. The suppos'd enemy prov'd a friend, so there was no fighting; but when the secretary went down to communicate the intelligence, William Penn rebuk'd him severely for staying upon deck, and undertaking to assist in defending the vessel, contrary to the principles of *Friends,* especially as it had not been required by the captain. This reproof, being before all the company, piqu'd the secretary, who answer'd, "*I being thy servant, why did thee not order me to come down? But thee was willing enough that I should stay and help to fight the ship when thee thought there was danger.*"

My being many years in the Assembly, the majority of which were constantly Quakers, gave me frequent opportunities of seeing the embarrassment given them by their principle against war, whenever application was made to them, by order of the crown, to grant aids for military purposes. They were unwilling to offend government, on the one hand, by a direct refusal; and their friends, the body of the Quakers, on the other, by a compliance contrary to their principles; hence a variety of evasions to avoid complying, and modes of disguising the compliance when it became unavoidable. The common mode at last was, to grant money under the phrase of its being "*for the king's use,*" and never to inquire how it was applied.

But, if the demand was not directly from the crown, that phrase was found not so proper, and some other was to be invented. As, when powder was wanting (I think it was for the garrison at Louisburg), and the government of New England solicited a grant of some from Pennsilvania, which was much urg'd on the House by Governor Thomas, they could not grant money to buy powder, because that was an ingredient of war; but they voted an aid to New England of three thousand pounds, to be put into the hands of the governor, and appropriated it for the purchasing of bread, flour, wheat, or *other grain.* Some of the council, desirous of giving the House still further embarrassment, advis'd the governor not to accept provision, as not being the thing he had demanded; but he reply'd, "I shall take the money, for I understand very well their meaning; other grain is gunpowder," which he accordingly bought, and they never objected to it.

It was in allusion to this fact that, when in our fire company we feared the success of our proposal in favour of the lottery, and I had said to my friend Mr. Syng, one of our members, "If we fail, let us move the purchase of a fire-engine with the money; the Quakers can have no objection to that; and then, if you nominate me and I you as a committee for that purpose, we will buy a great gun, which is certainly a *fire-engine.*" "I see," says he, "you have improv'd by being so long in the Assembly; your equivocal project would be just a match for their wheat or *other grain.*"

These embarrassments that the Quakers suffer'd from having establish'd and published it as one of their principles that no kind of war was lawful, and which, being once published, they could not afterwards, however they might change their minds, easily get rid of, reminds me of what I think a more prudent conduct in another sect among us, that of the Dunkers. I was acquainted with one of its founders, Michael Welfare, soon after it appear'd. He complain'd to me that they were grievously calumniated by the zealots of other persuasions, and charg'd with abominable principles and practices, to which they were utter strangers. I told him this had always been the case with new sects, and that, to put a stop to such abuse, I imagin'd it might be well to publish the articles of their belief, and the rules of their discipline. He said that it had been propos'd among them, but not agreed to, for this reason: "When we were first drawn together as a society," says he, "it had pleased God to enlighten our minds so far as to see that some doctrines, which we once esteemed truths, were errors; and that others, which we had esteemed errors, were real truths. From time to time He has been pleased to afford us farther light, and our principles have been improving, and our errors diminishing. Now we are not sure that we are arrived at the end of this progression, and at the perfection of spiritual or theological knowledge; and we fear that, if we should once print our confession of faith, we should feel ourselves as if bound and confin'd by it, and perhaps be unwilling to receive farther improvement, and our successors still more so, as conceiving what we their elders and founders had done, to be something sacred, never to be departed from."

This modesty in a sect is perhaps a singular instance in the history of mankind, every other sect supposing itself in possession of all truth, and that those who differ are so far in the wrong; like a man traveling in foggy weather, those at some distance before him on the road he sees wrapped up in the fog, as well as those behind him, and also the people in the fields on each side, but near him all appears clear, tho' in truth he is as much in the fog as any of them. To avoid this kind of embarrassment, the Quakers have of late years been gradually declining the public service in the Assembly and in the magistracy, choosing rather to quit their power than their principle.

In order of time, I should have mentioned before, that having, in 1742, invented an open stove for the better warming of rooms, and at the same time saving fuel, as the fresh air admitted was warmed in entering, I made a present of the model to Mr. Robert Grace, one of my early friends, who, having an iron-furnace, found the casting of the plates for these stoves a profitable thing, as they were growing in demand. To promote that demand, I wrote and published a pamphlet, entitled *"An Account of the new-invented Pennsylvania Fireplaces; wherein their Construction and Manner of Operation is particularly explained; their Advantages above every other Method of warming Rooms demonstrated; and all Objections that have been raised against the Use of them answered and obviated,"* etc. This pamphlet had a good effect. Gov'r. Thomas was so pleas'd with the construction of this stove, as described in it, that he offered to give me a patent for the sole vending of them for a term of years; but I declin'd it from a principle which has ever weighed with me on such occasions, viz., *That, as we enjoy*

great advantages from the inventions of others, we should be glad of an
opportunity to serve others by any invention of ours; and this we should
do freely and generously.

An ironmonger in London however, assuming a good deal of my pamphlet, and working it up into his own, and making some small changes in the machine, which rather hurt its operation, got a patent for it there, and made, as I was told, a little fortune by it. And this is not the only instance of patents taken out for my inventions by others, tho' not always with the same success, which I never contested, as having no desire of profiting by patents myself, and hating disputes. The use of these fireplaces in very many houses, both of this and the neighboring colonies, has been, and is, a great saving of wood to the inhabitants.

Peace being concluded, and the association business therefore at an end, I turn'd my thoughts again to the affair of establishing an academy. The first step I took was to associate in the design a number of active friends, of whom the Junto furnished a good part; the next was to write and publish a pamphlet, entitled *Proposals relating to the Education of Youth in Pennsylvania.* This I distributed among the principal inhabitants gratis; and as soon as I could suppose their minds a little prepared by the perusal of it, I set on foot a subscription for opening and supporting an academy: it was to be paid in quotas yearly for five years; by so dividing it, I judg'd the subscription might be larger, and I believe it was so, amounting to no less, if I remember right, than five thousand pounds.

In the introduction to these proposals, I stated their publication, not as an act of mine, but of some *publick-spirited gentlemen,* avoiding as much as I could, according to my usual rule, the presenting myself to the publick as the author of any scheme for their benefit.

The subscribers, to carry the project into immediate execution, chose out of their number twenty-four trustees, and appointed Mr. Francis, then attorney-general, and myself to draw up constitutions for the government of the academy; which being done and signed, a house was hired, masters engag'd, and the schools opened, I think, in the same year, 1749.

The scholars increasing fast, the house was soon found too small, and we were looking out for a piece of ground, properly situated, with intention to build, when Providence threw into our way a large house ready built, which, with a few alterations, might well serve our purpose. This was the building before mentioned, erected by the hearers of Mr. Whitefield, and was obtained for us in the following manner.

It is to be noted that the contributions to this building being made by people of different sects, care was taken in the nomination of trustees, in whom the building and ground was to be vested, that a predominancy should not be given to any sect, lest in time that predominancy might be a means of appropriating the whole to the use of such sect, contrary to the original intention. It was therefore that one of each sect was appointed, viz., one Church-of-England man, one Presbyterian, one Baptist, one Moravian, etc., those, in case of vacancy by death, were to fill it by election from

among the contributors. The Moravian happen'd not to please his colleagues, and on his death they resolved to have no other of that sect. The
difficulty then was, how to avoid having two of some other sect, by means
of the new choice.

Several persons were named, and for that reason not agreed to. At length
one mention'd me, with the observation that I was merely an honest man,
and of no sect at all, which prevail'd with them to chuse me. The enthusiasm which existed when the house was built had long since abated, and its
trustees had not been able to procure fresh contributions for paying the
ground-rent, and discharging some other debts the building had occasion'd,
which embarrass'd them greatly. Being now a member of both setts of
trustees, that for the building and that for the academy, I had a good opportunity of negotiating with both, and brought them finally to an agreement, by which the trustees for the building were to cede it to those
of the academy, the latter undertaking to discharge the debt, to keep for
ever open in the building a large hall for occasional preachers, according
to the original intention, and maintain a free-school for the instruction of
poor children. Writings were accordingly drawn, and on paying the debts
the trustees of the academy were put in possession of the premises; and by
dividing the great and lofty hall into stories, and different rooms above
and below for the several schools, and purchasing some additional ground,
the whole was soon made fit for our purpose, and the scholars remov'd
into the building. The care and trouble of agreeing with the workmen,
purchasing materials, and superintending the work, fell upon me; and I
went thro' it the more cheerfully, as it did not then interfere with my
private business, having the year before taken a very able, industrious, and
honest partner, Mr. David Hall, with whose character I was well acquainted,
as he had work'd for me four years. He took off my hands all care of the
printing-office, paying me punctually my share of the profits. This partnership continued eighteen years, successfully for us both.

The trustees of the academy, after a while, were incorporated by a
charter from the governor; their funds were increas'd by contributions
in Britain and grants of land from the proprietaries, to which the Assembly
has since made considerable addition; and thus was established the present
University of Philadelphia. I have been continued one of its trustees from
the beginning, now near forty years, and have had the very great pleasure
of seeing a number of the youth who have receiv'd their education in it,
distinguish'd by their improv'd abilities, serviceable in public stations,
and ornaments to their country.

When I disengaged myself, as above mentioned, from private business,
I flatter'd myself that, by the sufficient tho' moderate fortune I had acquir'd,
I had secured leisure during the rest of my life for philosophical studies
and amusements. I purchased all Dr. Spence's apparatus, who had come
from England to lecture here, and I proceeded in my electrical experiments
with great alacrity; but the publick, now considering me as a man of leisure,
laid hold of me for their purposes, every part of our civil government, and

almost at the same time, imposing some duty upon me. The governor put me into the commission of the peace; the corporation of the city chose me of the common council, and soon after an alderman; and the citizens at large chose me a burgess to represent them in Assembly. This latter station was the more agreeable to me, as I was at length tired with sitting there to hear debates, in which, as clerk, I could take no part, and which were often so unentertaining that I was induc'd to amuse myself with making magic squares or circles, or any thing to avoid weariness; and I conceiv'd my becoming a member would enlarge my power of doing good. I would not, however, insinuate that my ambition was not flatter'd by all these promotions; it certainly was; for, considering my low beginning, they were great things to me; and they were still more pleasing, as being so many spontaneous testimonies of the public good opinion, and by me entirely unsolicited.

The office of justice of the peace I try'd a little, by attending a few courts, and sitting on the bench to hear causes; but finding that more knowledge of the common law than I possess'd was necessary to act in that station with credit, I gradually withdrew from it, excusing myself by my being oblig'd to attend the higher duties of a legislator in the Assembly. My election to this trust was repeated every year for ten years, without my ever asking any elector for his vote, or signifying, either directly or indirectly, any desire of being chosen. On taking my seat in the House, my son was appointed their clerk.

The year following, a treaty being to be held with the Indians at Carlisle, the governor sent a message to the House, proposing that they should nominate some of their members, to be join'd with some members of council, as commissioners for that purpose. The House named the speaker (Mr. Norris) and myself; and, being commission'd, we went to Carlisle, and met the Indians accordingly.

As those people are extreamly apt to get drunk, and, when so, are very quarrelsome and disorderly, we strictly forbad the selling any liquor to them; and when they complain'd of this restriction, we told them that if they would continue sober during the treaty, we would give them plenty of rum when business was over. They promis'd this, and they kept their promise, because they could get no liquor, and the treaty was conducted very orderly, and concluded to mutual satisfaction. They then claim'd and receiv'd the rum; this was in the afternoon: they were near one hundred men, women, and children, and were lodg'd in temporary cabins, built in the form of a square, just without the town. In the evening, hearing a great noise among them, the commissioners walk'd out to see what was the matter. We found they had made a great bonfire in the middle of the square; they were all drunk, men and women, quarreling and fighting. Their dark-colour'd bodies, half naked, seen only by the gloomy light of the bonfire, running after and beating one another with firebrands, accompanied by their horrid yellings, form'd a scene the most resembling our ideas of hell that could well be imagin'd; there was no appeasing the tumult, and we retired to our lodging. At midnight a number of them came thundering at our door, demanding more rum, of which we took no notice.

The next day, sensible they had misbehav'd in giving us that disturbance, they sent three of their old counselors to make their apology. The orator acknowledg'd the fault, but laid it upon the rum; and then endeavored to excuse the rum by saying, "*The Great Spirit, who made all things, made every thing for some use, and whatever use he design'd any thing for, that use it should always be put to. Now, when he made rum, he said, 'Let this be for the Indians to get drunk with,' and it must be so.*" And, indeed, if it be the design of Providence to extirpate these savages in order to make room for cultivators of the earth, it seems not improbable that rum may be the appointed means. It has already annihilated all the tribes who formerly inhabited the sea-coast.

In 1751, Dr. Thomas Bond, a particular friend of mine, conceived the idea of establishing a hospital in Philadelphia (a very beneficent design, which has been ascrib'd to me, but was originally his), for the reception and cure of poor sick persons, whether inhabitants of the province or strangers. He was zealous and active in endeavoring to procure subscriptions for it, but the proposal being a novelty in America, and at first not well understood, he met but with small success.

At length he came to me with the compliment that he found there was no such thing as carrying a public-spirited project through without my being concern'd in it. "For," says he, "I am often ask'd by those to whom I propose subscribing, Have you consulted Franklin upon this business? And what does he think of it? And when I tell them that I have not (supposing it rather out of your line), they do not subscribe, but say they will consider of it." I enquired into the nature and probable utility of his scheme, and receiving from him a very satisfactory explanation, I not only subscrib'd to it myself, but engag'd heartily in the design of procuring subscriptions from others. Previously, however, to the solicitation, I endeavoured to prepare the minds of the people by writing on the subject in the newspapers, which was my usual custom in such cases, but which he had omitted.

The subscriptions afterwards were more free and generous; but, beginning to flag, I saw they would be insufficient without some assistance from the Assembly, and therefore propos'd to petition for it, which was done. The country members did not at first relish the project; they objected that it could only be serviceable to the city, and therefore the citizens alone should be at the expense of it; and they doubted whether the citizens themselves generally approv'd of it. My allegation on the contrary, that it met with such approbation as to leave no doubt of our being able to raise two thousand pounds by voluntary donations, they considered as a most extravagant supposition, and utterly impossible.

On this I form'd my plan; and, asking leave to bring in a bill for incorporating the contributors according to the prayer of their petition, and granting them a blank sum of money, which leave was obtained chiefly on the consideration that the House could throw the bill out if they did not like it, I drew it so as to make the important clause a conditional one, viz., "And be it enacted, by the authority aforesaid, that when the said contributors shall have met and chosen their managers and treasurer, *and shall have raised by their contributions a capital stock of* —— *value* (the yearly interest of which is to be applied to the accommodating of the sick poor in the said hospital, free of charge for diet, attendance, advice, and medicines), *and shall make the same appear to the satisfaction of the speaker of the Assembly for the time being,* that *then* it shall and may be lawful for the said speaker, and he is hereby required, to sign an order on the provincial treasurer for the payment of two thousand pounds, in two yearly payments, to the treasurer of the said hospital, to be applied to the founding, building, and finishing of the same."

This condition carried the bill through; for the members, who had oppos'd the grant, and now conceiv'd they might have the credit of being charitable without the expense, agreed to its passage; and then, in soliciting subscriptions among the people, we urg'd the conditional promise of the law as an additional motive to give, since every man's donation would be doubled; thus the clause work'd both ways. The subscriptions accordingly soon exceeded the requisite sum, and we claim'd and receiv'd the public gift, which enabled us to carry the design into execution. A convenient and handsome building was soon erected; the institution has by constant experience been found useful, and flourishes to this day; and I do not remember any of my political manœuvres, the success of which gave me at the time more pleasure, or wherein, after thinking of it, I more easily excus'd myself for having made some use of cunning.

It was about this time that another projector, the Rev. Gilbert Tennent, came to me with a request that I would assist him in procuring a subscription for erecting a new meeting-house. It was to be for the use of a congregation he had gathered among the Presbyterians, who were originally disciples of Mr. Whitefield. Unwilling to make myself disagreeable to my fellow-citizens by too frequently soliciting their contributions, I absolutely refus'd. He then desired I would furnish him with a list of the names of persons I knew by experience to be generous and public-spirited. I thought it would be unbecoming in me, after their kind compliance with my solicitations, to mark them out to be worried by other beggars, and therefore refus'd also to give such a list. He then desir'd I would at least give him my advice. "That I will readily do," said I; "and, in the first place, I advise you to apply to all those who you know will give something; next, to those whom you are uncertain whether they will give any thing or not, and show them the list of those who have given; and, lastly, do not neglect those who you are sure will give nothing, for in some of them you may be mistaken." He laugh'd and thank'd me, and said he would take my advice. He did so, for he ask'd of *everybody*, and he obtain'd a much larger sum than he expected, with which he erected the capacious and very elegant meeting-house that stands in Arch-street.

Our city, tho' laid out with a beautifull regularity, the streets large, strait, and crossing each other at right angles, had the disgrace of suffering those streets to remain long unpav'd, and in wet weather the wheels of heavy carriages plough'd them into a quagmire, so that it was difficult to cross them; and in dry weather the dust was offensive. I had liv'd near what was call'd the Jersey Market, and saw with pain the inhabitants wading in mud while purchasing their provisions. A strip of ground down the middle of that market was at length pav'd with brick, so that, being once in the market, they had firm footing, but were often over shoes in dirt to get there. By talking and writing on the subject, I was at length instrumental in getting the street pav'd with stone between the market and the brick'd foot-pavement, that was on each side next the houses. This, for some time, gave an easy access to the market dry-shod; but, the rest of the street not being pav'd, whenever a carriage came out of the mud upon this pavement, it shook off and left its dirt upon it, and it was soon cover'd with mire, which was not remov'd, the city as yet having no scavengers.

After some inquiry, I found a poor, industrious man, who was willing to undertake keeping the pavement clean, by sweeping it twice a week, carrying off the dirt from before all the neighbours' doors, for the sum of sixpence per month, to be paid by each house. I then wrote and printed a paper setting forth the advantages to the neighbourhood that might be obtain'd by this small expense; the greater ease in keeping our houses clean, so much dirt not being brought in by people's feet; the benefit to the shops by more custom, etc., etc., as buyers could more easily get at them; and by not having, in windy weather, the dust blown in upon their goods, etc., etc. I sent one of these papers to each house, and in a day or two went round to see who would subscribe an agreement to pay these sixpences; it was unanimously sign'd, and for a time well executed. All the inhabitants of the city were delighted with the cleanliness of the pavement that surrounded the market, it being a convenience to all, and this rais'd a general desire to have all the streets paved, and made the people more willing to submit to a tax for that purpose.

After some time I drew a bill for paving the city, and brought it into the Assembly. It was just before I went to England, in 1757, and did not pass till I was gone, and then with an alteration in the mode of assessment, which I thought not for the better, but with an additional provision for lighting as well as paving the streets, which was a great improvement. It was by a private person, the late Mr. John Clifton, his giving a sample of the utility of lamps, by placing one at his door, that the people were first impress'd with the idea of enlighting all the city. The honour of this public benefit has also been ascrib'd to me, but it belongs truly to that gentleman. I did but follow his example, and have only some merit to claim respecting the form of our lamps, as differing from the globe lamps we were at first supply'd with from London. Those we found inconvenient in these respects: they admitted no air below; the smoke, therefore, did not readily go out above, but circulated in the globe, lodg'd on its inside, and soon obstructed the light they were intended to afford; giving, besides, the daily trouble of wiping them clean; and an accidental stroke on one of them would demolish it, and render it totally useless. I therefore suggested the composing them of four flat panes, with a long funnel above to draw up the smoke, and crevices admitting air below, to facilitate the ascent of the smoke; by this means they were kept clean, and did not grow dark in a few hours, as the London lamps do, but continu'd bright till morning, and an accidental stroke would generally break but a single pane, easily repair'd.

I have sometimes wonder'd that the Londoners did not, from the effect holes in the bottom of the globe lamps us'd at Vauxhall have in keeping them clean, learn to have such holes in their street lamps. But, these holes being made for another purpose, viz., to communicate flame more suddenly to the wick by a little flax hanging down thro' them, the other use, of letting in air, seems not to have been thought of; and therefore, after the lamps have been lit a few hours, the streets of London are very poorly illuminated.

The mention of these improvements puts me in mind of one I propos'd, when in London, to Dr. Fothergill, who was among the best men I have known, and a great promoter of useful projects. I had observ'd that the streets, when dry, were never swept, and the light dust carried away; but it was suffer'd to accumulate till wet weather reduc'd it to mud, and then, after lying some days so deep on the pavement that there was no crossing but in paths kept clean by poor people with brooms, it was with great labour rak'd together and thrown up into carts open above, the sides of which suffer'd some of the slush at every jolt on the pavement to shake out and fall, sometimes to the annoyance of foot-passengers. The reason given for not sweeping the dusty streets was, that the dust would fly into the windows of shops and houses.

An accidental occurrence had instructed me how much sweeping might be done in a little time. I found at my door in Craven-street, one morning, a poor woman sweeping my pavement with a birch broom; she appeared very pale and feeble, as just come out of a fit of sickness. I ask'd who employ'd her to sweep there; she said, "Nobody; but I am very poor and in distress, and I sweeps before gentlefolkses doors, and hopes they will give me something." I bid her sweep the whole street clean, and I would give her a shilling; this was at nine o'clock; at 12 she came for the shilling. From the slowness I saw at first in her working, I could scarce believe that the work was done so soon, and sent my servant to examine it, who reported that the whole street was swept perfectly clean, and all the dust plac'd in the gutter, which was in the middle; and the next rain wash'd it quite away, so that the pavement and even the kennel were perfectly clean.

I then judg'd that, if that feeble woman could sweep such a street in three hours, a strong, active man might have done it in half the time. And here let me remark the convenience of having but one gutter in such a narrow street, running down its middle, instead of two, one on each side, near the footway; for where all the rain that falls on a street runs from the sides and meets in the middle, it forms there a current strong enough to wash away all the mud it meets with; but when divided into two channels, it is often too weak to cleanse either, and only makes the mud it finds more fluid, so that the wheels of carriages and feet of horses throw and dash it upon the foot-pavement, which is thereby rendered foul and slippery, and sometimes splash it upon those who are walking. My proposal, communicated to the good doctor, was as follows:

"For the more effectual cleaning and keeping clean the streets of London and Westminster, it is proposed that the several watchmen be contracted with to have the dust swept up in dry seasons, and the mud rak'd up at other times, each in the several streets and lanes of his round; that they be furnish'd with brooms and other proper instruments for these purposes, to be kept at their respective stands, ready to furnish the poor people they may employ in the service.

"That in the dry summer months the dust be all swept up into heaps at proper distances, before the shops and windows of houses are usually opened, when the scavengers, with close-covered carts, shall also carry it all away.

"That the mud, when rak'd up, be not left in heaps to be spread abroad again by the wheels of carriages and trampling of horses, but that the scavengers be provided with bodies of carts, not plac'd high upon wheels, but low upon sliders, with lattice bottoms, which, being cover'd with straw, will retain the mud thrown into them, and permit the water to drain from it, whereby it will become much lighter, water making the greatest part of its weight; these bodies of carts to be plac'd at convenient distances, and the mud brought to them in wheel-barrows; they remaining where plac'd till the mud is drain'd, and then horses brought to draw them away."

I have since had doubts of the practicability of the latter part of this proposal, on account of the narrowness of some streets, and the difficulty of placing the draining-sleds so as not to encumber too much the passage; but I am still of opinion that the former, requiring the dust to be swept up and carry'd away before the shops are open, is very practicable in the summer, when the days are long; for, in walking thro' the Strand and Fleet-street one morning at seven o'clock, I observ'd there was not one shop open, tho' it had been daylight and the sun up above three hours; the inhabitants of London chusing voluntarily to live much by candle-light, and sleep by sunshine, and yet often complain, a little absurdly, of the duty on candles, and the high price of tallow.

Some may think these trifling matters not worth minding or relating; but when they consider that tho' dust blown into the eyes of a single person, or into a single shop on a windy day, is but of small importance, yet the great number of the instances in a populous city, and its frequent repetitions give it weight and consequence, perhaps they will not censure very severely those who bestow some attention to affairs of this seemingly low nature. Human felicity is produc'd not so much by great pieces of good fortune that seldom happen, as by little advantages that occur every day. Thus, if you teach a poor young man to shave himself, and keep his razor in order, you may contribute more to the happiness of his life than in giving him a thousand guineas. The money may be soon spent, the regret only remaining of having foolishly consumed it; but in the other case, he escapes the frequent vexation of waiting for barbers, and of their sometimes dirty fingers, offensive breaths, and dull razors; he shaves when most convenient to him, and enjoys daily the pleasure of its being done with a good instrument. With these sentiments I have hazarded the few preceding pages, hoping they may afford hints which some time or other may be useful to a city I love, having lived many years in it very happily, and perhaps to some of our towns in America.

Having been for some time employed by the postmaster-general of America as his comptroller in regulating several offices, and bringing the officers to account, I was, upon his death in 1753, appointed, jointly with Mr. William Hunter, to succeed him, by a commission from the postmaster-general in England. The American office never had hitherto paid any thing to that of Britain. We were to have six hundred pounds a year between us, if we could make that sum out of the profits of the office. To do this, a variety of improvements were necessary; some of these were inevitably at first expensive, so that in the first four years the office became above nine hundred pounds in debt to us. But it soon after began to repay us; and before I was displac'd by a freak of the ministers, of which I shall speak hereafter, we had brought it to yield *three times* as much clear revenue to the crown as the postoffice of Ireland. Since that imprudent transaction, they have receiv'd from it—not one farthing!

The business of the postoffice occasion'd my taking a journey this year to New England, where the College of Cambridge, of their own motion, presented me with the degree of Master of Arts. Yale College, in Connecticut, had before made me a similar compliment. Thus, without studying in any college, I came to partake of their honours. They were conferr'd in consideration of my improvements and discoveries in the electric branch of natural philosophy.

In 1754, war with France being again apprehended, a congress of commissioners from the different colonies was, by an order of the Lords of Trade, to be assembled at Albany, there to confer with the chiefs of the Six Nations concerning the means of defending both their country and ours. Governor Hamilton, having receiv'd this order, acquainted the House with it, requesting they would furnish proper presents for the Indians, to be given on this occasion; and naming the speaker (Mr. Norris) and myself to join Mr. Thomas Penn and Mr. Secretary Peters as commissioners to act for Pennsylvania. The House approv'd the nomination, and provided the goods for the present, and tho' they did not much like treating out of the provinces; and we met the other commissioners at Albany about the middle of June.

In our way thither, I projected and drew a plan for the union of all the colonies under one government, so far as might be necessary for defense, and other important general purposes. As we pass'd thro' New York, I had there shown my project to Mr. James Alexander and Mr. Kennedy, two gentlemen of great knowledge in public affairs, and, being fortified by their approbation, I ventur'd to lay it before the Congress. It then appeared that several of the commissioners had form'd plans of the same kind. A previous question was first taken, whether a union should be established, which pass'd in the affirmative unanimously. A committee was then appointed, one member from each colony, to consider the several plans and report. Mine happen'd to be preferr'd, and, with a few amendments, was accordingly reported.

By this plan the general government was to be administered by a president-general, appointed and supported by the crown, and a grand council was to be chosen by the representatives of the people of the several colonies, met in their respective assemblies. The debates upon it in Congress went on daily, hand in hand with the Indian business. Many objections and difficulties were started, but at length they were all overcome, and the plan was unanimously agreed to, and copies ordered to be transmitted to the Board of Trade and to the assemblies of the several provinces. Its fate was singular: the assemblies did not adopt it, as they all thought there was too much *prerogative* in it, and in England it was judg'd to have too much of the *democratic*. The Board of Trade therefore did not approve of it, nor recommend it for the approbation of his majesty; but another scheme was form'd, supposed to answer the same purpose better, whereby the governors of the provinces, with some members of their respective councils, were to meet and order the raising of troops, building of forts, etc., and to draw on the treasury of Great Britain for the expense, which was afterwards to be refunded by an act of Parliament laying a tax on America. My plan, with my reasons in support of it, is to be found among my political papers that are printed.

Being the winter following in Boston, I had much conversation with Governor Shirley upon both the plans. Part of what passed between us on the occasion may also be seen among those papers. The different and contrary reasons of dislike to my plan make me suspect that it was really the true medium; and I am still of opinion it would have been happy for both sides the water if it had been adopted. The colonies, so united, would have been sufficiently strong to have defended themselves; there would then have been no need of troops from England; of course, the subsequent pretence for taxing America, and the bloody contest it occasioned, would have been avoided. But such mistakes are not new: history is full of the errors of states and princes.

> "Look round the habitable world, how few
> Know their own good, or, knowing it, pursue!"

Those who govern, having much business on their hands, do not generally like to take the trouble of considering and carrying into execution new projects. The best public measures are therefore seldom *adopted from previous wisdom, but forc'd by the occasion.*

The Governor of Pennsylvania, in sending it down to the Assembly, express'd his approbation of the plan, "as appearing to him to be drawn up with great clearness and strength of judgment, and therefore recommended it as well worthy of their closest and most serious attention." The House, however, by the management of a certain member, took it up when I happen'd to be absent, which I thought not very fair, and reprobated it without paying any attention to it at all, to my no small mortification.

In my journey to Boston this year, I met at New York with our new governor, Mr. Morris, just arriv'd there from England, with whom I had been before intimately acquainted. He brought a commission to supersede Mr. Hamilton, who, tir'd with the disputes his proprietary instructions subjected him to, had resign'd. Mr. Morris ask'd me if I thought he must expect as uncomfortable an administration. I said, "No; you may, on the contrary, have a very comfortable one, if you will only take care not to enter into any dispute with the Assembly." "My dear friend," says he, pleasantly, "how can you advise my avoiding disputes? You know I love disputing; it is one of my greatest pleasures; however, to show the regard I have for your counsel, I promise you I will, if possible, avoid them." He had some reason for loving to dispute, being eloquent, an acute sophister, and, therefore, generally successful in argumentative conversation. He had been brought up to it from a boy, his father, as I have heard, accustoming his children to dispute with one another for his diversion, while sitting at table after dinner; but I think the practice was not wise; for, in the course of my observation, these disputing, contradicting, and confuting people are generally unfortunate in their affairs. They get victory sometimes, but they never get good will, which would be of more use to them. We parted, he going to Philadelphia, and I to Boston.

In returning, I met at New York with the votes of the Assembly, by which it appear'd that, notwithstanding his promise to me, he and the House were already in high contention; and it was a continual battle between them as long as he retain'd the government. I had my share of it; for, as soon as I got back to my seat in the Assembly, I was put on every committee for answering his speeches and messages, and by the committees always desired to make the drafts. Our answers, as well as his messages, were often tart, and sometimes indecently abusive; and, as he knew I wrote for the Assembly, one might have imagined that, when we met, we could hardly avoid cutting throats; but he was so good-natur'd a man that no personal difference between him and me was occasion'd by the contest, and we often din'd together.

One afternoon, in the height of this public quarrel, we met in the street. "Franklin," says he, "you must go home with me and spend the evening; I am to have some company that you will like"; and, taking me by the arm, he led me to his house. In gay conversation over our wine, after supper, he told us, jokingly, that he much admir'd the idea of Sancho Panza, who, when it was proposed to give him a government, requested it might be a government of *blacks*, as then, if he could not agree with his people, he might sell them. One of his friends, who sat next to me, says, "Franklin, why do you continue to side with these damn'd Quakers? Had not you better sell them? The proprietor would give you a good price." "The governor," says I, "has not yet *blacked* them enough." He, indeed, had labored hard to blacken the Assembly in all his messages, but they wip'd off his coloring as fast as he laid it on, and plac'd it, in return, thick upon his own face; so that, finding he was likely to be negrofied himself, he, as well as Mr. Hamilton, grew tir'd of the contest, and quitted the government.

These public quarrels were all at bottom owing to the proprietaries, our hereditary governors, who, when any expense was to be incurred for the defense of their province, with incredible meanness instructed their deputies to pass no act for levying the necessary taxes, unless their vast estates were in the same act expressly excused; and they had even taken bonds of these deputies to observe such instructions. The Assemblies for three years held out against this injustice, tho' constrained to bend at last. At length Captain Denny, who was Governor Morris's successor, ventured to disobey those instructions: how that was brought about I shall show hereafter.

But I am got forward too fast with my story: there are still some transactions to be mention'd that happened during the administration of Governor Morris.

War being in a manner commenced with France, the government of Massachusetts Bay projected an attack upon Crown Point, and sent Mr. Quincy to Pennsylvania, and Mr. Pownall, afterward Governor Pownall, to New York, to solicit assistance. As I was in the Assembly, knew its temper, and was Mr. Quincy's countryman, he appli'd to me for my influence and assistance. I dictated his address to them, which was well received. They voted an aid of ten thousand pounds, to be laid out in provisions. But the governor refusing his assent to their bill (which included this with other sums granted for the use of the crown), unless a clause were inserted exempting the proprietary estate from bearing any part of the tax that would be necessary, the Assembly, tho' very desirous of making their grant to New England effectual, were at a loss how to accomplish it. Mr. Quincy labored hard with the governor to obtain his assent, but he was obstinate.

I then suggested a method of doing the business without the governor, by orders on the trustees of the Loan Office, which, by law, the Assembly had the right of drawing. There was, indeed, little or no money at that time in the office, and therefore I propos'd that the orders should be payable in a year, and to bear an interest of five per cent. With these orders I suppos'd the provisions might easily be purchas'd. The Assembly, with very little hesitation, adopted the proposal. The orders were immediately printed, and I was one of the committee directed to sign and dispose of them. The fund for paying them was the interest of all the paper currency then extant in the province upon loan, together with the revenue arising from the excise, which being known to be more than sufficient, they obtain'd instant credit, and were not only receiv'd in payment for the provisions, but many money'd people, who had cash lying by them, vested it in those orders, which they found advantageous, as they bore interest while upon hand, and might on any occasion be used as money; so that they were eagerly all bought up, and in a few weeks none of them were to be seen. Thus the important affair was by my means compleated. Mr. Quincy return'd thanks to the Assembly in a handsome memorial, went home highly pleas'd with the success of his embassy, and ever after bore for me the most cordial and affectionate friendship.

The British government, not chusing to permit the union of the colonies as propos'd at Albany, and to trust that union with their defense, lest they should thereby grow too military, and feel their own strength, suspicions and jealousies at this time being entertain'd of them, sent over General Braddock with two regiments of regular English troops for that purpose. He landed at Alexandria, in Virginia, and thence march'd to Frederictown, in Maryland, where he halted for carriages. Our Assembly apprehending, from some information, that he had conceived violent prejudices against them, as averse to the service, wish'd me to wait upon him, not as from them, but as postmaster-general, under the guise of proposing to settle with him the mode of conducting with most celerity and certainty the despatches between him and the governors of the several provinces, with whom he must necessarily have continual correspondence, and of which they pro-pos'd to pay the expense. My son accompanied me on this journey.

We found the general at Frederictown, waiting impatiently for the return of those he had sent thro' the back parts of Maryland and Virginia to collect waggons. I stayed with him several days, din'd with him daily, and had full opportunity of removing all his prejudices, by the information of what the Assembly had before his arrival actually done, and were still willing to do, to facilitate his operations. When I was about to depart, the returns of waggons to be obtained were brought in, by which it appear'd that they amounted only to twenty-five, and not all of those were in serviceable con-dition. The general and all the officers were surpris'd, declar'd the expedi-tion was then at an end, being impossible, and exclaim'd against the ministers for ignorantly landing them in a country destitute of the means of conveying their stores, baggage, etc., not less than one hundred and fifty waggons being necessary.

I happen'd to say I thought it was a pity they had not been landed rather in Pennsylvania, as in that country almost every farmer had his waggon. The general eagerly laid hold of my words, and said, "Then you, sir, who are a man of interest there, can probably procure them for us; and I beg you will undertake it." I ask'd what terms were to be offer'd the owners of the waggons; and I was desir'd to put on paper the terms that appeared to me necessary. This I did, and they were agreed to, and a commission and instructions accordingly prepar'd immediately. What those terms were will appear in the advertisement I publish'd as soon as I arriv'd at Lancaster, which being, from the great and sudden effect it produc'd, a piece of some curiosity, I shall insert it at length, as follows:

"ADVERTISEMENT.

"*Lancaster, April 26, 1755.*

"Whereas, one hundred and fifty waggons, with four horses to each waggon, and fifteen hundred saddle or pack horses, are wanted for the service of his majesty's forces now about to rendezvous at Will's Creek, and his excellency General Braddock having been pleased to empower me to contract for the hire of the same, I hereby give notice that I shall attend for that purpose at Lancaster from this day to next Wednesday evening, and at York from next Thursday morning till Friday evening, where I shall be ready to agree for waggons and teams, or single horses, on the following terms, viz: 1. That there shall be paid for each waggon, with four good horses and a driver, fifteen shillings per diem; and for each able horse with a pack-saddle, or other saddle and furniture, two shillings per diem; and for each able horse without a saddle, eighteen pence per diem. 2. That the pay commence from the time of their joining the forces at Will's Creek, which must be on or before the 20th of May ensuing, and that a reasonable allowance be paid over and above for the time necessary for their travelling to Will's Creek and home again after their discharge. 3. Each waggon and team, and every saddle or pack horse, is to be valued by indifferent persons chosen between me and the owner; and in case of the loss of any waggon, team, or other horse in the service, the price according to such valuation is to be allowed and paid. 4. Seven days' pay is to be advanced and paid in hand by me to the owner of each waggon and team, or horse, at the time of contracting, if required, and the remainder to be paid by General Braddock, or by the paymaster of the army, at the time of their discharge, or from time to time, as it shall be demanded. 5. No drivers of waggons, or persons taking care of the hired horses, are on any account to be called upon to do the duty of soldiers, or be otherwise employed than in conducting or taking care of their carriages or horses. 6. All oats, Indian corn, or other forage that waggons or horses bring to the camp, more than is necessary for the subsistence of the horses, is to be taken for the use of the army, and a reasonable price paid for the same.

"Note.—My son, William Franklin, is empowered to enter into like contracts with any person in Cumberland county.   B. FRANKLIN."

"*To the inhabitants of the Counties of Lancaster, York, and Cumberland.*

"Friends and Countrymen,
    "Being occasionally at the camp at Frederic a few days since, I found the general and officers extremely exasperated on account of their not being supplied with horses and carriages, which had been expected from this

province, as most able to furnish them; but, through the dissensions between our governor and Assembly, money had not been provided, nor any steps taken for that purpose.

"It was proposed to send an armed force immediately into these counties, to seize as many of the best carriages and horses as should be wanted, and compel as many persons into the service as would be necessary to drive and take care of them.

"I apprehended that the progress of British soldiers through these counties on such an occasion, especially considering the temper they are in, and their resentment against us, would be attended with many and great inconveniences to the inhabitants, and therefore more willingly took the trouble of trying first what might be done by fair and equitable means. The people of these back counties have lately complained to the Assembly that a sufficient currency was wanting; you have an opportunity of receiving and dividing among you a very considerable sum; for, if the service of this expedition should continue, as it is more than probable it will, for one hundred and twenty days, the hire of these waggons and horses will amount to upward of thirty thousand pounds, which will be paid you in silver and gold of the king's money.

"The service will be light and easy, for the army will scarce march above twelve miles per day, and the waggons and baggage-horses, as they carry those things that are absolutely necessary to the welfare of the army, must march with the army, and no faster; and are, for the army's sake, always placed where they can be most secure, whether in a march or in a camp.

"If you are really, as I believe you are, good and loyal subjects to his majesty, you may now do a most acceptable service, and make it easy to yourselves; for three or four of such as can not separately spare from the business of their plantations a waggon and four horses and a driver, may do it together, one furnishing the waggon, another one or two horses, and another the driver, and divide the pay proportionably between you; but if you do not this service to your king and country voluntarily, when such good pay and reasonable terms are offered to you, your loyalty will be strongly suspected. The king's business must be done; so many brave troops, come so far for your defense, must not stand idle through your backwardness to do what may be reasonably expected from you; waggons and horses must be had; violent measures will probably be used, and you will be left to seek for a recompense where you can find it, and your case, perhaps, be little pitied or regarded.

"I have no particular interest in this affair, as, except the satisfaction of endeavoring to do good, I shall have only my labor for my pains. If this method of obtaining the waggons and horses is not likely to succeed, I am obliged to send word to the general in fourteen days; and I suppose Sir John St. Clair, the hussar, with a body of soldiers, will immediately enter the province for the purpose, which I shall be sorry to hear, because I am very sincerely and truly your friend and well-wisher,

"B. FRANKLIN."

I received of the general about eight hundred pounds, to be disbursed in advance-money to the waggon owners, etc.; but that sum being insufficient, I advanc'd upward of two hundred pounds more, and in two weeks the one hundred and fifty waggons, with two hundred and fifty-nine carrying horses, were on their march for the camp. The advertisement promised payment according to the valuation, in case any waggon or horse should be lost. The owners, however, alleging they did not know General Braddock, or what dependence might be had on his promise, insisted on my bond for the performance, which I accordingly gave them.

While I was at the camp, supping one evening with the officers of Colonel Dunbar's regiment, he represented to me his concern for the subalterns, who, he said, were generally not in affluence, and could ill afford, in this dear country, to lay in the stores that might be necessary in so long a march, thro' a wilderness, where nothing was to be purchas'd. I commiserated their case, and resolved to endeavor procuring them some relief. I said nothing, however, to him of my intention, but wrote the next morning to the committee of the Assembly, who had the disposition of some public money, warmly recommending the case of these officers to their consideration, and proposing that a present should be sent them of necessaries and refreshments. My son, who had some experience of a camp life, and of its wants, drew up a list for me, which I enclos'd in my letter. The committee approv'd, and used such diligence that, conducted by my son, the stores arrived at the camp as soon as the waggons. They consisted of twenty parcels, each containing

6 lbs. loaf sugar.	1 Gloucester cheese.
6 lbs. good Muscovado do.	1 kegg containing 20 lbs. good butter.
1 lb. good green tea.	2 doz. old Madeira wine.
1 lb. good bohea do.	2 gallons Jamaica spirits.
6 lbs. good ground coffee.	1 bottle flour of mustard.
6 lbs. chocolate.	2 well-cur'd hams.
1-2 cwt. best white biscuit.	1-2 dozen dry'd tongues.
1-2 lb. pepper.	6 lbs. rice.
1 quart best white wine vinegar.	6 lbs. raisins.

These twenty parcels, well pack'd, were placed on as many horses, each parcel, with the horse, being intended as a present for one officer. They were very thankfully receiv'd, and the kindness acknowledg'd by letters to me from the colonels of both regiments, in the most grateful terms. The general, too, was highly satisfied with my conduct in procuring him the waggons, etc., and readily paid my account of disbursements, thanking me repeatedly, and requesting my farther assistance in sending provisions after him. I undertook this also, and was busily employ'd in it till we heard of his defeat, advancing for the service of my own money, upwards of one thousand pounds sterling, of which I sent him an account. It came to his hands, luckily for me, a few days before the battle, and he return'd me immediately an order on the paymaster for the round sum of one thousand pounds, leaving the remainder to the next account. I consider this payment as good luck, having never been able to obtain that remainder, of which more hereafter.

This general was, I think, a brave man, and might probably have made a figure as a good officer in some European war. But he had too much self-confidence, too high an opinion of the validity of regular troops, and too mean a one of both Americans and Indians. George Croghan, our Indian interpreter, join'd him on his march with one hundred of those people, who might have been of great use to his army as guides, scouts, etc., if he had treated them kindly; but he slighted and neglected them, and they gradually left him.

In conversation with him one day, he was giving me some account of his intended progress. "After taking Fort Duquesne," says he, "I am to proceed to Niagara; and, having taken that, to Frontenac, if the season will allow time; and I suppose it will, for Duquesne can hardly detain me above three or four days; and then I see nothing that can obstruct my march to Niagara." Having before revolv'd in my mind the long line his army must make in their march by a very narrow road, to be cut for them thro' the woods and bushes, and also what I had read of a former defeat of fifteen hundred French, who invaded the Iroquois country, I had conceiv'd some doubts and some fears for the event of the campaign. But I ventur'd only to say, "To be sure, sir, if you arrive well before Duquesne, with these fine troops, so well provided with artillery, that place not yet completely fortified, and as we hear with no very strong garrison, can probably make but a short resistance. The only danger I apprehend of obstruction to your march is from ambuscades of Indians, who, by constant practice, are dexterous in laying and executing them; and the slender line, near four miles long, which your army must make, may expose it to be attack'd by surprise in its flanks, and to be cut like a thread into several pieces, which, from their distance, can not come up in time to support each other."

He smil'd at my ignorance, and reply'd, "These savages may, indeed, be a formidable enemy to your raw American militia, but upon the king's regular and disciplin'd troops, sir, it is impossible they should make any impression." I was conscious of an impropriety in my disputing with a military man in matters of his profession, and said no more. The enemy, however, did not take the advantage of his army which I apprehended its long line of march expos'd it to, but let it advance without interruption till within nine miles of the place; and then, when more in a body (for it had just passed a river, where the front had halted till all were come over), and in a more open part of the woods than any it had pass'd, attack'd its advanced guard by a heavy fire from behind trees and bushes, which was the first intelligence the general had of an enemy's being near him. This guard being disordered, the general hurried the troops up to their assistance, which was done in great confusion, thro' waggons, baggage, and cattle; and presently the fire came upon their flank: the officers, being on horseback, were more easily distinguish'd, pick'd out as marks, and fell very fast; and the soldiers were crowded together in a huddle, having or hearing no orders, and stand-ing to be shot at till two-thirds of them were killed; and then, being seiz'd with a panick, the whole fled with precipitation.

The waggoners took each a horse out of his team and scamper'd; their example was immediately followed by others; so that all the waggons, pro-visions, artillery, and stores were left to the enemy. The general, being wounded, was brought off with difficulty; his secretary, Mr. Shirley, was killed by his side; and out of eighty-six officers, sixty-three were killed or wounded, and seven hundred and fourteen men killed out of eleven hun-dred. These eleven hundred had been picked men from the whole army; the rest had been left behind with Colonel Dunbar, who was to follow with the heavier part of the stores, provisions, and baggage. The flyers, not being pursu'd, arrived at Dunbar's camp, and the panick they brought with them instantly seiz'd him and all his people; and, tho' he had now above one thou-sand men, and the enemy who had beaten Braddock did not at most exceed four hundred Indians and French together, instead of proceeding, and en-deavoring to recover some of the lost honour, he ordered all the stores, ammunition, etc., to be destroy'd, that he might have more horses to assist his flight towards the settlements, and less number to remove. He was there met with requests from the governors of Virginia, Maryland, and Pennsyl-vania, that he would post his troops on the frontiers, so as to afford some protection to the inhabitants; but he continu'd his hasty march thro' all the country, not thinking himself safe till he arriv'd at Philadelphia, where the inhabitants could protect him. This whole transaction gave us Americans the first suspicion that our exalted ideas of the prowess of the British regu-lars had not been well founded.

In their first march, too, from their landing till they got beyond the set-tlements, they had plundered and stripped the inhabitants, totally ruining some poor families, besides insulting, abusing, and confining the people if they remonstrated. This was enough to put us out of conceit of such de-fenders, if we had really wanted any. How different was the conduct of our French friends in 1781, who, during a march thro' the most inhabited part of our country from Rhode Island to Virginia, near seven hundred miles, occasioned not the smallest complaint for the loss of a pig, a chicken, or even an apple.

Captain Orme, who was one of the general's aids-de-camp, and, being grievously wounded, was brought off with him, and continu'd with him to his death, which happen'd in a few days, told me that he was totally silent all the first day, and at night only said, *"Who would have thought it?"* That he was silent again the following day, saying only at last, *"We shall better know how to deal with them another time"*; and dy'd in a few min-utes after.

The secretary's papers, with all the general's orders, instructions, and cor-respondence, falling into the enemy's hands, they selected and translated into French a number of the articles, which they printed, to prove the hostile intentions of the British court before the declaration of war. Among these

I saw some letters of the general to the ministry, speaking highly of the great service I had rendered the army, and recommending me to their notice. David Hume, too, who was some years after secretary to Lord Hertford, when minister in France, and afterward to General Conway, when secretary of state, told me he had seen among the papers in that office, letters from Braddock highly recommending me. But, the expedition having been unfortunate, my service, it seems, was not thought of much value, for those recommendations were never of any use to me.

As to rewards from himself, I ask'd only one, which was, that he would give orders to his officers not to enlist any more of our bought servants, and that he would discharge such as had been already enlisted. This he readily granted, and several were accordingly return'd to their masters, on my application. Dunbar, when the command devolv'd on him, was not so generous. He being at Philadelphia, on his retreat, or rather flight, I apply'd to him for the discharge of the servants of three poor farmers of Lancaster county that he had enlisted, reminding him of the late general's orders on that head. He promised me that, if the masters would come to him at Trenton, where he should be in a few days on his march to New York, he would there deliver their men to them. They accordingly were at the expense and trouble of going to Trenton, and there he refus'd to perform his promise, to their great loss and disappointment.

As soon as the loss of the waggons and horses was generally known, all the owners came upon me for the valuation which I had given bond to pay. Their demands gave me a great deal of trouble, my acquainting them that the money was ready in the paymaster's hands, but that orders for paying it must first be obtained from General Shirley, and my assuring them that I had apply'd to that general by letter; but, he being at a distance, an answer could not soon be receiv'd, and they must have patience, all this was not sufficient to satisfy, and some began to sue me. General Shirley at length relieved me from this terrible situation by appointing commissioners to examine the claims, and ordering payment. They amounted to near twenty thousand pound, which to pay would have ruined me.

Before we had the news of this defeat, the two Doctors Bond came to me with a subscription paper for raising money to defray the expense of a grand firework, which it was intended to exhibit at a rejoicing on receipt of the news of our taking Fort Duquesne. I looked grave, and said it would, I thought, be time enough to prepare for the rejoicing when we knew we should have occasion to rejoice. They seem'd surpris'd that I did not immediately comply with their proposal. "Why the d—l!" says one of them, "you surely don't suppose that the fort will not be taken?" "I don't know that it will not be taken, but I know that the events of war are subject to great uncertainty." I gave them the reasons of my doubting; the subscription was dropt, and the projectors thereby missed the mortification they would have undergone if the firework had been prepared. Dr. Bond, on some other occasion afterward, said that he did not like Franklin's forebodings.

Governor Morris, who had continually worried the Assembly with message after message before the defeat of Braddock, to beat them into the making of acts to raise money for the defense of the province, without taxing, among others, the proprietary estates, and had rejected all their bills for not having such an exempting clause, now redoubled his attacks with more hope of success, the danger and necessity being greater. The Assembly, however, continu'd firm, believing they had justice on their side, and that it would be giving up an essential right if they suffered the governor to amend their money-bills. In one of the last, indeed, which was for granting fifty thousand pounds, his propos'd amendment was only of a single word. The bill express'd "that all estates, real and personal, were to be taxed, those of the proprietaries *not* excepted." His amendment was, for *not* read *only:* a small, but very material alteration. However, when the news of this disaster reached England, our friends there, whom we had taken care to furnish with all the Assembly's answers to the governor's messages, rais'd a clamor against the proprietaries for their meanness and injustice in giving their governor such instructions; some going so far as to say that, by obstructing the defense of their province, they forfeited their right to it. They were intimidated by this, and sent orders to their receiver-general to add five thousand pounds of their money to whatever sum might be given by the Assembly for such purpose.

This, being notified to the House, was accepted in lieu of their share of a general tax, and a new bill was form'd, with an exempting clause, which passed accordingly. By this act I was appointed one of the commissioners for disposing of the money, sixty thousand pounds. I had been active in modelling the bill and procuring its passage, and had, at the same time, drawn a bill for establishing and disciplining a voluntary militia, which I carried thro' the House without much difficulty, as care was taken in it to leave the Quakers at their liberty. To promote the association necessary to form the militia, I wrote a dialogue, stating and answering all the objections I could think of to such a militia, which was printed, and had, as I thought, great effect.

While the several companies in the city and country were forming, and learning their exercise, the governor prevail'd with me to take charge of our North-western frontier, which was infested by the enemy, and provide for the defense of the inhabitants by raising troops and building a line of forts. I undertook this military business, tho' I did not conceive myself well qualified for it. He gave me a commission with full powers, and a parcel of blank commissions for officers, to be given to whom I thought fit. I had but little difficulty in raising men, having soon five hundred and sixty under my command. My son, who had in the preceding war been an officer in the army rais'd against Canada, was my aid-de-camp, and of great use to me. The Indians had burned Gnadenhut, a village settled by the Moravians, and massacred the inhabitants; but the place was thought a good situation for one of the forts.

In order to march thither, I assembled the companies at Bethlehem, the chief establishment of those people. I was surprised to find it in so good a posture of defense; the destruction of Gnadenhut had made them apprehend danger. The principal buildings were defended by a stockade; they had purchased a quantity of arms and ammunition from New York, and had even plac'd quantities of small paving stones between the windows of their high stone houses, for their women to throw down upon the heads of any Indians that should attempt to force into them. The armed brethren, too, kept watch, and reliev'd as methodically as in any garrison town. In conversation with the bishop, Spangenberg, I mention'd this my surprise; for, knowing they had obtained an act of Parliament exempting them from military duties in the colonies, I had suppos'd they were conscientiously scrupulous of bearing arms. He answer'd me that it was not one of their established principles, but that, at the time of their obtaining that act, it was thought to be a principle with many of their people. On this occasion, however, they, to their surprise, found it adopted by but a few. It seems they were either deceiv'd in themselves, or deceiv'd the Parliament; but common sense, aided by present danger, will sometimes be too strong for whimsical opinions.

It was the beginning of January when we set out upon this business of building forts. I sent one detachment toward the Minisink, with instructions to erect one for the security of that upper part of the country, and another to the lower part, with similar instructions; and I concluded to go myself with the rest of my force to Gnadenhut, where a fort was tho't more immediately necessary. The Moravians procur'd me five waggons for our tools, stores, baggage, etc.

Just before we left Bethlehem, eleven farmers, who had been driven from their plantations by the Indians, came to me requesting a supply of firearms, that they might go back and fetch off their cattle. I gave them each a gun with suitable ammunition. We had not march'd many miles before it began to rain, and it continued raining all day; there were no habitations on the road to shelter us, till we arriv'd near night at the house of a German, where, and in his barn, we were all huddled together, as wet as water could make us. It was well we were not attack'd in our march, for our arms were of the most ordinary sort, and our men could not keep their gun locks dry. The Indians are dextrous in contrivances for that purpose, which we had not. They met that day the eleven poor farmers above mentioned, and killed ten of them. The one who escap'd inform'd that his and his companions' guns would not go off, the priming being wet with the rain.

The next day being fair, we continu'd our march, and arriv'd at the desolated Gnadenhut. There was a saw-mill near, round which were left several piles of boards, with which we soon hutted ourselves; an operation the more necessary at that inclement season, as we had no tents. Our first work was to bury more effectually the dead we found there, who had been half interr'd by the country people.

The next morning our fort was plann'd and mark'd out, the circumference measuring four hundred and fifty-five feet, which would require as many palisades to be made of trees, one with another, of a foot diameter each. Our axes, of which we had seventy, were immediately set to work to cut down trees, and, our men being dextrous in the use of them, great despatch was made. Seeing the trees fall so fast, I had the curiosity to look at my watch when two men began to cut at a pine; in six minutes they had it upon the ground, and I found it of fourteen inches diameter. Each pine made three palisades of eighteen feet long, pointed at one end. While these were preparing, our other men dug a trench all round, of three feet deep, in which the palisades were to be planted; and, our waggons, the bodys being taken off, and the fore and hind wheels separated by taking out the pin which united the two parts of the perch, we had ten carriages, with two horses each, to bring the palisades from the woods to the spot. When they were set up, our carpenters built a stage of boards all round within, about six feet high, for the men to stand on when to fire thro' the loopholes. We had one swivel gun, which we mounted on one of the angles, and fir'd it as soon as fix'd, to let the Indians know, if any were within hearing, that we had such pieces; and thus our fort, if such a magnificent name may be given to so miserable a stockade, was finish'd in a week, though it rain'd so hard every other day that the men could not work.

This gave me occasion to observe, that, when men are employ'd, they are best content'd; for on the days they worked they were good-natur'd and cheerful, and, with the consciousness of having done a good day's work, they spent the evening jollily; but on our idle days they were mutinous and quarrelsome, finding fault with their pork, the bread, etc., and in continual ill-humor, which put me in mind of a sea-captain, whose rule it was to keep his men constantly at work; and, when his mate once told him that they had done every thing, and there was nothing further to employ them about, "Oh," says he, "make them scour the anchor."

This kind of fort, however contemptible, is a sufficient defense against Indians, who have no cannon. Finding ourselves now posted securely, and having a place to retreat to on occasion, we ventur'd out in parties to scour the adjacent country. We met with no Indians, but we found the places on the neighboring hills where they had lain to watch our proceedings. There was an art in their contrivance of those places that seems worth mention. It being winter, a fire was necessary for them; but a common fire on the surface of the ground would by its light have discover'd their position at a distance. They had therefore dug holes in the ground about three feet in diameter, and somewhat deeper; we saw where they had with their hatchets cut off the charcoal from the sides of burnt logs lying in the woods. With these coals they had made small fires in the bottom of the holes, and we observ'd among the weeds and grass the prints of their bodies, made by their laying all round, with their legs hanging down in the holes to keep their feet warm, which, with them, is an essential point. This kind of fire, so manag'd, could not discover them, either by its light, flame, sparks, or even smoke: it appear'd that their number was not great, and it seems they saw we were too many to be attacked by them with prospect of advantage.

We had for our chaplain a zealous Presbyterian minister, Mr. Beatty, who complained to me that the men did not generally attend his prayers and exhortations. When they enlisted, they were promised, besides pay and provisions, a gill of rum a day, which was punctually serv'd out to them, half in the morning, and the other half in the evening; and I observ'd they were as punctual in attending to receive it; upon which I said to Mr. Beatty, "It is, perhaps, below the dignity of your profession to act as steward of the rum, but if you were to deal it out and only just after prayers, you would have them all about you." He liked the tho't, undertook the office, and, with the help of a few hands to measure out the liquor, executed it to satisfaction, and never were prayers more generally and more punctually attended; so that I thought this method preferable to the punishment inflicted by some military laws for non-attendance on divine service.

I had hardly finish'd this business, and got my fort well stor'd with provisions, when I receiv'd a letter from the governor, acquainting me that he had call'd the Assembly, and wished my attendance there, if the posture of affairs on the frontiers was such that my remaining there was no longer necessary. My friends, too, of the Assembly, pressing me by their letters to be, if possible, at the meeting, and my three intended forts being now compleated, and the inhabitants contented to remain on their farms under that protection, I resolved to return; the more willingly, as a New England officer, Colonel Clapham, experienced in Indian war, being on a visit to our establishment, consented to accept the command. I gave him a commission, and, parading the garrison, had it read before them, and introduc'd him to them as an officer who, from his skill in military affairs, was much more fit to command them than myself; and, giving them a little exhortation, took my leave. I was escorted as far as Bethlehem, where I rested a few days to recover from the fatigue I had undergone. The first night, being in a good bed, I could hardly sleep, it was so different from my hard lodging on the floor of our hut at Gnadenhut wrapt only in a blanket or two.

While at Bethlehem, I inquir'd a little into the practice of the Moravians: some of them had accompanied me, and all were very kind to me. I found they work'd for a common stock, eat at common tables, and slept in common dormitories, great numbers together. In the dormitories I observed loopholes, at certain distances all along just under the ceiling, which I thought judiciously placed for change of air. I was at their church, where I was entertain'd with good musick, the organ being accompanied with violins, hautboys, flutes, clarinets, etc. I understood that their sermons were not usually preached to mixed congregations of men, women, and children, as is our common practice, but that they assembled sometimes the married men, at other times their wives, then the young men, the young women, and the little children, each division by itself. The sermon I heard was to the latter, who came in and were plac'd in rows on benches; the boys under the conduct of a young man, their tutor, and the girls conducted by a young woman. The discourse seem'd well adapted to their capacities, and was delivered in a pleasing, familiar manner, coaxing them, as it were, to be good. They behav'd very orderly, but looked pale and unhealthy, which made me suspect they were kept too much within doors, or not allow'd sufficient exercise.

I inquir'd concerning the Moravian marriages, whether the report was true that they were by lot. I was told that lots were us'd only in particular cases; that generally, when a young man found himself dispos'd to marry, he inform'd the elders of his class, who consulted the elder ladies that govern'd the young women. As these elders of the different sexes were well acquainted with the tempers and dispositions of their respective pupils, they could best judge what matches were suitable, and their judgments were generally acquiesc'd in; but if, for example, it should happen that two or three young women were found to be equally proper for the young man, the lot was then recurred to. I objected, if the matches are not made by the mutual choice of the parties, some of them may chance to be very unhappy. "And so they may," answer'd my informer, "if you let the parties chuse for themselves"; which, indeed, I could not deny.

Being returned to Philadelphia, I found the association went on swimmingly, the inhabitants that were not Quakers having pretty generally come into it, formed themselves into companies, and chose their captains, lieutenants, and ensigns, according to the new law. Dr. B. visited me, and gave me an account of the pains he had taken to spread a general good liking to the law, and ascribed much to those endeavors. I had had the vanity to ascribe all to my *Dialogue;* however, not knowing but that he might be in the right, I let him enjoy his opinion, which I take to be generally the best way in such cases. The officers, meeting, chose me to be colonel of the regiment, which I this time accepted. I forget how many companies we had, but we paraded about twelve hundred well-looking men, with a company of artillery, who had been furnished with six brass field-pieces, which they had become so expert in the use of as to fire twelve times in a minute. The first time I reviewed my regiment they accompanied me to my house, and would salute me with some rounds fired before my door, which shook down and broke several glasses of my electrical apparatus. And my new honour proved not much less brittle; for all our commissions were soon after broken by a repeal of the law in England.

During this short time of my colonelship, being about to set out on a journey to Virginia, the officers of my regiment took it into their heads that it would be proper for them to escort me out of town, as far as the Lower Ferry. Just as I was getting on horseback they came to my door, between thirty and forty, mounted, and all in their uniforms. I had not been previously acquainted with the project, or I should have prevented it, being naturally averse to the assuming of state on any occasion; and I was a good deal chagrin'd at their appearance, as I could not avoid their accompanying me. What made it worse was, that, as soon as we began to move, they drew their swords and rode with them naked all the way. Somebody wrote an account of this to the proprietor, and it gave him great offense. No such honor had been paid him when in the province, nor to any of his governors; and he said it was only proper to princes of the blood royal, which may be true for aught I know, who was, and still am, ignorant of the etiquette in such cases.

This silly affair, however, greatly increased his rancour against me, which was before not a little, on account of my conduct in the Assembly respecting the exemption of his estate from taxation, which I had always oppos'd very warmly, and not without severe reflections on his meanness and injustice of contending for it. He accused me to the ministry as being the great obstacle to the king's service, preventing, by my influence in the House, the proper form of the bills for raising money, and he instanced this parade with my officers as a proof of my having an intention to take the government of the province out of his hands by force. He also applied to Sir Everard Fawkener, the postmaster-general, to deprive me of my office; but it had no other effect than to procure from Sir Everard a gentle admonition.

Notwithstanding the continual wrangle between the governor and the House, in which I, as a member, had so large a share, there still subsisted a civil intercourse between that gentleman and myself, and we never had any personal difference. I have sometimes since thought that his little or no resentment against me, for the answers it was known I drew up to his messages, might be the effect of professional habit, and that, being bred a lawyer, he might consider us both as merely advocates for contending clients in a suit, he for the proprietaries and I for the Assembly. He would, therefore, sometimes call in a friendly way to advise with me on difficult points, and sometimes, tho' not often, take my advice.

We acted in concert to supply Braddock's army with provisions; and, when the shocking news arrived of his defeat, the governor sent in haste for me, to consult with him on measures for preventing the desertion of the back counties. I forget now the advice I gave; but I think it was, that Dunbar should be written to, and prevail'd with, if possible, to post his troops on the frontiers for their protection, till, by re-enforcements from the colonies, he might be able to proceed on the expedition. And, after my return from the frontier, he would have had me undertake the conduct of such an expedition with provincial troops, for the reduction of Fort Duquesne, Dunbar and his men being otherwise employed; and he proposed to commission me as general. I had not so good an opinion of my military abilities as he profess'd to have, and I believe his professions must have exceeded his real sentiments; but probably he might think that my popularity would facilitate the raising of the men, and my influence in Assembly, the grant of money to pay them, and that, perhaps, without taxing the proprietary estate. Finding me not so forward to engage as he expected, the project was dropt, and he soon after left the government, being superseded by Captain Denny.

Before I proceed in relating the part I had in public affairs under this new governor's administration, it may not be amiss here to give some account of the rise and progress of my philosophical reputation.

In 1746, being at Boston, I met there with a Dr. Spence, who was lately arrived from Scotland, and show'd me some electric experiments. They were imperfectly performed, as he was not very expert; but, being on a subject quite new to me, they equally surpris'd and pleased me. Soon after my return to Philadelphia, our library company receiv'd from Mr. P. Collinson, Fellow of the Royal Society of London, a present of a glass tube, with some account of the use of it in making such experiments. I eagerly seized the opportunity of repeating what I had seen at Boston; and, by much practice, acquir'd great readiness in performing those, also, which we had an account of from England, adding a number of new ones. I say much practice, for my house was continually full, for some time, with people who came to see these new wonders.

To divide a little this incumbrance among my friends, I caused a number of similar tubes to be blown at our glass-house, with which they furnish'd themselves, so that we had at length several performers. Among these, the principal was Mr. Kinnersley, an ingenious neighbor, who, being out of business, I encouraged to undertake showing the experiments for money, and drew up for him two lectures, in which the experiments were rang'd in such order, and accompanied with such explanations in such method, as that the foregoing should assist in comprehending the following. He procur'd an elegant apparatus for the purpose, in which all the little machines that I had roughly made for myself were nicely form'd by instrument-makers. His lectures were well attended, and gave great satisfaction; and after some time he went thro' the colonies, exhibiting them in every capital town, and pick'd up some money. In the West India islands, indeed, it was with difficulty the experiments could be made, from the general moisture of the air.

Oblig'd as we were to Mr. Collinson for his present of the tube, etc., I thought it right he should be inform'd of our success in using it, and wrote him several letters containing accounts of our experiments. He got them read in the Royal Society, where they were not at first thought worth so much notice as to be printed in their Transactions. One paper, which I wrote for Mr. Kinnersley, on the sameness of lightning with electricity, I sent to Dr. Mitchel, an acquaintance of mine, and one of the members also of that society, who wrote me word that it had been read, but was laughed at by the connoisseurs. The papers, however, being shown to Dr. Fothergill, he thought them of too much value to be stifled, and advis'd the printing of them. Mr. Collinson then gave them to *Cave* for publication in his Gentleman's Magazine; but he chose to print them separately in a pamphlet, and Dr. Fothergill wrote the preface. Cave, it seems, judged rightly for his profit, for by the additions that arrived afterward, they swell'd to a quarto volume, which has had five editions, and cost him nothing for copy-money.

It was, however, some time before those papers were much taken notice of in England. A copy of them happening to fall into the hands of the Count de Buffon, a philosopher deservedly of great reputation in France, and, indeed, all over Europe, he prevailed with M. Dalibard to translate them into French, and they were printed at Paris. The publication offended the Abbé Nollet, preceptor in Natural Philosophy to the royal family, and an able experimenter, who had form'd and publish'd a theory of electricity, which then had the general vogue. He could not at first believe that such a work came from America, and said it must have been fabricated by his enemies at Paris, to decry his system. Afterwards, having been assur'd that there really existed such a person as Franklin at Philadelphia, which he had doubted, he wrote and published a volume of Letters, chiefly address'd to me, defending his theory, and denying the verity of my experiments, and of the positions deduc'd from them.

I once purpos'd answering the abbé, and actually began the answer; but, on consideration that my writings contain'd a description of experiments which any one might repeat and verify, and if not to be verifi'd, could not be defended; or of observations offer'd as conjectures, and not delivered dogmatically, therefore not laying me under any obligation to defend them; and reflecting that a dispute between two persons, writing in different languages, might be lengthened greatly by mistranslations, and thence misconceptions of one another's meaning, much of one of the abbé's letters being founded on an error in the translation, I concluded to let my papers shift for themselves, believing it was better to spend what time I could spare from public business in making new experiments, than in disputing about those already made. I therefore never answered M. Nollet, and the event gave me no cause to repent my silence; for my friend M. le Roy, of the Royal Academy of Sciences, took up my cause and refuted him; my book was translated into the Italian, German, and Latin languages; and the doctrine it contain'd was by degrees universally adopted by the philosophers of Europe, in preference to that of the abbé; so that he lived to see himself the last of his sect, except Monseur B——, of Paris, his *élève* and immediate disciple.

What gave my book the more sudden and general celebrity, was the success of one of its proposed experiments, made by Messrs. Dalibard and De Lor at Marly, for drawing lightning from the clouds. This engag'd the public attention every where. M. de Lor, who had an apparatus for experimental philosophy, and lectur'd in that branch of science, undertook to repeat what he called the *Philadelphia Experiments;* and, after they were performed before the king and court, all the curious of Paris flocked to see them. I will not swell this narrative with an account of that capital experiment, nor of the infinite pleasure I receiv'd in the success of a similar one I made soon after with a kite at Philadelphia, as both are to be found in the histories of electricity.

Dr. Wright, an English physician, when at Paris, wrote to a friend, who was of the Royal Society, an account of the high esteem my experiments were in among the learned abroad, and of their wonder that my writings had been so little noticed in England. The society, on this, resum'd the consideration of the letters that had been read to them; and the celebrated Dr. Watson drew up a summary account of them, and of all I had afterwards sent to England on the subject, which he accompanied with some praise of the writer. This summary was then printed in their Transactions; and some members of the society in London, particularly the very ingenious Mr. Canton, having verified the experiment of procuring lightning from the clouds by a pointed rod, and acquainting them with the success, they soon made me more than amends for the slight with which they had before treated me. Without my having made any application for that honor, they chose me a member, and voted that I should be excus'd the customary payments, which would have amounted to twenty-five guineas; and ever since have given me their Transactions gratis. They also presented me with the gold medal of Sir Godfrey Copley for the year 1753, the delivery of which was accompanied by a very handsome speech of the president, Lord Macclesfield, wherein I was highly honoured.

Our new governor, Captain Denny, brought over for me the before-mentioned medal from the Royal Society, which he presented to me at an entertainment given him by the city. He accompanied it with very polite expressions of his esteem for me, having, as he said, been long acquainted with my character. After dinner, when the company, as was customary at that time, were engag'd in drinking, he took me aside into another room, and acquainted me that he had been advis'd by his friends in England to cultivate a friendship with me, as one who was capable of giving him the best advice, and of contributing most effectually to the making his administration easy; that he therefore desired of all things to have a good understanding with me, and he begg'd me to be assur'd of his readiness on all occasions to render me every service that might be in his power. He said much to me, also, of the proprietor's good disposition towards the province, and of the advantage it might be to us all, and to me in particular, if the opposition that had been so long continu'd to his measures was dropt, and harmony restor'd between him and the people; in effecting which, it was thought no one could be more serviceable than myself; and I might depend on adequate acknowledgments and recompenses, etc., etc. The drinkers, finding we did not return immediately to the table, sent us a decanter of Madeira, which the governor made liberal use of, and in proportion became more profuse of his solicitations and promises.

My answers were to this purpose: that my circumstances, thanks to God, were such as to make proprietary favours unnecessary to me; and that, being a member of the Assembly, I could not possibly accept of any; that, however, I had no personal enmity to the proprietary, and that, whenever the public measures he propos'd should appear to be for the good of the people, no one should espouse and forward them more zealously than myself; my past opposition having been founded on this, that the measures which had been urged were evidently intended to serve the proprietary interest, with great prejudice to that of the people; that I was much obliged to him (the governor) for his professions of regard to me, and that he might rely on every thing in my power to make his administration as easy as possible, hoping at the same time that he had not brought with him the same unfortunate instruction his predecessor had been hamper'd with.

On this he did not then explain himself; but when he afterwards came to do business with the Assembly, they appear'd again, the disputes were renewed, and I was as active as ever in the opposition, being the penman, first, of the request to have a communication of the instructions, and then of the remarks upon them, which may be found in the votes of the time, and in the Historical Review I afterward publish'd. But between us personally no enmity arose; we were often together; he was a man of letters, had seen much of the world, and was very entertaining and pleasing in conversation. He gave me the first information that my old friend Jas. Ralph was still alive; that he was esteem'd one of the best political writers in England; had been employ'd in the dispute between Prince Frederic and the king, and had obtain'd a pension of three hundred a year; that his reputation was indeed small as a poet, Pope having damned his poetry in the Dunciad; but his prose was thought as good as any man's.

The Assembly finally finding their proprietary obstinately persisted in manacling their deputies with instructions inconsistent not only with the privileges of the people, but with the service of the crown, resolv'd to petition the king against them, and appointed me their agent to go over to England, to present and support the petition. The House had sent up a bill to the governor, granting a sum of sixty thousand pounds for the king's use (ten thousand pounds of which was subjected to the orders of the then general, Lord Loudoun), which the governor absolutely refus'd to pass, in compliance with his instructions.

I had agreed with Captain Morris, of the paquet at New York, for my passage, and my stores were put on board, when Lord Loudoun arriv'd at Philadelphia, expressly, as he told me, to endeavor an accommodation between the governor and Assembly, that his majesty's service might not be obstructed by their dissensions. Accordingly, he desir'd the governor and myself to meet him, that he might hear what was to be said on both sides. We met and discuss'd the business. In behalf of the Assembly, I urg'd all the various arguments that may be found in the public papers of that time, which were of my writing, and are printed with the minutes of the Assembly; and the governor pleaded his instructions; the bond he had given to observe them, and his ruin if he disobey'd, yet seemed not unwilling to hazard himself if Lord Loudoun would advise it. This his lordship did not chuse to do, though I once thought I had nearly prevail'd with him to do it; but finally he rather chose to urge the compliance of the Assembly; and he entreated me to use my endeavours with them for that purpose, declaring that he would spare none of the king's troops for the defense of our frontiers, and that, if we did not continue to provide for that defense ourselves, they must remain expos'd to the enemy.

I acquainted the House with what had pass'd, and, presenting them with a set of resolutions I had drawn up, declaring our rights, and that we did not relinquish our claim to those rights, but only suspended the exercise of them on this occasion thro' *force,* against which we protested, they at length agreed to drop that bill, and frame another conformable to the proprietary instructions. This of course the governor pass'd, and I was then at liberty to proceed on my voyage. But, in the mean time, the paquet had sailed with my sea-stores, which was some loss to me, and my only recompense was his lordship's thanks for my service, all the credit of obtaining the accommodation falling to his share.

He set out for New York before me; and, as the time for dispatching the paquet-boats was at his disposition, and there were two then remaining there, one of which, he said, was to sail very soon, I requested to know the precise time, that I might not miss her by any delay of mine. His answer was, "I have given out that she is to sail on Saturday next; but I may let you know, *entre nous*, that if you are there by Monday morning, you will be in time, but do not delay longer." By some accidental hinderance at a ferry, it was Monday noon before I arrived, and I was much afraid she might have sailed, as the wind was fair; but I was soon made easy by the information that she was still in the harbor, and would not move till the next day. One would imagine that I was now on the very point of departing for Europe. I thought so; but I was not then so well acquainted with his lordship's character, of which *indecision* was one of the strongest features. I shall give some instances. It was about the beginning of April that I came to New York, and I think it was near the end of June before we sail'd. There were then two of the paquet-boats, which had been long in port, but were detained for the general's letters, which were always to be ready to-morrow. Another paquet arriv'd; she too was detain'd; and, before we sail'd, a fourth was expected. Ours was the first to be dispatch'd, as having been there longest. Passengers were engag'd in all, and some extremely impatient to be gone, and the merchants uneasy about their letters, and the orders they had given for insurance (it being war time) for fall goods; but their anxiety avail'd nothing; his lordship's letters were not ready; and yet whoever waited on him found him always at his desk, pen in hand, and concluded he must needs write abundantly.

Going myself one morning to pay my respects, I found in his antechamber one Innis, a messenger of Philadelphia, who had come from thence express with a paquet from Governor Denny for the general. He delivered to me some letters from my friends there, which occasion'd my inquiring when he was to return, and where he lodg'd, that I might send some letters by him. He told me he was order'd to call to-morrow at nine for the general's answer to the governor, and should set off immediately. I put my letters into his hands the same day. A fortnight after I met him again in the same place. "So, you are soon return'd, Innis?" "*Return'd!* no, I am not *gone* yet." "How so?" "I have called here by order every morning these two weeks past for his lordship's letter, and it is not yet ready." "Is it possible, when he is so great a writer? for I see him constantly at his escritoire." "Yes," says Innis, "but he is like St. George on the signs, *always on horseback, and never rides on*." This observation of the messenger was, it seems, well founded; for, when in England, I understood that Mr. Pitt gave it as one reason for removing this general, and sending Generals Amherst and Wolfe, *that the minister never heard from him, and could not know what he was doing*.

This daily expectation of sailing, and all the three paquets going down to

Sandy Hook, to join the fleet there, the passengers thought it best to be on board, lest by a sudden order the ships should sail, and they be left behind. There, if I remember right, we were about six weeks, consuming our sea-stores, and oblig'd to procure more. At length the fleet sail'd, the general and all his army on board, bound to Louisburg, with intent to besiege and take that fortress; all the paquet-boats in company ordered to attend the general's ship, ready to receive his dispatches when they should be ready. We were out five days before we got a letter with leave to part, and then our ship quitted the fleet and steered for England. The other two paquets he still detained, carried them with him to Halifax, where he stayed some time to exercise the men in sham attacks upon sham forts, then alter'd his mind as to besieging Louisburg, and return'd to New York, with all his troops, together with the two paquets above mentioned, and all their passengers! During his absence the French and savages had taken Fort George, on the frontier of that province, and the savages had massacred many of the garrison after capitulation.

I saw afterwards in London Captain Bonnell, who commanded one of those paquets. He told me that, when he had been detain'd a month, he acquainted his lordship that his ship was grown foul, to a degree that must necessarily hinder her fast sailing, a point of consequence for a paquet-boat, and requested an allowance of time to heave her down and clean her bottom. He was asked how long a time that would require. He answer'd, three days. The general replied, "If you can do it in one day, I give leave; otherwise not; for you must certainly sail the day after to-morrow." So he never obtain'd leave, though detained afterwards from day to day during full three months.

I saw also in London one of Bonnell's passengers, who was so enrag'd against his lordship for deceiving and detaining him so long at New York, and then carrying him to Halifax and back again, that he swore he would sue him for damages. Whether he did or not, I never heard; but, as he represented the injury to his affairs, it was very considerable.

On the whole, I wonder'd much how such a man came to be intrusted with so important a business as the conduct of a great army; but, having since seen more of the great world, and the means of obtaining, and motives for giving places, my wonder is diminished. General Shirley, on whom the command of the army devolved upon the death of Braddock, would, in my opinion, if continued in place, have made a much better campaign than that of Loudoun in 1757, which was frivolous, expensive, and disgraceful to our nation beyond conception; for, tho' Shirley was not a bred soldier, he was sensible and sagacious in himself, and attentive to good advice from others, capable of forming judicious plans, and quick and active in carrying them into execution. Loudoun, instead of defending the colonies with his great army, left them totally expos'd, while he paraded idly at Halifax, by which means Fort George was lost, besides, he derang'd all our mercantile operations, and distress'd our trade, by a long embargo on the exportation of provisions, on pretence of keeping supplies from being obtain'd by the enemy, but in reality for beating down their price in favor of the contractors, in whose profits, it was said, perhaps from suspicion only, he had a share. And, when at length the embargo was taken off, by neglecting to send notice of it to Charlestown, the Carolina fleet was detain'd near three months longer, whereby their bottoms were so much damaged by the worm that a great part of them foundered in their passage home.

Shirley was, I believe, sincerely glad of being relieved from so burdensome a charge as the conduct of an army must be to a man unacquainted with military business. I was at the entertainment given by the city of New York to Lord Loudoun, on his taking upon him the command. Shirley, tho' thereby superseded, was present also. There was a great company of officers, citizens, and strangers, and, some chairs having been borrowed in the neighborhood, there was one among them very low, which fell to the lot of Mr. Shirley. Perceiving it as I sat by him, I said, "They have given you, sir, too low a seat." "No matter," says he, "Mr. Franklin, I find *a low seat* the easiest."

While I was, as afore mention'd, detain'd at New York, I receiv'd all the accounts of the provisions, etc., that I had furnish'd to Braddock, some of which accounts could not sooner be obtain'd from the different persons I had employ'd to assist in the business. I presented them to Lord Loudoun, desiring to be paid the balance. He caus'd them to be regularly examined by the proper officer, who, after comparing every article with its voucher, certified them to be right; and the balance due for which his lordship promis'd to give me an order on the paymaster. This was, however, put off from time to time; and, tho' I call'd often for it by appointment, I did not get it. At length, just before my departure, he told me he had, on better consideration, concluded not to mix his accounts with those of his predecessors. "And you," says he, "when in England, have only to exhibit your accounts at the treasury, and you will be paid immediately."

I mentioned, but without effect, the great and unexpected expense I had been put to by being detain'd so long at New York, as a reason for my desiring to be presently paid; and on my observing that it was not right I should be put to any further trouble or delay in obtaining the money I had advanc'd, as I charged no commission for my service, "O, sir," says he, "you must not think of persuading us that you are no gainer; we understand better those affairs, and know that every one concerned in supplying the army finds means, in the doing it, to fill his own pockets." I assur'd him that was not my case, and that I had not pocketed a farthing; but he appear'd clearly not to believe me; and, indeed, I have since learnt that immense fortunes are often made in such employments. As to my balance, I am not paid it to this day, of which more hereafter.

Our captain of the paquet had boasted much, before we sailed, of the swiftness of his ship; unfortunately, when we came to sea, she proved the dullest of ninety-six sail, to his no small mortification. After many conjectures respecting the cause, when we were near another ship almost as dull as ours, which, however, gain'd upon us, the captain ordered all hands to come aft, and stand as near the ensign staff as possible. We were, passengers included, about forty persons. While we stood there, the ship mended her pace, and soon left her neighbour far behind, which prov'd clearly what our captain suspected, that she was loaded too much by the head. The casks of water, it seems, had been all plac'd forward; these he therefore order'd to be mov'd further aft, on which the ship recover'd her character, and proved the best sailer in the fleet.

The captain said she had once gone at the rate of thirteen knots, which is accounted thirteen miles per hour. We had on board, as a passenger, Captain Kennedy, of the Navy, who contended that it was impossible, and that no ship ever sailed so fast, and that there must have been some error in the division of the log-line, or some mistake in heaving the log. A wager ensu'd between the two captains, to be decided when there should be sufficient wind. Kennedy thereupon examin'd rigorously the log-line, and, being satisfi'd with that, he determin'd to throw the log himself. Accordingly some days after, when the wind blew very fair and fresh, and the captain of the paquet, Lutwidge, said he believ'd she then went at the rate of thirteen knots, Kennedy made the experiment, and own'd his wager lost.

The above fact I give for the sake of the following observation. It has been remark'd, as an imperfection in the art of ship-building, that it can never be known, till she is tried, whether a new ship will or will not be a good sailer; for that the model of a good-sailing ship has been exactly follow'd in a new one, which has prov'd, on the contrary, remarkably dull. I apprehend that this may partly be occasion'd by the different opinions of seamen respecting the modes of lading, rigging, and sailing of a ship; each has his system; and the same vessel, laden by the judgment and orders of one captain, shall sail better or worse than when by the orders of another. Besides, it scarce ever happens that a ship is form'd, fitted for the sea, and sail'd by the same person. One man builds the hull, another rigs her, a third lades and sails her. No one of these has the advantage of knowing all the ideas and experience of the others, and, therefore, can not draw just conclusions from a combination of the whole.

Even in the simple operation of sailing when at sea, I have often observ'd different judgments in the officers who commanded the successive watches, the wind being the same. One would have the sails trimm'd sharper or flatter than another, so that they seem'd to have no certain rule to govern by. Yet I think a set of experiments might be instituted, first, to determine the most proper form of the hull for swift sailing; next, the best dimensions and properest place for the masts; then the form and quantity of sails, and their position, as the wind may be; and, lastly, the disposition of the lading. This is an age of experiments, and I think a set accurately made and combin'd would be of great use. I am persuaded, therefore, that ere long some ingenious philosopher will undertake it, to whom I wish success.

We were several times chas'd in our passage, but outsail'd every thing, and in thirty days had soundings. We had a good observation, and the captain judg'd himself so near our port, Falmouth, that, if we made a good run in the night, we might be off the mouth of that harbor in the morning, and by running in the night might escape the notice of the enemy's privateers, who often cruis'd near the entrance of the channel. Accordingly, all the sail was set that we could possibly make, and the wind being very fresh and fair, we went right before it, and made great way. The captain, after his observation, shap'd his course, as he thought, so as to pass wide of the Scilly Isles; but it seems there is sometimes a strong indraught setting up St. George's Channel, which deceives seamen and caused the loss of Sir Cloudesley Shovel's squadron. This indraught was probably the cause of what happened to us.

We had a watchman plac'd in the bow, to whom they often called, "*Look well out before there*," and he as often answered, "*Ay, ay*"; but perhaps had his eyes shut, and was half asleep at the time, they sometimes answering, as is said, mechanically; for he did not see a light just before us, which had been hid by the studding-sails from the man at the helm, and from the rest of the watch, but by an accidental yaw of the ship was discover'd, and occasion'd a great alarm, we being very near it, the light appearing to me as big as a cart-wheel. It was midnight, and our captain fast asleep; but Captain Kennedy, jumping upon deck, and seeing the danger, ordered the ship to wear round, all sails standing; an operation dangerous to the masts, but it carried us clear, and we escaped shipwreck, for we were running right upon the rocks on which the lighthouse was erected. This deliverance impressed me strongly with the utility of light-houses, and made me resolve to encourage the building more of them in America, if I should live to return there.

In the morning it was found by the soundings, etc., that we were near our port, but a thick fog hid the land from our sight. About nine o'clock the fog began to rise, and seem'd to be lifted up from the water like the curtain at a play-house, discovering underneath, the town of Falmouth, the vessels in its harbor, and the fields that surrounded it. This was a most pleasing spectacle to those who had been so long without any other prospects than the uniform view of a vacant ocean, and it gave us the more pleasure as we were now free from the anxieties which the state of war occasion'd.

I set out immediately, with my son, for London, and we only stopt a little by the way to view Stonehenge on Salisbury Plain, and Lord Pembroke's house and gardens, with his very curious antiquities at Wilton. We arrived in London the 27th of July, 1757.

Philadelphia, 1789.

(This continuation of the *Autobiography* was written in the last year of Franklin's life.)

As soon as I was settled in a lodging Mr. Charles had provided for me, I went to visit Dr. Fothergill, to whom I was strongly recommended, and whose counsel respecting my proceedings I was advis'd to obtain. He was against an immediate complaint to government, and thought the proprietaries should first be personally appli'd to, who might possibly be induc'd by the interposition and persuasion of some private friends, to accommodate matters amicably. I then waited on my old friend and correspondent, Mr. Peter Collinson, who told me that John Hanbury, the great Virginia merchant, had requested to be informed when I should arrive, that he might carry me to Lord Granville's, who was then President of the Council and wished to see me as soon as possible. I agreed to go with him the next morning. Accordingly Mr. Hanbury called for me and took me in his carriage to that nobleman's, who receiv'd me with great civility; and after some questions respecting the present state of affairs in America and discourse thereupon, he said to me: "You Americans have wrong ideas of the nature of your constitution; you contend that the king's instructions to his governors are not laws, and think yourselves at liberty to regard or disregard them at your own discretion. But those instructions are not like the pocket instructions given to a minister going abroad, for regulating his conduct in some trifling point of ceremony. They are first drawn up by judges learned in the laws; they are then considered, debated, and perhaps amended in Council, after which they are signed by the king. They are then, so far as they relate to you, the *law of the land*, for the king is the LEGISLATOR OF THE COLONIES." I told his lordship this was new doctrine to me. I had always understood from our charters that our laws were to be made by our Assemblies, to be presented indeed to the king for his royal assent, but that being once given the king could not repeal or alter them. And as the Assemblies could not make permanent laws without his assent, so neither could he make a law for them without theirs. He assur'd me I was totally mistaken. I did not think so, however, and his lordship's conversation having a little alarm'd me as to what might be the sentiments of the court concerning us, I wrote it down as soon as I return'd to my lodgings. I recollected that about 20 years before, a clause in a bill brought into Parliament by the ministry had propos'd to make the king's instructions laws in the colonies, but the clause was thrown out by the Commons, for which we adored them as our friends and friends of liberty, till by their conduct towards us in 1765 it seem'd that they had refus'd that point of sovereignty to the king only that they might reserve it for themselves.

After some days, Dr. Fothergill having spoken to the proprietaries, they agreed to a meeting with me at Mr. T. Penn's house in Spring Garden. The conversation at first consisted of mutual declarations of disposition to reasonable accommodations, but I suppose each party had its own ideas of what should be meant by *reasonable*. We then went into consideration of our several points of complaint, which I enumerated. The proprietaries justify'd their conduct as well as they could, and I the Assembly's. We now appeared very wide, and so far from each other in our opinions as to discourage all hope of agreement. However, it was concluded that I should give them the heads of our complaints in writing, and they promis'd then to consider them. I did so soon after, but they put the paper into the hands of their solicitor, Ferdinand John Paris, who managed for them all their law business in their great suit with the neighbouring proprietary of Maryland, Lord Baltimore, which had subsisted 70 years, and wrote for them all their papers and messages in their dispute with the Assembly. He was a proud, angry man, and as I had occasionally in the answers of the Assembly treated his papers with some severity, they being really weak in point of argument and haughty in expression, he had conceived a mortal enmity to me, which discovering itself whenever we met, I declin'd the proprietary's proposal that he and I should discuss the heads of complaint between our two selves, and refus'd treating with any one but them. They then by his advice put the paper into the hands of the Attorney and Solicitor-General for their opinion and counsel upon it, where it lay unanswered a year wanting eight days, during which time I made frequent demands of an answer from the proprietaries, but without obtaining any other than that they had not yet received the opinion of the Attorney and Solicitor-General. What it was when they did receive it I never learnt, for they did not communicate it to me, but sent a long message to the Assembly drawn and signed by Paris, reciting my paper, complaining of its want of formality, as a rudeness on my part, and giving a flimsy justification of their conduct, adding that they should be willing to accommodate matters if the Assembly would send out *some person of candour* to treat with them for that purpose, intimating thereby that I was not such.

The want of formality or rudeness was, probably, my not having address'd the paper to them with their assum'd titles of True and Absolute Proprietaries of the Province of Pennsylvania, which I omitted as not thinking it necessary in a paper, the intention of which was only to reduce to a certainty by writing, what in conversation I had delivered *viva voce*.

But during this delay, the Assembly having prevailed with Gov'r Denny to pass an act taxing the proprietary estate in common with the estates of the people, which was the grand point in dispute, they omitted answering the message.

When this act however came over, the proprietaries, counselled by Paris, determined to oppose its receiving the royal assent. Accordingly they petition'd the king in Council, and a hearing was appointed in which two lawyers were employ'd by them against the act, and two by me in support of it. They alledg'd that the act was intended to load the proprietary estate in order to spare those of the people, and that if it were suffer'd to continue in force, and the proprietaries who were in odium with the people, left to their mercy in proportioning the taxes, they would inevitably be ruined. We reply'd that the act had no such intention, and would have no such effect. That the assessors were honest and discreet men under an oath to assess fairly and equitably, and that any advantage each of them might expect in lessening his own tax by augmenting that of the proprietaries was too trifling to induce them to perjure themselves. This is the purport of what I remember as urged by both sides, except that we insisted strongly on the mischievous consequences that must attend a repeal, for that the money,

£100,000, being printed and given to the king's use, expended in his service, and now spread among the people, the repeal would strike it dead in their hands to the ruin of many, and the total discouragement of future grants, and the selfishness of the proprietors in soliciting such a general catastrophe, merely from a groundless fear of their estate being taxed too highly, was insisted on in the strongest terms. On this, Lord Mansfield, one of the Council, rose, and beckoning me took me into the clerk's chamber, while the lawyers were pleading, and asked me if I was really of opinion that no injury would be done the proprietary estate in the execution of the act. I said certainly. "Then," says he, "you can have little objection to enter into an engagement to assure that point." I answer'd, "None at all." He then call'd in Paris, and after some discourse, his lordship's proposition was accepted on both sides; a paper to the purpose was drawn up by the Clerk of the Council, which I sign'd with Mr. Charles, who was also an Agent of the Province for their ordinary affairs, when Lord Mansfield returned to the Council Chamber, where finally the law was allowed to pass. Some changes were however recommended and we also engaged they should be made by a subsequent law, but the Assembly did not think them necessary; for one year's tax having been levied by the act before the order of Council arrived, they appointed a committee to examine the proceedings of the assessors, and on this committee they put several particular friends of the proprietaries. After a full enquiry, they unanimously sign'd a report that they found the tax had been assess'd with perfect equity.

The Assembly looked into my entering into the first part of the engagement, as an essential service to the Province, since it secured the credit of the paper money then spread over all the country. They gave me their thanks in form when I return'd. But the proprietaries were enraged at Governor Denny for having pass'd the act, and turn'd him out with threats of suing him for breach of instructions which he had given bond to observe. He, however, having done it at the instance of the general, and for His Majesty's service, and having some powerful interest at court, despis'd the threats and they were never put in execution.

LETTERS AND JOURNALS
1757–1790

Mission to London

To his wife. London, 22 Nov., 1757.

During my illness, which continued near eight weeks, I wrote several letters as I was able. The last was by the packet which sailed from Falmouth above a week since. . . .

I should have read Sally's French letter with more pleasure, but that I thought the French rather too good to be all her own composing. I suppose her master must have corrected it. But I am glad she is improving in that and her music; I send her a French Pamela.

December 3d.—I write by little and little as I can find time. I have now gone through all your agreeable letters, which give me fresh pleasure every time I read them. Last night I received another, dated October 16th, which brings me the good news, that you and Sally were got safe home; your last, of the 9th, being from Elizabethtown.

I am glad to hear that Miss Ray is well, and that you correspond. It is not convenient to be forward in giving advice in such cases. She has prudence enough to judge for herself, and I hope she will judge and act for the best.

I hear there is a miniature painter gone over to Philadelphia, a relation to John Reynolds. If Sally's picture is not done to your mind by the young man, and the other gentleman is a good hand and follows the business, suppose you get Sally's done by him, and send it to me with your small picture, that I may here get all our little family drawn in one conversation piece. I am sorry to hear of the general sickness; I hope it is over before this time; and that little Franky is recovered.

I was as much disappointed in my intention of writing by the packet, as you were in not receiving letters, and it has since given me a great deal of vexation. I wrote to you by way of New York, the day after my arrival in London, which I do not find you have received.

I do not use to be a backward correspondent, though my sickness has brought me behindhand with my friends in that respect. Had I been well, I intended to have gone round among the shops, and bought some pretty things for you and my dear good Sally (whose little hands you say eased your headache), to send by this ship, but I must now defer it to the next, having only got a crimson satin cloak for you, the newest fashion, and the black silk for Sally; but Billy sends her a scarlet feather, muff, and tippet, and a box of fashionable linen for her dress. In the box is a thermometer for Mr. Taylor, and one for Mr. Schlatter, which you will carefully deliver; as also a watch for Mr. Schlatter. I shall write to them. The black silk was sent to Mr. Neates, who undertook to forward it in some package of his.

To his wife. London, 14 Jan., 1758.

I AM THANKFUL to God for sparing my little family in that time of general sickness, and hope to find them all well at my return. The New York paper you sent me was the latest that came, and of use to our friend Strahan. He has offered to lay me a considerable wager, that a letter he has wrote to you will bring you immediately over hither; but I tell him I will not pick his pocket; for I am sure there is no inducement strong enough to prevail with you to cross the seas. I should be glad if I could tell you when I expected to be at home, but that is still in the dark; it is possible I may not be able to get away this summer; but I hope, if I stay another winter, it will be more agreeable than the greatest part of the time I have hitherto spent in England.

To his wife. London, 21 Jan., 1758.

I BEGIN to think I shall hardly be able to return before this time twelve months. I am for doing effectually what I came about; and I find it requires both time and patience. You may think, perhaps, that I can find many amusements here to pass the time agreeably. It is true, the regard and friendship I meet with from persons of worth, and the conversation of ingenious men, give me no small pleasure; but, at this time of life, domestic comforts afford the most solid satisfaction, and my uneasiness at being absent from my family, and longing desire to be with them, make me often sigh in the midst of cheerful company.

My love to my dear Sally. I confide in you the care of her and her education. I promise myself the pleasure of finding her much improved at my return. When you write to Boston, give my love to sister Jenny, as I have not often time to write to her. If you please, you may send her the enclosed little picture.

To his wife. London, 19 Feb., 1758.

YOUR kind advice about getting a chariot, I had taken some time before; for I found, that, every time I walked out, I got fresh cold; and the hackney coaches at this end of the town, where most people keep their own, are the worst in the whole city, miserable, dirty, broken, shabby things, unfit to go into when dressed clean, and such as one would be ashamed to get out of at any gentleman's door. As to burning wood, it would answer no end, unless one would furnish all one's neighbours and the whole city with the same. The whole town is one great smoky house, and every street a chimney, the air full of floating seacoal soot, and you never get a sweet breath of what is pure, without riding some miles for it into the country.

I am sorry to hear, that a storm has damaged a house of my good friend Mr. Bartram. Acquaint him that I have received the seeds, and shall write to him shortly. I hope the Speaker is recovered of the illness you mention.

Give my thanks to Dr. Bond for the care he takes of you. I have wrote to him by this vessel. Mr. Hunter and Polly talk of returning this spring. He is wonderfully recruited. They both desire to be remembered to you. She received your letter and answered it. Her answer I enclosed in one of mine to you. Her daughter Rachel, who plays on the harpsichord and sings prettily, sends Sally one of her songs, that I fancied.

I send you by Captain Budden a large case, and a small box. In the large case is another small box, containing some English china; viz. melons and leaves for a desert of fruit and cream, or the like; a bowl remarkable for the neatness of the figures, made at Bow, near this city; some coffee cups of the same; a Worcester bowl, ordinary. To show the difference of workmanship, there is something from all the china works in England; and one old true china bason mended, of an odd color. The same box contains four silver salt ladles, newest, but ugliest, fashion; a little instrument to core apples; another to make little turnips out of great ones; six coarse diaper breakfast cloths; they are to spread on the tea-table, for nobody breakfasts here on the naked table, but on the cloth they set a large tea board with the cups. There is also a little basket, a present from Mrs. Stevenson to Sally, and a pair of garters for you, which were knit by the young lady, her daughter, who favored me with a pair of the same kind, the only ones I have been able to wear; as they need not be bound tight, the ridges in them preventing their slipping. We send them therefore as a curiosity for the form, more than for the value. Goody Smith may, if she pleases, make such for me hereafter. My love to her.

In the great case, besides the little box, is contained some carpeting for a best room floor. There is enough for one large or two small ones, it is to be sewed together, the edges being first felled down, and care taken to make the figures meet exactly; there is bordering for the same. This was my fancy. Also two large fine Flanders bed ticks, and two pair of large superfine blankets, two fine damask table-cloths and napkins, and forty-three ells of Ghentish sheeting Holland. These you ordered. There are also fifty-six yards of cotton, printed curiously from copper plates, a new invention, to make bed and window curtains; and seven yards of chair bottoms, printed in the same way, very neat. These were my fancy; but Mrs. Stevenson tells me I did wrong not to buy both of the same color. Also seven yards of printed cotton, blue ground, to make you a gown. I bought it by candlelight, and liked it then, but not so well afterwards. If you do not fancy it, send it as a present from me to sister Jenny. There is a better gown for you, of flowered tissue, sixteen yards, of Mrs. Stevenson's fancy, cost nine guineas; and I think it a great beauty. There was no more of the sort, or you should have had enough for a *negligée* or suit.

There are also snuffers, a snuffstand, and extinguisher, of steel, which I send for the beauty of the work. The extinguisher is for spermaceti candles only, and is of a new contrivance, to preserve the snuff upon the candle. There is some music Billy bought for his sister, and some pamphlets for the Speaker and for Susy Wright. A mahogany and a little shagreen box, with microscopes and other optical instruments loose, are for Mr. Alison, if he likes them; if not, put them in my room till I return. I send the invoice of them, and I wrote to him formerly the reason of my exceeding his orders. There are also two sets of books, a present from me to Sally, "The World" and "The Connoisseur." My love to her.

I forgot to mention another of my fancyings, viz. a pair of silk blankets, very fine. They are of a new kind, were just taken in a French prize, and such were never seen in England before. They are called blankets, but I think they will be very neat to cover a summer bed, instead of a quilt or counterpane. I had no choice, so you will excuse the soil on some of the folds; your neighbour Foster can get it off. I also forgot, among the china, to mention a large fine jug for beer, to stand in the cooler. I fell in love with it at first sight; for I thought it looked like a fat jolly dame, clean and tidy, with a neat blue and white calico gown on, good natured and lovely, and put me in mind of—somebody. It has the coffee cups in it, packed in best crystal salt, of a peculiar nice flavor, for the table, not to be powdered.

I hope Sally applies herself closely to her French and music, and that I shall find she has made great proficiency. The harpsichord I was about, and which was to have cost me forty guineas, Mr. Stanley advises me not to buy; and we are looking out for another, one that has been some time in use, and is a tried good one, there being not so much dependence on a new one, though made by the best hands. Sally's last letter to her brother is the best wrote that of late I have seen of hers. I only wish she was a little more careful of her spelling. I hope she continues to love going to church, and would have her read over and over again the "Whole Duty of Man," and the "Lady's Library."

Look at the figures on the china bowl and coffee cups, with your spectacles on; they will bear examining.

I have made your compliments to Mrs. Stevenson. She is indeed very obliging, takes great care of my health, and is very diligent when I am any way indisposed; but yet I have a thousand times wished you with me, and my little Sally with her ready hands and feet to do, and go, and come, and get what I wanted.

To his wife. London, 10 June, 1758.

I HAVE sent, in a trunk of the Library Company's, some of the best writing paper for letters, and best quills and wax, all for Mrs. Moore, which I beg she would accept; having received such civilities here from her sister and brother Scott, as are not in my power to return. I shall send some to Sally by the next opportunity. By Captain Lutwidge I sent my dear girl a newest fashioned white hat and cloak, and sundry little things, which I hope will get safe to hand. I now send her a pair of buckles, made of French paste stones, which are next in lustre to diamonds. They cost three guineas, and are said to be cheap at that price. I fancy I see more likeness in her picture than I did at first, and I look at it often with pleasure, as at least it reminds me of her. Yours is at the painter's, who is to copy it and do me of the same size; but, as to family pieces, it is said they never look well, and are quite out of fashion, and I find the limner very unwilling to undertake any thing of the kind. However, when Franky's comes, and that of Sally by young Hesselius, I shall see what can be done. I wonder how you came by Ben Lay's picture.

You are very prudent not to engage in party disputes. Women never should meddle with them, except in endeavours to reconcile their husbands, brothers, and friends, who happen to be of contrary sides. If your sex keep cool, you may be a means of cooling ours the sooner, and restoring more speedily that social harmony among fellow-citizens, that is so desirable after long and bitter dissensions.

I have ordered two large print Common Prayer Books to be bound, on purpose for you and Goody Smith; and, that the largeness of the print may not make them too bulky, the christenings, matrimonies, and every thing else that you and she have not immediate and constant occasion for, are to be omitted. So you will both of you be reprieved from the use of spectacles in church a little longer.

Travel in England

To his wife. London, 6 Sept., 1758.

IN MINE of June 10th, by the Mercury, Captain Robinson, I mentioned our having been at Cambridge. We stayed there a week, being entertained with great kindness by the principal people, and shown all the curiosities of the place; and, returning by another road to see more of the country, we came again to London. I found the journey advantageous to my health, increasing both my health and spirits, and therefore, as all the great folks were out of town, and public business at a stand, I the more easily prevailed with myself to take another journey, and accept of the invitation we had, to be again at Cambridge at the Commencement, the beginning of July. We went accordingly, were present at all the ceremonies, dined every day in their halls, and my vanity was not a little gratified by the particular regard shown me by the chancellor and vice-chancellor of the University, and the heads of colleges.

After the Commencement, we went from Cambridge through Huntingdonshire into Northumberlandshire,* and at Wellingborough, on inquiry, we found still living Mary Fisher, whose maiden name was Franklin, daughter and only child of Thomas Franklin, my father's eldest brother. She is five years older than sister Dowse, and remembers her going away with my father and his then wife, and two other children to New England about the year 1685. We have had no correspondence with her since my uncle Benjamin's death, now near thirty years. I knew she had lived at Wellingborough, and had married there to one Mr. Richard Fisher, a grazier and tanner, about fifty years ago, but did not expect to see either of them alive, so inquired for their posterity. I was directed to their house, and we found them both alive, but weak with age, very glad however to see us. She seems to have been a very smart, sensible woman. They are wealthy, have left off business, and live comfortably. They have had only one child, a daughter, who died, when about thirty years of age, unmarried. She gave me several of my uncle Benjamin's letters to her, and acquainted me where the other remains of the family lived, of which I have, since my return to London, found out a daughter of my father's only sister, very old, and never married. She is a good, clever woman, but poor, though vastly contented with her situation, and very cheerful. The others are in different parts of the country. I intend to visit them, but they were too much out of our tour in that journey.

From Wellingborough we went to Ecton, about three or four miles, being the village where my father was born, and where his father, grandfather, and great-grandfather had lived, and how many of the family before them we know not. We went first to see the old house and grounds; they came to Mr. Fisher with his wife, and, after letting them for some years, finding his rent something ill paid, he sold them. The land is now added to another farm, and a school kept in the house. It is a decayed old stone building, but still known by the name of Franklin House. Thence we went to visit the rector of the parish, who lives close by the church, a very ancient building. He entertained us very kindly, and showed us the old church register, in which were the births, marriages, and burials of our ancestors for two hundred years, as early as his book began. His wife, a goodnatured, chatty, old lady (granddaughter of the famous Archdeacon Palmer, who formerly had that parish, and lived there), remembered a great deal about the family; carried us out into the churchyard, and showed us several of their gravestones, which were so covered with moss that we could not read the letters, till she ordered a hard brush and basin of water, with which Peter scoured them clean, and then Billy copied them. She entertained and diverted us highly with stories of Thomas Franklin, Mrs. Fisher's father, who was a conveyancer, something of a lawyer, clerk of the county courts, and clerk to the archdeacon in his visitations; a very leading man in all county affairs, and much employed in public business. He set on foot a subscription for erecting chimes in their steeple, and completed

*Should be Northamptonshire.

it, and we heard them play. He found out an easy method of saving their village meadows from being drowned, as they used to be sometimes by the river, which method is still in being; but, when first proposed, nobody could conceive how it could be; "but however," they said, "if Franklin says he knows how to do it, it will be done." His advice and opinion were sought for on all occasions, by all sorts of people, and he was looked upon, she said, by some, as something of a conjurer. He died just four years before I was born, on the same day of the same month.

Since our return to London, I have had a kind letter from cousin Fisher, and another from the rector, which I send you.

From Ecton we went to Northampton, where we stayed part of the day; then went to Coventry, and from thence to Birmingham. Here, upon inquiry, we soon found out yours, and cousin Wilkinson's, and cousin Cash's relations. First, we found out one of the Cashes, and he went with us to Rebecca Flint's, where we saw her and her husband. She is a turner and he a buttonmaker; they have no children; were very glad to see any person that knew their sister Wilkinson; told us what letters they had received, and showed us some of them; and even showed us that they had, out of respect, preserved a keg, in which they had received a present of some sturgeon. They sent for their brother, Joshua North, who came with his wife immediately to see us; he is a turner also, and has six children, a lively, active man. Mrs. Flint desired me to tell her sister, that they live still in the old house she left them in, which I think she says was their father's. From thence Mr. North went with us to your cousin Benjamin's.

Portrait of Penn

To Lord Kames. London, 3 Jan., 1760.

YOU HAVE been pleased kindly to desire to have all my publications. I had daily expectations of procuring some of them from a friend to whom I formerly sent them when I was in America, and postponed writing to you, till I should obtain them; but at length he tells me he cannot find them; very mortifying this to an author, that his works should so soon be lost! So I can only send you my "Observations on the Peopling of Countries," which happens to have been reprinted here; "The Description of the Pennsylvania Fireplace," a machine of my contriving; and some little sketches that have been printed in the "Grand Magazine," which I should hardly own, did I not know that your friendly partiality would make them seem at least tolerable.

How unfortunate I was, that I did not press you and Lady Kames more strongly to favor us with your company farther. How much more agreeable would our journey have been, if we could have enjoyed you as far as York. We could have beguiled the way, by discoursing on a thousand things, that now we may never have an opportunity of considering together; for conversation warms the mind, enlivens the imagination, and is continually starting fresh game, that is immediately pursued and taken, and which would never have occurred in the duller intercourse of epistolary correspondence. So that whenever I reflect on the great pleasure and advantage I received from the free communication of sentiment, in the conversation we had at Kames, and in the agreeable little rides to the Tweed side, I shall for ever regret our premature parting.

No one can more sincerely rejoice than I do, on the reduction of Canada; and this is not merely as I am a colonist, but as I am a Briton. I have long been of opinion, that the *foundations of the future grandeur and stability of the British empire lie in America;* and though, like other foundations, they are low and little now, they are, nevertheless, broad and strong enough to support the greatest political structure that human wisdom ever yet erected. I am, therefore, by no means for restoring Canada. If we keep it, all the country from the St. Lawrence to the Mississippi will in another century be filled with British people. Britain itself will become vastly more populous, by the immense increase of its commerce; the Atlantic sea will be covered with your trading ships; and your naval power, thence continually increasing, will extend your influence round the whole globe, and awe the world! If the French remain in Canada, they will continually harass our colonies by the Indians, and impede if not prevent their growth; your progress to greatness will at best be slow, and give room for many accidents that may for ever prevent it. But I refrain, for I see you begin to think my notions extravagant, and look upon them as the ravings of a mad prophet.

Your Lordship's kind offer of Penn's picture is extremely obliging. But, were it certainly his picture, it would be too valuable a curiosity for me to think of accepting it. I should only desire the favor of leave to take a copy of it. I could wish to know the history of the picture before it came into your hands, and the grounds for supposing it his. I have at present some doubts about it; first, because the primitive Quakers declared against pictures as a vain expense; a man's suffering his portrait to be taken was conceived as pride; and I think to this day it is very little practised among them. Then, it is on a board; and I imagine the practice of painting portraits on boards did not come down so low as Penn's time; but of this I am not certain. My other reason is an anecdote I have heard, viz. that when old Lord Cobham was adorning his gardens at Stow with busts of famous men, he made inquiry of the family for the picture of William Penn, in order to get a bust formed from it, but could find none; that Sylvanus Bevan, an old Quaker apothecary, remarkable for the notice he takes of countenances, and a knack he has of cutting in ivory, strong likenesses of persons he has once seen, hearing of Lord Cobham's desire, set himself to recollect Penn's face, with which he had been well acquainted; and cut a little bust of him in ivory, which he sent to Lord Cobham, without any letter or notice that it was Penn's. But my Lord, who had personally known Penn, on seeing it, immediately cried out, "Whence comes this? It is William Penn himself!"

And from this little bust, they say, the large one in the gardens was formed.

I doubt, too, whether the whisker was not quite out of use at the time when Penn must have been of an age appearing in the face of that picture. And yet, notwithstanding these reasons, I am not without some hope that it may be his; because I know some eminent Quakers have had their pictures privately drawn and deposited with trusty friends; and know, also, that there is extant at Philadelphia a very good picture of Mrs. Penn, his last wife. After all, I own I have a strong desire to be satisfied concerning this picture; and as Bevan is yet living here, and some other old Quakers that remember William Penn, who died but 1718, I would wish to have it sent to me carefully packed up in a box by the wagon (for I would not trust it by sea), that I may obtain their opinion. The charges I shall very cheerfully pay; and if it proves to be Penn's picture, I shall be greatly obliged to your Lordship for leave to take a copy of it, and will carefully return the original.

On a Premature Peace

To the printer of the London Chronicle.

I met lately with an old quarto book on a stall, the titlepage and the author's name wanting, but containing discourses, addressed to some king of Spain, extolling the greatness of monarchy, translated into English, and said in the last leaf to be printed at London by Bonham Norton and John Bill, "Printers to the King's most excellent Majestie, MDCXXIX." The author appears to have been a Jesuit, for, speaking of that order in two places, he calls it *our Society*. Give me leave to communicate to the public a chapter of it, so *apropos* to our present situation (only changing Spain for France) that I think it well worth general attention and observation, as it discovers the arts of our enemies, and may therefore help in some degree to put us on our guard against them.

What effect the artifices here recommended might have had in the times when our author wrote, I cannot pretend to say; but I believe, the present age being more enlightened and our people better acquainted than formerly with our true national interest, such arts can now hardly prove so generally successful; for we may with pleasure observe, and to the honor of the British people, that, though writings and discourses like these have lately not been wanting, yet few in any of the classes he particularizes seem to be affected by them, but all ranks and degrees among us persist hitherto in declaring for a vigorous prosecution of the war, in preference to an unsafe, disadvantageous, or dishonorable peace; yet, as a little change of fortune may make such writings more attended to, and give them greater weight, I think the publication of this piece, as it shows the spring from whence these scribblers draw their poisoned waters, may be of public utility.   A Briton.

"Chap. XXXIV.

"On the Meanes of disposing the Enemie to Peace.

"Warres, with whatsoever Prudence undertaken and conducted, do not always succeed. Many Thinges out of Man's Power to governe, such as Dearth of Provision, Tempests, Pestilence, and the like, oftentimes interfering and totally overthrowing the best Designes; so that these Enemies (England and Holland) of our Monarchy though apparently at first the weaker, may by disastrous Events of Warre, on our Parte, become the stronger, and though not in such degree, as to endanger the Bodie of this great Kingdom, yet, by their greater Power of Shipping and Aptness in Sea Affairs, to be able to cut off, if I may so speake, some of its smaller Limbs and Members that are remote therefrom and not easily defended, to wit, our Islands and Colonies in the Indies; thereby however depriving the Bodie of its wonted Nourishment, so that it must thenceforthe languish and grow weake, if those Parts are not recovered, which possibly may by continuance of Warre be found unlikelie to be done. And the Enemie, puffed up with their successes, and hoping still for more, may not be disposed to Peace on such Termes as would be suitable to the honor of your Majestie, and to the Welfare of your State and Subjects. In such Case, the following Meanes may have good Effect.

"It is well knowne, that these Northerne People, though hardie of Bodie and bold in Fight, be nevertheless, through overmuch Eating and other Intemperance, slowe of Wit, and dull in Understanding, so that they are ofttimes more easilie to be governed and turned by Skill than by Force. There is therefore always Hope, that, by wise Counsel and dexterous Management, those Advantages, which through crosse Accidents in Warre have been lost, may again with Honour be recovered. In this Place I shall say little of the Power of Money secretly distributed among Grandees, or their Friends or Paramours; that Method being in all Ages known and practised. If the *minds* of Enemies can be *changed*, they may be brought to grant willingly and for nothing what much Gold would scarcely have otherwise prevailed to obtaine. Yet, as the procuring this Change is to be by fitte Instruments, some few Doubloones will not unprofitably be distributed by your Majestie. The manner whereof I shall now briefly recite.

"In those Countries, and particularly in England, there are not wanting Menne of Learning, ingenious Speakers and Writers, who are nevertheless in lowe Estate, and pinched by Fortune. These, being privately gained by proper Meanes, must be instructed in their Sermons, Discourses, Writings, Poems, and Songs, to handle and specially inculcate Points like these which followe. Let them magnifie the Blessings of Peace, and enlarge mightilie thereon, which is not unbecoming grave Divines and other Christian Menne. Let them expatiate on the Miseries of Warre, the Waste of Christian Blood, the growing Scarcitie of Labourers and Workmen, the Dearness of all foreign Wares and Merchandise, the Interruption of Commerce, the Captures of Ships, the Increase and great Burthen of Taxes. Let them represent the Warre as an unmeasurable Advantage to Particulars, and to Particulars only (thereby to excite envie against those, who manage and provide for the same), while so prejudicial to the Commonweale and People in general. Let them represent the Advantages gained against us, as trivial and of little Import; the Places taken from us, as of small Trade and Produce, inconvenient for Situation, unwholesome for Ayre and Climate, useless to their Nations, and greatlie chargeable to keepe, draining the home Countrie both of Menne and Money.

"Let them urge, that, if a Peace be forced on us, and those Places withheld, it will nourishe secret Griefe and Malice in the King and Grandees of Spain, which will ere long breake forthe in new Warres, when those Places may again be retaken, without the Merit and Grace of restoring them willingly for Peace's Sake. Let them represent the making or Continuance of Warres, from views of Gaine, to be base and unworthy a brave People, as those made from Views of Ambition are mad and wicked. Let them insinuate, that the Continuance of the present Warre, on their Parte, hath these Ingredients in its Nature. Then let them magnifie the great Power of your Majestie, and the Strength of your Kingdome, the inexhaustible Wealthe of your Mines, the Greatness of your Incomes, and thence your Abilitie of continuing the Warre; hinting withal the new Alliances you may possiblie make; at the same time setting forth the sincere Disposition you have for Peace, and that it is only a Concerne for your Honour, and the Honour of your Realme, that induceth you to insist on the Restitution of the places taken.

"If, with all this, they shrewdly intimate, and cause it to be understood by artful Wordes and believed, that their own Prince is himself in Heart for Peace, on your Majestie's Termes, and grieved at the Obstinacy and Perverseness of those among his people, who are for continuing the Warre, a marvellous Effect shall by these Discourses and Writings be produced; and a wonderful strong Partie shall your Majestie raise among your Enemies in Favour of the Peace you desire; insomuch that their own Princes and wisest Counsellours will in a Sorte be constrained to yeeld thereto. For, in this Warre of Wordes, the Avarice and Ambition, the Hope and Fears, and all the Crowd of humane Passions will be raised and put in Array to fight for your Interests against the reall and substantiall Interest of their own Countries. The simple and undiscerning Many shall be carried away by the Plausibilitie and Wellseeming of these Discourses; and the Opinions becoming more popular, all the Rich Menne, who have great Possessions, and fear the Continuance of Taxes, and hope Peace will end them, shall be emboldened thereby to crie aloud for Peace; their Dependents, who are many, must do the same.

"All Merchaunts, fearing Loss of Ships and greater Burthens on Trade by further Duties and Subsidies, and hoping greater Profits by the ending of the Warre, shall join in the crie for Peace. All the Usurers and Lenders of Money to the State, who on a Peace hope great Profits on their Bargains, and fear if the Warre be continued the State shall become bankeroute, and unable to pay them; these, who have no small Weighte, shall join the crie for Peace. All, who maligne the bold Conductors of the Warre, and envie the Glorie they may have thereby obtained; these shall crie aloud for Peace, hoping, that, when the Warre shall cease, such Menne becoming less necessarie shall be more lightly esteemed, and themselves more sought after. All the Officers of the Enemie's Armies and Fleets, who wish for Repose and to enjoy their Salaries or Rewardes in Quietnesse, and without Peril; these, and their Friends and Families, who desire their Safetie and the Solace of their Societie, shall all crie for Peace.

"All those, who be timorous by Nature, amongste whom be reckoned Menne of Learning that lead sedentaire Lives, doing little Exercise of Bodie, and thence obtaining but few and weake Spirits; great Statesmen, whose natural Spirits be exhausted by much Thinking, or depressed by overmuch Feasting; together with all Women, whose Power, weake as they are, is not a little amongste the Menne; these shall incessantly speake for Peace. And finally all Courtiers, who suppose they conforme thereby to the Inclinations of the Prince (*ad Exemplum Regis,* &c.); all who are in Places, fear to lose them, or hope for better; all who are out of Places, and hope to obtaine them; with all the worldly minded Clergy, who seeke Preferment; these, with all the Weighte of their Character and Influence, shall join the crie for Peace; till it becomes one universal Clamour, and no Sound, but that of Peace, Peace, Peace, shall be heard from every Quarter.

"Then shall your Majestie's Termes of Peace be listened to with much Readinesse, the Places taken from you be willingly restored, and your Kingdome, recovering its Strength, shall only need to waite a few Years for more favourable Occasions, when the Advantages to your Power, proposed by beginning the Warre, but lost by its bad Successe, shall, with better Fortune, be finally obtained."

On Good Company

To Hugh Roberts. London, 26 Feb., 1761.

YOU TELL me you sometimes visit the ancient Junto. I wish you would do it oftener. I know they all love and respect you, and regret your absenting yourself so much. People are apt to grow strange, and not understand one another so well, when they meet but seldom. Since we have held that Club, till we are grown gray together, let us hold it out to the end. For my own part, I find I love company, chat, a laugh, a glass, and even a song, as well as ever; and at the same time relish better than I used to do the grave observations and wise sentences of old men's conversation; so that I am sure the Junto will be still as agreeable to me as it ever has been.

I therefore hope it will not be discontinued, as long as we are able to crawl together.

On Lightning Rods

To David Hume. London, 19 May, 1762.

IT IS no small pleasure to me to hear from you that my paper on the means of preserving buildings from damage by lightning, was acceptable to the Philosophical Society. Mr. Russel's proposals of improvement are very sensible and just. A leaden spout or pipe is undoubtedly a good conductor, so far as it goes. If the conductor enters the ground just at the foundation, and from thence is carried horizontally to some well, or to a distant rod driven downright into the earth, I would then propose, that the part under the ground should be lead, as less liable to consume with rust than iron. Because, if the conductor near the foot of the wall should be wasted, the lightning might act on the moisture of the earth, and by suddenly rarefying it occasion an explosion, that may damage the foundation. In the experiment of discharging my large case of electrical bottles through a piece of small glass tube filled with water, the suddenly rarefied water has exploded with a force equal, I think, to that of so much gunpowder; bursting the tube into many pieces, and driving them with violence in all directions and to all parts of the room. The shivering of trees into small splinters, like a broom, is probably owing to this rarefaction of the sap in the longitudinal pores, or capillary pipes, in the substance of the wood. And the blowing up of bricks or stones in a hearth, rending stones out of a foundation, and splitting of walls, are also probably effects sometimes of rarefied moisture in the earth, under the hearth, or in the walls. We should therefore have a durable conductor under ground, or convey the lightning to the earth at some distance.

It must afford Lord Marischal a good deal of diversion to preside in a dispute so ridiculous as that you mention. Judges in their decisions often use precedents. I have somewhere met with one, that is what the lawyers call a *case in point*. The Church people and the Puritans in a country town had once a bitter contention concerning the erecting of a Maypole, which the former desired and the latter opposed. Each party endeavoured to strengthen itself by obtaining the authority of the mayor, directing or forbidding a Maypole. He heard their altercation with great patience, and then gravely determined thus: "You, that are for having no Maypole, shall have no Maypole; and you, that are for having a Maypole, shall have a Maypole. Get about your business, and let me hear no more of this quarrel."

Your compliment of *gold* and *wisdom* is very obliging to me, but a little injurious to your country. The various value of every thing in every part of this world arises, you know, from the various proportions of the quantity to the demand. We are told, that gold and silver in Solomon's time were so plenty, as to be of no more value in his country than the stones in the street. You have here at present just such a plenty of wisdom. Your people are, therefore, not to be censured for desiring no more among them than they have; and if I have *any*, I should certainly carry it where, from its scarcity, it may probably come to a better market.

Return to America

To Mary Stevenson. London, 7 June, 1762.

* * * Our ships for America do not sail so soon as I expected; it will be yet five or six weeks before we embark, and leave the old world for the new. I fancy I feel a little like dying saints, who, in parting with those they love in this world, are only comforted with the hope of more perfect happiness in the next. I have, in America, connexions of the most engaging kind; and, happy as I have been in the friendships here contracted, *those* promise me greater and more lasting felicity. But God only knows whether these promises shall be fulfilled.

To Lord Kames. Portsmouth, 17 August, 1762.

I am now waiting here only for a wind to waft me to America, but cannot leave this happy island and my friends in it, without extreme regret, though I am going to a country and a people that I love. I am going from the old world to the new; and I fancy I feel like those, who are leaving this world for the next; grief at the parting; fear of the passage; hope of the future. These different passions all affect their minds at once; and these have *tendered* me down exceedingly. It is usual for the dying to beg forgiveness of their surviving friends, if they have ever offended them.

Can you, my Lord, forgive my long silence, and my not acknowledging till now the favor you did me in sending me your excellent book? Can you make some allowance for a fault in others, which you have never experienced in yourself; for the bad habit of postponing from day to day, what one every day resolves to do to-morrow? A habit that grows upon us with years, and whose only excuse is we know not how to mend it. If you are disposed to favor me, you will also consider how much one's mind is taken up and distracted by the many little affairs one has to settle before the undertaking such a voyage, after so long a residence in a country; and how little, in such a situation, one's mind is fitted for serious and attentive reading; which, with regard to the "Elements of Criticism," I intended before I should write. I can now only confess and endeavour to amend. In packing up my books, I have reserved yours to read on the passage. I hope I shall therefore be able to write to you upon it soon after my arrival. At present I can only return my thanks, and say that the parts I have read gave me both pleasure and instruction; that I am convinced of your position, new as it was to me, that a good taste in the arts contributes to the improvement of morals; and that I have had the satisfaction of hearing the work universally commended by those who have read it.

And now, my dear Sir, accept my sincere thanks for the kindness you have shown me, and my best wishes of happiness to you and yours. Wherever I am, I shall esteem the friendship you honor me with as one of the felicities of my life; I shall endeavour to cultivate it by a more punctual correspondence; and I hope frequently to hear of your welfare and prosperity.

American Journey

To Lord Kames. London, 2 June, 1765.

YOU REQUIRE my history from the time I set sail for America. I left England about the end of August, 1762, in company with ten sail of merchant ships, under a convoy of a man-of-war. We had a pleasant passage to Madeira, where we were kindly received and entertained; our nation being then in high honor with the Portuguese, on account of the protection we were then affording them against the united invasions of France and Spain. It is a fertile island, and the different heights and situations among its mountains afford such temperaments of air, that all the fruits of northern and southern countries are produced there; corn, grapes, apples, peaches, oranges, lemons, plantains, bananas, &c. Here we furnished ourselves with fresh provisions, and refreshments of all kinds; and, after a few days, proceeded on our voyage, running southward until we got into the trade winds, and then with them westward, till we drew near the coast of America. The weather was so favorable, that there were few days in which we could not visit from ship to ship, dining with each other, and on board of the man-of-war; which made the time pass agreeably, much more so than when one goes in a single ship; for this was like travelling in a moving village, with all one's neighbors about one.

On the 1st of November, I arrived safe and well at my own home, after an absence of near six years, found my wife and daughter well; the latter grown quite a woman, with many amiable accomplishments acquired in my absence; and my friends as hearty and affectionate as ever, with whom my house was filled for many days, to congratulate me on my return. I had been chosen yearly during my absence to represent the city of Philadelphia in our provincial Assembly; and, on my appearance in the House, they voted me three thousand pounds sterling for my services in England, and their thanks, delivered by the Speaker. In February following, my son arrived with my new daughter; for, with my consent and approbation, he married soon after I left England a very agreeable West India lady, with whom he is very happy. I accompanied him to his government, where he met with the kindest reception from the people of all ranks, and has lived with them ever since in the greatest harmony. A river only parts that province and ours, and his residence is within seventeen miles of me, so that we frequently see each other.

In the spring of 1763, I set out on a tour through all the northern Colonies to inspect and regulate the post-offices in the several provinces. In this journey I spent the summer, travelled about sixteen hundred miles, and did not get home till the beginning of November. The Assembly sitting through the following winter, and warm disputes arising between them and the governor, I became wholly engaged in public affairs; for, besides my duty as an Assemblyman, I had another trust to execute, that of being one of the commissioners appointed by law to dispose of the public money appropriated to the raising and paying an army to act against the Indians, and defend the frontiers. And then, in December, we had two insurrections of the back inhabitants of our province, by whom twenty poor Indians were murdered, that had, from the first settlement of the province, lived among us, under the protection of our government. This gave me a good deal of employment; for, as the rioters threatened further mischief, and their actions seemed to be approved by an ever-acting party, I wrote a pamphlet entitled "A Narrative, &c." (which I think I sent to you) to strengthen the hands of our weak government, by rendering the proceedings of the rioters unpopular and odious. This had a good effect; and afterwards, when a great body of them with arms marched towards the capital, in defiance of the government, with an avowed resolution to put to death one hundred and forty Indian converts then under its protection, I formed an Association at the governor's request, for his and their defence, we having no militia. Near one thousand of the citizens accordingly took arms; Governor Penn made my house for some time his head-quarters, and did every thing by my advice; so that, for about forty-eight hours, I was a very great man; as I had been once some years before, in a time of public danger.

But the fighting face we put on, and the reasonings we used with the insurgents (for I went at the request of the governor and council, with three others, to meet and discourse with them) having turned them back and restored quiet to the city, I became a less man than ever; for I had, by this transaction, made myself many enemies among the populace; and the governor (with whose family our public disputes had long placed me in an unfriendly light, and the services I had lately rendered him not being of the kind that make a man acceptable) thinking it a favorable opportunity, joined the whole weight of the proprietary interest to get me out of the Assembly; which was accordingly effected at the last election, by a majority of about twenty-five in four thousand voters. The House, however, when they met in October, approved of the resolutions taken, while I was Speaker, of petitioning the crown for a change of government, and requested me to return to England, to prosecute that petition; which service I accordingly undertook, and embarked at the beginning of November last, being accompanied to the ship, sixteen miles, by a cavalcade of three hundred of my friends, who filled our sails with their good wishes, and I arrived in thirty days at London.

Here I have been ever since, engaged in that and other public affairs relating to America, which are like to continue some time longer upon my hands; but I promise you, that when I am quit of these, I will engage in no other; and that, as soon as I have recovered the ease and leisure I hope for, the task you require of me, of finishing my "Art of Virtue," shall be performed. In the mean time, I must request you would excuse me on this consideration, that the powers of the mind are possessed by different men in different degrees, and that every one cannot, like Lord Kames, intermix literary pursuits and important business without prejudice to either.

I send you herewith two or three other pamphlets of my writing on our political affairs, during my short residence in America; but I do not insist on your reading them; for I know you employ all your time to some useful purpose.

The English People

To Mary Stevenson. Philadelphia, 25 March, 1763.

YOUR PLEASING favor of November 11th is now before me. It found me, as you supposed it would, happy with my American friends and family about me; and it made me more happy in showing me, that I am not yet forgotten by the dear friends I left in England. And, indeed, why should I fear they will ever forget me, when I feel so strongly that I shall ever remember them?

Of all the enviable things England has, I envy it most its people. Why should that petty Island, which, compared to America, is but like a stepping-stone in a brook, scarce enough of it above water to keep one's shoes dry; why, I say, should that little Island enjoy, in almost every neighbourhood, more sensible, virtuous, and elegant minds, than we can collect in ranging a hundred leagues of our vast forests? But it is said the Arts delight to travel westward. You have effectually defended us in this glorious war, and in time you will improve us. After the first cares for the necessaries of life are over, we shall come to think of the embellishments. Already, some of our young geniuses begin to lisp attempts at painting, poetry, and music. We have a young painter now studying at Rome. Some specimens of our poetry I send you, which, if Dr. Hawkesworth's fine taste cannot approve, his good heart will at least excuse.

Religious Hope

To George Whitefield. Philadelphia, 19 June, 1764.

YOUR FREQUENTLY repeated wishes for my eternal, as well as my temporal happiness, are very obliging, and I can only thank you for them and offer you mine in return. I have myself no doubt, that I shall enjoy as much of both as is proper for me. That Being, who gave me existence, and through almost threescore years has been continually showering his favors upon me, whose very chastisements have been blessings to me; can I doubt that he loves me? And, if he loves me, can I doubt that he will go on to take care of me, not only here but hereafter? This to some may seem presumption; to me it appears the best grounded hope; hope of the future built on experience of the past.

Connecticut Religion

To Jared Ingersoll. Philadelphia, Dec. 11, 1762.

I SHOULD be glad to know what it is that distinguishes Connecticut religion from common religion:—communicate, if you please, some of these particulars that you think will amuse me as a virtuoso. When I traveled in Flanders I thought of your excessively strict observation of Sunday; and that a man could hardly travel on that day among you upon his lawful occasions without hazard of punishment, while where I was every one traveled, if he pleased, or diverted himself in any other way; and in the afternoon both high and low went to the play or the opera, where there was plenty of singing, fiddling, and dancing. I looked round for God's judgments but saw no signs of them. The cities were well built and full of inhabitants, the markets filled with plenty, the people well favoured and well clothed; the fields well tilled; the cattle fat and strong; the fences, houses and windows all in repair; and no *Old Tenor* anywhere in the country,—which would almost make one suspect that the Deity is not so angry at that offence as a New England Justice.

On Public Opinion

To the editor of a newspaper. Monday, 20 May, 1765.

SIR,—In your paper of Wednesday last, an ingenious correspondent who calls himself THE SPECTATOR, and dates from *Pimlico*, under the guise of good will to the news-writers, whom he calls a "useful body of men in this great city," has, in my opinion, artfully attempted to turn them and their works into ridicule, wherein, if he could succeed, great injury might be done to the public as well as to these good people.

Supposing, Sir, that the "*we hears*" they give us of this or the other intended tour or voyage of this and the other great personage were mere inventions, yet they at least offer us an innocent amusement while we read, and useful matter for conversation when we are disposed to converse.

Englishmen, Sir, are too apt to be silent when they have nothing to say, and too apt to be sullen when they are silent; and, when they are sullen, to hang themselves. But, by these *we hears*, we are supplied with abundant funds for discourse. . . .

And here, quitting Mr. Spectator of Pimlico, give me leave to instance the various accounts the news-writers have given us, with so much honest zeal for the welfare of *Poor Old England*, of the establishing manufactures in the colonies to the prejudice of those of the kingdom. It is objected by superficial readers, who yet pretend to some knowledge of those countries, that such establishments are not only improbable, but impossible, for that their sheep have but little wool, not in the whole sufficient for a pair of stockings a year to each inhabitant; that, from the universal dearness of labor among them, the working of iron and other materials, except in a few coarse instances, is impracticable to any advantage.

Dear Sir, do not let us suffer ourselves to be amused with such groundless objections. The very tails of the American sheep are so laden with wool, that each has a little car or wagon on four little wheels, to support and keep it from trailing on the ground. Would they caulk their ships, would they even litter their horses with wool, if it were not both plenty and cheap? And what signifies the dearness of labor, when an English shilling passes for five and twenty? Their engaging three hundred silk throwsters here in one week for New York was treated as a fable, because, forsooth, they have "no silk to there to throw." Those, who make this objection, perhaps do not know, that, at the same time the agents from the King of Spain were at Quebec to contract for one thousand pieces of cannon to be made there for the fortification of Mexico, and at New York engaging the usual supply of woollen floor-carpets for their West India houses, other agents from the emperor of China were at Boston treating about an exchange of raw silk for wool, to be carried in Chinese junks through the Straits of Magellan.

And yet all this is as certainly true, as the account said to be from Quebec, in all the papers of last week, that the inhabitants of Canada are making preparations for a cod and whale fishery this "summer in the upper Lakes." Ignorant people may object, that the upper Lakes are fresh, and that cod and whales are salt water fish; but let them know, Sir, that cod, like other fish when attacked by their enemies, fly into any water where they can be safest; that whales, when they have a mind to eat cod, pursue them wherever they fly; and that the grand leap of the whale in the chase up the Falls of Niagara is esteemed, by all who have seen it, as one of the finest spectacles in nature. Really, Sir, the world is grown too incredulous. It is like the pendulum ever swinging from one extreme to another. Formerly every thing printed was believed, because it was in print. Now things seem to be disbelieved for just the very same reason. Wise men wonder at the present growth of infidelity. They should have considered, when they taught the people to doubt the authority of newspapers and the truth of predictions in the almanacs, that the next step might be a disbelief of the well vouched accounts of ghosts and witches, and doubts even of the truths of the Creed.

Thus much I thought it necessary to say in favor of an honest set of writers, whose comfortable living depends on collecting and supplying the printers with news at the small price of sixpence an article, and who always show their regard to truth, by contradicting in a subsequent article such as are wrong, for another sixpence, to the great satisfaction and improvement of us coffee-house students in history and politics, and all future Livys, Rapins, Robertsons, Humes, and Macaulays, who may be sincerely inclined to furnish the world with that *rara avis*, a true history. I am, Sir, your humble servant,

A Traveller.

Letter to a person unknown, concerning the probability and effects of a union with Great Britain, and concerning the repeal or suspension of the Stamp Act, dated London, Jan. 6, 1766.

Sir,—I have attentively perused the paper you sent me, and am of opinion, that the measure it proposes, of an union with the colonies, is a wise one; but I doubt it will hardly be thought so here, till it is too late to attempt it. The time has been, when the colonies would have esteemed it a great advantage, as well as honor to be permitted to send members to Parliament; and would have asked for that privilege, if they could have had the least hopes of obtaining it. The time is now come, when they are indifferent about it, and will probably not ask it, though they might accept it if offered them; and the time will come, when they will certainly refuse it. But if such an union were now established (which methinks it highly imports this country to establish) it would probably subsist as long as Britain shall continue a nation. This people, however, is too proud, and too much despises the Americans, to bear the thought of admitting them to such an equitable participation in the government of the whole.

Then the next best thing seems to be, leaving them in the quiet enjoyment of their respective constitutions; and when money is wanted for any public service, in which they ought to bear a part, calling upon them by requisitorial letters from the crown (according to the long-established custom) to grant such aids as their loyalty shall dictate, and their abilities permit. The very sensible and benevolent author of that paper seems not to have known, that such a constitutional custom subsists, and has always hitherto been practised in America; or he would not have expressed himself in this manner; "It is evident, beyond a doubt, to the intelligent and impartial, that after the very extraordinary efforts, which were effectually made by Great Britain in the late war to save the colonists from destruction, and attended of necessity with an enormous load of debts in consequence, that the same colonists, now firmly secured from foreign enemies, should be somehow induced to contribute some proportion towards the exigencies of state in future." This looks as if he conceived the war had been carried on at the sole expense of Great Britain, and the colonies only reaped the benefit, without hitherto sharing the burden, and were therefore now indebted to Britain on that account. And this is the same kind of argument that is used by those, who would fix on the colonies the heavy charge of unreasonableness and ingratitude, which I think your friend did not intend.

Please to acquaint him, then, that the fact is not so; that, every year during the war, requisitions were made by the crown on the colonies for raising money and men; that accordingly they made more extraordinary efforts, in proportion to their abilities, than Britain did; that they raised, paid, and clothed, for fixe or six years, near twenty-five thousand men, besides providing for other services, as building forts, equipping guard-ships, paying transports, &c. And that this was more than their fair proportion is not merely an opinion of mine, but was the judgment of government here, in full knowledge of all the facts; for the then ministry, to make the burthen more equal, recommended the case to Parliament, and obtained a reimbursement to the Americans, of about two hundred thousand pounds sterling every year; which amounted only to about two-fifths of their expense; and great part of the rest lies still a load of debt upon them; heavy taxes on all their estates, real and personal, being laid by acts of their assemblies to discharge it, and yet will not discharge it in many years.

While, then, these burdens continue; while Britain restrains the colonies in every branch of commerce and manufactures that she thinks interferes with her own; while she drains the colonies, by her trade with them, of all the cash they can procure by every art and industry in any part of the world, and thus keeps them always in her debt (for they can make no law to discourage the importation of your to *them* ruinous superfluities, as *you* do the superfluities of France; since such a law would immediately be reported against by your Board of Trade, and repealed by the crown); I say, while these circumstances continue, and while there subsists the established method of royal requisitions for raising money on them by their own assemblies on every proper occasion; can it be necessary or prudent to distress and vex them by taxes laid here, in a Parliament wherein they have no representative, and in a manner which they look upon to be unconstitutional and subversive of their most valuable rights? And are they to be thought unreasonable and ungrateful if they oppose such taxes?

Wherewith, they say, shall we show our loyalty to our gracious King, if our money is to be given by others, without asking our consent? And, if the Parliament has a right thus to take from us a penny in the pound, where is the line drawn that bounds that right, and what shall hinder their calling, whenever they please, for the other nineteen shillings and eleven pence? Have we then any thing that we can call our own? It is more than probable, that bringing representatives from the colonies to sit and act here as members of Parliament, thus uniting and consolidating your dominions, would in a little time remove these objections and difficulties, and make the future government of the colonies easy; but, till some such thing is done, I apprehend no taxes, laid there by Parliament here, will ever be collected, but such as must be stained with blood; and I am sure the profit of such taxes will never answer the expense of collecting them, and that the respect and affection of the Americans to this country will in the struggle be totally lost, perhaps never to be recovered; and therewith all the commercial and political advantages, that might have attended the continuance of this respect and this affection.

In my own private judgment, I think an immediate repeal of the Stamp Act would be the best measure for this country; but a suspension of it for three years, the best for that. The repeal would fill them with joy and gratitude, reëstablish their respect and veneration for Parliament, restore at once their ancient and natural love for this country, and their regard for every thing that comes from it; hence the trade would be renewed in all its branches; they would again indulge in all the expensive superfluities you supply them with, and their own new-assumed home industry would languish. But the suspension, though it might continue their fears and anxieties, would at the same time keep up their resolutions of industry and frugality; which in two or three years would grow into habits, to their lasting advantage. However, as the repeal will probably not be now agreed to, from what I think a mistaken opinion, that the honor and dignity of government is better supported by persisting in a wrong measure once entered into, than by rectifying an error as soon as it is discovered; we must allow the next best thing for the advantage of both countries, is the suspension; for, as to executing the act by force, it is madness, and will be ruin to the whole.

House of Commons Hearing

The examination of Dr. Benjamin Franklin, in the British House of Commons, relative to the repeal of the American Stamp Act, in 1766.

From the journal of the House of Commons, as given by Mr. Vaughan:
"*February 3d, 1766.* Benjamin Franklin and a number of other persons ordered to attend the committee of the whole House, to whom it was referred to consider farther the several papers, which were presented to the House by Mr. Secretary Conway.

"*February 13th.* Benjamin Franklin, having passed through his examination, was excepted from farther attendance.

"*February 24th.* The resolutions of the committee were reported by the chairman, Mr. Fuller; their seventh and last resolution setting forth, that it was their opinion that the House be moved, that leave be given to bring in a bill to repeal the Stamp Act."

1. *Q.* What is your name, and place of abode?
  A. Franklin, of Philadelphia.
2. *Q.* Do the Americans pay any considerable taxes among themselves?
  A. Certainly many, and very heavy taxes.
3. *Q.* What are the present taxes in Pennsylvania, laid by the laws of the colony?
  A. There are taxes on all estates real and personal; a poll tax; a tax on all

offices, professions, trades, and businesses, according to their profits; an excise on all wine, rum, and other spirits; and a duty of ten pounds per head on all negroes imported, with some other duties.

4. *Q.* For what purposes are those taxes laid?

A. For the support of the civil and military establishments of the country, and to discharge the heavy debt contracted in the last war.

5. *Q.* How long are those taxes to continue?

A. Those for discharging the debt are to continue till 1772, and longer, if the debt should not be then all discharged. The others must always continue.

6. *Q.* Was it not expected that the debt would have been sooner discharged?

A. It was, when the peace was made with France and Spain. But, a fresh war breaking out with the Indians, a fresh load of debt was incurred; and the taxes, of course, continued longer by a new law.

7. *Q.* Are not all the people very able to pay those taxes?

A. No. The frontier counties, all along the continent, having been frequently ravaged by the enemy and greatly impoverished, are able to pay very little tax. And therefore, in consideration of their distresses, our late tax laws do expressly favor those counties, excusing the sufferers; and I suppose the same is done in other governments.

8. *Q.* Are not you concerned in the management of the post-office in America?

A. Yes. I am deputy-postmaster-general of North America.

9. *Q.* Don't you think the distribution of stamps by post to all the inhabitants very practicable, if there was no opposition?

A. The posts only go along the seacoasts; they do not, except in a few instances, go back into the country; and, if they did, sending for stamps by post would occasion an expense of postage amounting in many cases to much more than that of the stamps themselves.

10. *Q.* Are you acquainted with Newfoundland?

A. I never was there.

11. *Q.* Do you know whether there are any post-roads on that island?

A. I have heard that there are no roads at all, but that the communication between one settlement and another is by sea only.

12. *Q.* Can you disperse the stamps by post in Canada?

A. There is only a post between Montreal and Quebec. The inhabitants live so scattered and remote from each other in that vast country, that posts cannot be supported among them, and therefore they cannot get stamps per post. The English colonies, too, along the frontiers are very thinly settled.

13. *Q.* From the thinness of the back settlements, would not the Stamp Act be extremely inconvenient to the inhabitants, if executed?

A. To be sure it would; as many of the inhabitants could not get stamps when they had occasion for them without taking long journeys, and spending perhaps three or four pounds, that the crown might get sixpence.

14.   *Q.* Are not the colonies, from their circumstances, very able to pay the stamp duty?

A. In my opinion there is not gold and silver enough in the colonies to pay the stamp duty for one year.

15.   *Q.* Don't you know that the money arising from the stamps was all to be laid out in America?

A. I know it is appropriated by the act to the American service; but it will be spent in the conquered colonies, where the soldiers are; not in the colonies that pay it.

16.   *Q.* Is there not a balance of trade due from the colonies where the troops are posted, that will bring back the money to the old colonies?

A. I think not. I believe very little would come back. I know of no trade likely to bring it back. I think it would come, from the colonies where it was spent, directly to England; for I have always observed, that in every colony the more plenty the means of remittance to England, the more goods are sent for, and the more trade with England carried on.

17.   *Q.* What number of white inhabitants do you think there are in Pennsylvania?

A. I suppose there may be about one hundred and sixty thousand.

18.   *Q.* What number of them are Quakers?

A. Perhaps a third.

19.   *Q.* What number of Germans?

A. Perhaps another third; but I cannot speak with certainty.

20.   *Q.* Have any number of the Germans seen service, as soldiers, in Europe?

A. Yes, many of them, both in Europe and America.

21.   *Q.* Are they as much dissatisfied with the stamp duty as the English?

A. Yes, and more; and with reason, as their stamps are, in many cases, to be double.*

22.   *Q.* How many white men do you suppose there are in North America?

A. About three hundred thousand, from sixteen to sixty years of age.

23.   *Q.* What may be the amount of one year's imports into Pennsylvania from Britain?

A. I have been informed that our merchants compute the imports from Britain to be above five hundred thousand pounds.

24.   *Q.* What may be the amount of the produce of your province exported to Britain?

A. It must be small, as we produce little that is wanted in Britain. I suppose it cannot exceed forty thousand pounds.

25.   *Q.* How then do you pay the balance?

A. The balance is paid by our produce carried to the West Indies, and sold in our own islands, or to the French, Spaniards, Danes, and Dutch; by

*The Stamp Act provided, that a double duty should be laid "where the instrument, proceedings, &c., shall be engrossed, written, or printed within the said colonies and plantations, in any other than the English language."

the same produce carried to other colonies in North America, as to New England, Nova Scotia, Newfoundland, Carolina, and Georgia; by the same, carried to different parts of Europe, as Spain, Portugal, and Italy. In all which places we receive either money, bills of exchange, or commodities that suit for remittance to Britain; which, together with all the profits on the industry of our merchants and mariners, arising in those circuitous voyages, and the freights made by their ships, centre finally in Britain to discharge the balance, and pay for British manufactures continually used in the provinces, or sold to foreigners by our traders.

26. *Q.* Have you heard of any difficulties lately laid on the Spanish trade?

A. Yes; I have heard, that it has been greatly obstructed by some new regulations, and by the English men-of-war and cutters stationed all along the coast in America.

27. *Q.* Do you think it right that America should be protected by this country and pay no part of the expense?

A. That is not the case. The colonies raised, clothed, and paid, during the last war, near twenty-five thousand men, and spent many millions.

28. *Q.* Were you not reimbursed by Parliament?

A. We were only reimbursed what, in your opinion, we had advanced beyond our proportion, or beyond what might reasonably be expected from us; and it was a very small part of what we spent. Pennsylvania, in particular, disbursed about five hundred thousand pounds, and the reimbursements, in the whole, did not exceed sixty thousand pounds.

29. *Q.* You have said that you pay heavy taxes in Pennsylvania; what do they amount to in the pound?

A. The tax on all estates, real and personal, is eighteen pence in the pound, fully rated; and the tax on the profits of trades and professions, with other taxes, do, I suppose, make full half a crown in the pound.

30. *Q.* Do you know any thing of the rate of exchange in Pennsylvania, and whether it has fallen lately?

A. It is commonly from one hundred and seventy to one hundred and seventy-five. I have heard, that it has fallen lately from one hundred and seventy-five to one hundred and sixty-two and a half; owing, I suppose, to their lessening their orders for goods; and, when their debts to this country are paid, I think the exchange will probably be at par.

31. *Q.* Do you not think the people of America would submit to pay the stamp duty, if it was moderated?

A. No, never, unless compelled by force of arms.

32. *Q.* Are not the taxes in Pennsylvania laid on unequally, in order to burden the English trade; particularly the tax on professions and business?

A. It is not more burdensome in proportion than the tax on lands. It is intended and supposed to take an equal proportion of profits.

33. *Q.* How is the assembly composed? Of what kinds of people are the members; landholders or traders?

A. It is composed of landholders, merchants, and artificers.

34. *Q.* Are not the majority landholders?

A. I believe they are.

35. *Q.* Do not they, as much as possible, shift the tax off from the land, to ease that, and lay the burden heavier on trade?

A. I have never understood it so. I never heard such a thing suggested. And indeed an attempt of that kind could answer no purpose. The merchant or trader is always skilled in figures, and ready with his pen and ink. If unequal burdens are laid on his trade, he puts an additional price on his goods; and the consumers, who are chiefly landholders, finally pay the greatest part, if not the whole.

36. *Q.* What was the temper of America towards Great Britain before the year 1763?

A. The best in the world. They submitted willingly to the government of the crown, and paid, in their courts, obedience to the acts of Parliament. Numerous as the people are in the several old provinces, they cost you nothing in forts, citadels, garrisons, or armies, to keep them in subjection. They were governed by this country at the expense only of a little pen, ink, and paper; they were led by a thread. They had not only a respect, but an affection for Great Britain; for its laws, its customs and manners, and even a fondness for its fashions, that greatly increased the commerce. Natives of Britain were always treated with particular regard; to be an *Old-England man* was, of itself, a character of some respect, and gave a kind of rank among us.

37. *Q.* And what is their temper now?

A. O, very much altered.

38. *Q.* Did you ever hear the authority of Parliament to make laws for America questioned till lately?

A. The authority of Parliament was allowed to be valid in all laws, except such as should lay internal taxes. It was never disputed in laying duties to regulate commerce.

39. *Q.* In what proportion hath population increased in America?

A. I think the inhabitants of all the provinces together, taken at a medium, double in about twenty-five years. But their demand for British manufactures increases much faster; as the consumption is not merely in proportion to their numbers, but grows with the growing abilities of the same numbers to pay for them. In 1723, the whole importation from Britain to Pennsylvania was about fifteen thousand pounds sterling; it is now near half a million.

40. *Q.* In what light did the people of America use to consider the Parliament of Great Britain?

A. They considered the Parliament as the great bulwark and security of their liberties and privileges, and always spoke of it with the utmost respect and veneration. Arbitrary ministers, they thought, might possibly, at times, attempt to oppress them; but they relied on it, that the Parliament, on application, would always give redress. They remembered, with gratitude, a strong instance of this, when a bill was brought into Parliament, with a clause to make royal instructions laws in the colonies, which the House of Commons would not pass, and it was thrown out.

41. *Q.* And have they not still the same respect for Parliament?

A. No, it is greatly lessened.

42. *Q.* To what cause is that owing?

A. To a concurrence of causes; the restraints lately laid on their trade, by which the bringing of foreign gold and silver into the colonies was prevented; the prohibition of making paper money among themselves, and then demanding a new and heavy tax by stamps, taking away, at the same time, trials by juries, and refusing to receive and hear their humble petitions.

43. *Q.* Don't you think they would submit to the Stamp Act, if it was modified, the obnoxious parts taken out, and the duty reduced to some particulars of small moment?

A. No, they will never submit to it.

44. *Q.* What do you think is the reason that the people in America increase faster than in England?

A. Because they marry younger, and more generally.

45. *Q.* Why so?

A. Because any young couple, that are industrious, may easily obtain land of their own, on which they can raise a family.

46. *Q.* Are not the lower ranks of people more at their ease in America than in England?

A. They may be so, if they are sober and diligent, as they are better paid for their labor.

47. *Q.* What is your opinion of a future tax, imposed on the same principle with that of the Stamp Act? How would the Americans receive it?

A. Just as they do this. They would not pay it.

48. *Q.* Have not you heard of the resolutions of this House, and of the House of Lords, asserting the right of Parliament relating to America, including a power to tax the people there?

A. Yes, I have heard of such resolutions.

49. *Q.* What will be the opinion of the Americans on those resolutions?

A. They will think them unconstitutional and unjust.

50. *Q.* Was it an opinion in America before 1763, that the Parliament had no right to lay taxes and duties there?

A. I never heard any objection to the right of laying duties to regulate commerce; but a right to lay internal taxes was never supposed to be in Parliament, as we are not represented there.

51. *Q.* On what do you found your opinion, that the people in America made any such distinction?

A. I know that whenever the subject has occurred in conversation where I have been present, it has appeared to be the opinion of every one, that we could not be taxed by a Parliament wherein we were not represented. But the payment of duties laid by an act of Parliament, as regulations of commerce, was never disputed.

52.   *Q.* But can you name any act of assembly, or public act of any of your governments, that made such distinction?

A. I do not know that there was any; I think there was never an occasion to make any such act, till now that you have attempted to tax us; that has occasioned resolutions of assembly, declaring the distinction, in which I think every assembly on the continent, and every member in every assembly, have been unanimous.

53.   *Q.* What, then, could occasion conversations on that subject before that time?

A. There was in 1754 a proposition made (I think it came from hence), that in case of a war, which was then apprehended, the governors of the colonies should meet, and order the levying of troops, building of forts, and taking every other necessary measure for the general defence; and should draw on the treasury here for the sums expended, which were afterwards to be raised in the colonies by a general tax, to be laid on them by *act of Parliament.* This occasioned a good deal of conversation on the subject; and the general opinion was, that the Parliament neither would nor could lay any tax on us, till we were duly represented in Parliament; because it was not just, nor agreeable to the nature of an English constitution.

54.   *Q.* Don't you know there was a time in New York, when it was under consideration to make an application to Parliament to lay taxes on that colony, upon a deficiency arising from the assembly's refusing or neglecting to raise the necessary supplies for the support of the civil government?

A. I never heard of it.

55.   *Q.* There was such an application under consideration in New York; and do you apprehend they could suppose the right of Parliament to lay a tax in America was only local, and confined to the case of a deficiency in a particular colony, by a refusal of its assembly to raise the necessary supplies?

A. They could not suppose such a case, as that the assembly would not raise the necessary supplies to support its own government. An assembly that would refuse it must want common sense; which cannot be supposed. I think there was never any such case at New York, and that it must be a misrepresentation, or the fact must be misunderstood. I know there have been some attempts, by ministerial instructions from hence, to oblige the assemblies to settle permanent salaries on governors, which they wisely refused to do; but I believe no assembly of New York, or any other colony, ever refused duly to support government by proper allowances, from time to time, to public officers.

56.   *Q.* But, in case a governor, acting by instruction, should call on an assembly to raise the necessary supplies, and the assembly should refuse to do it, do you not think it would then be for the good of the people of the colony, as well as necessary to government, that the Parliament should tax them?

A. I do not think it would be necessary. If an assembly could possibly be so absurd, as to refuse raising the supplies requisite for the maintenance of government among them, they could not long remain in such a situation; the disorders and confusion occasioned by it must soon bring them to reason.

57. *Q*. If it should not, ought not the right to be in Great Britain of applying a remedy?

A. A right, only to be used in such a case, I should have no objection to; supposing it to be used merely for the good of the people of the colony.

58. *Q*. But who is to judge of that, Britain or the colony?

A. Those that feel can best judge.

59. *Q*. You say the colonies have always submitted to external taxes, and object to the right of Parliament only in laying internal taxes; now can you show, that there is any kind of difference between the two taxes to the colony on which they may be laid?

A. I think the difference is very great. An *external* tax is a duty laid on commodities imported; that duty is added to the first cost and other charges on the commodity, and, when it is offered to sale, makes a part of the price. If the people do not like it at that price, they refuse it; they are not obliged to pay it. But an *internal* tax is forced from the people without their consent, if not laid by their own representatives. The Stamp Act says, we shall have no commerce, make no exchange of property with each other, neither purchase, nor grant, nor recover debts; we shall neither marry nor make our wills, unless we pay such and such sums; and thus it is intended to extort our money from us, or ruin us by the consequences of refusing to pay it.

60. *Q*. But supposing the external tax or duty to be laid on the necessaries of life, imported into your colony, will not that be the same thing in its effects as an internal tax?

A. I do not know a single article imported into the northern colonies, but what they can either do without, or make themselves.

61. *Q*. Don't you think cloth from England absolutely necessary to them?

A. No, by no means absolutely necessary; with industry and good management, they may very well supply themselves with all they want.

62. *Q*. Will it not take a long time to establish that manufacture among them; and must they not in the mean while suffer greatly?

A. I think not. They have made a surprising progress already. And I am of the opinion, that before their old clothes are worn out, they will have new ones of their own making.

63. *Q*. Can they possibly find wool enough in North America?

A. They have taken steps to increase the wool. They entered into general combinations to eat no more lamb; and very few lambs were killed last year. This course, persisted in, will soon make a prodigious difference in the quantity of wool. And the establishing of great manufactories, like those in the clothing towns here, is not necessary, as it is where the business is to be carried on for the purposes of trade. The people will all spin, and work for themselves, in their own houses.

64. Q. Can there be wool and manufacture enough in one or two years?

A. In three years, I think there may.

65. Q. Does not the severity of the winter, in the northern colonies, occasion the wool to be of bad quality?

A. No; the wool is very fine and good.

66. Q. In the more southern colonies, as in Virginia, don't you know, that the wool is coarse, and only a kind of hair?

A. I don't know it. I never heard it. Yet I have been sometimes in Virginia. I cannot say I ever took particular notice of the wool there, but I believe it is good, though I cannot speak positively of it; but Virginia and the colonies south of it have less occasion for wool; their winters are short, and not very severe; and they can very well clothe themselves with linen and cotton of their own raising for the rest of the year.

67. Q. Are not the people in the more northern colonies obliged to fodder their sheep all the winter?

A. In some of the most northern colonies they may be obliged to do it, some part of the winter.

68. Q. Considering the resolutions of Parliament, *as to the right*, do you think, if the Stamp Act is repealed, that the North Americans will be satisfied?

A. I believe they will.

69. Q. Why do you think so?

A. I think the resolutions of *right* will give them very little concern, if they are never attempted to be carried into practice. The colonies will probably consider themselves in the same situation, in that respect, with Ireland; they know you claim the same right with regard to Ireland, but you never exercise it, and they may believe you never will exercise it in the colonies, any more than in Ireland, unless on some very extraordinary occasion.

70. Q. But who are to be the judges of that extraordinary occasion? Is not the Parliament?

A. Though the Parliament may judge of the occasion, the people will think it can never exercise such right, till representatives from the colonies are admitted into Parliament; and that, whenever the occasion arises, representatives *will* be ordered.

71. Q. Did you never hear that Maryland, during the last war, had refused to furnish a quota towards the common defence?

A. Maryland has been much misrepresented in that matter. Maryland, to my knowledge, never refused to contribute or grant aids to the crown. The assemblies, every year during the war, voted considerable sums, and formed bills to raise them. The bills were, according to the constitution of that province, sent up to the Council, or Upper House, for concurrence, that they might be presented to the governor, in order to be enacted into laws. Unhappy disputes between the two Houses, arising from the defects of that constitution principally, rendered all the bills but one or two, abortive. The proprietary's council rejected them. It is true, Maryland did not then contribute its proportion; but it was, in my opinion, the fault of the government, not of the people.

72. *Q.* Was it not talked of in the other provinces, as a proper measure, to apply to Parliament to compel them?

A. I have heard such discourse; but, as it was well known that the people were not to blame, no such application was ever made, nor any step taken towards it.

73. *Q.* Was it not proposed at a public meeting?

A. Not that I know of.

74. *Q.* Do you remember the abolishing of the paper currency in New England, by act of assembly?

A. I do remember its being abolished in the Massachusetts Bay.

75. *Q.* Was not Lieutenant-Governor Hutchinson principally concerned in that transaction?

A. I have heard so.

76. *Q.* Was it not at that time a very unpopular law?

A. I believe it was, though I can say little about it, as I lived at a distance from that province.

77. *Q.* Was not the scarcity of gold and silver an argument used against abolishing the paper?

A. I suppose it was.

78. *Q.* What is the present opinion there of that law? Is it as unpopular as it was at first?

A. I think it is not.

79. *Q.* Have not instructions from hence been sometimes sent over to governors, highly oppressive and unpolitical?

A. Yes.

80. *Q.* Have not some governors dispensed with them for that reason?

A. Yes, I have heard so.

81. *Q.* Did the Americans ever dispute the controlling power of Parliament to regulate the commerce?

A. No.

82. *Q.* Can any thing less than a military force carry the Stamp Act into execution?

A. I do not see how a military force can be applied to that purpose.

83. *Q.* Why may it not?

A. Suppose a military force sent into America, they will find nobody in arms; what are they then to do? They cannot force a man to take stamps who chooses to do without them. They will not find a rebellion; they may indeed make one.

84. *Q.* If the act is not repealed, what do you think will be the consequences?

A. A total loss of the respect and affection the people of America bear to this country, and of all the commerce that depends on that respect and affection.

85.   Q. How can the commerce be affected?

A. You will find, that if the act is not repealed, they will take a very little of your manufactures in a short time.

86.   Q. Is it in their power to do without them?

A. I think they may very will do without them.

87.   Q. Is it their interest not to take them?

A. The goods they take from Britain are either necessaries, mere conveniences, or superfluities. The first, as cloth, &c., with a little industry they can make at home; the second they can do without, till they are able to provide them among themselves; and the last, which are much the greatest part, they will strike off immediately. They are mere articles of fashion, purchased and consumed because the fashion in a respected country; but will now be detested and rejected. The people have already struck off, by general agreement, the use of all goods fashionable in mournings, and many thousands pounds' worth are sent back as unsalable.

88.   Q. Is it their interest to make cloth at home?

A. I think they may at present get it cheaper from Britain; I mean, of the same fineness and workmanship; but, when one considers other circumstances, the restraints on their trade, and the difficulty of making remittances, it is their interest to make every thing.

89.   Q. Suppose an act of internal regulations connected with a tax; how would they receive it?

A. I think it would be objected to.

90.   Q. Then no regulation with a tax would be submitted to?

A. Their opinion is, that, when aids to the crown are wanted, they are to be asked of the several assemblies, according to the old established usage; who will, as they always have done, grant them freely. And that their money ought not to be given away, without their consent, by persons at a distance, unacquainted with their circumstances and abilities. The granting aids to the crown is the only means they have of recommending themselves to their sovereign; and they think it extremely hard and unjust, that a body of men, in which they have no representatives, should make a merit to itself of giving and granting what is not its own, but theirs; and deprive them of a right they esteem of the utmost value and importance, as it is the security of all their other rights.

91.   Q. But is not the post-office, which they have long received, a tax as well as a regulation?

A. No; the money paid for the postage of a letter is not of the nature of a tax; it is merely a *quantum meruit* for a service done; no person is compellable to pay the money if he does not choose to receive the service. A man may still, as before the act, send his letter by a servant, a special messenger, or a friend, if he thinks it cheaper and safer.

92.   Q. But do they not consider the regulations of the post-office, by the act of last year, as a tax?

A. By the regulations of last year the rate of postage was generally abated near thirty per cent through all America; they certainly cannot consider such abatement *as a tax*.

93. *Q.* If an excise was laid by Parliament, which they might likewise avoid paying, by not consuming the articles excised, would they then not object to it?

A. They would certainly object to it, as an excise is unconnected with any service done, and is merely an aid, which they think ought to be asked of them, and granted by them, if they are to pay it; and can be granted for them by no others whatsoever, whom they have not empowered for that purpose.

94. *Q.* You say they do not object to the right of Parliament, in laying duties on goods to be paid on their importation; now, is there any kind of difference between a duty on the importation of goods, and an excise on their consumption?

A. Yes, a very material one; an excise, for the reasons I have just mentioned, they think you can have no right to lay within their country. But the sea is yours; you maintain, by your fleets, the safety of navigation in it, and keep it clear of pirates; you may have, therefore, a natural and equitable right to some toll or duty on merchandises carried through that part of your dominions, towards defraying the expense you are at in ships to maintain the safety of that carriage.

95. *Q.* Does this reasoning hold in the case of a duty laid on the produce of their lands exported? And would they not then object to such a duty?

A. If it tended to make the produce so much dearer abroad, as to lessen the demand for it, to be sure they would object to such a duty; not to your right of laying it, but they would complain of it as a burden, and petition you to lighten it.

96. *Q.* Is not the duty paid on the tobacco exported, a duty of that kind?

A. That, I think, is only on tobacco carried coastwise, from one colony to another, and appropriated as a fund for supporting the college at Williamsburg in Virginia.

97. *Q.* Have not the assemblies in the West Indies the same natural rights with those in North America?

A. Undoubtedly.

98. *Q.* And is there not a tax laid there on their sugars exported?

A. I am not much acquainted with the West Indies; but the duty of four and a half per cent on sugars exported was, I believe, granted by their own assemblies.

99. *Q.* How much is the poll-tax in your province laid on unmarried men?

A. It is, I think, fifteen shillings, to be paid by every single freeman, upwards of twenty-one years old.

100. *Q.* What is the annual amount of all the taxes in Pennsylvania?

A. I suppose about twenty thousand pounds sterling.

101. *Q.* Supposing the Stamp Act continued and enforced, do you

imagine that ill humor will induce the Americans to give as much for worse manufactures of their own, and use them, preferable to better of ours?

A. Yes, I think so. People will pay as freely to gratify one passion as another, their resentment as their pride.

102. *Q.* Would the people at Boston discontinue their trade?

A. The merchants are a very small number compared with the body of the people, and must discontinue their trade, if nobody will buy their goods.

103. *Q.* What are the body of the people in the colonies?

A. They are farmers, husbandmen, or planters.

104. *Q.* Would they suffer the produce of their lands to rot?

A. No; but they would not raise so much. They would manufacture more, and plough less.

105. *Q.* Would they live without the administration of justice in civil matters, and suffer all the inconveniences of such a situation for any considerable time, rather than take the stamps, supposing the stamps were protected by a sufficient force, where every one might have them?

A. I think the supposition impracticable, that the stamps should be so protected as that every one might have them. The act requires sub-distributors to be appointed in every county, town, district, and village, and they would be necessary. But the principal distributors, who were to have had a considerable profit on the whole, have not thought it worth while to continue in the office; and I think it impossible to find sub-distributors fit to be trusted, who, for the trifling profit that must come to their share, would incur the odium, and run the hazard, that would attend it; and, if they could be found, I think it impracticable to protect the stamps in so many distant and remote places.

106. *Q.* But in places where they could be protected, would not the people use them, rather than remain in such a situation, unable to obtain any right, or recover by law any debt?

A. It is hard to say what they would do. I can only judge what other people will think, and how they will act, by what I feel within myself. I have a great many debts due to me in America, and I had rather they should remain unrecoverable by any law, than submit to the Stamp Act. They will be debts of honor. It is my opinion the people will either continue in that situation, or find some way to extricate themselves; perhaps by generally agreeing to proceed in the courts without stamps.

107. *Q.* What do you think a sufficient military force to protect the distribution of the stamps in every part of America?

A. A very great force, I can't say what, if the disposition of America is for a general resistance.

108. *Q.* What is the number of men in America able to bear arms, or of disciplined militia?

A. There are, I suppose, at least . . .

[*Question objected to. He withdrew. Called in again.*]

109. *Q.* Is the American Stamp Act an equal tax on the country?

A. I think not.

110. *Q.* Why so?

A. The greatest part of the money must arise from lawsuits for the recovery of debts, and be paid by the lower sort of people, who were too poor easily to pay their debts. It is, therefore, a heavy tax on the poor, and a tax upon them for being poor.

111. *Q.* But will not this increase of expense be a means of lessening the number of lawsuits?

A. I think not; for as the costs all fall upon the debtor, and are to be paid by him, they would be no discouragement to the creditor to bring his action.

112. *Q.* Would it not have the effect of excessive usury?

A. Yes; as an oppression of the debtor.

113. *Q.* How many ships are there laden annually in North America with flax-seed for Ireland?

A. I cannot speak to the number of ships; but I know, that, in 1752, ten thousand hogsheads of flax-seed, each containing seven bushels, were exported from Philadelphia to Ireland. I suppose the quantity is greatly increased since that time, and it is understood, that the exportation from New York is equal to that from Philadelphia.

114. *Q.* What becomes of the flax that grows with that flax-seed?

A. They manufacture some into coarse, and some into a middling kind of linen.

115. *Q.* Are there any slitting-mills in America?

A. I think there are three, but I believe only one at present employed. I suppose they will all be set to work, if the interruption of the trade continues.

116. *Q.* Are there any fulling-mills there?

A. A great many.

117. *Q.* Did you never hear, that a great quantity of stockings were contracted for, for the army, during the war, and manufactured in Philadelphia?

A. I have heard so.

118. *Q.* If the Stamp Act should be repealed, would not the Americans think they could oblige the Parliament to repeal every external tax law now in force?

A. It is hard to answer questions of what people at such a distance will think.

119. *Q.* But what do you imagine they will think were the motives of repealing the act?

A. I suppose they will think, that it was repealed from a conviction of its inexpediency; and they will rely upon it, that, while the same inexpediency subsists, you will never attempt to make such another.

120. *Q.* What do you mean by its inexpediency?

A. I mean its inexpediency on several accounts; the poverty and inability of those who were to pay the tax, the general discontent it has occasioned, and the impracticability of enforcing it.

121. *Q.* If the act should be repealed, and the legislature should show

its resentment to the opposers of the Stamp Act, would the colonies acquiesce in the authority of the legislature? What is your opinion they would do?

A. I don't doubt at all, that if the legislature repeal the Stamp Act, the colonies will acquiesce in the authority.

122. *Q.* But if the legislature should think fit to ascertain its right to lay taxes, by any act laying a small tax, contrary to their opinion, would they submit to pay the tax?

A. The proceedings of the people in America have been considered too much together. The proceedings of the assemblies have been very different from those of the mobs, and should be distinguished, as having no connexion with each other. The assemblies have only peaceably resolved what they take to be their rights; they have taken no measures for opposition by force, they have not built a fort, raised a man, or provided a grain of ammunition, in order to such opposition. The ringleaders of riots, they think ought to be punished; they would punish them themselves, if they could. Every sober, sensible man would wish to see rioters punished, as, otherwise, peaceable people have no security of person or estate; but as to an internal tax, how small soever, laid by the legislature here on the people there, while they have no representatives in this legislature, I think it will never be submitted to; they will oppose it to the last; they do not consider it as at all necessary for you to raise money on them by your taxes; because they are, and always have been, ready to raise money by taxes among themselves, and to grant large sums, equal to their abilities, upon requisition from the crown.

They have not only granted equal to their abilities, but, during all the last war, they granted far beyond their abilities, and beyond their proportion with this country (you yourselves being judges), to the amount of many hundred thousand pounds; and this they did freely and readily, only on a sort of promise, from the Secretary of State, that it should be recommended to Parliament to make them compensation. It was accordingly recommended to Parliament, in the most honorable manner for them. America has been greatly misrepresented and abused here, in papers, and pamphlets, and speeches, as ungrateful, and unreasonable, and unjust; in having put this nation to an immense expense for their defence, and refusing to bear any part of that expense. The colonies raised, paid, and clothed near twenty-five thousand men during the last war; a number equal to those sent from Britain, and far beyond their proportion; they went deeply into debt in doing this, and all their taxes and estates are mortgaged for many years to come, for discharging that debt.

Government here was at that time very sensible of this. The colonies were recommended to Parliament. Every year the King sent down to the House a written message to this purpose; "that his Majesty, being highly sensible of the zeal and vigor with which his faithful subjects in North America had exerted themselves, in defence of his Majesty's just rights and possessions, recommended it to the House to take the same into consideration, and enable him to give them a proper compensation." You will find those messages on your own journals every year of the war to the very last; and you did accordingly give two hundred thousand pounds annually to the crown, to be distributed in such compensation to the colonies.

This is the strongest of all proofs, that the colonies, far from being unwilling to bear a share of the burden, did exceed their proportion; for if they had done less, or had only equalled their proportion, there would have been no room or reason for compensation. Indeed, the sums, reimbursed them, were by no means adequate to the expense they incurred beyond their proportion; but they never murmured at that; they esteemed their sovereign's approbation of their zeal and fidelity, and the approbation of this House, far beyond any other kind of compensation; therefore there was no occasion for this act, to force money from a willing people. They had not refused giving money for the purposes of the act; no requisition had been made; they were always willing and ready to do what could reasonably be expected from them, and in this light they wish to be considered.

123. *Q.* But suppose Great Britain should be engaged in a war in Europe, would North America contribute to the support of it?

A. I do think they would as far as their circumstances would permit. They consider themselves as a part of the British empire, and as having one common interest with it; they may be looked on here as foreigners, but they do not consider themselves as such. They are zealous for the honor and prosperity of this nation; and, while they are well used, will always be ready to support it, as far as their little power goes. In 1739 they were called upon to assist in the expedition against Carthagena, and they sent three thousand men to join your army. It is true, Carthagena is in America, but as remote from the northern colonies, as if it had been in Europe. They make no distinction of wars, as to their duty of assisting in them.

I know the last war is commonly spoken of here, as entered into for the defence, or for the sake, of the people in America. I think it is quite misunderstood. It began about the limits between Canada and Nova Scotia; about territories to which the *crown* indeed laid claim, but which were not claimed by any British *colony;* none of the lands had been granted to any colonist; we had therefore no particular concern or interest in that dispute. As to the Ohio, the contest there began about your right of trading in the Indian country, a right you had by the treaty of Utrecht, which the French infringed; they seized the traders and their goods, which were your manufactures; they took a fort which a company of your merchants, and their factors, and correspondents, had erected there to secure that trade. Braddock was sent with an army to retake that fort (which was looked on here as another encroachment on the King's territory), and to protect your trade. It was not till after his defeat that the colonies were attacked. They were before in perfect peace with both French and Indians; the troops were not, therefore, sent for their defence.

The trade with the Indians, though carried on in America, is not an American interest. The people of America are chiefly farmers and planters; scarce any thing that they raise or produce is an article of commerce with the Indians. The Indian trade is a British interest; it is carried on with British manufactures, for the profit of British merchants and manufacturers; therefore the war, as it commenced for the defence of territories of the crown (the property of no American), and for the defence of a trade purely British, was really a British war, and yet the people of America made no scruple of contributing their utmost towards carrying it on, and bringing it to a happy conclusion.

124. Q. Do you think, then, that the taking possession of the King's territorial rights, and strengthening the frontiers, is not an American interest?

A. Not particularly, but conjointly a British and an American interest.

125. Q. You will not deny, that the preceding war, the war with Spain, was entered into for the sake of America; was it not occasioned by captures made in the American seas?

A. Yes; captures of ships carrying on the British trade there with British manufactures.

126. Q. Was not the late war with the Indians, since the peace with France, a war for America only?

A. Yes; it was more particularly for America than the former; but was rather a consequence or remains of the former war, the Indians not having been thoroughly pacified; and the Americans bore by much the greatest share of the expense. It was put an end to by the army under General Bouquet; there were not above three hundred regulars in that army, and above one thousand Pennsylvanians.

127. Q. Is it not necessary to send troops to America, to defend the Americans against the Indians?

A. No, by no means; it never was necessary. They defended themselves when they were but a handful, and the Indians much more numerous. They continually gained ground, and have driven the Indians over the mountains, without any troops sent to their assistance from this country. And can it be thought necessary now to send troops for their defence from those diminished Indian tribes, when the colonies have become so populous and so strong? There is not the least occasion for it; they are very able to defend themselves.

128. Q. Do you say there were not more than three hundred regular troops employed in the late Indian war?

A. Not on the Ohio, or the frontiers of Pennsylvania, which was the chief part of the war that affected the colonies. There were garrisons at Niagara, Fort Detroit, and those remote posts kept for the sake of your trade; I did not reckon them; but I believe, that on the whole the number of Americans or provincial troops, employed in the war, was greater than that of the regulars. I am not certain, but I think so.

129. Q. Do you think the assemblies have a right to levy money on the subject there, to grant to the crown?

A. I certainly think so; they have always done it.

130. *Q.* Are they acquainted with the Declaration of Rights? And do they know, that, by that statute, money is not to be raised on the subject but by consent of Parliament?

A. They are very well acquainted with it.

131. *Q.* How then can they think they have a right to levy money for the crown, or for any other than local purposes?

A. They understand that clause to relate to subjects only within the realm; that no money can be levied on them for the crown, but by consent of Parliament. The colonies are not supposed to be within the realm; they have assemblies of their own, which are their parliaments, and they are, in that respect, in the same situation with Ireland. When money is to be raised for the crown upon the subject in Ireland, or in the colonies, the consent is given in the Parliament of Ireland, or in the assemblies of the colonies. They think the Parliament of Great Britain cannot properly give that consent, till it has representatives from America; for the Petition of Right expressly says, it is to be by common consent in Parliament; and the people of America have no representatives in Parliament, to make a part of that common consent.

132. *Q.* If the Stamp Act should be repealed, and an act should pass, ordering the assemblies of the colonies to indemnify the sufferers by the riots, would they obey it?

A. That is a question I cannot answer.

133. *Q.* Suppose the King should require the colonies to grant a revenue, and the Parliament should be against their doing it, do they think they can grant a revenue to the King, without the consent of the Parliament of Great Britain?

A. That is a deep question. As to my own opinion, I should think myself at liberty to do it, and should do it, if I liked the occasion.

134. *Q.* When money has been raised in the colonies, upon requisitions, has it not been granted to the King?

A. Yes, always; but the requisitions have generally been for some service expressed, as to raise, clothe, and pay troops, and not for money only.

135. *Q.* If the act should pass requiring the American assemblies to make compensation to the sufferers, and they should disobey it, and then the Parliament should, by another act, lay an internal tax, would they then obey it?

A. The people will pay no internal tax; and, I think, an act to oblige the assemblies to make compensation is unnecessary; for I am of opinion, that, as soon as the present heats are abated, they will take the matter into consideration, and if it is right to be done, they will do it of themselves.

136. *Q.* Do not letters often come into the post-offices in America, directed to some inland town where no post goes?

A. Yes.

137. *Q.* Can any private person take up those letters and carry them as directed?

A. Yes; any friend of the person may do it, paying the postage that has accrued.

138.   *Q.* But must not he pay an additional postage for the distance to such inland town?

A. No.

139.   *Q.* Can the postmaster answer for delivering the letter, without being paid such additional postage?

A. Certainly he can demand nothing, where he does no service.

140.   *Q.* Suppose a person, being far from home, finds a letter in a post-office directed to him, and he lives in a place to which the post generally goes, and the letter is directed to that place; will the postmaster deliver him the letter, without his paying the postage receivable at the place to which the letter is directed?

A. Yes; the office cannot demand postage for a letter that it does not carry, or farther than it does carry it.

141.   *Q.* Are not ferry-men in America obliged, by act of Parliament, to carry over the posts without pay?

A. Yes.

142.   *Q.* Is not this a tax on the ferry-men?

A. They do not consider it as such, as they have an advantage from persons travelling with the post.

143.   *Q.* If the Stamp Act should be repealed, and the crown should make a requisition to the colonies for a sum of money, would they grant it?

A. I believe they would.

144.   *Q.* Why do you think so?

A. I can speak for the colony I live in; I had it in *instruction* from the assembly to assure the ministry, that, as they always had done, so they should always think it their duty, to grant such aids to the crown as were suitable to their circumstances and abilities, whenever called upon for that purpose, in the usual constitutional manner; and I had the honor of communicating this instruction to that honorable gentleman then minister.

145.   *Q.* Would they do this for a British concern, as suppose a war in some part of Europe, that did not affect them?

A. Yes, for any thing that concerned the general interest. They consider themselves a part of the whole.

146.   *Q.* What is the usual constitutional manner of calling on the colonies for aids?

A. A letter from the Secretary of State.

147.   *Q.* Is this all you mean; a letter from the Secretary of State?

A. I mean the usual way of requisition, in a circular letter from the Secretary of State, by his Majesty's command, reciting the occasion, and recommending it to the colonies to grant such aids as became their loyalty, and were suitable to their abilities.

148.   *Q.* Did the Secretary of State ever write for money for the crown?

A. The requisitions have been to raise, clothe, and pay men, which cannot be done without money.

149. *Q.* Would they grant money alone, if called on?

A. In my opinion they would, money as well as men, when they have money, or can make it.

150. *Q.* If the Parliament should repeal the Stamp Act, will the assembly of Pennsylvania rescind their resolutions?

A. I think not.

151. *Q.* Before there was any thought of the Stamp Act, did they wish for a representation in Parliament?

A. No.

152. *Q.* Don't you know, that there is, in the Pennsylvania charter, an express reservation of the right of Parliament to lay taxes there?

A. I know there is a clause in the charter, by which the King grants, that he will levy no taxes on the inhabitants, unless it be with the consent of the assembly, or by act of Parliament.

153. *Q.* How, then, could the assembly of Pennsylvania assert, that laying a tax on them by the Stamp Act was an infringement of their rights?

A. They understand it thus; by the same charter, and otherwise, they are entitled to all the privileges and liberties of Englishmen; they find in the Great Charters, and the Petition and Declaration of Rights, that one of the privileges of English subjects is, that they are not to be taxed but by their common consent; they have therefore relied upon it, from the first settlement of the province, that the Parliament never would, nor could, by color of that clause in the charter, assume a right of taxing them, till it had qualified itself to exercise such right, by admitting representatives from the people to be taxed, who ought to make a part of that common consent.

154. *Q.* Are there any words in the charter that justify that construction?

A. "The common rights of Englishmen," as declared by *Magna Charta*, and the Petition of Right, all justify it.

155. *Q.* Does the distinction between internal and external taxes exist in the words of the charter?

A. No, I believe not.

156. *Q.* Then, may they not, by the same interpretation, object to the Parliament's right of external taxation?

A. They never have hitherto. Many arguments have been lately used here to show them, that there is no difference, and that, if you have no right to tax them internally, you have none to tax them externally, or make any other law to bind them. At present they do not reason so; but in time they may possibly be convinced by these arguments.

157. *Q.* Do not the resolutions of the Pennsylvania assembly say, "all taxes"?

A. If they do, they mean only internal taxes; the same words have not always the same meaning here and in the colonies. By taxes, they mean internal taxes; by duties, they mean customs; these are their ideas of the language.

158.   Q. Have you not seen the resolutions of the Massachusetts Bay assembly?

A. I have.

159.   Q. Do they not say, that neither external nor internal taxes can be laid on them by Parliament?

A. I don't know that they do; I believe not.

160.   Q. If the same colony should say, neither tax nor imposition could be laid, does not that province hold the power of Parliament can lay neither?

A. I suppose, that, by the word *imposition*, they do not intend to express duties to be laid on goods imported, as *regulations of commerce*.

161.   Q. What can the colonies mean then by imposition, as distinct from taxes?

A. They may mean many things, as impressing of men or of carriages, quartering troops on private houses, and the like; there may be great impositions that are not properly taxes.

162.   Q. Is not the post-office rate an internal tax laid by act of Parliament?

A. I have answered that.

163.   Q. Are all parts of the colonies equally able to pay taxes?

A. No, certainly; the frontier parts, which have been ravaged by the enemy, are greatly disabled by that means; and therefore, in such cases, are usually favored in our tax laws.

164.   Q. Can we, at this distance, be competent judges of what favors are necessary?

A. The Parliament have supposed it, by claiming a right to make tax laws for America; I think it impossible.

165.   Q. Would the repeal of the Stamp Act be any discouragement of your manufactures? Will the people that have begun to manufacture decline it?

A. Yes, I think they will; especially if, at the same time, the trade is opened again, so that remittances can be easily made. I have known several instances that make it probable. In the war before last, tobacco being low, and making little remittance, the people of Virginia went generally into family manufactures. Afterwards, when tobacco bore a better price, they returned to the use of British manufactures. So fulling-mills were very much disused in the last war in Pennsylvania, because bills were then plenty, and remittances could easily be made to Britain for English cloth and other goods.

166.   Q. If the Stamp Act should be repealed, would it induce the assemblies of America to acknowledge the rights of Parliament to tax them, and would they erase their resolutions?

A. No, never.

167.   Q. Are there no means of obliging them to erase those resolutions?

A. None that I know of; they will never do it, unless compelled by force of arms.

168. *Q.* Is there a power on earth that can force them to erase them?

A. No power, how great soever, can force men to change their opinions.

169. *Q.* Do they consider the post-office as a tax, or as a regulation?

A. Not as a tax, but as a regulation and conveniency; every assembly encouraged it, and supported it in its infancy, by grants of money, which they would not otherwise have done; and the people have always paid the postage.

170. *Q.* When did you receive the instructions you mentioned?

A. I brought them with me, when I came to England, about fifteen months since.

171. *Q.* When did you communicate that instruction to the minister?

A. Soon after my arrival, while the stamping of America was under consideration, and before the bill was brought in.

172. *Q.* Would it be most for the interest of Great Britain, to employ the hands of Virginia in tobacco, or in manufactures?

A. In tobacco, to be sure.

173. *Q.* What used to be the pride of the Americans?

A. To indulge in the fashions and manufactures of Great Britain.

174. *Q.* What is now their pride?

A. To wear their old clothes over again, till they can make new ones.

Domestic Matters

To his wife. London, 6 April, 1766.

As THE Stamp Act is at length repealed, I am willing you should have a new gown, which you may suppose I did not send sooner, as I knew you would not like to be finer than your neighbours, unless in a gown of your own spinning. Had the trade between the two countries totally ceased, it was a comfort to me to recollect, that I had once been clothed from head to foot in woollen and linen of my wife's manufacture, that I never was prouder of any dress in my life, and that she and her daughter might do it again if it was necessary. I told the Parliament, that it was my opinion, before the old clothes of the Americans were worn out, they might have new ones of their own making. I have sent you a fine piece of Pompadour satin, fourteen yards, cost eleven shillings a yard; a silk *negligée* and petticoat of brocaded lutestring for my dear Sally, with two dozen gloves, four bottles of lavender water, and two little reels. The reels are to screw on the edge of the table, when she would wind silk or thread. The skein is to be put over them, and winds better than if held in two hands. There is also a gimcrack corkscrew, which you must get some brother gimcrack to show you the use of. In the chest is a parcel of books for my friend Mr. Coleman, and another for cousin Colbert. Pray did he receive those I sent him before? I send you also a box with three fine cheeses. Perhaps a bit of them may be left when I come home. Mrs. Stevenson has been very diligent and serviceable in getting these things together for you, and presents her best respects, as does her daughter, to both you and Sally.

To his wife. London, 22 June, 1767.

It seems now as if I should stay here another winter, and therefore I must leave it to your judgment to act in the affair of our daughter's match, as shall seem best.* If you think it a suitable one, I suppose the sooner it is completed the better. In that case I would advise, that you do not make an expensive feasting wedding, but conduct every thing with frugality and economy, which our circumstances now require to be observed in all our expenses. For, since my partnership with Mr. Hall is expired, a great source of our income is cut off; and, if I should lose the postoffice, which, among the many changes here, is far from being unlikely, we should be reduced to our rents and interest of money for a subsistence, which will by no means afford the chargeable housekeeping and entertainments we have been used to.

For my own part, I live here as frugally as possible not to be destitute of the comforts of life, making no dinners for anybody and contenting myself with a single dish when I dine at home; and yet such is the dearness of living here in every article, that my expenses amaze me. I see, too, by the sums you have received in my absence, that yours are very great; and I am very sensible that your situation naturally brings you a great many visitors, which occasions an expense not easily to be avoided, especially when one has been long in the practice and habit of it. But, when people's incomes are lessened, if they cannot proportionably lessen their outgoings, they must come to poverty. If we were young enough to begin business again, it might be another matter; but I doubt we are past it, and business not well managed ruins one faster than no business. In short, with frugality and prudent care we may subsist decently on what we have, and leave it entire to our children; but without such care we shall not be able to keep it together; it will melt away like butter in the sunshine, and we may live long enough to feel the miserable consequences of our indiscretion.

I know very little of the gentleman or his character, nor can I at this distance. I hope his expectations are not great of any fortune to be had with our daughter before our death. I can only say, that, if he proves a good husband to her and a good son to me, he shall find me as good a father as I can be; but at present, I suppose you would agree with me, that we cannot do more than fit her out handsomely in clothes and furniture, not exceeding in the whole five hundred pounds of value. For the rest, they must depend, as you and I did, on their own industry and care, as what remains in our hands will be barely sufficient for our support, and not enough for them when it comes to be divided at our decease.

I suppose the blue room is too blue, the wood being of the same color with the paper, and so looks too dark. I would have you finish it as soon as

*Sally Franklin married Richard Bache, October 29, 1767.

you can, thus; paint the wainscot a dead white; paper the walls blue, and tack the gilt border round just above the surbase and under the cornice. If the paper is not equally colored when pasted on, let it be brushed over again with the same color, and let the *papier mâché* musical figures be tacked to the middle of the ceiling. When this is done, I think it will look very well.

I am glad to hear that Sally keeps up and increases the number of her friends. The best wishes of a fond father for her happiness always attend her.

Journey in France

To Miss Mary Stevenson. Paris, 14 September, 1767.

SOON AFTER I left you in that agreeable society at Bromley, I took the resolution of making a trip with Sir John Pringle into France. We set out on the 28th past. All the way to Dover we were furnished with postchaises, hung so as to lean forward, the top coming down over one's eyes, like a hood, as if to prevent one's seeing the country; which being one of my great pleasures, I was engaged in perpetual disputes with the innkeepers, ostlers, and postilions, about getting the straps taken up a hole or two before, and let down as much behind, they insisting that the chaise leaning forward was an ease to the horses, and that the contrary would kill them. I suppose the chaise leaning forward looks to them like a willingness to go forward, and that its hanging back shows reluctance. They added other reasons, that were no reasons at all, and made me, as upon a hundred other occasions, almost wish that mankind had never been endowed with a reasoning faculty, since they know so little how to make use of it, and so often mislead themselves by it, and that they had been furnished with a good sensible instinct instead of it.

At Dover, the next morning, we embarked for Calais with a number of passengers, who had never before been at sea. They would previously make a hearty breakfast, because, if the wind should fail, we might not get over till supper time. Doubtless they thought, that, when they had paid for their breakfast, they had a right to it, and that, when they had swallowed it, they were sure of it. But they had scarce been out half an hour, before the sea laid claim to it, and they were obliged to deliver it up. So that it seems there are uncertainties, even beyond those between the cup and the lip. If ever you go to sea, take my advice, and live sparingly a day or two beforehand. The sickness, if any, will be lighter and sooner over. We got to Calais that evening.

Various impositions we suffered from boatmen, porters, and the like, on both sides the water. I know not which are most rapacious, the English or French, but the latter have, with their knavery, most politeness.

The roads we found equally good with ours in England, in some places paved with smooth stones, like our new streets, for many miles together, and rows of trees on each side, and yet there are no turnpikes. But then the poor peasants complained to us grievously, that they were obliged to work upon the roads full two months in the year, without being paid for their labor. Whether this is truth, or whether, like Englishmen, they grumble, cause or no cause, I have not yet been able fully to inform myself.

The women we saw at Calais, on the road, at Boulogne, and in the inns and villages, were generally of dark complexions; but arriving at Abbeville we found a sudden change, a multitude of both women and men in that place appearing remarkably fair. Whether this is owing to a small colony of spinners, wool-combers, and weavers, brought hither from Holland with the woollen manufactory about sixty years ago, or to their being less exposed to the sun, than in other places, their business keeping them much within doors, I know not. Perhaps, as in some other cases, different causes may club in producing the effect, but the effect itself is certain. Never was I in a place of greater industry, wheels and looms going in every house.

As soon as we left Abbeville, the swarthiness returned. I speak generally; for here are some fair women at Paris, who, I think, are not whitened by art. As to rouge, they don't pretend to imitate nature in laying it on. There is no gradual diminution of the color, from the full bloom in the middle of the cheek to the faint tint near the sides, nor does it show itself differently in different faces. I have not had the honor of being at any lady's toilette to see how it is laid on, but I fancy I can tell you how it is or may be done. Cut a hole of three inches diameter in a piece of paper; place it on the side of your face in such a manner, as that the top of the hole may be just under the eye; then, with a brush dipped in the color, paint face and paper together; so when the paper is taken off, there will remain a round patch of red exactly the form of the hole. This is the mode, from the actresses on the stage upwards through all ranks of ladies to the princesses of the blood; but it stops there, the Queen not using it, having in the serenity, complacence, and benignity, that shine so eminently in, or rather through her countenance, sufficient beauty, though now an old woman, to do extremely well without it.

You see I speak of the Queen as if I had seen her; and so I have, for you must know I have been at court. We went to Versailles last Sunday, and had the honor of being presented to the King; he spoke to both of us very graciously and very cheerfully, is a handsome man, has a very lively look, and appears younger than he is. In the evening we were at the *Grand Couvert*, where the family sup in public. The table was half a hollow square, the service gold. When either made a sign for drink, the word was given by one of the waiters; *A boire pour le Roi*, or *A boire pour la Reine*. Then two persons came from within, the one with wine and the other with water in *carafes;* each drank a little glass of what he brought, and then put both the *carafes* with a glass on a salver, and then presented it. Their distance from each other was such, as that other chairs might have been placed between any two of them. An officer of the court brought us up through the crowd of spectators, and placed Sir John so as to stand between the Queen and Madame Victoire. The King talked a good deal to Sir John, asking many questions about our royal family; and did me too the honor of taking some notice of me; that is saying enough; for I would not have you think me so much pleased with this King and Queen, as to have a whit less regard than I used to have for ours. No Frenchman shall go beyond me in thinking my own King and Queen the very best in the world, and the most amiable.

Versailles has had infinite sums laid out in building it and supplying it with water. Some say the expenses exceeded eighty millions sterling. The range of buildings is immense; the garden-front most magnificent, all of hewn stone; the number of statues, figures, urns, &c., in marble and bronze of exquisite workmanship, is beyond conception. But the water-works are out of repair, and so is a great part of the front next the town, looking with its shabby, half-brick walls, and broken windows, not much better than the houses in Durham Yard. There is, in short, both at Versailles and Paris, a prodigious mixture of magnificence and negligence, with every kind of elegance except that of cleanliness, and what we call *tidiness*. Though I must do Paris the justice to say, that in two points of cleanliness they exceed us. The water they drink, though from the river, they render as pure as that of the best spring, by filtering it through cisterns filled with sand; and the streets with constant sweeping are fit to walk in, though there is no paved footpath. Accordingly, many well dressed people are constantly seen walking in them. The crowd of coaches and chairs for this reason is not so great. Men, as well as women, carry umbrellas in their hands, which they extend in case of rain or too much sun; and, a man with an umbrella not taking up more than three foot square, or nine square feet of the street, when, if in a coach, he would take up two hundred and forty square feet, you can easily conceive, that, though the streets here are narrow, they may be much less encumbered. They are extremely well paved, and the stones, being generally cubes, when worn on one side, may be turned and become new.

The civilities we everywhere receive give us the strongest impressions of the French politeness. It seems to be a point settled here universally, that strangers are to be treated with respect; and one has just the same deference shown one here by being a stranger, as in England by being a lady. The custom-house officers at Port St. Denis, as we entered Paris, were about to seize two dozen of excellent Bordeaux wine given us at Boulogne, and which we brought with us; but, as soon as they found we were strangers, it was immediately remitted on that account. At the Church of Notre Dame, where we went to see a magnificent illumination, with figures, &c., for the deceased Dauphiness, we found an immense crowd, who were kept out by guards; but, the officer being told that we were strangers from England, he immediately admitted us, accompanied and showed us every thing. Why don't we practise this urbanity to Frenchmen? Why should they be allowed to outdo us in any thing?

Here is an exhibition of painting, like ours in London, to which multitudes flock daily. I am not connoisseur enough to judge which has most merit. Every night, Sundays not excepted, here are plays or operas; and, though the weather has been hot, and the houses full, one is not incommoded by the heat so much as with us in winter. They must have some way of changing the air, that we are not acquainted with. I shall inquire into it.

Travelling is one way of lengthening life, at least in appearance. It is but about a fortnight since we left London, but the variety of scenes we have gone through makes it seem equal to six months living in one place. Perhaps I have suffered a greater change, too, in my own person, than I could have done in six years at home. I had not been here six days, before my tailor and perruquier had transformed me into a Frenchman. Only think what a figure I make in a little bag-wig and with naked ears! They told me I was become twenty years younger, and looked very gallant.

This letter shall cost you a shilling, and you may consider it cheap, when you reflect, that it has cost me at least fifty guineas to get into the situation, that enables me to write it. Besides, I might, if I had stayed at home, have won perhaps two shillings of you at cribbage. By the way, now I mention cards, let me tell you that quadrille is now out of fashion here, and English whist all the mode at Paris and the court.

And pray look upon it as no small matter, that, surrounded as I am by the glories of the world, and amusements of all sorts, I remember you, and Dolly, and all the dear good folks at Bromley. It is true, I cannot help it, but must and ever shall remember you all with pleasure.

Newspaper Libels

To William Franklin. London, 25 Nov., 1767.

I THINK the New Yorkers have been very discreet in forbearing to write and publish against the late act of Parliament. I wish the Boston people had been as quiet, since Governor Bernard has sent over all their violent papers to the ministry, and wrote them word that he daily expected a rebellion. He did indeed afterwards correct this extravagance, by writing again, that he now understood those papers were approved by few, and disliked by all the sober, sensible people of the province. A certain noble Lord expressed himself to me with some disgust and contempt of Bernard on this occasion, saying he ought to have known his people better, than to impute to the whole country sentiments, that perhaps are only scribbled by some madman in a garret. . . .

At the same time that we Americans wish not to be judged of, in the gross, by particular papers written by anonymous scribblers and published in the colonies, it would be well if we could avoid falling into the same mistake in America, in judging of ministers here by the libels printed against them. The enclosed is a very abusive one, in which if there is any foundation of truth, it can only be in the insinuation contained in the words *"after eleven adjournments,"* that they are too apt to postpone business; but, if they have given any occasion for this reflection, there are reasons and circumstances that may be urged in their excuse.

It gives me pleasure to hear, that the people of the other colonies are not insensible of the zeal, with which I occasionally espouse their respective interests, as well as the interests of the whole. I shall continue to do so as long as I reside here and am able.

American Food

To his wife. London, 13 Feb., 1768.

I RECEIVED your kind letter by Captain Story, of November 19th, and a subsequent one by Captain Falconer without date. I have received also the Indian and buckwheat meal, that they brought from you, with the apples, cranberries, and nuts, for all which I thank you. They all prove good, and the apples were particularly welcome to me and my friends, as there happens to be scarce any of any kind in England this year. We are much obliged to the captains, who are so good as to bring these things for us, without charging any thing for their trouble. . . .

P. S. I forgot to tell you that a certain very great lady, the best woman in England, was graciously pleased to accept some of your nuts, and to say they were excellent. This is to yourself only.

The following note explains this postscript:
"Dr. Franklin presents his respectful compliments to Lord Bathurst, with some American nuts; and to Lady Bathurst with some American apples; which he prays they will accept as a tribute from that country, small indeed, but *voluntary*."

Colonial Problems

To William Franklin. London, 13 March, 1768.

THE PURPOSE of settling the new colonies seems at present to be dropped, the change of American administration not appearing favorable to it. There seems rather to be an inclination to abandon the posts in the back country, as more expensive than useful; but counsels are so continually fluctuating here, that nothing can be depended on. . . .

I know not what the Boston people mean by the "subordination" they acknowledge in their Assembly to Parliament, while they deny its power to make laws for them, nor what bounds the Farmer sets to the power he acknowledges in Parliament to "regulate the trade of the colonies," it being difficult to draw lines between duties for regulation and those for revenue; and, if the Parliament is to be the judge, it seems to me that establishing such principles of distinction will amount to little.

The more I have thought and read on the subject, the more I find myself confirmed in opinion, that no middle doctrine can be well maintained, I mean not clearly with intelligible arguments. Something might be made of either of the extremes; that Parliament has a power to make *all laws* for us, or that it has a power to make *no laws* for us; and I think the arguments for the latter more numerous and weighty, than those for the former. Supposing that doctrine established, the colonies would then be so many separate states, only subject to the same king, as England and Scotland were before the union. And then the question would be, whether a union like that with Scotland would or would not be advantageous to *the whole*. I should have no doubt of the affirmative, being fully persuaded that it would be best for *the whole*, and that though particular parts might find particular disadvantages in it, they would find greater advantages in the security arising to every part from the increased strength of the whole. But such union is not likely to take place, while the nature of our present relation is so little understood on both sides of the water, and sentiments concerning it remain so widely different. . . .

Mr. Grenville complained in the House, that the governors of New Jersey, New Hampshire, East and West Florida, had none of them obeyed the orders sent them, to give an account of the manufactures carried on in their respective provinces. Upon hearing this, I went after the House was up, and got a sight of the reports made by the other governors. They are all much in the same strain, that there are no manufactures of any consequence; in Massachusetts a little coarse woollen only, made in families for their own wear; glass and linen have been tried and failed. Rhode Island, Connecticut, and New York much the same. Pennsylvania has tried a linen manufactory, but it is dropped, it being imported cheaper; there is a glasshouse in Lancaster county, but it makes only a little coarse ware for the country neighbours. Maryland is clothed all with English manufactures. Virginia the same, except that in their families they spin a little cotton of their own growing. South Carolina and Georgia none. All speak of the dearness of labor, that makes manufactures impracticable. Only the governor of North Carolina parades with a large manufacture in his country, that may be useful to Britain, of *pine boards;* they having fifty sawmills on one river.

These accounts are very satisfactory here, and induce the Parliament to despise and take no notice of the Boston resolutions. I wish you would send your account before the meeting of next Parliament. You have only to report a glasshouse for coarse window glass and bottles, and some domestic manufactures of linen and woollen for family use, that do not half clothe the inhabitants, all the finer goods coming from England and the like. I believe you will be puzzled to find any other, though I see great puffs in the papers.

The Parliament is up, and the nation in a ferment with the new elections. Great complaints are made that the natural interests of country gentlemen in their neighbouring boroughs is overborne by the moneyed interests of the new people, who have got sudden fortunes in the Indies, or as contractors. *Four thousand pounds* is now the *market price* for a borough. In short, this whole venal nation is now at market, will be sold for about two millions, and might be bought out of the hands of the present bidders (if he would offer half a million more) by the very Devil himself.

English Politics

To Joseph Galloway. London, 13 March, 1768.

THE old Parliament is gone, and its enemies now find themselves at liberty to abuse it. I enclose you a pamphlet, published the very hour of its prorogation. All the members are now in their counties and boroughs among their drunken electors; much confusion and disorder in many places, and such profusion of money as never was known before on any similar occasion. The first instance of bribery to be chosen a member, taken notice of on the journals, is no longer ago than Queen Elizabeth's time, when the being sent to Parliament was looked upon as a troublesome service, and therefore not sought after. It is said that such a one, "being a simple man, and conceiving it might be of some advantage to him, had given *four pounds* to the mayor and corporation, that they might choose him to serve them in Parliament."

The price is monstrously risen since that time, for it is now no less than *four thousand pounds!* It is thought, that near two millions will be spent this election; but those, who understand figures and act by computation, say the crown has *two millions a year in places and pensions to dispose of,* and it is well worth while to engage in such a seven years' lottery, though all that have tickets should not get prizes.

To William Franklin. London, 16 April, 1768.

SINCE MY last, a long one, of March 13th, nothing has been talked or thought of here but elections. There have been amazing contests all over the kingdom, *twenty* or *thirty thousand pounds* of a side spent in several places, and inconceivable mischief done by debauching the people and making them idle, besides the immediate actual mischief done by drunken mad mobs to houses, windows, &c. The scenes have been horrible. London was illuminated two nights running, at the command of the mob, for the success of Wilkes, in the Middlesex election. The second night exceeded any thing of the kind ever seen here on the greatest occasions of rejoicing, as even the small cross-streets, lanes, courts, and other out-of-the-way places were all in a blaze with lights, and the principal streets all night long, as the mobs went round again after two o'clock, and obliged people who had extinguished their candles to light them again. Those who refused had all their windows destroyed. The damage done, and expense of candles, have been computed at fifty thousand pounds. It must have been great, though probably not so much.

The ferment is not yet over, for he has promised to surrender himself to the court next Wednesday, and another tumult is then expected; and what the upshot will be no one can yet foresee. It is really an extraordinary event, to see an outlaw and an exile, of bad personal character, not worth a farthing, come over from France, set himself up as candidate for the capital of the kingdom, miss his election only by being too late in his application, and immediately carrying it for the principal county; the mob (spirited up by numbers of different ballads sung or roared in every street) requiring gentlemen and ladies of all ranks, as they passed in their carriages, to shout for Wilkes and liberty, marking the same words on all their coaches with chalk. . . .

To Joseph Galloway. London, 14 May, 1768.

I RECEIVED your favor of March 31st. It is now, with the messages, in the hands of the minister, so that I cannot be more particular at present in answering it than to say, I should have a melancholy prospect in going home to such public confusion, if I did not leave greater confusion behind me. The newspapers, and my letter of this day to Mr. Ross, will inform you of the miserable situation this country is in. While I am writing, a great mob of coal porters fills the street, carrying a wretch of their business upon poles to be ducked, and otherwise punished at their pleasure, for working at the old wages. All respect to law and government seems to be lost among the common people, who are moreover continually inflamed by seditious scribblers, to trample on authority and every thing that used to keep them in order.

The Parliament is now sitting, but will not continue long together, nor undertake any material business. The court of King's Bench postponed giving sentence against Wilkes on his outlawry till the next term, intimidated, as some say, by his popularity, and willing to get rid of the affair for a time, till it should be seen what the Parliament would conclude as to his membership. The Commons, at least some of them, resent that conduct, which has thrown a burthen on them it might have eased them of, by pillorying or punishing him in some infamous manner, that would have given better ground for expelling him the House. His friends complain of it as a delay of justice, say the court knew the outlawry to be defective, and that they must finally pronounce it void, but would punish him by long confinement. Great mobs of his adherents have assembled before the prison, the guards have fired on them; it is said five or six are killed, and sixteen or seventeen wounded; and some circumstances have attended this military execution, such as its being done by the Scotch regiment, the pursuing a lad, and killing him at his father's house, &c. &c., that exasperate people exceedingly, and more mischief seems brewing. Several of the soldiers are imprisoned. If they are not hanged, it is feared there will be more and greater mobs; and, if they are, that no soldier will assist in suppressing any mob hereafter. The prospect either way is gloomy. It is said the English soldiers cannot be confided in, to act against these mobs, being suspected as rather inclined to favor and join them.

The tumults and disorders, that prevailed here lately, have now pretty well subsided. Wilkes's outlawry is reversed, but he is sentenced to twenty-two months imprisonment, and *one thousand pounds'* fine, which his friends, who feared he would be pilloried, seem rather satisfied with. The importation of corn, a pretty good hay harvest, now near over, and the prospect of plenty from a fine crop of wheat, make the poor more patient, in hopes of an abatement in the price of provisions; so that, unless want of employment by the failure of American orders should distress them, they are like to be tolerably quiet.

On Early Marriage

To John Alleyne. Craven St., 9 August, 1768.

You DESIRE, you say, my impartial thoughts on the subject of an early marriage, by way of answer to the numberless objections that have been made by numerous persons to your own. You may remember, when you consulted me on the occasion, that I thought youth on both sides to be no objection. Indeed, from the marriages that have fallen under my observation, I am rather inclined to think, that early ones stand the best chance of happiness. The temper and habits of the young are not become so stiff and uncomplying, as when more advanced in life; they form more easily to each other, and hence many occasions of disgust are removed. And, if youth has less of that prudence, which is necessary to manage a family, yet the parents and elder friends of young married persons are generally at hand to afford their advice, which amply supplies that defect; and, by early marriage, youth is sooner formed to regular and useful life; and possibly some of those accidents or connexions, that might have injured the constitution, or reputation, or both, are thereby happily prevented.

Particular circumstances of particular persons may possibly sometimes make it prudent to delay entering into that state; but in general, when nature has rendered our bodies fit for it, the presumption is in nature's favor, that she has not judged amiss in making us desire it. Late marriages are often attended, too, with this further inconvenience, that there is not the same chance that the parents will live to see their offspring educated. "*Late children,*" says the Spanish proverb, "*are early orphans.*" A melancholy reflection to those, whose case it may be! With us in America, marriages are generally in the morning of life; our children are therefore educated and settled in the world by noon; and thus, our business being done, we have an afternoon and evening of cheerful leisure to ourselves; such as our friend at present enjoys. By these early marriages we are blessed with more children; and from the mode among us, founded by nature, every mother suckling and nursing her own child, more of them are raised. Thence the swift progress of population among us, unparalleled in Europe.

In fine, I am glad you are married, and congratulate you most cordially upon it. You are now in the way of becoming a useful citizen; and you have escaped the unnatural state of celibacy for life, the fate of many here, who never intended it, but who, having too long postponed the change of their condition, find at length, that it is too late to think of it, and so live all their lives in a situation that greatly lessens a man's value. An odd volume of a set of books bears not the value of its proportion to the set. What think you of the odd half of a pair of scissors? It cannot well cut any thing; it may possibly serve to scrape a trencher.

Pray make my compliments and best wishes acceptable to your bride. I am old and heavy, or I should ere this have presented them in person. I shall make but small use of the old man's privilege, that of giving advice to younger friends. Treat your wife always with respect; it will procure respect to you, not only from her, but from all that observe it. Never use a slighting expression to her, even in jest, for slights in jest, after frequent bandyings, are apt to end in angry earnest. Be studious in your profession, and you will be learned. Be industrious and frugal, and you will be rich. Be sober and temperate, and you will be healthy. Be in general virtuous, and you will be happy. At least, you will, by such conduct, stand the best chance for such consequences. I pray God to bless you both; being ever your affectionate friend.

Family Problem

To Miss Mary Stevenson. London, Oct., 1768.

I SEE very clearly the unhappiness of your situation, and that it does not arise from any fault in you. I pity you most sincerely. I should not, however, have thought of giving you advice on this occasion, if you had not requested it, believing, as I do, that your own good sense is more than sufficient to direct you in every point of duty to others and yourself. If, then, I should advise you to any thing, that may be contrary to your own opinion, do not imagine, that I shall condemn you if you do not follow such advice. I shall only think, that, from a better acquaintance with circumstances, you form a better judgment of what is fit for you to do.

Now, I conceive with you, that ——, both from her affection to you, and from the long habit of having you with her, would really be miserable without you. Her temper, perhaps, was never of the best; and, when that is the case, age seldom mends it. Much of her unhappiness must arise from thence; and, since wrong turns of mind, when confirmed by time, are almost as little in our power to cure, as those of the body, I think with you, that her case is a compassionable one.

If she had, through her own imprudence, brought on herself any grievous sickness, I know you would think it your duty to attend and nurse her with filial tenderness, even were your own health to be endangered by it. Your apprehension, therefore, is right, that it may be your duty to live with her, though inconsistent with your happiness and your interest; but this can only mean present interest and present happiness; for I think your future, greater, and more lasting interest and happiness will arise from the reflection, that you have done your duty, and from the high rank you will ever hold in the esteem of all that know you, for having persevered in doing that duty under so many and great discouragements.

My advice, then, must be, that you return to her as soon as the time proposed for your visit is expired; and that you continue, by every means in your power, to make the remainder of her days as comfortable to her as possible. Invent amusements for her; be pleased when she accepts of them, and patient when she perhaps peevishly rejects them. I know this is hard, but I think you are equal to it; not from any servility of temper, but from abundant goodness. In the mean time, all your friends, sensible of your present uncomfortable situation, should endeavour to ease your burden, by acting in concert with you, and to give her as many opportunities as possible of enjoying the pleasures of society, for your sake.

Nothing is more apt to sour the temper of aged people, than the apprehension that they are neglected; and they are extremely apt to entertain such suspicions. It was therefore that I proposed asking her to be of our late party; but, your mother disliking it, the motion was dropped, as some others have been, by my too great easiness, contrary to my judgment. Not but that I was sensible her being with us might have lessened our pleasure, but I hoped it might have prevented you some pain.

In fine, nothing can contribute to true happiness, that is inconsistent with duty; nor can a course of action, conformable to it, be finally without an ample reward. For God governs; and he is *good*. I pray him to direct you; and, indeed, you will never be without his direction, if you humbly ask it, and show yourself always ready to obey it. Farewell, *my* dear friend, and believe me ever sincerely and affectionately *yours*.

Hope for Peace

To a friend. London, 28 Nov., 1768.

YOUR SENTIMENTS of the importance of the present dispute between Great Britain and the colonies appear to me extremely just. There is nothing I wish for more, than to see it amicably and equitably settled.

But Providence will bring about its own ends by its own means; and if it intends the downfall of a nation, that nation will be so blinded by its pride and other passions, as not to see its danger, or how its fall may be prevented.

Being born and bred in one of the countries, and having lived long and made many agreeable connexions of friendship in the other, I wish all prosperity to both; but I have talked and written so much and so long on the subject, that my acquaintance are weary of hearing, and the public of reading any more of it, which begins to make me weary of talking and writing; especially as I do not find that I have gained any point, in either country, except that of rendering myself suspected by my impartiality; in England, of being too much an American, and in America, of being too much an Englishman. Your opinion, however, weighs with me, and encourages me to try one effort more, in a full, though concise statement of facts, accompanied with arguments drawn from those facts; to be published about the meeting of Parliament, after the holidays. If any good may be done I shall rejoice; but at present I almost despair.

Have you ever seen the barometer so low as of late? The 22d instant, mine was at 28.41, and yet the weather fine and fair.

Virginia Currency

To Lord Kames. London, 1 January, 1769.

I am glad to find you are turning your thoughts to political subjects, and particularly to those of money, taxes, manufactures, and commerce. The world is yet much in the dark on these important points; and many mischievous mistakes are continually made in the management of them. Most of our acts of Parliament for regulating them are, in my opinion, little better than political blunders, owing to ignorance of the science, or to the designs of crafty men, who mislead the legislature, proposing something under the specious appearance of public good, while the real aim is, to sacrifice that to their own private interest. I hope a good deal of light may be thrown on these subjects by your sagacity and acuteness. I only wish I could first have engaged you in discussing the weighty points in dispute between Britain and the colonies. But the long letter I wrote you for that purpose, in February or March, 1767, perhaps never reached your hand, for I have not yet had a word from you in answer to it.

The act you inquire about had its rise thus. During the war, Virginia issued great sums of paper money for the payment of their troops, to be sunk in a number of years by taxes. The British merchants trading thither received these bills in payment for their goods, purchasing tobacco with them to send home. The crop of tobacco one or two years falling short, the factors, who were desirous of making a speedy remittance, sought to pay, with the paper money, bills of exchange. The number of bidders for these bills raised the price of them thirty per cent above par. This was deemed so much loss to the purchasers, and supposed to arise from a depreciation of the paper money. The merchants, on this supposition, founded a complaint against that currency to the Board of Trade. Lord Hillsborough, then at the head of that Board, took up the matter strongly, and drew a report, which was presented to the King in Council, against all paper currency in the colonies. And, though there was no complaint against it from any merchants, but those trading to Virginia, all those trading to the other colonies being satisfied with its operation, yet the ministry proposed, and the Parliament came into the making a general act, forbidding all future emissions of paper money, that should be a legal tender in any colony whatever.

The Virginia merchants have since had the mortification to find, that, if they had kept the paper money a year or two, the abovementioned loss would have been avoided; for, as soon as tobacco became more plenty, and of course bills of exchange also, the exchange fell as much as it before had risen. I was in America when the act passed. On my return to England, I got the merchants trading to New York, Pennsylvania, Maryland, Virginia, &c., to meet, to consider and join in an application to have the restraining act repealed. To prevent this application, a copy was put into the merchants' hands of Lord Hillsborough's report, by which it was supposed they might be convinced, that such an application would be wrong. They desired my sentiments on it, which I gave in the paper I send you enclosed. I have no copy by me of the report itself; but in my answer you will see a faithful abridgment of all the arguments or reasons it contained. Lord Hillsborough has read my answer, but says he is not convinced by it, and adheres to his former opinion. We know nothing can be done in Parliament, that the minister is absolutely against, and therefore we let that point rest for the present. And, as I think a scarcity of money will work with our other present motives for lessening our fond extravagance in the use of the superfluous manufactures of this country, which unkindly grudges us the enjoyment of common rights, and will tend to lead us naturally into industry and frugality, I am grown more indifferent about the repeal of the act, and, if my countrymen will be advised by me, we shall never ask it again.

There is not, as I conceive, any new principle wanting, to account for the operations of air, and all the affections of smoke in rooms and chimneys; but it is difficult to advise in particular cases at a distance, where one cannot have all the circumstances under view. If two rooms and chimneys are "perfectly similar" in situation, dimension, and all other circumstances, it seems not possible, that, "in summer, when no fire had been in either of them for some months, and in a calm day, a current of air should at the same time go up the chimney of the one, and down the chimney of the other." But such difference may and often does take place, from circumstances in which they are dissimilar, and which dissimilarity is not very obvious to those who have little studied the subject. As to your particular case, which you describe to be, that, "after a whole day's fire, which must greatly heat the vent, yet, when the fire becomes low, so as not to emit any smoke, neighbour smoke immediately begins to descend and fill the room"; this, if not owing to particular winds, may be occasioned by a stronger fire in another room, communicating with yours by a door, the outer air being excluded by the outward door's being shut, whereby the stronger fire finds it easier to be supplied with air down through the vent, in which the weak fire is, and thence through the communicating door, than through the crevices. If this is the circumstance, you will find that a supply of air is only wanting, that may be sufficient for both vents. If this is not the circumstance, send me, if you please, a complete description of your room, its situation, and connexion, and possibly I may form a better judgment. Though I imagine your Professor of Natural Philosophy, Mr. Russel, or Mr. George Clark, may give you as good advice on the subject as I can. But I shall take the liberty of sending you, by the first convenient opportunity, a collection of my philosophical papers lately published, in which you will find something more relating to the motions of air in chimneys.

To commence a conversation with you on your new project, I have thrown some of my present sentiments into the concise form of aphorisms, to be examined between us, if you please, and rejected or corrected and confirmed, as we shall find most proper. I send them enclosed.

Farm Problem

To the same. London, 21 Feb., 1769.

I RECEIVED your excellent paper on the preferable use of oxen in agriculture, and have put it in the way of being communicated to the public here. I have observed in America, that the farmers are more thriving in those parts of the country where horned cattle are used, than in those where the labor is done by horses. The latter are said to require twice the quantity of land to maintain them; and after all are not good to eat, at least we do not think them so. Here is a waste of land that might afford subsistence for so many of the human species. Perhaps it was for this reason, that the Hebrew lawgiver, having promised that the children of Israel should be as numerous as the sands of the sea, not only took care to secure the health of individuals by regulating their diet, that they might be fitter for producing children, but also forbade their using horses, as those animals would lessen the quantity of subsistence for men. Thus we find, when they took any horses from their enemies, they destroyed them; and in the commandments, where the labor of the ox and ass is mentioned, and forbidden on the Sabbath, there is no mention of the horse, probably because they were to have none. And, by the great armies suddenly raised in that small territory they inhabited, it appears to have been very full of people.

Food is *always* necessary to *all*, and much the greatest part of the labor of mankind is employed in raising provisions for the mouth. Is not this kind of labor, then, the fittest to be the standard by which to measure the values of all other labor, and consequently of all other things whose value depends on the labor of making or procuring them? May not even gold and silver be thus valued? If the labor of the farmer, in producing a bushel of wheat, be equal to the labor of the miner in producing an ounce of silver, will not the bushel of wheat just measure the value of the ounce of silver? The miner must eat; the farmer indeed can live without the ounce of silver, and so perhaps will have some advantage in settling the price. But these discussions

I leave to you, as being more able to manage them; only, I will send you a little scrap I wrote some time since on the laws prohibiting foreign commodities.

I congratulate you on your election as president of your Edinburgh Society. I think I formerly took notice to you in conversation, that I thought there had been some similarity in our fortunes, and the circumstances of our lives. This is a fresh instance, for, by letters just received, I find that I was about the same time chosen president of our American Philosophical Society, established at Philadelphia.

I have sent by sea, to the care of Mr. Alexander, a little box, containing a few copies of the late edition of my books, for my friends in Scotland. One is directed for you, and one for your Society, which I beg that you and they would accept as a small mark of my respect.

On Fashions

To Samuel Cooper. London, 27 April, 1769.

THE Parliament remain fixed in their resolution not to repeal the duty acts this session, and will rise next Tuesday. I hope my country folks will remain as fixed in their resolutions of industry and frugality, till these acts are repealed. And, if I could be sure of that, I should almost wish them never to be repealed; being persuaded, that we shall reap more solid and extensive advantages from the steady practice of those two great virtues, than we can possibly suffer damage from all the duties the Parliament of this kingdom can levy on us. They flatter themselves you cannot long subsist without their manufactures. They believe you have not virtue enough to persist in such agreements. They imagine the colonies will differ among themselves, deceive and desert one another, and quietly one after the other submit to the yoke, and return to the use of British fineries. They think, that, though the men may be contented with homespun stuffs, the women will never get the better of their vanity and fondness for English modes and gewgaws. The ministerial people all talk in this strain, and many even of the merchants. I have ventured to assert, that they will all find themselves mistaken; and I rely so much on the spirit of my country, as to be confident I shall not be found a false prophet, though at present not believed.

Pretty Good World

To Mrs. Jane Mecom. London, March 1, 1766.

As TO the reports you mention, that are spread to my disadvantage, I give myself as little concern about them as possible. I have often met with such treatment from people, that I was all the while endeavouring to serve. At other times I have been extolled extravagantly, where I had little or no merit. These are the operations of nature. It sometimes is cloudy, it rains, it hails; again it is clear and pleasant, and the sun shines on us. Take one thing with another, and the world is a pretty good sort of a world, and it is our duty to make the best of it, and be thankful. One's true happiness depends more upon one's own judgment of one's self, or a consciousness of rectitude in action and intention, and the approbation of those few, who judge impartially, than upon the applause of the unthinking, undiscerning multitude, who are apt to cry *Hosanna* to-day, and to-morrow, *Crucify him.*

On Silkworms

To Cadwallader Evans. London, 7 Sept., 1769.

BY A ship just sailed from hence (the captain a stranger, whose name I have forgotten), I send you a late French treatise on the management of silkworms. It is said to be the best hitherto published, being written in the silk country by a gentleman well acquainted with the whole affair. It seems to me to be, like many other French writings, rather too much drawn out in words; but some extracts from it, of the principal directions, might be of use, if you would translate and publish them. I think the bounty is offered for silk from all the colonies in general. I will send you the act. But I believe it must be wound from the cocoons, and sent over in skeins. The cocoons would spoil on the passage, by the dead worm corrupting and staining the silk. A public filature should be set up for winding them there; or every family should learn to wind their own. In Italy they are all brought to market, from the neighbouring country, and bought up by those that keep the filatures. In Sicily each family winds its own silk, for the sake of having the remains to card and spin for family use. If some provision were made by the Assembly for promoting the growth of mulberry trees in all parts of the province, the culture of silk might afterwards follow easily. For the great discouragement to breeding worms at first is the difficulty of getting leaves and the being obliged to go far for them.

There is no doubt with me but that it might succeed in our country. It is the happiest of all inventions for clothing. Wool uses a good deal of land to produce it, which, if employed in raising corn, would afford much more subsistence for man, than the mutton amounts to. Flax and hemp require good land, impoverish it, and at the same time permit it to produce no food at all. But mulberry trees may be planted in hedgerows on walks or avenues, or for shade near a house, where nothing else is wanted to grow. The food for the worms, which produce the silk, is in the air, and the ground under the trees may still produce grass, or some other vegetable good for man or beast. Then the wear of silken garments continues so much longer, from the strength of the materials, as to give it greatly the preference. Hence it is that the most populous of all countries, China, clothes its inhabitants with silk, while it feeds them plentifully, and has besides a vast quantity both raw and manufactured to spare for exportation. Raw silk here, in skeins well wound, sells from twenty to twenty-five shillings per pound; but, if badly wound, is not worth five shillings. Well wound is, when the threads are made to cross each other every way in the skein, and only touch where they cross. Badly wound is, when they are laid parallel to each other; for so they are glued together, break in unwinding them, and take a vast deal of time more than the other, by losing the end every time the thread breaks. When once you can raise plenty of silk, you may have manufactures enough from hence.

Colonial Trade

To a friend in America. London, 18 March, 1770.

YOUR VERY judicious letter of November 26th, being communicated by me to some member of Parliament, was handed about among them, so that it was some time before I got it again into my hands. It had due weight with several, and was of considerable use. You will see that I printed it at length in the London *Chronicle*, with the merchants' letter. When the American affairs came to be debated in the House of Commons, the majority, notwithstanding all the weight of ministerial influence, was only sixty-two for continuing the whole last act; and would not have been so large, nay, I think the repeal would have been carried, but that the ministry were persuaded by Governor Bernard, and some lying letters said to be from Boston, that the associations not to import were all breaking to pieces, that America was in the greatest distress for want of the goods, that we could not possibly subsist any longer without them, and must of course submit to any terms Parliament should think fit to impose upon us. This, with the idle notion of the dignity and sovereignty of Parliament, which they are so fond of, and imagine will be endangered by any further concessions, prevailed, I know, with many, to vote with the ministry, who, otherwise, on account of the commerce, wish to see the difference accommodated.

But, though both the Duke of Grafton and Lord North were and are, in my opinion, rather inclined to satisfy us, yet the Bedford party are so violent against us, and so prevalent in the council, that more moderate measures could not take place. This party never speak of us but with evident malice; "rebels" and "traitors" are the best names they can afford us, and I believe they only wish for a colorable pretence and occasion of ordering the soldiers to make a massacre among us.

On the other hand, the Rockingham and Shelburne people, with Lord Chatham's friends, are disposed to favor us, if they were again in power, which at present they are not like to be; though they, too, would be for keeping up the claim of Parliamentary sovereignty, but without exercising it in any mode of taxation. Besides these, we have for sincere friends and well-wishers the body of Dissenters generally throughout England, with many others, not to mention Ireland and all the rest of Europe, who, from various motives, join in applauding the spirit of liberty, with which we have claimed and insisted on our privileges, and wish us success, but whose suffrage cannot have much weight in our affairs.

The merchants here were at length prevailed on to present a petition, but they moved slowly, and some of them, I thought, reluctantly; perhaps from a despair of success, the city not being much in favor with the court at present. The manufacturing towns absolutely refused to move at all; some pretending to be offended with our attempting to manufacture for ourselves; others saying, that they had employment enough, and that our trade was of little importance to them, whether we continued or refused it. Those, who began a little to feel the effects of our forbearing to purchase, were persuaded to be quiet by the ministerial people, who gave out, that certain advices were received of our beginning to break our agreements; of our attempts to manufacture proving all abortive and ruining the undertakers; of our distress for want of goods, and dissensions among ourselves, which promised the total defeat of all such kind of combinations, and the prevention of them for the future, if the government were not urged imprudently to repeal the duties. But now that it appears from late and authentic accounts, that agreements continue in full force, that a ship is actually returned from Boston to Bristol with nails and glass (articles that were thought of the utmost necessity), and that the ships, which were waiting here for the determination of Parliament, are actually returning to North America in their ballast, the tone of the manufacturers begins to change, and there is no doubt, that, if we are steady, and persevere in our resolutions, these people will soon begin a clamor, that much pains has hitherto been used to stifle.

In short, it appears to me, that if we do not now persist in this measure till it has had its full effect, it can never again be used on any future occasion with the least prospect of success, and that, if we do persist another year, we shall never afterwards have occasion to use it.

To Samuel Cooper. London, 8 June, 1770.

WITH this I send you two speeches in Parliament on our affairs by a member that you know. The repeal of the whole late act would undoubtedly have been a prudent measure, and I have reason to believe that Lord North was for it, but some of the other ministers could not be brought to agree to it; so the duty on tea, with that obnoxious preamble, remains to continue the dispute. But I think the next session will hardly pass over without repealing them; for the Parliament must finally comply with the sense of the nation.

As to the standing army kept up among us in time of peace, without the consent of our Assemblies, I am clearly of opinion that it is not agreeable to the constitution. Should the King, by the aid of his Parliaments in Ireland and the colonies, raise an army, and bring it into England, quartering it here in time of peace without the consent of the Parliament of Great Britain, I am persuaded he would soon be told, that he had no right so to do, and the nation would ring with clamors against it. I own, that I see no difference in the cases; and, while we continue so many distinct and separate states, our having the same head, or sovereign, the King, will not justify such an invasion of the separate right of each state to be consulted on the establishment of whatever force is proposed to be kept up within its limits, and to give or refuse its consent, as shall appear most for the public good of that state.

That the colonies originally were constituted distinct states, and intended to be continued such, is clear to me from a thorough consideration of their original charters, and the whole conduct of the crown and nation towards them until the restoration. Since that period, the Parliament here has usurped an authority of making laws for them, which before it had not. We have for some time submitted to that usurpation, partly through ignorance and inattention, and partly from our weakness and inability to contend. I hope, when our rights are better understood here, we shall, by prudent and proper conduct, be able to obtain from the equity of this nation a restoration of them. And, in the mean time, I could wish, that such expressions as *the Supreme authority of Parliament, the subordinacy of our Assemblies to the Parliament,* and the like, which in reality mean nothing, if our Assemblies, with the King, have a true legislative authority; I say, I could wish that such expressions were no more seen in our public pieces. They are too strong for compliment, and tend to confirm a claim of subjects in one part of the King's dominions to be sovereigns over their fellow subjects in another part of his dominions, when in truth they have no such right, and their claim is founded only in usurpation, the several states having equal rights and liberties, and being only connected, as England and Scotland were before the union, by having one common sovereign, the King.

To M. Dubourg. London, Oct. 2, 1770.

I SEE with pleasure, that we think pretty much alike on the subject of English America. We of the colonies have never insisted, that we ought to be exempt from contributing to the common expenses necessary to support the prosperity of the empire. We only assert, that, having Parliaments of our own, and not having representatives in that of Great Britain, our Parliaments are the only judges of what we can and what we ought to contribute in this case; and that the English Parliament has no right to take our money without our consent. In fact, the British empire is not a single state; it comprehends many; and, though the Parliament of Great Britain has arrogated to itself the power of taxing the colonies, it has no more right to do so, than it has to tax Hanover. We have the same King, but not the same legislatures.

The dispute between the two countries has already lost England many millions sterling, which it has lost in its commerce, and America has in this respect been a proportionable gainer. This commerce consisted principally of superfluities; objects of luxury and fashion, which we can well do without; and the resolution we have formed of importing no more, till our grievances are redressed, has enabled many of our infant manufactures to take root; and it will not be easy to make our people abandon them in future, even should a connexion more cordial than ever succeed the present troubles.

On Grandmothers

To his wife. London, 3 Oct., 1770.

I AM glad your little grandson recovered so soon of his illness, as I see you are quite in love with him, and that your happiness is wrapped up in his; since your whole long letter is made up of the history of his pretty actions. It was very prudently done of you not to interfere, when his mother thought fit to correct him; which pleased me the more, as I feared, from your fondness of him, that he would be too much humored, and perhaps spoiled. There is a story of two little boys in the street; one was crying bitterly; the other came to him to ask what was the matter; "I have been," says he, "for a pennyworth of vinegar, and I have broke the glass, and spilled the vinegar, and my mother will whip me." "No she won't whip you," says the other. "Indeed, she will," says he. "What," says the other, "have you then got ne'er a grandmother?"

Independence of Office

To Mrs. Jane Mecom. London, 30 Dec., 1770.

As TO the rumor you mention (which was, as Josiah tells me, that I had been deprived of my place in the postoffice on account of a letter I wrote to Philadelphia), it might have this foundation, that some of the ministry had been displeased on my writing such letters, and there were really some thoughts among them of showing that displeasure in that manner. But I had some friends, too, who, unrequested by me, advised the contrary. And my enemies were forced to content themselves with abusing me plentifully in the newspapers, and endeavouring to provoke me to resign. In this they are not likely to succeed, I being deficient in that Christian virtue of resignation. If they would have my office, they must take it.

I have heard of some great man, whose rule it was, with regard to offices, *never to ask for them, and never to refuse them;* to which I have always added, in my own practice, *never to resign them.* As I told my friends, I rose to that office through a long course of service in the inferior degrees of it. Before my time, through bad management, it never produced the salary annexed to it; and, when I received it, no salary was to be allowed, if the office did not produce it. During the first four years it was so far from defraying itself, that it became nine hundred and fifty pounds sterling in debt to me and my colleague. I had been chiefly instrumental in bringing it to its present flourishing state, and therefore thought I had some kind of right to it. I had hitherto executed the duties of it faithfully, and to the perfect satisfaction of my superiors, which I thought was all that should be expected of me on that account. As to the letters complained of, it was true I did write them, and they were written in compliance with another duty, that to my country; a duty quite distinct from that of postmaster.

My conduct in this respect was exactly similar to that I held on a similar occasion but a few years ago, when the then ministry were ready to hug me for the assistance I afforded them in repealing a former revenue act. My sentiments were still the same, that no such acts should be made here for America; or, if made, should as soon as possible be repealed; and I thought it should not be expected of me to change my political opinions every time his Majesty thought fit to change his ministers. This was my language on the occasion; and I have lately heard, that, though I was thought much to blame, it being understood that every man who holds an office should act with the ministry, whether agreeable or not to his own judgment, yet, in consideration of the goodness of my private character (as they were pleased to compliment me), the office was not to be taken from me.

Possibly they may still change their minds, and remove me; but no apprehension of that sort will, I trust, make the least alteration in my political conduct. My rule, in which I have always found satisfaction, is, never to turn aside in public affairs through views of private interest; but to go straight forward in doing what appears to me right at the time, leaving the consequences with Providence. What in my younger days enabled me more easily to walk upright, was, that I had a trade, and that I knew I could live upon little; and thence (never having had views of making a fortune) I was free from avarice, and contented with the plentiful supplies my business afforded me. And now it is still more easy for me to preserve my freedom and integrity, when I consider that I am almost at the end of my journey, and therefore need less to complete the expense of it; and that what I now possess, through the blessing of God, may, with tolerable economy, be sufficient for me (great misfortunes excepted), though I should add nothing more to it by any office or employment whatsoever.

I send you by this opportunity the two books you wrote for. They cost three shillings apiece. When I was first in London, about forty-five years since, I knew a person, who had an opinion something like your author's. Her name was Ilive, a printer's widow. She died soon after I left England, and by her *will* obliged her son to deliver publicly, in Salters' Hall, a solemn discourse, the purport of which was to prove, that this world is the true Hell, or place of punishment for the spirits, who had transgressed in a better state, and were sent here to suffer for their sins in animals of all sorts. It is long since I saw the discourse, which was printed. I think a good deal of

Scripture was cited in it, and that the supposition was, that, though we now remembered nothing of such a preëxistent state, yet after death we might recollect it, and remember the punishments we had suffered, so as to be the better for them; and others, who had not yet offended, might now behold and be warned by our sufferings.

In fact, we see here, that every lower animal has its enemy, with proper inclinations, faculties, and weapons, to terrify, wound, and destroy it; and that men, who are uppermost, are devils to one another; so that, on the established doctrine of the goodness and justice of the great Creator, this apparent state of general and systematical mischief seemed to demand some such supposition as Mrs. Ilive's, to account for it consistently with the honor of the Deity. But our reasoning powers, when employed about what may have been before our existence here, or shall be after it, cannot go far, for want of history and facts. Revelation only can give us the necessary information, and that, in the first of these points especially, has been very sparingly afforded us.

I hope you continue to correspond with your friends at Philadelphia. My love to your children.

English Diplomacy

To Samuel Cooper. London, 5 Feb., 1771.

I wrote to you some weeks since in answer to yours of July and November, expressing my sentiments without the least reserve on points that require free discussion, as I know I can confide in your prudence not to hurt my usefulness here, by making me more obnoxious than I must necessarily be from that known attachment to the American interest, which my duty as well as inclination demands of me.

In the same confidence I send you the enclosed extract from my Journal, containing a late conference between the Secretary* and your friend, in which you will see a little of his temper. It is one of the many instances of his behaviour and conduct, that have given me the very mean opinion I entertain of his abilities and fitness for his station. His character is conceit, wrongheadedness, obstinacy, and passion. Those, who would speak most favorably of him, allow all this; they only add, that he is an honest man, and means well. If that be true, as perhaps it may, I wish him a better place, where only honesty and well-meaning are required, and where his other qualities can do no harm. Had the war taken place, I have reason to believe he would have been removed. He had, I think, some apprehensions of it himself at the time I was with him. I hope, however, that our affairs will not much longer be perplexed and embarrassed by his perverse and senseless management. I have since heard, that his Lordship took great offence at some of my last words, which he calls extremely rude and abusive. He assured a

*Lord Hillsborough.

friend of mine, that they were equivalent to telling him to his face, that the colonies could expect neither favor nor justice during his administration. I find he did not mistake me.

It is true, as you have heard, that some of my letters to America have been echoed back hither; but that has not been the case with any that were written to you. Great umbrage was taken, but chiefly by Lord Hillsborough, who was disposed before to be angry with me, and therefore the inconvenience was the less; and, whatever the consequences are of his displeasure, putting all my offences together, I must bear them as well as I can. Not but that, if there is to be war between us, I shall do my best to defend myself and annoy my adversary, little regarding the story of the Earthen Pot and Brazen Pitcher. One encouragement I have, the knowledge, that he is not a whit better liked by his colleagues in the ministry, than he is by me, that he cannot probably continue where he is much longer, and that he can scarce be succeeded by anybody, who will not like me the better for his having been at variance with me.

Minutes of the Conference mentioned above.

Wednesday, 16 January, 1771.—I went this morning to wait on Lord Hillsborough. The porter at first denied his Lordship, on which I left my name and drove off. But, before the coach got out of the square, the coachman heard a call, turned, and went back to the door, when the porter came and said, "His Lordship will see you, Sir." I was shown into the levee room, where I found Governor Bernard, who, I understand, attends there constantly. Several other gentlemen were there attending, with whom I sat down a few minutes, when Secretary Pownall came out to us, and said his Lordship desired I would come in.

I was pleased with this ready admission and preference, having sometimes waited three or four hours for my turn; and, being pleased, I could more easily put on the open, cheerful countenance, that my friends advised me to wear. His Lordship came towards me and said, "I was dressing in order to go to court; but, hearing that you were at the door, who are a man of business, I determined to see you immediately." I thanked his Lordship, and said that my business at present was not much; it was only to pay my respects to his Lordship, and to acquaint him with my appointment by the House of Representatives of Massachusetts Bay to be their agent here, in which station if I could be of any service—(I was going on to say—"to the public, I should be very happy"; but his Lordship, whose countenance changed at my naming that province, cut me short by saying, with something between a smile and a sneer),

L. H. I must set you right there, Mr. Franklin, you are not agent.

B. F. Why, my Lord?

L. H. You are not appointed.

B. F. I do not understand your Lordship; I have the appointment in my pocket.

L. H. You are mistaken; I have later and better advices. I have a letter from Governor Hutchinson; he would not give his assent to the bill.

B. F. There was no bill, my Lord; it was a vote of the House.

L. H. There was a bill presented to the governor for the purpose of appointing you and another, one Dr. Lee, I think he is called, to which the governor refused his assent.

B. F. I cannot understand this, my Lord; I think there must be some mistake in it. Is your Lordship quite sure that you have such a letter?

L. H. I will convince you of it directly. (*Rings the bell.*) Mr. Pownall will come in and satisfy you.

B. F. It is not necessary, that I should now detain your Lordship from dressing. You are going to court. I will wait on your Lordship another time.

L. H. No, stay; he will come immediately. (*To the servant.*) Tell Mr. Pownall I want him.

(*Mr. Pownall comes in.*)

L. H. Have not you at hand Governor Hutchinson's letter, mentioning his refusing his assent to the bill for appointing Dr. Franklin agent?

Sec. P. My Lord?

L. H. Is there not such a letter?

Sec. P. No, my Lord; there is a letter relating to some bill for the payment of a salary to Mr. De Berdt, and I think to some other agent, to which the governor had refused his assent.

L. H. And is there nothing in the letter to the purpose I mention?

Sec. P. No, my Lord.

B. F. I thought it could not well be, my Lord; as my letters are by the last ships, and they mention no such thing. Here is the authentic copy of the vote of the House appointing me, in which there is no mention of any act intended. Will your Lordship please to look at it? (*With seeming unwillingness he takes it, but does not look into it.*)

L. H. An information of this kind is not properly brought to me as Secretary of State. The Board of Trade is the proper place.

B. F. I will leave the paper then with Mr. Pownall to be——

L. H. (*Hastily.*) To what end would you leave it with him?

B. F. To be entered on the minutes of that Board, as usual.

L. H. (*Angrily.*) It shall not be entered there. No such paper shall be entered there, while I have any thing to do with the business of that Board. The House of Representatives has no right to appoint an agent. We shall take no notice of any agents, but such as are appointed by acts of Assembly, to which the governor gives his assent. We have had confusion enough already. Here is one agent appointed by the Council, another by the House of Representatives. Which of these is agent for the province? Who are we to hear in provincial affairs? An agent appointed by act of Assembly we can understand. No other will be attended to for the future, I can assure you.

B. F. I cannot conceive, my Lord, why the consent of the governor should be thought necessary to the appointment of an agent for the people. It seems to me that——

L. H. (*With a mixed look of anger and contempt.*) I shall not enter into a dispute with you, Sir, upon this subject.

B. F. I beg your Lordship's pardon; I do not presume to dispute with your Lordship; I would only say, that it seems to me, that every body of men, who cannot appear in person, where business relating to them may be transacted, should have a right to appear by an agent. The concurrence of the governor does not seem to me necessary. It is the business of the people, that is to be done; he is not one of them; he is himself an agent.

L. H. (*Hastily.*) Whose agent is he?

B. F. The King's, my Lord.

L. H. No such matter. He is one of the corporation by the province charter. No agent can be appointed but by an act, nor any act pass without his assent. Besides, this proceeding is directly contrary to express instructions.

B. F. I did not know there had been such instructions. I am not concerned in any offence against them, and——

L. H. Yes, your offering such a paper to be entered is an offence against them. (*Folding it up again without having read a word of it.*) No such appointment shall be entered. When I came into the administration of American affairs, I found them in great disorder. By *my firmness* they are now something mended; and, while I have the honor to hold the seals, I shall continue the same conduct, the same *firmness.* I think my duty to the master I serve, and to the government of this nation, requires it of me. If that conduct is not approved, *they* may take my office from me when they please. I shall make them a bow, and thank them; I shall resign with pleasure. That gentleman knows it (*pointing to Mr. Pownall*), but, while I continue in it, I shall resolutely persevere in the same FIRMNESS. (*Spoken with great warmth, and turning pale in his discourse, as if he was angry at something or somebody besides the agent, and of more consequence to himself.*)

B. F. (*Reaching out his hand for the paper, which his Lordship returned to him.*) I beg your Lordship's pardon for taking up so much of your time. It is, I believe, of no great importance whether the appointment is acknowledged or not, for I have not the least conception that an agent can *at present* be of any use to any of the colonies. I shall therefore give your Lordship no further trouble. (*Withdrew.*)

English Winter

To William Franklin. London, 20 April, 1771.

It is long since I have heard from you. The last packet brought me no letter, and there are two packets now due. It is supposed that the long easterly winds have kept them back. We have had a severe and tedious winter. There is not yet the smallest appearance of spring. Not a bud has pushed out, nor a blade of grass. The turnips, that used to feed the cattle, have been destroyed by the frost. The hay in most parts of the country is gone, and the cattle perishing for want, the lambs dying by thousands through cold and scanty nourishment. On Tuesday last I went to dine at our friend Sir Matthew Featherstone's through a heavy storm of snow. His windows, you know, look into the park. Towards evening, I observed the snow still lying over all the park, for the ground was before too cold to thaw, it being itself frozen, and ice in the canal. You cannot imagine a more winterlike prospect.

Empires Crumble

To the Committee of Correspondence in Massachusetts. London, 15 May, 1771.*

I THINK one may clearly see, in the system of customs to be exacted in America by act of Parliament, the seeds sown of a total disunion of the two countries, though, as yet, that event may be at a considerable distance. The course and natural progress seems to be, first, the appointment of needy men as officers, for others do not care to leave England; then, their necessities make them rapacious, their office makes them proud and insolent, their insolence and rapacity make them odious, and, being conscious that they are hated, they become malicious; their malice urges them to a continual abuse of the inhabitants in their letters to administration, representing them as disaffected and rebellious, and (to encourage the use of severity) as weak, divided, timid, and cowardly. Government believes all; thinks it necessary to support and countenance its officers; their quarreling with the people is deemed a mark and consequence of their fidelity; they are therefore more highly rewarded, and this makes their conduct still more insolent and provoking.

The resentment of the people will, at times and on particular incidents, burst into outrages and violence upon such officers, and this naturally draws down severity and acts of further oppression from hence. The more the people are dissatisfied, the more rigor will be thought necessary; severe punishments will be inflicted to terrify; rights and privileges will be abolished; greater force will then be required to secure execution and submission; the expense will become enormous; it will then be thought proper, by fresh exactions, to make the people defray it; thence, the British nation and government will become odious, the subjection to it will be deemed no longer tolerable; war ensues, and the bloody struggle will end in absolute slavery to America, or ruin to Britain by the loss of her colonies; the latter most probable, from America's growing strength and magnitude.

But, as the whole empire must, in either case, be greatly weakened, I cannot but wish to see much patience and the utmost discretion in our general conduct, that the fatal period may be postponed, and that, whenever this

*Thomas Cushing, James Otis, and Samuel Adams.

catastrophe shall happen, it may appear to all mankind, that the fault has not been ours. And, since the collection of these duties has already cost Britain infinitely more, in the loss of commerce, than they amount to, and that loss is likely to continue and increase by the encouragement given to our manu-factures through resentment; and since the best pretence for establishing and enforcing the duties is the regulation of trade for the general advantage, it seems to me, that it would be much better for Britain to give them up, or condition of the colonies undertaking to enforce and collect such, as are thought fit to be continued, by laws of their own, and officers of their own appointment, for the public uses of their respective governments. This would alone destroy those seeds of disunion, and both countries might thence much longer continue to grow great together, more secure by their united strength, and more formidable to their common enemies. But the power of appointing friends and dependents to profitable offices is too pleas-ing to most administrations, to be easily parted with or lessened; and there-fore such a proposition, if it were made, is not very likely to meet with attention.

I do not pretend to the gift of prophecy. History shows, that, by these steps, great empires have crumbled heretofore; and the late transactions we have so much cause to complain of show, that we are in the same train, and that, without a greater share of prudence and wisdom, than we have seen both sides to be possessed of, we shall probably come to the same con-clusion.

Silk Culture

To Cadwallader Evans. London, 18 July, 1771.

I wrote to you on the 4th instant, and sent you a paper of observations on your specimens of silk, drawn up by Mr. Patterson, who is noted here in that trade, with a specimen of Italian silk as a copy for our people to imi-tate. But they must not be discouraged if they should not come up to the lustre of it, that being the very finest, and from a particular district in Italy, none other being equal to it from any other district or any other country.

The European silk I understand is all yellow, and most of the India silk. What comes from China is white. In Ogilby's account of that country, I find that, in the province of Chekiang, "they prune their mulberry trees once a year, as we do our vines in Europe, and suffer them not to grow up to high trees, because through long experience they have learned, that the leaves of the smallest and youngest trees make the best silk, and know there-by how to distinguish the first spinning of the threads from the second, viz. the first is that which comes from the young leaves, that are gathered in March, with which they feed their silkworms; and the second is of the old summer leaves. And it is only the change of food, as to the young and old leaves, which makes the difference in the silk. The prices of the first and second spinning differ among the Chinese. The best silk is that of March, the coarsest of June, yet both in one year." I have copied this passage to show, that in Chekiang they keep the mulberry trees low; but I suppose the reason to be, the greater facility of gathering the leaves. It appears too by this passage, that they raise two crops a year in that province, which may account for the great plenty of silk there. But perhaps this would not answer with us, since it is not practised in Italy, though it might be tried. Chekiang is from twenty-seven to thirty-one degrees of north latitude. Duhalde has a good deal on the Chinese management of the silk business.

Proverbial Debtor

To Mrs. Jane Mecom. London, 13 Jan., 1772.

I HAVE now been some weeks returned from my journey through Wales, Ireland, Scotland, and the North of England, which, besides being an agreeable tour with a pleasant companion, has contributed to the establishment of my health; and this is the first ship I have heard of, by which I could write to you.

I thank you for the receipts; they are as full and particular as one could wish; but they can easily be practised only in America, no bayberry wax, nor any Brasiletto, being here to be had, at least to my knowledge. I am glad, however, that those useful arts, which have so long been in our family, are now put down in writing. Some future branch may be the better for it.

It gives me pleasure, that those little things sent by Jonathan proved agreeable to you. I write now to cousin Williams to press the payment of the bond. There has been forbearance enough on my part; seven years or more, without receiving any principal or interest. It seems as if the debtor was like a whimsical man in Pennsylvania, of whom it was said that, it being against his principle to pay interest, and against his interest to pay the principal, he paid neither one nor the other. . . .

Two Commandments

To Samuel Cooper. London, 13 Jan., 1772.

As TO the agency, whether I am re-chosen or not, and whether the General Assembly is ever permitted to pay me or not, I shall nevertheless continue to exert myself in behalf of my country as long as I see a probability of my being able to do it any service. I have nothing to ask or expect of ministers. I have, thanks to God, a competency for the little time I may expect to live, and am grown too old for ambition of any kind, but that of leaving a good name behind me.

Your story of the clergyman and proclamation is a pleasant one. I can only match it with one I had from my father. I know not if it was ever printed. Charles the First ordered his proclamation, authorizing sport on a Sunday, to be read in all churches. Many clergymen complied, some refused, and others hurried it through as indistinctly as possible. But one, whose congregation expected no such thing from him, did, nevertheless, to their great surprise read it distinctly. He followed it, however, with the fourth commandment, *Remember to keep holy the Sabbath day*, and then said, "Brethren, I have laid before you the commandment of your King, and the commandment of your God. I leave it to yourselves to judge which of the two ought rather to be observed."

British System

To Joshua Babcock. London, 13 Jan., 1772.

I HAVE lately made a tour through Ireland and Scotland. In those countries, a small part of the society are landlords, great noblemen, and gentlemen, extremely opulent, living in the highest affluence and magnificence. The bulk of the people are tenants, extremely poor, living in the most sordid wretchedness, in dirty hovels of mud and straw, and clothed only in rags.

I thought often of the happiness of New England, where every man is a freeholder, has a vote in public affairs, lives in a tidy, warm house, has plenty of good food and fuel, with whole clothes from head to foot, the manufacture, perhaps, of his own family. Long may they continue in this situation! But, if they should ever envy the trade of these countries, I can put them in a way to obtain a share of it. Let them, with three fourths of the people of Ireland, live the year round on potatoes and buttermilk, without shirts, then may their merchants export beef, butter, and linen. Let them, with the generality of the common people of Scotland, go barefoot, then may they make large exports in shoes and stockings; and, if they will be content to wear rags, like the spinners and weavers of England, they may make cloths and stuffs for all parts of the world.

Farther, if my countrymen should ever wish for the honor of having among them a gentry enormously wealthy, let them sell their farms and pay racked rents; the scale of the landlords will rise, as that of the tenants is depressed, who will soon become poor, tattered, dirty, and abject in spirit. Had I never been in the American colonies, but were to form my judgment of civil society by what I have lately seen, I should never advise a nation of savages to admit of civilization; for I assure you, that, in the possession and enjoyment of the various comforts of life, compared to these people, every Indian is a gentleman, and the effect of this kind of civil society seems to be, the depressing multitudes below the savage state, that a few may be raised above it. My best wishes attend you and yours, being ever, with great esteem, &c.

Diplomatic Interview

To Thomas Cushing. London, 13 Jan., 1772.

LORD CLARENDON . . . was impeached for endeavouring to introduce arbitrary government into the colonies. Lord Hillsborough seems, by the late instructions, to have been treading in the paths that lead to the same unhappy situation, if the Parliament here should ever again feel for the colonies. Being in Dublin at the same time with his Lordship, I met with him accidentally at the Lord Lieutenant's, who had happened to invite us to dine with a large company on the same day. As there was something curious in our interview, I must give you an account of it. He was surprisingly civil, and urged my fellow travellers and me to call at his house in our intended journey northward, where we might be sure of better accommodations than the inns would afford us. He pressed us so politely, that it was not easy to refuse without apparent rudeness, as we must pass through his town, Hillsborough, and by his door; and therefore, as it might afford an opportunity of saying something on American affairs, I concluded to comply with his invitation.

His Lordship went home some time before we left Dublin. We called upon him, and were detained at his house four days, during which time he entertained us with great civility, and a particular attention to me, that appeared the more extraordinary, as I knew that just before we left London he had expressed himself concerning me in very angry terms, calling me a republican, a factious, mischievous fellow, and the like.

In our conversations he first showed himself a good Irishman, blaming England for its narrowness towards that country in restraining its commerce, and discouraging its woollen manufacture. When I applied his observations to America, he said he had always been of opinion, that America ought not to be restrained in manufacturing any thing she could manufacture to advantage; that he supposed, that, at present, she found more profit in agriculture; but, whenever she found that less profitable, or any particular manufacture more so, he had no objection to her pursuing it; and that the subjects in every part of the King's dominion had a natural right to make the best use they could of the productions of their country. He censured Lord Chatham for affecting in his speech, that the Parliament had a right or ought to restrain manufactures in the colonies; adding, that, as he knew the English were apt to be jealous on that head, he avoided every thing that might inflame that jealousy; and, therefore, though the Commons had requested the crown to order the governor to send over annually accounts of such manufactures, as were undertaken in the colonies, yet, as they had not ordered such accounts to be annually laid before them, he should never produce them till they were called for.

Then he gave me to understand, that the bounty on silk raised in America was a child of his, and he hoped it would prove of great advantage to that country; and that he wished to know in what manner a bounty on raising wine there might be contrived, so as to operate effectually for that purpose, desiring me to turn it in my thoughts, as he should be glad of my opinion and advice. Then he informed me, that Newfoundland was grown too populous to be left any longer without a regular government, but there were great difficulties in the forming such a kind of government as would be suitable to the particular circumstances of that country, which he wished me likewise to consider, and that I would favor him with my sentiments.

He seemed attentive to every thing, that might make my stay in his house agreeable to me, and put his eldest son Lord Killwarling into his phaeton with me, to drive me a round of forty miles, that I might see the country, the seats, and manufactures, covering me with his own greatcoat, lest I should take cold. In short, he seemed extremely solicitous to impress me, and the colonies through me, with a good opinion of him. All which I could not but wonder at, knowing that he likes neither them nor me; and I thought it inexplicable but on the supposition, that he apprehended an approaching storm, and was desirous of lessening beforehand the number of enemies he had so imprudently created. But, if he takes no steps towards withdrawing the troops, repealing the duties, restoring the Castle, or recalling the offensive instructions, I shall think all the plausible behaviour I have described is meant only, by patting and stroking the horse, to make him more patient, while the reins are drawn tighter, and the spurs set deeper into his sides.

Before leaving Ireland I must mention, that, being desirous of seeing the principal patriots there, I stayed till the opening of their Parliament. I found them disposed to be friends of America, in which I endeavoured to confirm them, with the expectation that our growing weight might in time be thrown into their scale, and, by joining our interests with theirs, a more equitable treatment from this nation might be obtained for them as well as for us. There are many brave spirits among them. The gentry are a very sensible, polite, and friendly people. Their Parliament makes a most respectable figure, with a number of very good speakers in both parties, and able men of business. And I must not omit acquainting you, that, it being a standing rule to admit members of the English Parliament to sit (though they do not vote) in the House among the members, while others are only admitted into the gallery, my fellow traveller, being an English member, was accordingly admitted as such. But I supposed I must go to the gallery, when the Speaker stood up, and acquainted the House, that he understood there was in town an American gentleman of (as he was pleased to say) distinguished character and merit, a member or delegate of some of the Parliaments of that country, who was desirous of being present at the debates of the House; that there was a rule of the House for admitting members of English Parliaments, and that he supposed the House would consider the American Assemblies as English Parliaments; but, as this was the first instance, he had chosen not to give any order in it without receiving their directions. On the question, the House gave a loud unanimous *ay*.

On Choosing a Wife

To Samuel Franklin. London, 13 Jan., 1772.

I RECEIVED your kind letter of November 8th, and rejoice to hear of the continued welfare of you and your good wife and four daughters. I hope they will all get good husbands. I dare say they will be educated so as to deserve them.

I knew a wise old man, who used to advise his young friends to choose wives out of a bunch; for where there were many daughters, he said, they improved each other, and from emulation acquired more accomplishments, knew more, could do more, and were not spoiled by parental fondness, as single children often are. Yours have my best wishes, and blessing, if that can be of any value.

Family Letters

To his wife. London, 28 Jan., 1772.

I RECEIVED your young neighbour Haddock's silk, and carried it to her relations, who live very well, keeping a linen-draper's shop in Bishop's-gate Street. They have a relation in Spitalfields, that is a manufacturer, who I believe will do it well. I shall honor much every young lady, that I find on my return dressed in silk of her own raising. I thank you for the sauceboats, and am pleased to find so good a progress made in the china manufactory. I wish it success most heartily. . . .

The squirrels came safe and well. You will see by the enclosed how welcome they were. A hundred thanks are sent you for them, and I thank you for the readiness with which you executed the commission. The buckwheat and Indian meal are come safe and good. They will be a great refreshment to me this winter; for, since I cannot be in America, everything that comes from thence comforts me a little, as being something like home. The dried peaches, too, are excellent; those dried without their skins. The parcel in their skins are not so good. The apples are the best I ever had, and came with the least damage.

To William Franklin. London, 30 Jan., 1772.

IN YOUR last you mention some complaisance of Lord Hillsborough towards you, that showed a disposition to be on better terms. His behaviour to me in Ireland corresponds exactly. We met first at the Lord Lieutenant's. Mr. Jackson and I were invited to dine there, and when we came, we were shown into a room where Lord Hillsborough was alone. He was extremely civil, wonderfully so to me, whom he had not long before abused to Mr. Strahan, as a factious, turbulent fellow, always in mischief, a republican, enemy to the King's service, and what not. He entered very frankly into conversation with us both, and invited us both to stop at his house in Hillsborough, as we should travel northward, and urged it in so polite a manner, that we could not avoid saying that we would wait on him if we went that way. In my own mind I was determined not to go that way; but Mr. Jackson thought himself obliged to call on his Lordship, considering the connexion his office forms between them. His Lordship dined with us at the Lord Lieutenant's. There were at table the Lord Chancellor, the Speaker, and all the great officers of state. He drank my health, and was otherwise particularly civil. He went from Dublin some days before us.

At Dublin we saw and were entertained by both parties, the courtiers and the patriots. The latter treated me with particular respect. We were admitted to sit among the members of the Commons' House; Mr. Jackson as member of the British Parliament, and I as member of some British Parliament in America. The Speaker proposed it in my behalf, with some very obliging expressions of respect for my character, and was answered by the House with a unanimous *ay* of consent, when two members came out to me, led me in between them, and placed me honorably and commodiously. I hope our Assemblies will not fall short of them in this politeness, if any Irish member should happen to be in our country.

In Scotland I spent five days with Lord Kames at his seat, Blair Drummond, near Stirling, two or three days at Glasgow, two days at Carron Iron Works, and the rest of the month in and about Edinburgh, lodging at David Hume's, who entertained me with the greatest kindness and hospitality, as did Lord Kames and his lady.

To William Franklin. London, 19 August, 1772.

As Lord Hillsborough in fact got nothing out of me, I should rather suppose he threw me away as an orange that would yield no juice, and therefore not worth more squeezing. When I had been a little while returned to London, I waited on him to thank him for his civilities in Ireland, and to discourse with him on a Georgia affair. The porter told me he was not at home. I left my card, went another time, and received the same answer, though I knew he was at home, a friend of mine being with him. After intermissions of a week each, I made two more visits, and received the same answer. The last time was on a levee day, when a number of carriages were at his door. My coachman driving up, alighted, and was opening the coach door, when the porter, seeing me, came out, and surlily chid the coachman for opening the door before he had inquired whether my Lord was at home; and then turning to me, said, "My Lord is not at home." I have never since been nigh him, and we have only abused one another at a distance.

The contrast, as you observe, is very striking between his conversation with the chief justice, and his letter to you concerning your province. I know him to be as double and deceitful as any man I ever met with. But we have done with him, I hope, for ever. His removal has, I believe, been meditated ever since the death of the Princess Dowager. For I recollect, that on my complaining of him about that time to a friend at court, whom you may guess, he told me, we Americans were represented by Hillsborough as an unquiet people, not easily satisfied with any ministry; that, however, it was thought too much occasion had been given us to dislike the present; and asked me, whether, if he should be removed, I could name another likely to be more acceptable to us. I said, "Yes, there is Lord Dartmouth; we liked him very well when he was at the head of the Board formerly, and probably should like him again." This I heard no more of, but I am pretty sure it was reported where I could wish it, though I know not that it had any effect.

As to my situation here, nothing can be more agreeable, especially as I hope for less embarrassment from the new minister; a general respect paid me by the learned, a number of friends and acquaintance among them, with whom I have a pleasing intercourse; a character of so much weight, that it has protected me when some in power would have done me injury, and continued me in an office they would have deprived me of; my company so much desired, that I seldom dine at home in winter, and could spend the whole summer in the country-houses of inviting friends, if I chose it. Learned and ingenious foreigners, that come to England, almost all make a point of visiting me; for my reputation is still higher abroad than here. Several of the foreign ambassadors have assiduously cultivated my acquaintance, treating me as one of their *corps*, partly I believe from the desire they have, from time to time, of hearing something of American affairs, an object become of importance in foreign courts, who begin to hope Britain's alarming power will be diminished by the defection of her colonies; and partly that they may have an opportunity of introducing me to the gentlemen of their country who desire it. The King, too, has lately been heard to speak of me with great regard.

These are flattering circumstances; but a violent longing for home sometimes seizes me, which I can no otherwise subdue but by promising myself a return next spring or next fall, and so forth. As to returning hither, if I once go back, I have no thoughts of it. I am too far advanced in life to propose three voyages more. I have some important affairs to settle at home, and, considering my double expenses here and there, I hardly think my salaries fully compensate the disadvantages. The late change, however, being thrown into the balance, determines me to stay another winter.

August 22d.—I find I omitted congratulating you on the honor of your election into the Society for propagating the Gospel. There you match indeed my Dutch honor. But you are again behind, for last night I received a letter from Paris, of which the enclosed is an extract, acquainting me that I am chosen *Associé Etranger* (foreign member) of the Royal Academy there. There are but eight of these *Associés Etrangers* in all Europe, and those of the most distinguished names for science. The vacancy I have the honor of filling was made by the death of the late celebrated Van Swieten of Vienna. This mark of respect from the first academy in the world, which Abbé Nollet, one of its members, took so much pains to prejudice against my doctrines, I consider as a kind of victory without ink-shed, since I never answered him. I am told he has but one of his sect now remaining in the Academy. All the rest, who have in any degree acquainted themselves with electricity, are as he calls them *Franklinists*.

On Slavery

To Anthony Benezet. London, 22 August, 1772.

I MADE a little extract from yours of April 27th, of the number of slaves imported and perishing, with some close remarks on the hypocrisy of this country, which encourages such a detestable commerce by laws for promoting the Guinea trade; while it piqued itself on its virtue, love of liberty, and the equity of its courts, in setting free a single negro. This was inserted in the *London Chronicle*, of the 20th of June last.

I thank you for the Virginia address, which I shall also publish with some remarks. I am glad to hear that the disposition against keeping negroes grows more general in North America. Several pieces have been lately printed here against the practice, and I hope in time it will be taken into consideration and suppressed by the legislature. Your labors have already been attended with great effects. I hope, therefore, you and your friends will be encouraged to proceed. My hearty wishes of success attend you, being ever, my dear friend, yours affectionately.

"Moral Algebra"

To Joseph Priestley. London, 19 September, 1772.

IN THE affair of so much importance to you, wherein you ask my advice, I cannot, for want of sufficient premises, counsel you *what* to determine; but, if you please, I will tell you *how*. When those difficult cases occur, they are difficult, chiefly because, while we have them under consideration, all the reasons *pro* and *con* are not present to the mind at the same time; but sometimes one set present themselves, and at other times another, the first being out of sight. Hence the various purposes or inclinations that alternately prevail, and the uncertainty that perplexes us.

To get over this, my way is, to divide half a sheet of paper by a line into two columns; writing over the one *pro*, and over the other *con;* then during three or four days' consideration, I put down under the different heads short hints of the different motives, that at different times occur to me, *for* or *against* the measure. When I have thus got them all together in one view, I endeavour to estimate their respective weights; and, where I find two (one on each side) that seem equal, I strike them both out. If I find a reason *pro* equal to some *two* reasons *con*, I strike out the *three*. If I judge some *two* reasons *con*, equal to some *three* reasons *pro*, I strike out the *five;* and thus proceeding I find at length where the *balance* lies; and if, after a day or two of farther consideration, nothing new that is of importance occurs on either side, I come to a determination accordingly. And, though the weight of reasons cannot be taken with the precision of algebraic quantities, yet, when each is thus considered separately and comparatively, and the whole lies before me, I think I can judge better, and am less liable to make a rash step; and in fact I have found great advantage from this kind of equation, in what may be called *moral* or *prudential algebra*.

Squirrel Friend

To Miss Georgiana Shipley. London, 26 September, 1772.

I LAMENT with you most sincerely the unfortunate end of poor MUNGO. Few squirrels were better accomplished; for he had had a good education, had travelled far, and seen much of the world. As he had the honor of being, for his virtues, your favorite, he should not go, like common skuggs, without an elegy or an epitaph. Let us give him one in the monumental style and measure, which, being neither prose nor verse, is perhaps the properest for grief; since to use common language would look as if we were not affected, and to make rhymes would seem trifling in sorrow.

EPITAPH,

ON THE LOSS OF AN AMERICAN SQUIRREL, WHO, ESCAPING FROM HIS CAGE, WAS KILLED BY A SHEPHERD'S DOG.

Alas! poor MUNGO!
Happy wert thou, hadst thou known
Thy own felicity.
Remote from the fierce bald eagle,
Tyrant of thy native woods,
Thou hadst nought to fear from his piercing talons,
Nor from the murdering gun
Of the thoughtless sportsman.
Safe in thy wired castle,
GRIMALKIN never could annoy thee.
Daily wert thou fed with the choicest viands,
By the fair hand of an indulgent mistress;
But, discontented,
Thou wouldst have more freedom.

Too soon, alas! didst thou obtain it;
And wandering,
Thou art fallen by the fangs of wanton, cruel RANGER!
Learn hence,
Ye who blindly seek more liberty,
Whether subjects, sons, squirrels, or daughters,
That apparent restraint may be real protection,
Yielding peace and plenty
With security.

You see, my dear Miss, how much more decent and proper this broken style is, than if we were to say, by way of epitaph,—

Here SKUGG
Lies snug,
As a bug
In a rug.

And yet, perhaps, there are people in the world of so little feeling as to think that this would be a good-enough epitaph for poor Mungo.

If you wish it, I shall procure another to succeed him; but perhaps you will now choose some other amusement.

Remember me affectionately to all the good family, and believe me ever your affectionate friend.

Stamp Revenue

To Joseph Galloway. London, 2 Dec., 1772.

Two circumstances have diverted me lately. One was, that, being at the court of exchequer on some business of my own, I there met with one of the commissioners of the stamp office, who told me he attended with a memorial from that board, to be allowed in their accounts the difference between their expense in endeavouring to establish those offices in America, and the amount of what they received, which from Canada and the West India Islands was but about *fifteen hundred pounds*, while the expense, if I remember right, was above *twelve thousand pounds*, being for stamps and stamping, with paper and parchment returned upon their hands, freight, &c. The other is the present difficulties of the India Company, and of government on their account. The Company have accepted bills, which they find themselves unable to pay, though they have the value of two millions in tea and other India goods in their stores, perishing under a want of demand; their credit thus suffering, and their stock falling one hundred and twenty per cent, whereby the government will lose the *four hundred thousand pounds* per annum, it having been stipulated that it should no longer be paid, if the dividend fell to that mark. And, although it is known, that the American market is lost by continuing the duty on tea, and that we are supplied by the Dutch, who doubtless take the opportunity of smuggling other India goods among us with the tea, so that for the five years past we might probably have otherwise taken off the greatest part of what the Company have on hand, and so have prevented their present embarrassment, yet the honor of government is supposed to forbid the repeal of the American tea duty; while the amount of all the duties goes on decreasing, so that the balance of this year does not (as I have it from good authority) exceed eighty pounds, after paying the collection; not reckoning the immense expense of *guardacostas*, &c. Can an American help smiling at these blunders? Though, in a national light, they are truly deplorable.

To Thomas Cushing. London, 5 Jan., 1773.

SOME circumstances are working in our favor with regard to the duties. It is found by the last year's accounts transmitted by the commissioners, that the balance in favor of Britain is but about eighty-five pounds, after payment of salaries, &c., exclusive of the charge of a fleet to enforce the collection. Then it is observed, that the India Company is so out of cash, that it cannot pay the bills drawn upon it, and its other debts; and at the same time so out of credit, that the Bank does not care to assist them, whence they find themselves obliged to lower their dividend; the apprehension of which has sunk their stock from two hundred and eighty to one hundred and sixty, whereby several millions of property are annihilated, occasioning private bankruptcies and other distress, besides a loss to the public treasury of four hundred thousand pounds per annum, which the Company are not to pay into it as heretofore, if they are not able to keep up their dividend at twelve and a half. And, as they have at the same time tea and other India goods in their warehouses, to the amount of four millions, as some say, for which they want a market, and which, if it had been sold, would have kept up their credit, I take the opportunity of remarking in all companies the great imprudence of losing the American market, by keeping up the duty on tea, which has thrown that trade into the hands of the Dutch, Danes, Swedes, and French, who, according to the reports and letters of some custom-house officers in America, now supply by smuggling the whole continent, not with tea only, but accompany that article with other India goods, amounting, as supposed, in the whole to five hundred thousand pounds sterling per annum. This gives some alarm, and begins to convince people more and more of the impropriety of quarrelling with America, who at that rate might have taken off two millions and a half of those goods within these five years that the combination has subsisted, if the duty had not been laid, or had been speedily repealed.

But our great security lies, I think, in our growing strength, both in numbers and wealth; that creates an increasing ability of assisting this nation in its wars, which will make us more respectable, our friendship more valued, and our enmity feared; thence it will soon be thought proper to treat us not with justice only, but with kindness, and thence we may expect in a few years a total change of measures with regard to us; unless, by a neglect of military discipline, we should lose all martial spirit, and our western people become as tame as those in the eastern dominions of Britain, when we may expect the same oppressions; for there is much truth in the Italian saying, *Make yourselves sheep, and the wolves will eat you.* In confidence of this coming change in our favor, I think our prudence is meanwhile to be quiet, only holding up our rights and claims on all occasions in resolutions, memorials, and remonstrances; but bearing patiently the little present notice that is taken of them. They will all have their weight in time, and that time is at no great distance.

Birthday Thought

To his wife. London, 6 Jan., 1773.

I FEEL some regard for this sixth of January, as my old nominal birthday, though the change of style has carried the real day forward to the 17th, when I shall be, if I live till then, sixty-seven years of age. It seems but the other day since you and I were ranked among the boys and girls, so swiftly does time fly! We have, however, great reason to be thankful, that so much of our lives has passed so happily; and that so great a share of health and strength remains, as to render life yet comfortable.

I received your kind letter of November 16th by Sutton. The apples are not yet come on shore, but I thank you for them. Captain All was so good as to send me a barrel of excellent ones, which serve me in the mean time. I rejoice to hear that you all continue well. But you have so used me to have something pretty about the boy, that I am a little disappointed in finding nothing more of him, than that he is gone up to Burlington. Pray give in your next, as usual, a little of his history.

All our friends here are pleased with your remembering them, and send their love to you. Give mine to all that inquire concerning me, and a good deal to our children.

Political Affairs

To William Franklin. London, 14 Feb., 1773.

. . . THE ministry are more embarrassed with the India affairs. The continued refusal of North America to take tea from hence, has brought infinite distress on the Company. They imported great quantities in faith that that agreement could not hold; and now they can neither pay their debts nor dividends; their stock has sunk to the annihilating near three millions of their property, and government will lose its four hundred thousand pounds a year; while their teas lie on hand. The bankruptcies, brought on partly by this means, have given such a shock to credit, as has not been experienced here since the South Sea year. And this has affected the great manufacturers so much, as to oblige them to discharge their hands, and thousands of Spital-fields and Manchester weavers are now starving, or subsisting on charity. Blessed effects of pride, pique, and passion in government, which should have no passions.

To Thomas Cushing. London, 4 June, 1773.

IT WAS thought at the beginning of the session, that the American duty on tea would be taken off. But now the wise scheme is, to take off so much duty here, as will make tea cheaper in America than foreigners can supply us, and to confine the duty there, to keep up the exercise of the right. They have no idea, that any people can act from any other principle but that of interest; and they believe, that three pence in a pound of tea, of which one does not perhaps drink ten pounds in a year, is sufficient to overcome all the patriotism of an American.

To Thomas Cushing. London, 7 July, 1773.

I AM GLAD to see the resolves of the Virginia House of Burgesses. There are brave spirits among that people. I hope their proposal will be readily complied with by all the colonies. It is natural to suppose, as you do, that, if the oppressions continue, a congress may grow out of that correspondence. Nothing would more alarm our ministers; but, if the colonies agree to hold a congress, I do not see how it can be prevented.

To Thomas Cushing. London, 7 July, 1773.

No ONE doubts the advantage of a strict union between the mother country and the colonies, if it may be obtained and preserved on equitable terms. In every fair connexion, each party should find its own interest. Britain will find hers in our joining with her in every war she makes, to the greater annoyance and terror of her enemies; in our employment of her manufactures, and enriching her merchants by our commerce; and her government will feel some additional strengthening of its hands by the disposition of our profitable posts and places. On our side, we have to expect the protection she can afford us, and the advantage of a common umpire in our disputes, thereby preventing wars we might otherwise have with each other; so that we can without interruption go on with our improvements, and increase our numbers. We ask no more of her, and she should not think of forcing more from us.

By the exercise of prudent moderation on her part, mixed with a little kindness; and by a decent behaviour on ours, excusing where we can excuse from a consideration of circumstances, and bearing a little with the infirmities of her government, as we would with those of an aged parent, though firmly asserting our privileges, and declaring that we mean at a proper time to vindicate them, this advantageous union may still be long continued. We wish it, and we may endeavour it; but God will order it as to his wisdom shall seem most suitable. The friends of liberty here wish we may long preserve it on our side of the water, that they may find it there, if adverse events should destroy it here. They are therefore anxious and afraid, lest we should hazard it by premature attempts in its favor. They think we may risk much by violent measures, and that the risk is unnecessary, since a little time must infallibly bring us all we demand or desire, and bring it to us in peace and safety. I do not presume to advise. There are many wiser men among you, and I hope you will be directed by a still superior wisdom.

With regard to the sentiments of people in general here, concerning America, I must say, that we have among them many friends and well-wishers. The Dissenters are all for us, and many of the merchants and manu-facturers. There seems to be, even among the country gentlemen, a general sense of our growing importance, a disapprobation of the harsh measures with which we have been treated, and a wish that some means may be found of perfect reconciliation. A few members of Parliament in both Houses, and perhaps some in high office, have in a degree the same ideas; but none of these seem willing as yet to be active in our favor, lest adversaries should take advantage, and charge it upon them as a betraying the interests of this nation. In this state of things, no endeavour of mine, or our other friends here, "to obtain a repeal of the acts so oppressive to the colonists, or the orders of the crown so destructive of the charter rights of our province in particular," can expect a sudden success. By degrees, and a judicious im-provement of events, we may work a change in minds and measures; but otherwise such great alterations are hardly to be looked for.

To Samuel Mather. London, 7 July, 1773.

I PERUSED your tracts with pleasure. I see you inherit all the various learn-ing of your famous ancestors, Cotton and Increase Mather. The father, In-crease, I once heard preach at the Old South Meeting for Mr. Pemberton; and I remember his mentioning the death of "that wicked old persecutor of God's people, Louis the Fourteenth"; of which news had just been received; but which proved premature. I was some years afterwards at his house at the North End, on some errand to him, and remember him sitting in an easy chair, apparently very old and feeble. But Cotton I remember in the vigor of his preaching and usefulness.

You have made the most of your argument, to prove that America might be known to the ancients. There is another discovery of it claimed by the Norwegians, which you have not mentioned, unless it be under the words, "of old viewed and observed," page 7. About twenty-five years since, Pro-fessor Kalm, a learned Swede, was with us in Pennsylvania. He contended, that America was discovered by their northern people, long before the time of Columbus; which I doubting, he drew up and gave me some time after a note of those discoveries, which I send you enclosed. It is his own hand-writing, and his own English; very intelligible for the time he had been among us. The circumstances give the account a great appearance of authenticity. And if one may judge by the description of the winter, the country they visited should be southward of New England, supposing no change since that time of the climate. But, if it be true, as Krantz, I think, and some other historians tell us, that old Greenland, once inhabited and populous, is now rendered uninhabited by ice, it should seem that almost perpetual northern winter had gained ground to the southward; and, if so, perhaps more northern countries might anciently have had vines, than can bear them in these days.

The remarks you have added, on the late proceedings against America, are very just and judicious; and I cannot see any impropriety in your making them, though a minister of the gospel. This kingdom is a good deal indebted for its liberties to the public spirit of its ancient clergy, who joined with the barons in obtaining Magna Charta, and joined heartily in forming the curses of excommunication against the infringers of it. There is no doubt but the claim of Parliament, of authority to make laws *binding on the colonies in all cases whatsoever*, includes an authority to change our religious constitution, and establish Popery or Mahomedanism, if they please, in its stead; but, as you intimate, *power* does not infer *right*; and, as the *right* is nothing, and the *power*, by our increase, continually diminishing, the one will soon be as insignificant as the *other*. You seem only to have made a small mistake, in supposing they modestly avoided to declare they had a right, the words of the act being, "that they have and of *right* ought to have, full power, &c."

Your suspicion that sundry others, besides Governor Bernard, "had written hither their opinions and counsels, encouraging the late measures to the prejudice of our country, which have been too much heeded and followed," is, I apprehend, but too well founded. You call them "traitorous individuals," whence I collect, that you suppose them of our own country. There was among the twelve Apostles one traitor, who betrayed with a kiss. It should be no wonder, therefore, if among so many thousand true patriots, as New England contains, there should be found even twelve Judases ready to betray their country for a few paltry pieces of silver. Their *ends*, as well as their views, ought to be similar. But all the oppressions evidently work for our good. Providence seems by every means intent on making us a great people. May our virtues public and private grow with us, and be durable, that liberty, civil and religious, may be secured to our posterity, and to all from every part of the Old World that take refuge among us.

To William Franklin. London, 14 July, 1773.

LET ME tell you a little of Lord Hillsborough. I went down to Oxford with and at the instance of Lord Le Despencer, who is on all occasions very good to me, and seems of late very desirous of my company. Mr. Todd too was there, who has some attachment to Lord Hillsborough, and, in a walk we were taking, told me, as a secret, that Lord Hillsborough was much chagrined at being out of place, and could never forgive me for writing that pamphlet against his Report about the Ohio. "I assured him," says Mr. Todd, "that I knew you did not write it; and the consequence is, that he thinks I know the contrary, and wanted to impose upon him in your favor; and so I find he is now displeased with me, and for no other cause in the world." His friend Bamber Gascoign, too, says, that they *well know* it was written by Dr. Franklin, who was one of the most mischievous men in England.

That same day Lord Hillsborough called upon Lord Le Despencer, whose chamber and mine were together in Queen's College. I was in the inner room shifting, and heard his voice, but did not see him, as he went down stairs immediately with Lord Le Despencer, who mentioning that I was above, he returned directly and came to me in the pleasantest manner imaginable. "Dr. Franklin," said he, "I did not know till this minute that you were here, and I am come back *to make you my bow.* I am glad to see you at Oxford, and that you look so well," &c. In return for this extravagance, I complimented him on his son's performance in the theatre, though indeed it was but indifferent, so that account was settled. For as people say, when they are angry, *If he strikes me, I'll strike him again;* I think sometimes it may be right to say, *If he flatters me, I'll flatter him again.* This is *lex talionis,* returning offences in kind.

To Samuel Danforth. London, 25 July, 1773.

I SEE by the papers, that you continue to afford that public your services, which makes me almost ashamed of my resolutions for retirement. But this exile, though an honorable one, is become grievous to me, in so long a separation from my family, friends, and country; all which you happily enjoy; and long may you continue to enjoy them. I hope for the great pleasure of once more seeing and conversing with you; and, though living on in one's children, as we both may do, is a good thing, I cannot but fancy it might be better to continue living ourselves at the same time. I rejoice, therefore, in your kind intentions of including me in the benefits of that inestimable stone, which, curing all diseases (even old age itself), will enable us to see the future glorious state of our America, enjoying in full security her own liberties, and offering in her bosom a participation of them to all the oppressed of other nations.

To William Franklin. London, 1 September, 1773.

IT IS said there is now a project on foot to form a union with Ireland, and that Lord Harcourt is to propose it at the next meeting of the Irish Parliament. The eastern side of Ireland are averse to it; supposing, that, when Dublin is no longer the seat of their government it will decline, the harbour being but indifferent, and that the western and southern ports will rise and flourish on its ruins, being good in themselves, and much better situated for commerce. For these same reasons, the western and southern people are inclined to the measure, and it is thought it may be carried. But these are difficult affairs, and usually take longer time than the projectors imagine. Mr. Crowley, the author of several proposals for uniting the colonies with the mother country, and who runs about much among the ministers, tells me, the union of Ireland is only the first step towards a general union. He is for having it done by the Parliament of England, without consulting the colonies, and he will warrant, he says, that if the terms proposed are equitable, they will all come in one after the other. He seems rather a little cracked upon the subject.

To William Franklin. London, 6 Oct., 1773.

I HAVE written two pieces here lately for the *Public Advertiser,* on American affairs, designed to expose the conduct of this country towards the colonies in a short, comprehensive, and striking view, and stated, therefore, in out-of-the-way forms, as most likely to take the general attention. The first was called "Rules by which a Great Empire may be reduced to a Small One"; the second, "An Edict of the King of Prussia." I sent you one of the first, but could not get enough of the second to spare you one, though my clerk went the next morning to the printer's, and wherever they were sold. They were all gone but two. In my own mind I preferred the first, as a composition, for the quantity and variety of the matter contained, and a kind of spirited ending of each paragraph. But I find that others here generally prefer the second.

I am not suspected as the author, except by one or two friends; and have heard the latter spoken of in the highest terms, as the keenest and severest piece that has appeared here in a long time. Lord Mansfield, I hear, said of it, that it *was very* ABLE *and very* ARTFUL *indeed;* and would do mischief by giving here a bad impression of the measures of government; and in the colonies, by encouraging them in their contumacy. It is reprinted in the *Chronicle,* where you will see it, but stripped of all the capitaling and italicking, that intimate the allusions and mark the emphasis of written discourses, to bring them as near as possible to those spoken. Printing such a piece all in one even small character, seems to me like repeating one of Whitefield's sermons in the monotony of a school-boy.

What made it the more noticed here was, that people in reading it were, as the phrase is, *taken in,* till they had got half through it, and imagined it a real edict, to which mistake I suppose the King of Prussia's *character* must have contributed. I was down at Lord Le Despencer's, when the post brought that day's papers. Mr. Whitehead was there, too (Paul Whitehead, the author of "Manners"), who runs early through all the papers, and tells the company what he finds remarkable. He had them in another room, and we were chatting in the breakfast parlour, when he came running in to us, out of breath, with the paper in his hand. "Here!" says he, "here's news for ye! Here's the King of Prussia, claiming a right to this kingdom!" All stared, and I as much as anybody; and he went on to read it. When he had read two or three paragraphs, a gentleman present said, "Damn his impudence, I dare say we shall hear by next post, that he is upon his march with one hundred thousand men to back this." Whitehead, who is very shrewd, soon after began to smoke it, and looking in my face, said, "I'll be hanged if this is not some of your American jokes upon us." The reading went on, and ended with abundance of laughing, and a general verdict that it was a fair hit; and the piece was cut out of the paper and preserved in my Lord's collection.

New Inventions

To an engraver. London, 3 Nov., 1773.

I was much pleased with the specimens you so kindly sent me of your new art of engraving. That on the china is admirable. No one would suppose it any thing but painting. I hope you meet with all the encouragement you merit, and that the invention will be, what inventions seldom are, profitable to the inventor.

Now we are speaking of inventions, I know not who pretends to that of copper-plate engravings for earthen ware, and I am not disposed to contest the honor with anybody, as the improvement in taking impressions not directly from the plate, but from printed paper, applicable by that means to other than flat forms, is far beyond my first idea. But I have reason to apprehend, that I might have given the hint, on which that improvement was made; for, more than twenty years since, I wrote to Dr. Mitchell from America, proposing to him the printing of square tiles, for ornamenting chimneys, from copper plates, describing the manner in which I thought it might be done, and advising the borrowing from the booksellers the plates, that had been used in a thin folio, called "Moral Virtue Delineated," for the purpose.

The Dutch Delft ware tiles were much used in America, which are only or chiefly Scripture histories, wretchedly scrawled. I wished to have those moral prints, which were originally taken from Horace's poetical figures, introduced on tiles, which, being about our chimneys and constantly in the eyes of children when by the fire side, might give parents an opportunity of explaining them, to impress moral sentiments, and I gave expectations of great demand for them if executed. Dr. Mitchell wrote to me, in answer, that he had communicated my scheme to one of the principal artists in the earthen way about London, who rejected it as impracticable; and it was not till some years after, that I first saw an enamelled snuff box, which I was sure was from a copper plate, though the curvature of the form made me wonder how the impression was taken. I understand the china work in Philadelphia is declined by the first owners. Whether any others will take it up and continue it, I know not.

Two Famous Satires

Rules for reducing a Great Empire to a Small One; presented to a Late Minister,* when he entered upon his Administration.

AN ANCIENT sage valued himself upon this, that, though he could not fiddle, he knew how to make a great city of a little one. The science that I, a modern simpleton, am about to communicate, is the very reverse.

I address myself to all ministers who have the management of extensive dominions, which from their very greatness have become troublesome to govern, because the multiplicity of their affairs leaves no time for fiddling.

1. In the first place, Gentlemen, you are to consider, that a great empire, like a great cake, is most easily diminished at the edges. Turn your attention, therefore, first to your *remotest* provinces; that, as you get rid of them, the next may follow in order.

2. That the possibility of this separation may always exist, take special care the provinces are *never incorporated with the mother country;* that they do not enjoy the same common rights, the same privileges in commerce; and that they are governed by severer laws, all of your enacting, without allowing them any share in the choice of the legislators. By carefully making and preserving such distinctions, you will (to keep to my simile of the cake) act like a wise gingerbread-baker, who, to facilitate a division, cuts his dough half through in those places where, when baked, he would have it broken to pieces.

3. Those remote provinces have perhaps been acquired, purchased, or conquered, at the sole expense of the settlers, or their ancestors; without the aid of the mother country. If this should happen to increase her strength, by their growing numbers, ready to join in her wars; her commerce, by their growing demand for her manufactures; or her naval power, by greater employment for her ships and seamen, they may probably suppose some merit in this, and that it entitles them to some favor; you are therefore to *forget it all, or resent it,* as if they had done you injury. If they happen to be zealous whigs, friends of liberty, nurtured in revolution principles, remember all that to their prejudice, and contrive to punish it; for such principles, after a revolution is thoroughly established, are of no more use; they are even odious and abominable.

4. However peaceably your colonies have submitted to your government, shown their affection to your interests, and patiently borne their grievances; you are to suppose them *always inclined to revolt,* and treat them accordingly. Quarter troops among them, who by their insolence may provoke the rising of mobs, and by their bullets and bayonets suppress them. By this

---

*Lord Hillsborough.

means, like the husband who uses his wife ill from suspicion, you may in time convert your suspicions into realities.

5. Remote provinces must have governors and judges, to represent the royal person, and execute everywhere the delegated parts of his office and authority. You ministers know, that much of the strength of government depends on the opinion of the people; and much of that opinion on the *choice of rulers* placed immediately over them. If you send them wise and good men for governors, who study the interest of the colonists, and advance their prosperity; they will think their King wise and good, and that he wishes the welfare of his subjects. If you send them learned and upright men for judges, they will think him a lover of justice. This may attach your provinces more to his government. You are therefore to be careful whom you recommend to those offices. If you can find prodigals, who have ruined their fortunes, broken gamesters or stock-jobbers, these may do well as governors; for they will probably be rapacious, and provoke the people by their extortions. Wrangling proctors and pettifogging lawyers, too, are not amiss; for they will be for ever disputing and quarrelling with their little Parliaments. If withal they should be ignorant, wrongheaded, and insolent, so much the better. Attorneys' clerks, and Newgate solicitors will do for chief justices, especially if they hold their places during your pleasure; and all will contribute to impress those ideas of your government, that are proper for a people you would wish to renounce it.

6. To confirm these impressions, and strike them deeper, whenever the injured come to the capital with complaints of mal-administration, oppression, or injustice, *punish such suitors* with long delay, enormous expense, and a final judgment in favor of the oppressor. This will have an admirable effect every way. The trouble of future complaints will be prevented, and governors and judges will be encouraged to farther acts of oppression and injustice; and thence the people may become more disaffected, and at length desperate.

7. When such governors have crammed their coffers, and made themselves so odious to the people that they can no longer remain among them, with safety to their persons, *recall and reward* them with pensions. You may make them baronets too, if that respectable order should not think fit to resent it. All will contribute to encourage new governors in the same practice, and make the supreme government detestable.

8. If, when you are engaged in war, your colonies should vie in liberal aids of men and money against the common enemy, upon your simple requisition, and give far beyond their abilities, reflect that a penny taken from them by your power is more honorable to you, than a pound presented by their benevolence; *despise therefore their voluntary grants*, and resolve to harass them with *novel taxes*. They will probably complain to your Parliament, that they are taxed by a body in which they have no representative, and that this is contrary to common right. They will petition for redress. Let the Parliament flout their claims, reject their petitions, refuse even to suffer the reading of them, and treat the petitioners with the

utmost contempt. Nothing can have a better effect in producing the alienation proposed; for, though many can forgive injuries, none ever forgave
contempt.

9. In laying these taxes, *never regard the heavy burdens* those remote
people already undergo, in defending their own frontiers, supporting their
own provincial government, making new roads, building bridges, churches,
and other public edifices; which in old countries have been done to your
hands by your ancestors, but which occasion constant calls and demands
on the purses of a new people. Forget the restraint you lay on their trade
for your own benefit, and the advantage a monopoly of this trade gives
your exacting merchants. Think nothing of the wealth those merchants and
your manufacturers acquire by the colony commerce; their increased
ability thereby to pay taxes at home; their accumulating, in the price of
their commodities, most of those taxes, and so levying them from their
consuming customers; all this, and the employment and support of thousands of your poor by the colonists, you are entirely to forget. But remember to make your arbitrary tax more grievous to your provinces, by public
declarations importing that your power of taxing them has *no limits;* so
that, when you take from them without their consent a shilling in the pound,
you have a clear right to the other nineteen. This will probably weaken
every idea of security in their property, and convince them, that under
such a government they have nothing they can call their own; which can
scarce fail of producing the happiest consequences!

10. Possibly, indeed, some of them might still comfort themselves, and
say, "Though we have no property, we have yet something left that is valuable; we have constitutional *liberty, both of person and of conscience.* This
King, these Lords, and these Commons, who it seems are too remote from
us to know us, and feel for us, cannot take from us our Habeas Corpus
right, or our right of trial by a jury of our neighbours; they cannot deprive
us of the exercise of our religion, alter our ecclesiastical constitution, and
compel us to be Papists, if they please, or Mahometans." To annihilate this
comfort, begin by laws to perplex their commerce with infinite regulations,
impossible to be remembered and observed; ordain seizures of their property for every failure; take away the trial of such property by jury, and give
it to arbitrary judges of your own appointing, and of the lowest characters
in the country, whose salaries and emoluments are to arise out of the duties
or condemnations, and whose appointments are during pleasure. Then let
there be a formal declaration of both Houses, that opposition to your edicts
is treason, and that persons suspected of treason in the provinces may, according to some obsolete law, be seized and sent to the metropolis of the
empire for trial; and pass an act, that those there charged with certain other
offences, shall be sent away in chains from their friends and country to be
tried in the same manner for felony. Then erect a new court of Inquisition
among them, accompanied by an armed force, with instructions to transport
all such suspected persons; to be ruined by the expense, if they bring over
evidences to prove their innocence, or be found guilty and hanged, if they

cannot afford it. And, lest the people should think you cannot possibly go any farther, pass another solemn declaratory act, "that King, Lords, Commons had, have, and of right ought to have, full power and authority to make statutes of sufficient force and validity to bind the unrepresented provinces *in all cases whatsoever.*" This will include spiritual with temporal, and, taken together, must operate wonderfully to your purpose; by convincing them, that they are at present under a power something like that spoken of in the Scriptures, which can not only kill their bodies, but damn their souls to all eternity, by compelling them, if it pleases, to worship the Devil.

11. To make your taxes more odious, and more likely to procure resistance, send from the capital a *board of officers* to superintend the collection, *composed of the most indiscreet,* ill-bred, and insolent you can find. Let these have large salaries out of the extorted revenue, and live in open, grating luxury upon the sweat and blood of the industrious; whom they are to worry continually with groundless and expensive prosecutions before the abovementioned arbitrary revenue judges; all at the cost of the party prosecuted, though acquitted, because the King is to pay no costs. Let these men, by your order, be exempted from all the common taxes and burdens of the province, though they and their property are protected by its laws. If any revenue officers are suspected of the least tenderness for the people, discard them. If others are justly complained of, protect and reward them. If any of the under officers behave so as to provoke the people to drub them, promote those to better offices; this will encourage others to procure for themselves such profitable drubbings, by multiplying and enlarging such provocations, and all will work towards the end you aim at.

12. Another way to make your tax odious, is to *misapply the produce of it.* If it was originally appropriated for the defence of the provinces, and the better support of government, and the administration of justice, where it may be necessary; then apply none of it to that defence; but bestow it where it is not necessary, in augmenting salaries or pensions to every governor, who has distinguished himself by his enmity to the people, and by calumniating them to their sovereign. This will make them pay it more unwillingly, and be more apt to quarrel with those that collect it and those that impose it; who will quarrel again with them; and all shall contribute to your own purpose, of making them weary of your government.

13. If the people of any province have been accustomed to *support their own governors and judges* to satisfaction, you are to apprehend that such governors and judges may be thereby influenced to treat the people kindly, and to do them justice. This is another reason for applying part of that revenue in larger salaries to such governors and judges, given, as their commissions are, during *your* pleasure only; forbidding them to take any salaries from their provinces; that thus the people may no longer hope any kindness from their governors, or (in crown cases) any justice from their judges. And, as the money thus misapplied in one province is extorted from all, probably all will resent the misapplication.

14. If the Parliaments of your provinces should dare to claim rights, or complain of your administration, order them to be harassed with *repeated dissolutions*. If the same men are continually returned by new elections, adjourn their meetings to some country village, where they cannot be accommodated, and there keep them during pleasure; for this, you know, is your prerogative; and an excellent one it is, as you may manage it to promote discontents among the people, diminish their respect, and increase their disaffection.

15. Convert the brave, honest officers of your *navy* into pimping tide-waiters and colony officers of the *customs*. Let those, who in time of war fought gallantly in defence of the commerce of their countrymen, in peace be taught to prey upon it. Let them learn to be corrupted by great and real smugglers; but (to show their diligence) scour with armed boats every bay, harbour, river, creek, cove, or nook throughout the coast of your colonies; stop and detain every coaster, every wood-boat, every fisherman; tumble their cargoes and even their ballast inside out and upside down; and, if a pennyworth of pins is found unentered, let the whole be seized and confiscated. Thus shall the trade of your colonists suffer more from their friends in time of peace, than it did from their enemies in war. Then let these boats' crews land upon every farm in their way, rob their orchards, steal their pigs and poultry, and insult the inhabitants. If the injured and exasperated farmers, unable to procure other justice, should attack the aggressors, drub them, and burn their boats; you are to call this *high treason and rebellion*, order fleets and armies into their country, and threaten to carry all the offenders three thousand miles to be hanged, drawn, and quartered. O! this will work admirably!

16. If you are told of *discontents* in your colonies, never believe that they are general, or that you have given occasion for them; therefore do not think of applying any remedy, or of changing any offensive measure. Redress no grievance, lest they should be encouraged to demand the redress of some other grievance. Grant no request that is just and reasonable, lest they should make another that is unreasonable. Take all your informations of the state of the colonies from your governors and officers in enmity with them. Encourage and reward these leasing-makers; secrete their lying accusations, lest they should be confuted; but act upon them as the clearest evidence; and believe nothing you hear from the friends of the people. Suppose all *their* complaints to be invented and promoted by a few factious demagogues, whom if you could catch and hang, all would be quiet. Catch and hang a few of them accordingly; and the blood of the martyrs shall work miracles in favor of your purpose.

17. If you see *rival nations* rejoicing at the prospect of your disunion with your provinces, and endeavouring to promote it; if they translate, publish, and applaud all the complaints of your discontented colonists, at the same time privately stimulating you to severer measures, let not that offend you. Why should it, since you all mean the same thing?

18. If any colony should *at their own charge erect a fortress* to secure

their *port* against the fleets of a foreign enemy, get your governor to betray that fortress into your hands. Never think of paying what it cost the country, for that would look, at least, like some regard for justice; but turn it into a citadel to awe the inhabitants and curb their commerce. If they should have lodged in such fortress the very arms they bought and used to aid you in your conquests, seize them all; it will provoke, like ingratitude added to robbery. One admirable effect of these operations will be, to discourage every other colony from erecting such defences, and so their and your enemies may more easily invade them; to the great disgrace of your government, and of course the furtherance of your project.

19. Send armies into their country under pretence of protecting the inhabitants; but, instead of garrisoning the forts on their frontiers with those troops, to prevent incursions, demolish those forts, and order the troops into the heart of the country, that the savages may be encouraged to attack the frontiers, and that the troops may be protected by the inhabitants. This will seem to proceed from your *ill will or your ignorance,* and contribute farther to produce and strengthen an opinion among them, that you are no longer fit to govern them.

20. Lastly, invest the *general of your army in the provinces,* with great and unconstitutional powers, and free him from the control of even your own civil governors. Let him have troops enough under his command, with all the fortresses in his possession; and who knows but (like some provincial generals in the Roman empire, and encouraged by the universal discontent you have produced) he may take it into his head to set up for himself? If he should, and you have carefully practised the few excellent rules of mine, take my word for it, all the provinces will immediately join him; and you will that day (if you have not done it sooner) get rid of the trouble of governing them, and all the plagues attending their commerce and connexion from thenceforth and forever.

An Edict by the King of Prussia

Dantzic, 5 Sept., 1773.

WE HAVE long wondered here at the supineness of the English nation, under the Prussian impositions upon its trade entering our port. We did not, till lately, know the claims, ancient and modern, that hang over that nation; and therefore could not suspect that it might submit to those impositions from a sense of duty or from principles of equity. The following Edict, just made public, may, if serious, throw some light upon this matter.

"FREDERIC, by the grace of God, King of Prussia, &c. &c. &c., to all present and to come (*à tous présens et à venir*), health. The peace now enjoyed throughout our dominions, having afforded us leisure to apply ourselves to the regulation of commerce, the improvement of our finances, and at the same time the easing our *domestic* subjects in their taxes; for these causes, and other good considerations us thereunto moving, we hereby make known, that, after having deliberated these affairs in our Council, present our dear brothers, and other great officers of the state, members of the same; we, of our certain knowledge, full power, and authority royal, have made and issued this present Edict, viz.

"Whereas it is well known to all the world, that the first German settlements made in the Island of Britain, were by colonies of people, subject to our renowned ducal ancestors, and drawn from their dominions, under the conduct of Hengist, Horsa, Hella, Uffa, Cerdicus, Ida, and others; and that the said colonies have flourished under the protection of our august house for ages past; have never been emancipated therefrom; and yet have hitherto yielded little profit to the same; and whereas we ourself have in the last war fought for and defended the said colonies, against the power of France, and thereby enabled them to make conquests from the said power in America, for which we have not yet received adequate compensation; and whereas it is just and expedient that a revenue should be raised from the said colonies in Britain, towards our indemnification; and that those who are descendants of our ancient subjects, and thence still owe us due obedience, should contribute to the replenishing of our royal coffers (as they must have done, had their ancestors remained in the territories now to us appertaining); we do therefore hereby ordain and command, that, from and after the date of these presents, there shall be levied and paid to our officers of the *customs*, on all goods, wares, and merchandises, and on all grain and other produce of the earth, exported from the said Island of Britain, and on all goods of whatever kind imported into the same, a duty of four and a half per cent *ad valorem*, for the use of us and our successors. And, that the said duty may more effectually be collected, we do hereby ordain, that all ships or vessels bound from Great Britain to any other part of the world, or from any other part of the world to Great Britain, shall in their respective voyages touch at our port of Koningsberg, there to be unladen, searched, and charged with the said duties.

"And whereas there hath been from time to time discovered in the said Island of Great Britain, by our colonists there, many mines or beds of iron-stone; and sundry subjects of our ancient dominion, skillful in converting the said stone into metal, have in time past transported themselves thither, carrying with them and communicating that art; and the inhabitants of the said Island, presuming that they had a natural right to make the best use they could of the natural productions of their country for their own benefit, have not only built furnaces for smelting the said stone into iron, but have erected plating-forges, slitting-mills, and steel-furnaces, for the more convenient manufacturing of the same; thereby endangering a diminution of the said manufacture in our ancient dominion;—We do therefore hereby farther ordain, that, from and after the date hereof, no mill or other engine for slitting or rolling of iron, or any plating-forge to work with a tilt-hammer, or any furnace for making steel, shall be erected or continued in the said Island of Great Britain. And the Lord Lieutenant of every county in the said Island is hereby commanded, on information of any such erection within his county, to order, and by force to cause, the same to be abated and destroyed; as he shall answer the neglect thereof to us at his peril. But we are nevertheless graciously pleased to permit the inhabitants of the said island to transport their iron into Prussia, there to be manufactured, and to them returned; they paying our Prussian subjects for the workmanship, with all the costs of commission, freight, and risk, coming and returning; any thing herein contained to the contrary notwithstanding.

"We do not, however, think fit to extend this our indulgence to the article of *wool;* but, meaning to encourage, not only the manufacturing of woollen cloth, but also the raising of wool, in our ancient dominions, and to prevent both, as much as may be, in our said island, we do hereby absolutely forbid the transportation of wool from thence, even to the mother country, Prussia; and, that those islanders may be farther and more effectually restrained in making any advantage of their own wool in the way of manufacture, we command that none shall be carried out of one county into another; nor shall any worsted, bay, or woollen yarn, cloth, says, bays, kerseys, serges, frizes, druggets, cloth-serges, shalloons, or any other drapery stuffs, or woollen manufactures whatsoever, made up or mixed with wool in any of the said counties, be carried into any other county, or be water-borne even across the smallest river or creek; on penalty of forfeiture of the same, together with the boats, carriages, horses, &c., that shall be employed in removing them. Nevertheless, our loving subjects there are hereby permitted (if they think proper) to use all their wool as manure for the improvement of their lands.

"And whereas the art and mystery of making *hats* hath arrived at great perfection in Prussia, and the making of hats by our remoter subjects ought to be as much as possible restrained; and forasmuch as the islanders before mentioned, being in possession of wool, beaver, and other furs, have presumptuously conceived they had a right to make some advantage thereof, by manufacturing the same into hats, to the prejudice of our domestic manufacture; we do therefore hereby strictly command and ordain, that no hats or felts whatsoever, dyed or undyed, finished or unfinished, shall be loaded or put into or upon any vessel, cart, carriage, or horse, to be transported or conveyed out of one county in the said island into another county, or to any other place whatsoever, by any person or persons whatsoever; on pain of forfeiting the same, with a penalty of five hundred pounds sterling for every offence. Nor shall any hat-maker, in any of the said counties, employ more than two apprentices, on penalty of five pounds sterling per month; we intending hereby, that such hat-makers, being so restrained, both in the production and sale of their commodity, may find no advantage in continuing their business. But, lest the said islanders should suffer inconveniency by the want of hats, we are farther graciously pleased to permit them to send their beaver furs to Prussia; and we also permit hats made thereof to be exported from Prussia to Britain; the people thus favored to pay all costs and charges of manufacturing, interest, commission to our merchants, insurance and freight going and returning, as in the case of iron.

"And, lastly, being willing farther to favor our said colonies in Britain, we do hereby also ordain and command, that all the *thieves,* highway and street robbers, housebreakers, forgerers, murderers, s—d—tes, and villains of every denomination, who have forfeited their lives to the law in Prussia; but whom we, in our great clemency, do not think fit here to hang; shall be emptied out of our gaols into the said Island of Great Britain, for the better peopling of that country.

"We flatter ourselves, that these our royal regulations and commands will be thought *just and reasonable* by our much-favored colonists in England; the said regulations being copied from their Statutes of 10th and 11th William III. c. 10, 5th George II. c. 22, 23d George II. c. 29, 4th George I. c. 11, and from other equitable laws made by their Parliaments; or from instructions given by their princes; or from resolutions of both Houses, entered into for the good government of their *own colonies in Ireland and America.*

"And all persons in the said Island are hereby cautioned not to oppose in any wise the execution of this our Edict, or any part thereof, such opposition being high treason; of which all who are suspected shall be transported in fetters from Britain to Prussia, there to be tried and executed according to the Prussian law.

"Such is our pleasure.
"Given at Potsdam, this twenty-fifth day of the month of August, one thousand seven hundred and seventy-three, and in the thirty-third year of our reign.

"By the King, in his Council.

"RECHTMAESSIG, *Sec.*"

Some take this Edict to be merely one of the King's *jeux d'esprit;* others suppose it serious, and that he means a quarrel with England; but all here think the assertion it concludes with, "that these regulations are copied from acts of the English Parliament respecting their colonies," a very injurious one; it being impossible to believe, that a people distinguished for their love of liberty, a nation so wise, so liberal in its sentiments, so just and equitable towards its neighbours, should, from mean and injudicious views of petty immediate profit, treat its own children in a manner so arbitrary and tyrannical!

Friendly Enemy

To Thomas Cushing. London, 5 January, 1774.

A LETTER of mine to you, printed in one of the Boston papers, has lately been reprinted here, to show, as the publisher expresses it, that I am *"one of the most determined enemies* of the welfare and prosperity of Great Britain." In the opinion of some, every one who wishes the good of the *whole empire* may nevertheless be an enemy to *the welfare of Great Britain*, if he does not wish its good *exclusively* of every other *part*, and to see its welfare built on their servitude and wretchedness. Such an enemy I certainly am. But methinks it is wrong to print letters of mine at Boston, which give occasion to these reflections.

I shall continue to do all I possibly can this winter towards an accommodation of our differences; but my hopes are small. Divine Providence first infatuates the power it resigns to ruin.

Right of Petition

To Thomas Cushing. London, 15 February, 1774.

WE HAD long imagined, that the King would have considered that petition,* as he had done the preceding one, in his cabinet, and have given an answer without a hearing, since it did not pray punishments or disabilities on the governors. But on Saturday the 8th of January, in the afternoon, I received notice from the clerk of the Council, that the Lords of the Committee for Plantation Affairs, would, on the Tuesday following at twelve, meet at the Cockpit, to take into consideration the petition referred to them by his Majesty. . . .

Their Lordships' Report, which I send you, contains a severe censure, as you will see, on the petition and the petitioners . . . It may be supposed, that I am very angry on this occasion, and therefore I did purpose to add no reflections of mine on the treatment the Assembly and their agent have received, lest they should be thought the effects of resentment and a desire of exasperating. But, indeed, what I feel on my own account is half lost in what I feel for the public. When I see, that all petitions and complaints of grievances are so odious to government, that even the mere pipe which conveys them becomes obnoxious, I am at a loss to know how peace and union are to be maintained or restored between the different parts of the empire. Grievances cannot be redressed unless they are known; and they cannot be known but through complaints and petitions. If these are deemed affronts, and the messengers punished as offenders, who will henceforth send petitions? And who will deliver them? It has been thought a dangerous thing in any state to stop up the vent of griefs. Wise governments have therefore generally received petitions with some indulgence, even when but slightly founded. Those, who think themselves injured by their rulers, are sometimes, by a mild and prudent answer, convinced of their error. But where complaining is a crime, hope becomes despair.

*Of the Assembly of Massachusetts for the recall of Governor Hutchinson.

To William Franklin. London, 7 September, 1774.

You MENTION, that my presence is wished for at the Congress; but no person besides in America has given me the least intimation of such a desire, and it is thought by the great friends of the colonies here, that I ought to stay till the result of the Congress arrives, when my presence here may be useful. All depends on the Americans themselves. If they make, and keep firmly, resolutions not to consume British manufactures till their grievances are redressed, this ministry must fall, and the laws be repealed. This is the opinion of all the wise men here.

Censorship

To Mrs. Jane Mecom. London, 26 September, 1774.

I HOPE you continue in health, as I do, thanks to God. But I wish to know how you fare in the present distress of our dear country. I am apprehensive, that the letters between us, though very innocent ones, are intercepted. They might restore to me yours at least, after reading them; especially as I never complain of broken, patched-up seals (of late very common), because I know not on whom to fix the fact.

I see in a Boston paper of August 18th, an article expressing, "that it is generally believed Dr. Franklin has received a promise of being restored to the royal favor, and promoted to an office superior to that which he resigned." I have made no public answer to any of the abuses I have received in the papers here, nor shall I to this. But as I am anxious to preserve your good opinion, and as I know your sentiments, and that you must be much afflicted yourself, and even despise me, if you thought me capable of accepting any office from this government, while it is acting with so much hostility towards my native country, I cannot miss this first opportunity of assuring you, that there is not the least foundation for such a report; that, so far from having any promise of royal favor, I hear of nothing but royal and ministerial displeasure; which, indeed, as things at present stand, I consider as an honor. I have seen no minister since January, nor had the least communication with them. The generous and noble friends of America in both Houses do indeed favor me with their notice and regard; but they are in disgrace at court, as well as myself. Be satisfied, that I shall do nothing to lessen me in your esteem, or my own. I shall not, by the least concurrence with the present measures, merit any court favor, nor accept of any, if it were offered me, which, however, is not at all likely to happen.

As those here, who most interest themselves in behalf of America, conceive, that my being present at the arrival of the proceedings of the Congress and the meeting of Parliament may be of use, I submit to their judgment, and think it now likely, that I shall not return till spring.

Recommendation

To Richard Bache. London, 30 September, 1774.

THE BEARER, Mr. Thomas Paine, is very well recommended to me, as an ingenious, worthy young man. He goes to Pennsylvania with a view of settling there. I request you to give him your best advice and countenance, as he is quite a stranger there. If you can put him in a way of obtaining employment as a clerk, or assistant tutor in a school, or assistant surveyor (of all which I think him very capable), so that he may procure a subsistence at least, till he can make acquaintance and obtain a knowledge of the country, you will do well, and much oblige your affectionate father. My love to Sally and the boys.

Firm Stand

To James Bowdoin. London, 25 Feb., 1775.

IF WE continue firm and united, and resolutely persist in the non-consumption agreement, this adverse ministry cannot possibly stand another year. And surely the great body of our people, the farmers and artificers, will not find it hard to keep an agreement by which they both *save* and *gain*. The traders only can suffer, and, where they do really suffer, some compensation should if possible be made them. Hitherto the conduct of the colonies has given them great reputation all over Europe. By a brave perseverance, with prudence and moderation, not forward in acting offensively, but resolute in defence when necessary, they will establish a respectable character both for wisdom and courage; and then they will find friends everywhere. The eyes of all Christendom are now upon us, and our honor as a people is become a matter of the utmost consequence to be taken care of. If we tamely give up our rights in this contest, a century to come will not restore us in the opinion of the world; we shall be stamped with the character of dastards, poltroons, and fools; and be despised and trampled upon, not by this haughty, insolent nation only, but by all mankind. Present inconveniences are, therefore, to be borne with fortitude, and better times expected.

A Game of Chess

On board the Pennsylvania Packet, Captain Osborne, bound to Philadelphia, March 22d, 1775.

DEAR SON,—Having now a little leisure for writing, I will endeavour, as I promised you, to recollect what particulars I can of the negotiations I have lately been concerned in, with regard to the *misunderstandings between Great Britain and America*. . . .

When I came to England in 1757, you may remember I made several attempts to be introduced to Lord Chatham (at that time first minister), on account of my Pennsylvania business, but without success. He was then too great a man, or too much occupied in affairs of greater moment. I was therefore obliged to content myself with a kind of non-apparent and unacknowledged communication through Mr. Potter and Mr. Wood, his secretaries, who seemed to cultivate an acquaintance with me by their civilities, and drew from me what information I could give relative to the American war, with my sentiments occasionally on measures that were proposed or advised by others, which gave me the opportunity of recommending and enforcing the utility of conquering Canada. I afterwards considered Mr. Pitt as an *inaccessible*. I admired him at a distance, and made no more attempts for a nearer acquaintance. I had only once or twice the satisfaction of hearing through Lord Shelburne, and I think Lord Stanhope, that he did me the honor of mentioning me sometimes as a person of respectable character.

But towards the end of August last, returning from Brighthelmstone, I called to visit my friend, Mr. Sargent, at his seat, Halsted in Kent, agreeable to a former engagement. He let me know, that he had promised to conduct me to Lord Stanhope's at Chevening, who expected I would call on him when I came into that neighbourhood. We accordingly waited on Lord Stanhope that evening, who told me Lord Chatham desired to see me, and that Mr. Sargent's house, where I was to lodge, being in the way, he would call for me there the next morning, and carry me to Hayes. This was done accordingly. That truly great man received me with abundance of civility, inquired particularly into the situation of affairs in America, spoke feelingly of the severity of the late laws against the Massachusetts, gave me some account of his speech in opposing them, and expressed great regard and esteem for the people of that country, who he hoped would continue firm and united in defending by all peaceable and legal means their constitutional rights. I assured him, that I made no doubt they would do so; which he said he was pleased to hear from me, as he was sensible I must be well acquainted with them.

I then took occasion to remark to him, that in former cases great empires had crumbled first at their extremities, from this cause; that countries remote from the seat and eye of government, which therefore could not well understand their affairs for want of full and true information, had never been well governed, but had been oppressed by bad governors, on presumption that complaint was difficult to be made and supported against them at such a distance. Hence, such governors had been encouraged to go on, till their oppressions became intolerable. But that this empire had happily found, and long been in the practice of, a method, whereby every province was well governed, being trusted in a great measure with the government of itself; and that hence had arisen such satisfaction in the subjects, and such encouragement to new settlements, that, had it not been for the late wrong politics (which would have Parliament to be *omnipotent*, though it ought not to be so unless it could at the same time be *omniscient*) we might have gone on extending our western empire, adding province to province, as far as the South Sea. That I lamented the ruin which seemed impending over so fine a plan, so well adapted to make all the subjects of the greatest empire happy; and I hoped that, if his Lordship, with the other great and wise men of the British nation, would unite and exert themselves, it might yet be rescued out of the mangling hands of the present set of blundering ministers; and that the union and harmony between Britain and her colonies, so necessary to the welfare of both, might be restored.

He replied, with great politeness, that my idea of extending our empire in that manner was a sound one, worthy of a great, benevolent, and comprehensive mind. He wished with me for a good understanding among the different parts of the opposition here, as a means of restoring the ancient harmony of the two countries, which he most earnestly desired; but he spoke of the coalition of our domestic parties, as attended with difficulty, and rather to be desired than expected. He mentioned an opinion prevailing here, that America aimed at setting up for itself as an *independent state;* or, at least, to get rid of the *Navigation Acts.* I assured him, that, having more than once travelled almost from one end of the continent to the other, and kept a great variety of company, eating, drinking, and conversing with them freely, I never had heard in any conversation, from any person, drunk or sober, the least expression of a wish for a separation, or hint that such a thing would be advantageous to America. And as to the Navigation Act, the main, material part of it, that of carrying on trade in British or plantation bottoms, excluding foreign ships from our ports, and navigating with three quarters British seamen, was as acceptable to us as it could be to Britain. That we were even not against regulations of the general commerce by Parliament, provided such regulations were *bona fide* for the benefit of the *whole empire,* not for the small advantage of one part to the great injury of another, such as the obliging our ships to call in England with our wine and fruit, from Portugal or Spain; the restraints on our manufactures, in the woollen and hatmaking branches, the prohibiting of slitting-mills, steel-works, &c. He allowed, that some amendment might be made in those acts; but said those relating to the slitting-mills, trip-hammers, and steel-works, were agreed to by our agents, in a compromise on the opposition made here to abating the duty.

In fine, he expressed much satisfaction in my having called upon him, and particularly in the assurances I had given him, that America did not aim at *independence;* adding, that he should be glad to see me again as often as might be. I said, I should not fail to avail myself of the permission he was pleased to give me of waiting upon his Lordship occasionally, being very sensible of the honor, and of the great advantages and improvement I should reap, from his instructive conversation; which indeed was not a mere compliment.

The new Parliament was to meet the 29th of November, 1774. About the beginning of that month, being at the Royal Society, Mr. Raper, one of our members, told me there was a certain lady who had a desire of playing with me at chess, fancying she could beat me, and had requested him to bring me to her. It was, he said, a lady with whose acquaintance he was sure I should be pleased, a sister of Lord Howe's, and he hoped I would not refuse the challenge. I said, I had been long out of practice, but would wait upon the lady when he and she should think fit. He told me where her house was, and would have me call soon, and without further introduction, which I undertook to do; but, thinking it a little awkward, I postponed it; and on the 30th, meeting him again at the feast of the Society election, being the day after the Parliament met, he put me in mind of my promise, and that I had not kept it, and would have me name a day when he said he would call for me, and conduct me. I named the Friday following. He called accordingly. I went with him, played a few games with the lady, whom I found of very sensible conversation and pleasing behaviour, which induced me to agree most readily to an appointment for another meeting a few days afterwards; though I had not the least apprehension that any political business could have any connexion with this new acquaintance.

On the Thursday preceding this chess party, Mr. David Barclay called on me to have some discourse concerning the meeting of merchants to petition Parliament. When that was over, he spoke of the dangerous situation of American affairs, the hazard that a civil war might be brought on by the present measures, and the great merit that person would have, who could contrive some means of preventing so terrible a calamity, and bring about a reconciliation. He was then pleased to add, that he was persuaded, from my knowledge of both countries, my character and influence in one of them, and my abilities in business, no man had it so much in his power as myself. I naturally answered, that I should be very happy if I could in any degree be instrumental in so good a work, but that I saw no prospect of it; for, though I was sure the Americans were always willing and ready to agree upon any equitable terms, yet I thought an accommodation impracticable, unless both sides wished it; and, by what I could judge from the proceedings of the ministry, I did not believe they had the least disposition towards it; that they rather wished to provoke the North American people into an open rebellion, which might justify a military execution, and thereby gratify a grounded malice, which I conceived to exist here against the Whigs and Dissenters of that country. Mr. Barclay apprehended I judged too hardly of the ministers; he was persuaded they were not all of that temper, and he fancied they would be very glad to get out of their present embarrassment on any terms, only saving the honor and dignity of government. He wished, therefore, that I would think of the matter, and he would call again and converse with me further upon it. I said I would do so, as he requested it, but I had no opinion of its answering any purpose. We parted upon this. But two days after I received a letter from him, enclosed in a note from Dr. Fothergill, both which follow.

"Youngsbury, near Ware, 3d 12th Month, 1774.

"Esteemed Friend,

"After we parted on Thursday last, I accidentally met our mutual friend, Dr. Fothergill, on my way home, and intimated to him the subject of our discourse; in consequence of which, I have received from him an invitation to a further conference on this momentous affair, and I intend to be in town to-morrow accordingly, to meet at his house between four and five o'clock; and we unite in the request of thy company. We are neither of us insensible, that the affair is of that *magnitude* as should almost deter private persons from meddling with it; at the same time we are respectively such well-wishers to the cause, that nothing in our power ought to be left undone, though the utmost of our efforts may be unavailable. I am thy respectful friend, DAVID BARCLAY.

"DR. FRANKLIN, *Craven Street.*"

"DR. FOTHERGILL presents his respects to Dr. Franklin, and hopes for the favor of his company in Harpur Street to-morrow evening, to meet their mutual friend, David Barclay, to confer on American affairs. As near five o'clock as may be convenient.

"*Harpur Street, 3d inst.*"

The time thus appointed was the evening of the day on which I was to have my second chess party with the agreeable Mrs. Howe, whom I met accordingly. After playing as long as we liked, we fell into a little chat, partly on a mathematical problem, and partly about the new Parliament, then just met, when she said, "And what is to be done with this dispute between Great Britain and the colonies? I hope we are not to have a civil war." "They should kiss and be friends," said I; "what can they do better? Quarrelling can be of service to neither, but is ruin to both." "I have often said," replied she, "that I wished government would employ you to settle the dispute for them; I am sure nobody could do it so well. Do not you think that the thing is practicable?" "Undoubtedly, Madam, if the parties are disposed to reconciliation; for the two countries have really no clashing interests to differ about. It is rather a matter of punctilio, which two or three reasonable people might settle in half an hour. I thank you for the good opinion you are pleased to express of me; but the ministers will never think of employing me in that good work; they choose rather to abuse me." "Ay," said she, "they have behaved shamefully to you. And indeed some of them are now ashamed of it themselves." I looked upon this as accidental conversation, thought no more of it, and went in the evening to the appointed meeting at Dr. Fothergill's, where I found Mr. Barclay with him.

The Doctor expatiated feelingly on the mischiefs likely to ensue from the present difference, the necessity of accommodating it, and the great merit of being instrumental in so good a work; concluding with some compliments to me; that nobody understood the subject so thoroughly, and had a better head for business of the kind; that it seemed therefore a duty incumbent on me, to do every thing I could to accomplish a reconciliation; and that, as he had with pleasure heard from David Barclay, that I had promised to think of it, he hoped I had put pen to paper, and formed some plan for consideration, and brought it with me. I answered, that I had formed no plan; as, the more I thought of the proceedings against the colonies, the more satisfied I was, that there did not exist the least disposition in the ministry to an accommodation; that therefore all plans must be useless. He said, I might be mistaken; that, whatever was the violence of some, he had reason, *good reason*, to believe others were differently disposed; and that, if I would draw a plan, which we three upon considering should judge reasonable, it might be made use of, and answer some good purpose, since he believed that either himself or David Barclay could get it communicated to some of the most moderate among the ministers, who would consider it with attention; and what appeared reasonable to us, two of us being Englishmen, might appear so to them.

As they both urged this with great earnestness, and, when I mentioned the impropriety of my doing any thing of the kind at the time we were in daily expectation of hearing from the Congress, who undoubtedly would be explicit on the means of restoring a good understanding, they seemed impatient, alleging, that it was uncertain when we should receive the result of the Congress, and what it would be; that the least delay might be dangerous; that additional punishments for New England were in contemplation, and accidents might widen the breach, and make it irreparable; therefore, something preventive could not be too soon thought of and applied. I was therefore finally prevailed with to promise doing what they desired, and to meet them again on Tuesday evening at the same place, and bring with me something for their consideration.

Accordingly, at the time, I met with them, and produced the following paper.

"Hints for Conversation *upon the Subject of Terms that might probably produce a Durable Union between Britain and the Colonies.*

"1. The tea destroyed to be paid for.

"2. The Tea-duty Act to be repealed, and all the duties that have been received upon it to be repaid into the treasuries of the several provinces from which they have been collected.

"3. The Acts of Navigation to be all reënacted in the colonies.

"4. A naval officer, appointed by the crown, to reside in each colony, to see that those acts are observed.

"5. All the acts restraining manufactures in the colonies to be repealed.

"6. All duties arising on the acts for regulating trade with the colonies, to be for the public use of the respective colonies, and paid into their treasuries. The collectors and custom-house officers to be appointed by each governor, and not sent from England.

"7. In consideration of the Americans maintaining their own peace establishment, and the monopoly Britain is to have of their commerce, no requisition to be made from them in time of peace.

"8. No troops to enter and quarter in any colony, but with the consent of its legislature.

"9. In time of war, on requisition made by the King, with the consent of Parliament, every colony shall raise money by the following rules or proportions, viz. If Britain, on account of the war, raises three shillings in the pound to its land tax, then the colonies to add to their last general provincial peace tax a sum equal to one fourth thereof; and if Britain, on the same account, pays four shillings in the pound, then the colonies to add to their said last peace tax a sum equal to half thereof, which additional tax is to be granted to his Majesty, and to be employed in raising and paying men for land or sea service, furnishing provisions, transports, or for such other purposes as the King shall require and direct. And, though no colony may contribute less, each may add as much by voluntary grant as they shall think proper.

"10. Castle William to be restored to the province of the Massachusetts Bay, and no fortress built by the crown in any province, but with the consent of its legislature.

"11. The late Massachusetts and Quebec Acts to be repealed, and a free government granted to Canada.

"12. All judges to be appointed during good behaviour, with equally permanent salaries, to be paid out of the province revenues by appointment of the Assemblies. Or, if the judges are to be appointed during the pleasure of the crown, let the salaries be during the pleasure of the Assemblies, as heretofore.

"13. Governors to be supported by the Assemblies of each province.

"14. If Britain will give up its monopoly of the American commerce, then the aid above mentioned to be given by America in time of peace as well as in time of war.

"15. The extension of the act of Henry the Eighth, concerning treasons, to the colonies, to be formally disowned by Parliament.

"16. The American admiralty courts reduced to the same powers they have in England, and the acts establishing them to be reënacted in America.

"17. All powers of internal legislation in the colonies to be disclaimed by Parliament."

In reading this paper a second time, I gave my reasons at length for each article. . . .

About this time, I received a letter from Mr. Barclay, then at Norwich, dated December 18th, expressing his opinion, that it might be best to postpone taking any further steps in the affair of procuring a meeting and petition of the merchants (on which we had had several consultations) till after the holidays, thereby to give the proceedings of Congress more time to work upon men's minds; adding, "I likewise consider, that our superiors will have some little time for reflection, and perhaps may contemplate on the propriety of the 'HINTS' in their possession. By a few lines I have received from Lord Hyde, he intimates his hearty wish that they may be productive of what may be practicable and advantageous for the mother country and the colonies."

On the 22d, Mr. Barclay was come to town, when I dined with him, and learnt that Lord Hyde thought the propositions too hard.

On the 24th, I received the following note from a considerable merchant in the city, viz:

"Mr. WILLIAM NEATE presents his most respectful compliments to Dr. Franklin, and, as a report prevailed yesterday evening, that all the disputes between Great Britain and the American colonies were, through his application and influence with Lord North, amicably settled, conformable to the wish and desire of the late Congress, W. N. desires the favor of Dr. Franklin to inform him by a line, per the bearer, whether there is any credit to be given to the report.

"*St. Mary Hill, 24th December, 1774.*"

My answer was to this effect; that I should be very happy to be able to inform him, that the report he had heard had some truth in it; but I could only assure him, that I knew nothing of the matter. Such reports, however, were confidentially circulated, and had some effect in recovering the stocks, which had fallen three or four per cent.

On Christmas-day evening, visiting Mrs. Howe, she told me as soon as I went in, that her brother, Lord Howe, wished to be acquainted with me; that he was a very good man, and she was sure we should like each other. I said, I had always heard a good character of Lord Howe, and should be proud of the honor of being known to him. "He is but just by," said she; "will you give me leave to send for him?" "By all means, Madam, if you think proper." She rang for a servant, wrote a note, and Lord Howe came in a few minutes.

After some extremely polite compliments, as to the general motives for his desiring an acquaintance with me, he said he had a particular one at this time, which was the alarming situation of our affairs with America, which no one, he was persuaded, understood better than myself; that it was the opinion of some friends of his, that no man could do more towards reconciling our differences than I could, if I would undertake it; that he was sensible I had been very ill treated by the ministry, but he hoped that would not be considered by me in the present case; that he himself, though not in opposition, had much disapproved of their conduct towards me; that some of them, he was sure, were ashamed of it, and sorry it had happened; which he supposed must be sufficient to abate resentment in a great and generous mind; that, if he were himself in administration, he should be ready to make me ample satisfaction, which, he was persuaded, would one day or other be done; that he was unconnected with the ministry, except by some personal friendships, wished well however to government, was anxious for

the general welfare of the whole empire, and had a particular regard for
New England, which had shown a very endearing respect to his family;
that he was merely an independent member of Parliament, desirous of doing
what good he could, agreeably to his duty in that station; that he therefore
had wished for an opportunity of obtaining my sentiments on the means of
reconciling our differences, which he saw must be attended with the most
mischievous consequences, if not speedily accommodated; that he hoped his
zeal for the public welfare would, with me, excuse the impertinence of a
mere stranger, who could have otherwise no reason to expect, or right to
request, me to open my mind to him on these topics; but he did conceive,
that, if I would indulge him with my ideas of the means proper to bring
about a reconciliation, it might be of some use; that perhaps I might not be
willing myself to have any *direct* communication with this ministry on this
occasion; that I might likewise not care to have it known, that I had any
indirect communication with them, till I could be well assured of their good
dispositions; that, being himself upon no ill terms with them, he thought it
not impossible that he might, by conveying my sentiments to them and
theirs to me, be a means of bringing on a good understanding, without committing either them or me, if his negotiation should not succeed; and that I
might rely on his keeping perfectly secret every thing I should wish to
remain so.

Mrs. Howe here offering to withdraw, whether of herself, or from any
sign from him, I know not, I begged she might stay, as I should have no
secret in a business of this nature, that I could not freely confide to her
prudence; which was truth; for I had never conceived a higher opinion of
the discretion and excellent understanding of any woman on so short an
acquaintance. I added, that, though I had never before the honor of being in
his Lordship's company, his manner was such as had already engaged my
confidence, and would make me perfectly easy and free in communicating
myself to him.

I begged him, in the first place, to give me credit for a sincere desire of
healing the breach between the two countries; that I would cheerfully and
heartily do every thing in my small power to accomplish it; but that I
apprehended from the King's speech, and from the measures talked of, as
well as those already determined on, no intention or disposition of the kind
existed in the present ministry, and therefore no accommodation could be
expected till we saw a change. That, as to what his Lordship mentioned of
the *personal injuries* done me, those done my country were so much greater,
that I did not think the other, at this time, worth mentioning; that, besides,
it was a fixed rule with me, not to mix my private affairs with those of the
public; that I could join with my personal enemy in serving the public, or,
when it was for its interest, with the public in serving that enemy; these
being my sentiments, his Lordship might be assured, that no private considerations of the kind should prevent my being as useful in the present case as
my small ability would permit.

He appeared satisfied and pleased with these declarations, and gave it me as his sincere opinion, that some of the ministry were extremely well disposed to any reasonable accommodation, preserving only the dignity of government; and he wished me to draw up in writing some propositions containing the terms on which I conceived a good understanding might be obtained and established, and the mode of proceeding to accomplish it; which propositions, as soon as prepared, we might meet to consider, either at his house, or at mine, or where I pleased; but, as his being seen at my house, or me at his, might, he thought, occasion some speculation, it was concluded to be best to meet at his sister's, who readily offered her house for the purpose, and where there was a good pretence with her family and friends for my being often seen, as it was known we played together at chess. I undertook, accordingly, to draw up something of the kind; and so for that time we parted, agreeing to meet at the same place again on the Wednesday following.

I dined about this time by invitation with Governor Pownall. There was no company but the family; and after dinner we had a *tête-à-tête*. He had been in the opposition; but was now about making his peace, in order to come into Parliament upon ministerial interest, which I did not then know. He told me, what I had before been told by several of Lord North's friends, that the American measures were not the measures of that minister, nor approved by him; that, on the contrary, he was well disposed to promote a reconciliation upon any terms honorable to government; that I had been looked upon as the great fomenter of the opposition in America, and as a great adversary to any accommodation; that he, Governor Pownall, had given a different account of me, and had told his Lordship that I was certainly much misunderstood. From the Governor's further discourse I collected, that he wished to be employed as an envoy or commissioner to America, to settle the differences, and to have me with him; but, as I apprehended there was little likelihood that either of us would be so employed by government, I did not give much attention to that part of his discourse.

I should have mentioned in its place (but one cannot recollect every thing in order), that, declining at first to draw up the propositions desired by Lord Howe, I alleged its being unnecessary, since the Congress in their petition to the King, just then received and presented through Lord Dartmouth, had stated their grievances, and pointed out very explicitly what would restore the ancient harmony; and I read a part of the petition to show their good dispositions, which, being very pathetically expressed, seemed to affect both the brother and sister. But still I was desired to give my ideas of the steps to be taken, in case some of the propositions in the petition should not be thought admissible. And this, as I said before, I undertook to do.

I had promised Lord Chatham to communicate to him the first important news I should receive from America. I therefore sent him the proceedings of the Congress as soon as I received them; but a whole week passed after I received the petition, before I could, as I wished to do, wait upon him with it, in order to obtain his sentiments on the *whole;* for my time was taken up in meetings with the other agents to consult about presenting the petition, in waiting three different days with them on Lord Dartmouth, in consulting upon and writing letters to the Speakers of Assemblies, and other business, which did not allow me a day to go to Hayes.

At last, on Monday the 26th, I got out, and was there about one o'clock. He received me with an affectionate kind of respect, that from so great a man was extremely engaging; but the opinion he expressed of the Congress was still more so. They had acted, he said, with so much temper, moderation, and wisdom, that he thought it the most honorable assembly of statesmen since those of the ancient Greeks and Romans, in the most virtuous times. That there were not in their whole proceedings above one or two things he could have wished otherwise; perhaps but one, and that was their assertion, that the keeping up a standing army in the colonies in time of peace, without consent of their legislatures, was against law. He doubted that was not well founded, and that the law alluded to did not extend to the colonies. The rest he admired and honored. He thought the petition decent, manly, and properly expressed. He inquired much and particularly concerning the state of America, the probability of their perseverance, the difficulties they must meet with in adhering for any long time to their resolutions, the resources they might have to supply the deficiency of commerce; to all which I gave him answers with which he seemed well satisfied. He expressed a great regard and warm affection for that country, with hearty wishes for their prosperity; and that government here might soon come to see its mistakes, and rectify them; and intimated that possibly he might, if his health permitted, prepare something for its consideration, when the Parliament should meet after the holidays; on which he should wish to have previously my sentiments.

I mentioned to him the very hazardous state I conceived we were in, by the continuance of the army in Boston; that, whatever disposition there might be in the inhabitants to give no just cause of offence to the troops, or in the general to preserve order among them, an unpremeditated, unforeseen quarrel might happen between perhaps a drunken porter and a soldier, that might bring on a riot, tumult, and bloodshed, and in its consequences produce a breach impossible to be healed; that the army could not possibly answer any good purpose *there*, and might be infinitely mischievous; that no accommodation could properly be proposed and entered into by the Americans, while the bayonet was at their breasts; that, to have any agreement binding, all force should be withdrawn. His Lordship seemed to think these sentiments had something in them that was reasonable.

From Hayes I went to Halsted, Mr. Sargent's place, to dine, intending thence a visit to Lord Stanhope at Chevening; but, hearing that his Lordship and the family were in town, I stayed at Halsted all night, and the next morning went to Chislehurst to call upon Lord Camden, it being in my way to town. I met his Lordship and family in two carriages just without his gate, going on a visit of congratulation to Lord Chatham and his lady, on the late marriage of their daughter to Lord Mahon, son of Lord Stanhope. They were to be back at dinner; so I agreed to go in, stay dinner, and spend the evening there, and not return to town till next morning. We had that afternoon and evening a great deal of conversation on American affairs, concerning which he was very inquisitive, and I gave him the best information in my power. I was charmed with his generous and noble sentiments; and had the great pleasure of hearing his full approbation of the proceedings of the Congress, the petition, &c. &c., of which, at his request, I afterwards sent him a copy. He seemed anxious that the Americans should continue to act with the same temper, coolness, and wisdom, with which they had hitherto proceeded in most of their public assemblies, in which case he did not doubt they would succeed in establishing their rights, and obtain a solid and durable agreement with the mother country; of the necessity and great importance of which agreement, he seemed to have the strongest impressions.

I returned to town the next morning, in time to meet at the hour appointed by Lord Howe. I apologized for my not being ready with the paper I had promised, by my having been kept longer than I intended in the country. We had, however, a good deal of conversation on the subject, and his Lordship told me he could now assure me, of a certainty, that there was a sincere disposition in Lord North and Lord Dartmouth to accommodate the differences with America, and to listen favorably to any proposition that might have a probable tendency to answer that salutary purpose. He then asked me what I thought of sending some person or persons over, commissioned to inquire into the grievances of America upon the spot, converse with the leading people, and endeavour with them to agree upon some means of composing our differences. I said, that a person of rank and dignity, who had a character of candor, integrity, and wisdom, might possibly, if employed in that service, be of great use.

He seemed to be of the same opinion, and that whoever was employed should go with a hearty desire of promoting a sincere reconciliation, on the foundation of mutual interests and mutual good-will; that he should endeavour, not only to remove their prejudices against government, but equally the prejudices of government against them, and bring on a perfect good understanding, &c. Mrs. Howe said, "I wish, brother, you were to be sent thither on such a service; I should like that much better than General Howe's going to command the army there." "I think, Madam," said I, "they ought to provide for General Howe some more honorable employment." Lord Howe here took out of his pocket a paper, and offering it to me said, smiling, "If it is not an unfair question, may I ask whether you know any thing of this paper?" Upon looking at it, I saw it was a copy, in David Barclay's hand, of the "Hints" before recited; and said, that I had seen it; adding, a little after, that, since I perceived his Lordship was acquainted with a transaction, my concern in which I had understood was to have been kept a secret, I should make no difficulty in owning to him, that I had been consulted on the subject, and had drawn up that paper. He said, he was rather sorry to find that the sentiments expressed in it were mine, as it gave him less hopes of promoting, by my assistance, the wished-for reconciliation; since he had reason to think there was no likelihood of the admission of those propositions. He hoped, however, that I would reconsider the subject, and form some plan that would be acceptable here. He expatiated on the infinite service it would be to the nation, and the great merit in being instrumental in so good a work; that he should not think of influencing me by any selfish motive, but certainly I might with reason expect any reward in the power of government to bestow.

This to me was what the French vulgarly call *spitting in the soup*. However, I promised to draw some sketch of a plan, at his request, though I much doubted, I said, whether it would be thought preferable to that he had in his hand. But he was willing to hope that it would; and, as he considered my situation, that I had friends here and constituents in America to keep well with, that I might possibly propose something improper to be seen in my handwriting; therefore, it would be better to send it to Mrs. Howe, who would copy it, send the copy to him to be communicated to the ministry, and return me the original. This I agreed to, though I did not apprehend the inconvenience he mentioned. In general, I liked much his manner, and found myself disposed to place great confidence in him on occasion; but in this particular the secrecy he proposed seemed not of much importance.

In a day or two, I sent the following paper, enclosed in a cover, directed to the Honorable Mrs. Howe.

"It is supposed to be the wish on both sides, not merely to put a stop to the mischief at present threatening the general welfare, but to cement a *cordial union*, and remove, not only every real grievance, but every cause of jealousy and suspicion.

"With this view, the first thing necessary is, to know what is, by the different parties in the dispute, thought essentially necessary for the obtaining such a union.

"The American Congress, in their petition to the King, have been explicit, declaring, that by a repeal of the oppressive acts therein complained of, '*the harmony between Great Britain and the colonies, so necessary to the happiness of both, and so ardently desired of them, will, with the usual intercourse, be immediately restored.*'

"If it has been thought reasonable here, to expect that, previous to an alteration of measures, the colonies should make some declaration respecting their future conduct, they have also done that, by adding, '*That, when the causes of their apprehensions are removed, their future conduct will prove them not unworthy of the regard they have been accustomed in their happier days to enjoy.*'

"For their sincerity in these declarations, they solemnly call to witness the Searcher of all hearts.

"If Britain can have any reliance on these declarations (and perhaps none to be extorted by force can be more relied on than these, which are thus freely made), she may, without hazard to herself, try the expedient proposed, since, if it fails, she has it in her power at any time to resume her present measures.

"It is then proposed; That Britain should show some confidence in these declarations, by repealing all the laws or parts of laws, that are requested to be repealed in the Petition of the Congress to the King;

"And that, at the same time, orders should be given to withdraw the fleet from Boston, and remove all the troops to Quebec, or the Floridas, that the colonies may be left at perfect liberty in their future stipulations.

"That this may, for the honor of Britain, appear not the effect of any apprehension from the measures entered into and recommended to the people by the Congress, but from good-will, and a change of disposition towards the colonies, with a sincere desire of reconciliation; let some of their other grievances, which in their petition they have left to the magnanimity and justice of the King and Parliament, be at the same time removed, such as those relating to the payment of governors' and judges' salaries, and the instructions for dissolving Assemblies, &c., with the declarations concerning the statute of Henry the Eighth.

"And to give the colonies an immediate opportunity of demonstrating the reality of their professions, let their proposed ensuing Congress be authorized by government (as was that held at Albany, in 1754), and a person of weight and dignity of character be appointed to preside at it on behalf of the crown.

"And then let requisition be made to the Congress, of such points as government wishes to obtain for its future security, for aids, for the advantage of general commerce, for reparation to the India Company, &c. &c.

"A generous confidence thus placed in the colonies, will give ground to the friends of government there, in their endeavours to procure from America every reasonable concession, or engagement, and every substantial aid, that can fairly be desired."

On the Saturday evening, I saw Mrs. Howe, who informed me she had transcribed and sent the paper to Lord Howe in the country, and she returned me the original. On the following Tuesday, January 3d, I received a note from her (enclosing a letter she had received from Lord Howe the last night), as follows.

"MRS. HOWE's compliments to Dr. Franklin; she encloses him a letter she received last night, and returns him many thanks for his very obliging present,* which has already given her great entertainment. If the Doctor has any spare time for chess, she will be exceedingly glad to see him any morning this week, and as often as will be agreeable to him, and rejoices in having so good an excuse for asking the favor of his company.

"*Tuesday*."

*Franklin's Philosophical Writings.

"TO THE HONORABLE MRS. HOWE.

"Grafton Street. Porter's Lodge, January 2d, 1775.

"I have received your packet; and it is with much concern that I collect, from sentiments of such authority as those of our worthy friend, that the desired accommodation threatens to be attended with much greater difficulty than I had flattered myself, in the progress of our intercourse, there would be reason to apprehend.

"I shall forward the propositions as intended, not desirous of trespassing further on our friend's indulgence; but retaining sentiments of regard, which his candid and obliging attention to my troublesome inquiries will render ever permanent in the memory of your affectionate, &c.

"HOWE.

"I ought to make excuses likewise to you."

His Lordship had, in his last conversation with me, acknowledged a communication between him and the ministry, to whom he wished to make my sentiments known. In this letter from the country he owns the receipt of them, and mentions his intention of forwarding them, that is, as I understood it, to the ministers; but expresses his apprehensions, that such propositions were not likely to produce any good effect. Some time after, perhaps a week, I received a note from Mrs. Howe, desiring to see me. I waited upon her immediately, when she showed me a letter from her brother, of which having no copy, I can only give from the best of my recollection the purport of it, which I think was this; that he desired to know from their friend, meaning me, through her means, whether it might not be expected, that if that friend would engage for their payment of the tea as a preliminary, relying on a promised redress of their grievances on future petitions from their Assembly, they would approve of his making such engagement; and whether the proposition in the former paper (the "HINTS") relating to aids, was still in contemplation of the author. As Mrs. Howe proposed sending to her brother that evening, I wrote immediately the following answer, which she transcribed and forwarded.

"The proposition in the former paper relating to aids, is still in contemplation of the author, and, as he thinks, is included in the last article of the present paper.

"The people of America, conceiving that Parliament has no right to tax them, and that therefore all that has been extorted from them by the operation of the duty acts, with the assistance of an armed force, *preceding* the destruction of the tea, is so much injury, which ought in order of time to be first repaired, before a demand on the tea account can be justly made of them, are not, he thinks, likely to approve of the measure proposed, and pay *in the first place* the value demanded, especially as twenty times as much injury has since been done them by blocking up their port; and their castle also, seized before by the crown, has not been restored, nor any satisfaction offered them for the same."

At the meeting of Parliament after the holidays, which was on the 19th of January, 1775, Lord Howe returned to town, when we had another meeting, at which he lamented, that my propositions were not such as probably could be accepted; intimated, that it was thought I had powers or instructions from the Congress to make concessions on occasion, that would be more satisfactory. I disclaimed the having any of any kind, but what related to the presenting of their petition. We talked over all the particulars in my paper, which I supported with reasons; and finally said, that, if what I had proposed would not do, I should be glad to hear what would do; I wished to see some propositions from the ministers themselves. His Lordship was not, he said, as yet fully acquainted with their sentiments, but should learn more in a few days. It was, however, some weeks before I heard any thing further from him.

In the mean while, Mr. Barclay and I were frequently together on the affair of preparing the merchants' petition, which took up so much of his time that he could not conveniently see Lord Hyde; so he had no information to give me concerning the "Hints," and I wondered I heard nothing of them from Dr. Fothergill. At length, however, but I cannot recollect about what time, the Doctor called on me, and told me he had communicated them, and with them had verbally given my arguments in support of them, to Lord Dartmouth, who, after consideration, had told him, some of them appeared reasonable, but others were inadmissible or impracticable. That having occasion to see frequently the Speaker,* he had also communicated them to him, as he found him very anxious for a reconciliation. That the Speaker had said it would be very humiliating to Britain to be obliged to submit to such terms; but the Doctor told him she had been unjust, and ought to bear the consequences, and alter her conduct; that the pill might be bitter, but it would be salutary, and must be swallowed. That these were the sentiments of impartial men, after thorough consideration and full information of all circumstances; and that sooner or later these or similar measures must be followed, or the empire would be divided and ruined. The Doctor, on the whole, hoped some good would be effected by our endeavours.

On the 19th of January, I received a card from Lord Stanhope, acquainting me, that Lord Chatham, having a motion to make on the morrow in the House of Lords, concerning America, greatly desired that I might be in the House, into which Lord Stanhope would endeavour to procure me admittance. At this time it was a rule of the House, that no person could introduce more than one friend. The next morning his Lordship let me know by another card, that, if I attended at two o'clock in the lobby, Lord Chatham would be there about that time, and would himself introduce me. I attended,

*Sir Fletcher Norton.

and met him there accordingly. On my mentioning to him what Lord Stanhope had written to me, he said, "Certainly; and I shall do it with the more pleasure, as I am sure your being present at this day's debate will be of more service to America than mine"; and so taking me by the arm was leading me along the passage to the door that enters near the throne, when one of the door-keepers followed, and acquainted him that, by the order, none were to be carried in at that door but the eldest sons or brothers of peers; on which he limped back with me to the door near the bar, where were standing a number of gentlemen, waiting for the peers who were to introduce them, and some peers waiting for friends they expected to introduce; among whom he delivered me to the door-keepers, saying, aloud, "This is Dr. Franklin, whom I would have admitted into the House"; when they readily opened the door for me accordingly.

As it had not been publicly known, that there was any communication between his Lordship and me, this I found occasioned some speculation. His appearance in the House, I observed, caused a kind of bustle among the officers, who were hurried in sending messengers for members, I suppose those in connexion with the ministry, something of importance being expected when that great man appears; it being but seldom that his infirmities permit his attendance. I had great satisfaction in hearing his motion and the debate upon it, which I shall not attempt to give here an account of, as you may find a better in the papers of the time. It was his motion for withdrawing the troops from Boston, as the first step towards an accommodation.

The day following, I received a note from Lord Stanhope expressing, that, "at the desire of Lord Chatham, was sent me enclosed the motion he made in the House of Lords, that I might be possessed of it in the most authentic manner, by the communication of the individual paper, which was read to the House by the mover himself." I sent copies of this motion to America, and was the more pleased with it, as I conceived it had partly taken its rise from a hint I had given his Lordship in a former conversation. . . .

I was quite charmed with Lord Chatham's speech in support of his motion. He impressed me with the highest idea of him, as a great and most able statesman. Lord Camden, another wonderfully good speaker and close reasoner, joined him in the same argument, as did several other Lords, who spoke excellently well; but all availed no more than the whistling of the winds. The motion was rejected. Sixteen Scotch peers, and twenty-four bishops, with all the lords in possession or expectation of places, when they vote together unanimously, as they generally do for ministerial measures, make a dead majority, that renders all debating ridiculous in itself, since it can answer no end. Full of the high esteem I had imbibed for Lord Chatham, I wrote back to Lord Stanhope the following note, viz.

"Dr. Franklin presents his best respects to Lord Stanhope, with many thanks to his Lordship and Lord Chatham for the communication of so authentic a copy of the motion. Dr. F. is filled with admiration of that truly great man. He has seen, in the course of life, sometimes eloquence without wisdom, and often wisdom without eloquence; in the present instance he sees both united, and both, as he thinks, in the highest degree possible.

"*Craven Street, January 23d, 1775.*"

As in the course of the debate some Lords in the administration had observed, that it was common and easy to censure their measures, but those who did so proposed nothing better, Lord Chatham mentioned, that he should not be one of those idle censurers; that he had thought long and closely upon the subject, and proposed soon to lay before their Lordships the result of his meditation, in a plan for healing our differences, and restoring peace to the empire, to which his present motion was preparatory. I much desired to know what his plan was, and intended waiting on him to see if he would communicate it to me; but he went the next morning to Hayes, and I was so much taken up with daily business and company, that I could not easily get out to him. A few days after, however, Lord Mahon called on me, and told me Lord Chatham was very desirous of seeing me; when I promised to be with him the Friday following, several engagements preventing my going sooner.

On Friday the 27th, I took a post-chaise about nine o'clock, and got to Hayes about eleven; but, my attention being engaged in reading a new pamphlet, the post-boy drove me a mile or two beyond the gate. His Lordship, being out on an airing in his chariot, had met me before I reached Hayes, unobserved by me, turned and followed me, and not finding me there, concluded, as he had seen me reading, that I had passed by mistake, and sent a servant after me. He expressed great pleasure at my coming, and acquainted me in a long conversation with the outlines of his plan, parts of which he read to me. He said he had communicated it only to Lord Camden, whose advice he much relied on, particularly in the law part; and that he would, as soon as he could get it transcribed, put it into my hands for my opinion and advice, but should show it to no other person before he presented it to the House; and he requested me to make no mention of it, otherwise parts might be misunderstood and blown upon beforehand, and others perhaps adopted and produced by ministers as their own. I promised the closest secrecy, and kept my word, not even mentioning to any one that I had seen him. I dined with him, his family only present, and returned to town in the evening.

On the Sunday following, being the 29th, his Lordship came to town, and called upon me in Craven Street. He brought with him his plan transcribed, in the form of an act of Parliament, which he put into my hands, requesting me to consider it carefully, and communicate to him such remarks upon it as should occur to me. His reason for desiring to give me that trouble was, as he was pleased to say, that he knew no man so thoroughly acquainted with the subject, or so capable of giving advice upon it; that he thought the errors of ministers in American affairs had been often owing to their not obtaining the best information; that, therefore, though he had considered the business thoroughly in all its parts, he was not so confident of his own judgment, but that he came to set it right by mine, as men set their watches by a regulator. He had not determined when he should produce it in the House of Lords; but in the course of our conversation, considering the precarious situation of his health, and that if presenting it was delayed, some intelligence might arrive which would make it seem less seasonable, or in all parts not so proper; or the ministry might engage in different measures, and then say, "if you had produced your plan sooner, we might have attended to it"; he concluded to offer it the Wednesday following; and therefore wished to see me upon it the preceding Tuesday, when he would again call upon me, unless I could conveniently come to Hayes. I chose the latter, in respect to his Lordship, and because there was less likelihood of interruptions; and I promised to be with him early, that we might have more time. He stayed with me near two hours, his equipage waiting at the door; and being there while people were coming from church, it was much taken notice of, and talked of, as at that time was every little circumstance that men thought might possibly any way affect American affairs. Such a visit from so great a man, on so important a business, flattered not a little my vanity; and the honor of it gave me the more pleasure, as it happened on the very day twelve months that the ministry had taken so much pains to disgrace me before the Privy Council.

I applied myself immediately to the reading and considering the plan, of which, when it was afterwards published, I sent you a copy, and therefore need not insert it here. I put down upon paper, as I went along, some short memorandums for my future discourse with him upon it, which follow, that you may, if you please, compare them with the plan; and, if you do so, you will see their drift and purpose, which otherwise would take me much writing to explain.

"Tuesday, January 31st, 1775.

"NOTES *for Discourse with Lord Chatham on his Plan.*

"Voluntary grants and forced taxes not to be expected of the same people at the same time.

"Permanent revenue will be objected to. Would not a temporary agreement be best, suppose for one hundred years?

"Does the whole of the rights claimed in the Petition of Rights relate to England only?

"The American Naturalization Act gives all the rights of natural-born subjects to foreigners residing there seven years. Can it be supposed, that the natives there have them not?

"If the King should raise armies in America, would Britain like their being brought hither? as the King might bring them when he pleased.

"An act of Parliament requires the colonies to furnish sundry articles of provision and accommodation to troops quartered among them; this may be made very burdensome to colonies that are out of favor.

"If a permanent revenue, why not the same privileges in trade with Scotland?

"Should not the lands, conquered by Britain and the colonies in conjunction, be given them (reserving a quitrent), whence they might form funds to enable them to pay?

"Instructions about agents to be withdrawn.

"Grants to be for three years, at the end of which a new Congress; and so from three to three years.

"Congress to have the general defence of the frontiers, making and regulating new settlements.

"Protection mutual.

"We go into all your wars.

"Our settlements cost you nothing.

"Take the plan of union.

" 'Defence, extension, and prosperity of.' The late Canada Act prevents their extension, and may check their prosperity.

"Laws should be secure as well as charters.

"Perhaps if the legislative power of Parliament is owned in the colonies, they may make a law to forbid the meeting of any Congress, &c."

I was at Hayes early on Tuesday, agreeably to my promise, when we entered into consideration of the plan; but, though I stayed near four hours, his Lordship, in the manner of, I think, all eloquent persons, was so full and diffuse in supporting every particular I questioned, that there was not time to go through half my memorandums. He is not easily interrupted; and I had such pleasure in hearing him, that I found little inclination to interrupt him. Therefore, considering that neither of us had much expectation, that the plan would be adopted entirely as it stood; that, in the course of its consideration, if it should be received, proper alterations might be introduced; that, before it would be settled, America should have opportunity to make her objections and propositions of amendment; that, to have it received at all here, it must seem to comply a little with some of the prevailing prejudices of the legislature; that, if it was not so perfect as might be wished, it would at least serve as a basis for treaty, and in the mean time prevent mischiefs; and that, as his Lordship had determined to offer it the next day, there was not time to make changes and another fair copy; I therefore ceased my querying; and, though afterwards many people were pleased to do me the honor of supposing I had a considerable share in composing it, I assure you, that the addition of a single word only was made at my instance, viz. *"constitutions"* after "charters"; for my filling up, at his request, a blank with the titles of acts proper to be repealed, which I took from the proceedings of the Congress, was no more than might have been done by any copying clerk.

On Wednesday, Lord Stanhope, at Lord Chatham's request, called upon me, and carried me down to the House of Lords, which was soon very full. Lord Chatham, in a most excellent speech, introduced, explained, and supported his plan. When he sat down, Lord Dartmouth rose, and very properly said, it contained matter of such weight and magnitude, as to require much consideration; and he therefore hoped the noble Earl did not expect their Lordships to decide upon it by an immediate vote, but would be willing it should lie upon the table for consideration. Lord Chatham answered readily, that he expected nothing more.

But Lord Sandwich rose, and in a petulant, vehement speech, opposed its being received at all, and gave his opinion, that it ought to be immediately *rejected*, with the contempt it deserved. That he could never believe it to be the production of any British Peer. That it appeared to him rather the work of some American; and, turning his face towards me, who was leaning on the bar, said, he fancied he had in his eye the person who drew it up, one of the bitterest and most mischievous enemies this country had ever known. This drew the eyes of many Lords upon me; but, as I had no inducement to take it to myself, I kept my countenance as immovable as if my features had been made of wood. Then several other Lords of the administration gave their sentiments also for rejecting it, of which opinion also was strongly the *wise* Lord Hillsborough. But the Dukes of Richmond and Manchester, Lord Shelbourne, Lord Camden, Lord Temple, Lord Lyttleton, and others, were for receiving it, some through approbation, and others for the character and dignity of the House. One Lord mentioning with applause, the candid proposal of one of the ministers, Lord Dartmouth, his Lordship rose again, and said, that having since heard the opinions of so many Lords against receiving it, to lie upon the table for consideration, he had altered his mind, could not accept the praise offered him for a candor of which he was now ashamed, and should therefore give his voice for rejecting the plan immediately.

I am the more particular in this, as it is a trait of that nobleman's character, who from his office is supposed to have so great a share in American affairs, but who has in reality no will or judgment of his own, being, with dispositions for the best measures, easily prevailed with to join in the worst.

Lord Chatham, in his reply to Lord Sandwich, took notice of his illiberal insinuation, that the plan was not the person's who proposed it; declared that it was entirely his own; a declaration he thought himself the more obliged to make, as many of their Lordships appeared to have so mean an opinion of it; for if it was so weak or so bad a thing, it was proper in him to take care that no other person should unjustly share in the censure it deserved. That it had been heretofore reckoned his vice, not to be apt to take advice; but he made no scruple to declare, that, if he were the first minister of this country, and had the care of settling this momentous business, he should not be ashamed of publicly calling to his assistance a person so perfectly acquainted with the whole of American affairs as the gentleman alluded to, and so injuriously reflected on; one, he was pleased to say, whom all Europe held in high estimation for his knowledge and wisdom.

and ranked with our Boyles and Newtons; who was an honor, not to the English nation only, but to human nature! I found it harder to stand this extravagant compliment than the preceding equally extravagant abuse; but kept as well as I could an unconcerned countenance, as not conceiving it to relate to me.

To hear so many of these *hereditary* legislators declaiming so vehemently against, not the adopting merely, but even the *consideration* of a proposal so important in its nature, offered by a person of so weighty a character, one of the first statesmen of the age, who had taken up this country when in the lowest despondency, and conducted it to victory and glory, through a war with two of the mightiest kingdoms in Europe; to hear them censuring his plan, not only for their own misunderstandings of what was in it, but for their imaginations of what was not in it, which they would not give themselves an opportunity of rectifying by a second reading; to perceive the total ignorance of the subject in some, the prejudice and passion of others, and the wilful perversion of plain truth in several of the ministers; and, upon the whole, to see it so ignominiously rejected by so great a majority, and so hastily too, in breach of all decency, and prudent regard to the character and dignity of their body, as a third part of the national legislature, gave me an exceeding mean opinion of their abilities, and made their claim of sovereignty over three millions of virtuous, sensible people in America seem the greatest of absurdities, since they appeared to have scarce discretion enough to govern a herd of swine. *Hereditary legislators!* thought I. There would be more propriety, because less hazard of mischief, in having (as in some university of Germany) *hereditary professors of mathematics!* But this was a hasty reflection; for the *elected* House of Commons is no better, nor ever will be while the electors receive money for their votes, and pay money wherewith ministers may bribe their representatives when chosen.

After this proceeding I expected to hear no more of any negotiation for settling our difference amicably; yet, in a day or two, I had a note from Mr. Barclay, requesting a meeting at Dr. Fothergill's, the 4th of February, in the evening. I attended accordingly, and was surprised by being told, that a very good disposition appeared in administration; that the "Hints" had been considered, and several of them thought reasonable, and that others might be admitted with small amendments. The good Doctor, with his usual philanthropy, expatiated on the miseries of war; that even a bad peace was preferable to the most successful war; that America was growing in strength; and, whatever she might be obliged to submit to at present, she would in a few years be in a condition to make her own terms.

Mr. Barclay hinted how much it was in my power to promote an agreement; how much it would be to my honor to effect it; and that I might expect, not only restoration of my old place, but almost any other I could wish for, &c. I need not tell you, who know me so well, how improper and disgusting this language was to me. The Doctor's was more suitable. Him I answered, that we did not wish for war, and desired nothing but what was reasonable and necessary for our security and well-being. To Mr. Barclay I replied, that the ministry, I was sure, would rather give me a place in a cart to Tyburn, than any other place whatever; and to both, that I sincerely wished to be serviceable; that I needed no other inducement than to be shown how I might be so; but saw they imagined more to be in my power than really was. I was then told again, that conferences had been held upon the "HINTS"; and the paper being produced was read, that I might hear the observations that had been made upon them. . . .

A week and more passed, in which I heard nothing further of any negotiation, and my time was much taken up among the members of Parliament, when Mr. Barclay sent me a note to say, that he was indisposed, but desirous of seeing me, and should be glad if I would call on him. I waited upon him the next morning, when he told me, that he had seen Lord Hyde, and had some further discourse with him on the ARTICLES; that he thought himself now fully possessed of what would do in this business; that he therefore wished another meeting with me and Dr. Fothergill, when he would endeavour to bring prepared a draft conformable chiefly to what had been proposed and conceded on both sides, with some propositions of his own. I readily agreed to the meeting, which was to be on Thursday evening, February 16th.

We met accordingly. . . . It was said, that the ministry only wanted some opening to be given them, some ground on which to found the commencement of conciliating measures; that a petition . . . would answer that purpose; that preparations were making to send over more troops and ships; that such a petition might prevent their going, especially if a commissioner were proposed. . . .

Weighing now the present dangerous situation of affairs in America, and the daily hazard of widening the breach there irreparably, I embraced the idea proposed in the paper of sending over a commissioner, as it might be a means of suspending military operations, and bring on a treaty, whereby mischief would be prevented, and an agreement by degrees be formed and established. I also concluded to do what had been desired of me as to the engagement, and essayed a draft of a memorial to Lord Dartmouth; . . . with some hints, on a separate paper, of further remarks to be made in conversation, when we should meet in the evening of the 17th:

"TO THE RIGHT HONORABLE LORD DARTMOUTH.

"MY LORD,

"Being deeply apprehensive of the impending calamities, that threaten the nation and its colonies through the present unhappy dissensions, I have attentively considered by what possible means those calamities may be prevented. The great importance of a business which concerns us all, will, I hope, in some degree excuse me to your Lordship, if I presume unasked to offer my humble opinion, that, should his Majesty think fit to authorize delegates from the several provinces to meet at such convenient time and place, as in his wisdom shall seem meet, then and there to confer with a commissioner or commissioners to be appointed and empowered by his Majesty, on the means of establishing a firm and lasting union between Britain and the American provinces, such a measure might be effectual for that purpose. I cannot therefore but wish it may be adopted, as no one can more ardently and sincerely desire the general prosperity of the British dominions, than, my Lord, your Lordship's most obedient, &c.

"B. FRANKLIN."

"REMARKS AND HINTS.

. . . "Massachusetts must suffer all the hazards and mischiefs of war, rather than admit the alteration of their charters and laws by Parliament. 'They, who can give up essential liberty to obtain a little temporary safety, deserve neither liberty nor safety.'

. . . "The Assemblies are many of them in a state of dissolution. It will require time to make new elections; then to meet and choose delegates, supposing all could meet. But the Assembly of the Massachusetts Bay cannot act under the new constitution, or meet the new Council for that purpose, without acknowledging the power of Parliament to alter their charter, which they never will do. The language of the proposal is, *Try on your fetters first, and then, if you don't like them, petition and we will consider. . . .*"

That afternoon I received the following note from Mrs. Howe, enclosing another from Lord Howe, viz.

"MRS. HOWE's compliments to Dr. Franklin; she has just received the enclosed note from Lord Howe, and hopes it will be convenient to him to come to her, either to-morrow or Sunday, at an hour most convenient to him, which she begs he will be so good to name.

"*Grafton Street, Friday, February 17th, 1775.*"

[*Enclosed in the foregoing.*]

"TO THE HONORABLE MRS. HOWE.

"I wish you to procure me an opportunity to see Dr. Franklin at your house to-morrow, or on Sunday morning, for an essential purpose.

"*Grafton Street, Friday, four o'clock.*"

The next morning I met Lord Howe, according to appointment. He seemed very cheerful, having, as I imagine, heard from Lord Hyde what that Lord might have heard from Mr. Barclay the evening of the 16th, viz. that I had consented to petition, and engage payment for the tea; whence it was hoped, the ministerial terms of accommodation might take place. He

On the morning of the same day, February 20th, it was currently and industriously reported all over the town, that Lord North would that day make a pacific motion in the House of Commons for healing all differences between Britain and America. The House was accordingly very full, and the members full of expectation. . . .

After a good deal of wild debate, in which this motion was supported upon various and inconsistent principles by the ministerial people, and even met with an opposition from some of them, which showed a want of concert, probably from the suddenness of the alterations above supposed, they all agreed at length, as usual, in voting it by a large majority.

Hearing nothing during all the following week from Messrs. Barclay and Fothergill (except that Lord Hyde, when acquainted with my willingness to engage for the payment of the tea, had said it gave him *new life*), nor any thing from Lord Howe, I mentioned his silence occasionally to his sister, adding, that I supposed it owing to his finding what he had proposed to me was not likely to take place; and I wished her to desire him, if that was the case, to let me know it by a line, that I might be at liberty to take other measures. She did so as soon as he returned from the country, where he had been for a day or two; and I received from her the following note.

"MRS. HOWE's compliments to Dr. Franklin; Lord Howe not quite understanding the message received from her, will be very glad to have the pleasure of seeing him, either between twelve and one this morning (the only hour he is at liberty this day), at her house, or at any hour to-morrow most convenient to him.

"*Grafton Street, Tuesday.*"

I met his Lordship at the hour appointed. He said, that he had not seen me lately, as he expected daily to have something more material to say to me than had yet occurred; and hoped that I would have called on Lord Hyde, as I had intimated I should do when I apprehended it might be useful, which he was sorry to find I had not done. That there was something in my verbal message by Mrs. Howe, which perhaps she had apprehended imperfectly; it was the hint of my purpose to take other measures. I answered, that having, since I had last seen his Lordship, heard of the death of my wife at Philadelphia, in whose hands I had left the care of my affairs there, it was become necessary for me to return thither as soon as conveniently might be; that what his Lordship had proposed of my accompanying him to America might, if likely to take place, postpone my voyage to suit his conveniency; otherwise, I should proceed by the first ship; that I did suppose by not hearing from him, and by Lord North's motion, all thoughts of that kind were laid aside, which was what I only desired to know from him.

He said, my last paper of "REMARKS" by Mr. Barclay, wherein I had made the indemnification of Boston, for the injury of stopping its port, a condition of my engaging to pay for the tea (a condition impossible to be complied with), had discouraged further proceeding on that idea. Having a copy of that paper in my pocket, I showed his Lordship, that I had proposed no such condition of my engagement, nor any other than the repeal of all the Massachusetts acts. That what followed relating to the indemnification was only expressing my private opinion, that it would be just, but by no means insisting upon it. He said the arrangements were not yet determined on; that, as I now explained myself, it appeared I had been much misapprehended; and he wished of all things I would see Lord Hyde, and asked if I would choose to meet him there (at Mrs. Howe's), or that he should call upon me. I said, that I would by no means give Lord Hyde that trouble. That, since he (Lord Hyde) seemed to think it might be of use, and wished it done soon, I would wait upon Lord Hyde. I knew him to be an early riser, and would be with him at eight o'clock the next morning; which Lord Howe undertook to acquaint him with. But I added, that, from what circumstances I could collect of the disposition of ministry, I apprehended my visit would answer no material purpose. He was of a different opinion; to which I submitted.

The next morning, March 1st, I accordingly was early with Lord Hyde, who received me with his usual politeness. We talked over a great part of the dispute between the countries. I found him ready with all the newspaper and pamphlet topics; of the expense of settling our colonies, the protection afforded them, the heavy debt under which Britain labored, the equity of our contributing to its alleviation; that many people in England were no more represented than we were, yet all were taxed and governed by Parliament, &c. &c. I answered all, but with little effect; for, though his Lordship seemed civilly to hear what I said, I had reason to believe he attended very little to the purport of it, his mind being employed the while in thinking on what he himself purposed to say next.

He had hoped, he said, that Lord North's motion would have been satisfactory; and asked what could be objected to it. I replied, the terms of it were, that we should grant money till Parliament had agreed we had given enough, without having the least share in judging of the propriety of the measure for which it was to be granted, or of our own abilities to grant; that these grants were also to be made under a threat of exercising a claimed right of taxing us at pleasure, and compelling such taxes by an armed force, if we did not give till it should be thought we had given enough; that the proposition was similar to no mode of obtaining aids that ever existed, except that of a highwayman, who presents his pistol and hat at a coach window, demanding no specific sum, but, if you will give all your money, or what he is pleased to think sufficient, he will civilly omit putting his own hand into your pockets; if not, there is his pistol. That the mode of raising contributions in an enemy's country was fairer than this, since there an explicit sum was demanded, and the people who were raising it knew what they were about, and when they should have done; and that, in short, no free people could ever think of beginning to grant upon such terms. That, besides, a new dispute had now been raised, by the Parliament's pretending to a power of altering our charters and established laws, which was of still more importance to us than their claim of taxation, as it set us all adrift, and left us without a privilege we could depend upon, but at their pleasure; this was a situation we could not possibly be in; and, as Lord North's proposition had no relation to this matter, if the other had been such as we could have agreed to, we should still be far from a reconciliation.

His Lordship thought I misunderstood the proposition; on which I took it out and read it. He then waived that point, and said he should be glad to know from me, what would produce a reconciliation. I said, that his Lordship, I imagined, had seen several proposals of mine for that purpose. He said he had; but some of my articles were such as would never be agreed to. That it was apprehended I had several instructions and powers to offer more acceptable terms, but was extremely reserved, and perhaps from a desire he did not blame, of doing better for my constituents; but my expectations might deceive me; and he did think I might be assured I should never obtain better terms than what were now offered by Lord North. That administration had a sincere desire of restoring harmony with America; and it was thought, if I would coöperate with them, the business would be easy. That he hoped I was above retaining resentment against them, for what nobody now approved, and for which satisfaction might be made me; that I was, as he understood, in high esteem among the Americans; that, if I would bring about a reconciliation on terms suitable to the dignity of government, I might be as highly and generally esteemed here, and be honored and *rewarded*, perhaps, *beyond my expectation*.

I replied, that I thought I had given a convincing proof of my sincere desire of promoting peace, when, on being informed that all wanted for the honor of government was, to obtain payment for the tea, I offered, without any instruction to warrant my so doing, or assurance that I should be reimbursed, or my conduct approved, to engage for that payment, if the Massachusetts acts were to be repealed; an engagement in which I must have risked my whole fortune, which I thought few besides me would have done. That, in truth, private resentments had no weight with me in public business; that I was not the reserved man imagined, having really no secret instructions to act upon. That I was certainly willing to do every thing that could reasonably be expected of me. But, if any supposed I could prevail with my countrymen to take black for white, and wrong for right, it was not knowing either them or me; they were not capable of being so imposed on, nor was I capable of attempting it.

He then asked my opinion of sending over a commissioner, for the purpose mentioned in a preceding part of this account, and my answer was to the same effect. By the way, I apprehend, that to give me an opportunity of discoursing with Lord Hyde on that point, was a principal motive with Lord Howe for urging me to make this visit. His Lordship did not express his own sentiments upon it. And thus ended this conversation.

Three or four days after, I received the following note from Mrs. Howe.

"Mrs. Howe's compliments to Dr. Franklin; Lord Howe begs to have the pleasure of meeting him once more before he goes, at her house; he is at present out of town, but returns on Monday; and any day or hour after that, that the Doctor will name, he will be very glad to attend him.

"*Grafton Street, Saturday, March 4th.*"

I answered, that I would do myself the honor of waiting on Lord Howe, at her house, the Tuesday following, at eleven o'clock. We met accordingly. He began by saying, that I had been a better prophet than himself, in foreseeing that my interview with Lord Hyde would be of no great use; and then said, that he hoped I would excuse the trouble he had given me, as his intentions had been good both towards me and the public. He was sorry, that at present there was no appearance of things going into the train he had wished, but that possibly they might yet take a more favorable turn; and, as he understood I was going soon to America, if he should chance to be sent thither on that important business, he hoped he might still expect my assistance. I assured him of my readiness at all times of coöperating with him in so good a work; and so, taking my leave, and receiving his good wishes, ended the negotiation with Lord Howe. And I heard no more of that with Messrs. Fothergill and Barclay. I could only gather, from some hints in their conversation, that neither of them were well pleased with the conduct of the ministers respecting these transactions. And, a few days before I left London, I met them by their desire, at the Doctor's house, when they desired me to assure their friends from them, that it was now their fixed opinion, that nothing could secure the privileges of America, but a firm, sober adherence to the terms of the association made at the Congress, and that the salvation of English liberty depended now on the perseverance and virtue of America.

During the whole, my time was otherwise much taken up, by friends calling continually to inquire news from America; members of both Houses of Parliament, to inform me what passed in the Houses, and discourse with me on the debates, and on motions made, or to be made; merchants of London and of the manufacturing and port towns, on their petitions; the Quakers, upon theirs, &c. &c.; so that I had no time to take notes of almost any thing. This account is therefore chiefly from recollection, in which doubtless much must have been omitted, from deficiency of memory; but what there is, I believe to be pretty exact; except that, discoursing with so many different persons about the same time, on the same subject, I may possibly have put down some things as said by or to one person, which passed in conversation with another.

A little before I left London, being at the House of Lords, during a debate in which Lord Camden was to speak, and who indeed spoke admirably on American affairs, I was much disgusted, from the ministerial side, by many base reflections on American courage, religion, understanding,

&c., in which we were treated with the utmost contempt, as the lowest of mankind, and almost of a different species from the English of Britain; but particularly the American honesty was abused by some of the Lords, who asserted that we were all knaves, and wanted only by this dispute to avoid paying our debts; that, if we had any sense of equity or justice, we should offer payment of the tea, &c. I went home somewhat irritated and heated; and, partly to retort upon this nation, on the article of *equity*, drew up a memorial to present to Lord Dartmouth before my departure; but, consulting my friend, Mr. Thomas Walpole, upon it, who is a member of the House of Commons, he looked at it and at me several times alternately, as if he apprehended me a little out of my senses. As I was in the hurry of packing up, I requested him to take the trouble of showing it to his neighbour, Lord Camden, and ask his advice upon it, which he kindly undertook to do; and returned it me with a note, which here follows the proposed memorial.

"To the Right Honorable the Earl of Dartmouth, one of his Majesty's principal Secretaries of State;

"A Memorial of Benjamin Franklin, Agent of the Province of Massachusetts Bay.

"Whereas an injury done can only give the party injured a right to full reparation; or, in case that be refused, a right to return an equal injury; and whereas the blockade of Boston, now continued nine months, hath every week of its continuance done damage to that town, equal to what was suffered there by the India Company; it follows that such *exceeding* damage is an *injury* done by this government, for which reparation ought to be made; and whereas reparation of injuries ought always (agreeably to the custom of all nations, savage as well as civilized) to be first required, before satisfaction is taken by a return of damage to the aggressors; which was not done by Great Britain in the instance above mentioned; I the underwritten do therefore, as their agent, in the behalf of my country and the said town of Boston, protest against the continuance of the said blockade; and I do hereby solemnly demand satisfaction for the accumulated injury done them, beyond the value of the India Company's tea destroyed.

"And whereas the conquest of the Gulf of St. Lawrence, the coasts of Labrador and Nova Scotia, and the fisheries possessed by the French there and on the Banks of Newfoundland, so far as they were more extended than at present, was made by the *joint forces* of Britain and the colonies, the latter having nearly an equal number of men in that service with the former; it follows, that the colonies have an equitable and just right to participate in the advantage of those fisheries; I do, therefore, in the behalf of the colony of the Massachusetts Bay, protest against the act now under consideration in Parliament, for depriving that province, with others, of that fishery (on pretence of their refusing to purchase British commodities), as an act highly unjust and injurious; and I give notice, that satisfaction will probably one day be demanded for all the injury that may be done and suffered in the execution of such act; and that the injustice of the proceeding is likely to give such umbrage to *all the colonies*, that in no future war, wherein other conquests may be meditated, either a man or a shilling will be obtained from any of them to aid such conquests, till full satisfaction be made as aforesaid.

"B. FRANKLIN.

"*Given in London, this 16th day of March, 1775.*"

"TO DR. FRANKLIN.

"DEAR SIR,

"I return you the memorial, which it is thought might be attended with dangerous consequences to your person, and contribute to exasperate the nation.

"I heartily wish you a prosperous voyage, a long health, and am, with the sincerest regard, your most faithful and obedient servant,

"THOMAS WALPOLE.

"*Lincoln's Inn Fields, 16th March, 1775.*"

Mr. Walpole called at my house the next day, and, hearing I was gone to the House of Lords, came there to me, and repeated more fully what was in his note; adding, that it was thought my having no instructions directing me to deliver such a protest, would make it appear still more unjustifiable, and be deemed a national affront. I had no desire to make matters worse, and, being grown cooler, took the advice so kindly given me.

The evening before I left London, I received a note from Dr. Fothergill, with some letters to his friends in Philadelphia. In that note he desired me to get those friends "and two or three more together, and inform them, that, whatever specious pretences are offered, they are all hollow; and that to get a larger field on which to fatten a herd of worthless parasites is all that is regarded. Perhaps it may be proper to acquaint them with David Barclay's and our united endeavours and the effects. They will stun at least, if not convince, the most worthy, that nothing very favorable is intended, if more unfavorable articles cannot be obtained." The Doctor, in the course of his daily visits among the great, in the practice of his profession, had full opportunity of being acquainted with their sentiments, the conversation everywhere turning upon the subject of America.

Declaration of War

To William Strahan. Philadelphia, 5 July, 1775.

YOU ARE a member of Parliament, and one of that majority, which has doomed my country to destruction. You have begun to burn our towns, and murder our people. Look upon your hands, they are stained with the blood of your relations! You and I were long friends; you are now my enemy, and I am, yours.

To Joseph Priestley. Philadelphia, 7 July, 1775.

THE CONGRESS met at a time when all minds were so exasperated by the perfidy of General Gage, and his attack on the country people, that propositions for attempting an accommodation were not much relished; and it has been with difficulty that we have carried another humble petition to the crown, to give Britain one more chance, one opportunity more, of recovering the friendship of the colonies; which, however, I think she has not sense enough to embrace, and so I conclude she has lost them for ever.

She has begun to burn our seaport towns; secure, I suppose, that we shall never be able to return the outrage in kind. She may doubtless destroy them all; but, if she wishes to recover our commerce, are these the probable means? She must certainly be distracted; for no tradesman out of Bedlam ever thought of increasing the number of his customers, by knocking them on the head; or of enabling them to pay their debts, by burning their houses. If she wishes to have us subjects, and that we should submit to her as our compound sovereign, she is now giving us such miserable specimens of her government, that we shall ever detest and avoid it, as a complication of robbery, murder, famine, fire, and pestilence.

You will have heard before this reaches you, of the treacherous conduct of General Gage to the remaining people in Boston, in detaining their goods, after stipulating to let them go out with their effects, on pretence that merchants' goods were not effects; the defeat of a great body of his troops by the country people at Lexington; some other small advantages gained in skirmishes with their troops; and the action at Bunker's Hill, in which they were twice repulsed, and the third time gained a dear victory. Enough has happened, one would think, to convince your ministers, that the Americans will fight, and that this is a harder nut to crack than they imagined.

We have not yet applied to any foreign power for assistance, nor offered our commerce for their friendship. Perhaps we never may; yet it is natural to think of it, if we are pressed. We have now an army on the establishment, which still holds yours besieged. My time was never more fully employed. In the morning at six, I am at the Committee of Safety, appointed by the Assembly to put the province in a state of defence; which committee holds till near nine, when I am at the Congress, and that sits till after four in the afternoon. Both these bodies proceed with the greatest unanimity, and their meetings are well attended. It will scarce be credited in Britain, that men can be as diligent with us from zeal for the public good, as with you for thousands per annum. Such is the difference between uncorrupted new states, and corrupted old ones.

Great frugality and great industry are now become fashionable here.

Gentlemen, who used to entertain with two or three courses, pride themselves now in treating with simple beef and pudding. By these means, and the stoppage of our consumptive trade with Britain, we shall be better able to pay our voluntary taxes for the support of our troops. Our savings in the articles of trade amount to near five millions sterling per annum.

I shall communicate your letter to Mr. Winthrop; but the camp is at Cambridge, and he has as little leisure for philosophy as myself.

To Joseph Priestley. Philadelphia, 3 Oct., 1775.

I AM to set out to-morrow for the camp, and, having but just heard of this opportunity, can only write a line to say that I am well and hearty. Tell our dear good friend, Dr. Price, who sometimes has his doubts and despondencies about our firmness, that America is determined and unanimous; a very few Tories and placemen excepted, who will probably soon export themselves. Britain, at the expense of three millions, has killed one hundred and fifty Yankees this campaign, which is twenty thousand pounds a head; and at Bunker's Hill she gained a mile of ground, half of which she lost again by our taking post on Ploughed Hill. During the same time sixty thousand children have been born in America. From these *data* his mathematical head will easily calculate the time and expense necessary to kill us all, and conquer our whole territory.

To a friend in England. Philadelphia, 3 Oct., 1775.

I WISH AS ardently as you can do for peace, and should rejoice exceedingly in coöperating with you to that end. But every ship from Britain brings some intelligence of new measures that tend more and more to exasperate; and it seems to me, that until you have found by dear experience the reducing us by force impracticable, you will think of nothing fair and reasonable.

We have as yet resolved only on defensive measures. If you would recall your forces and stay at home, we should meditate nothing to injure you. A little time so given for cooling on both sides would have excellent effects. But you will goad and provoke us. You despise us too much; and you are insensible of the Italian adage, that there is no *little enemy*. I am persuaded that the body of the British people are our friends; but they are changeable, and by your lying gazettes may soon be made our enemies. Our respect for them will proportionably diminish, and I see clearly we are on the high road to mutual family hatred and detestation. A separation of course will be inevitable. It is a million of pities so fair a plan as we have hitherto been engaged in, for increasing strength and empire with public felicity, should be destroyed by the mangling hands of a few blundering ministers. It will not be destroyed; God will protect and prosper it, you will only exclude yourselves from any share in it. We hear, that more ships and troops are coming out. We know, that you may do us a great deal of mischief, and are determined to bear it patiently as long as we can. But, if you flatter yourselves with beating us into submission, you know neither the people nor the country. The Congress are still sitting, and will wait the result of their *last* petition.

Congressional Record

To his most Serene Highness, Don Gabriel of Bourbon.
Philadelphia, 12 Dec., 1775

I HAVE JUST received, through the hands of the ambassador of Spain, the much esteemed present your most Serene Highness hath so kindly sent me, of your excellent version of Sallust.

I am extremely sensible of the honor done me, and beg you would accept my thankful acknowledgments. I wish I could send hence any American literary production worthy of your perusal; but as yet the Muses have scarcely visited these remote regions. Perhaps, however, the proceedings of our American Congress, just published, may be a subject of some curiosity at your court. I therefore take the liberty of sending your Highness a copy, with some other papers, which contain accounts of the successes wherewith Providence has lately favored us. Therein your wise politicians may contemplate the first efforts of a rising state, which seems likely soon to act a part of some importance on the stage of human affairs, and furnish materials for a future Sallust. I am very old, and can scarce hope to see the event of this great contest; but looking forward, I think I see a powerful dominion growing up here, whose interest it will be, to form a close and firm alliance with Spain (their territories bordering), and who, being united, will be able, not only to preserve their own people in peace, but to repel the force of all the other powers in Europe. It seems, therefore, prudent on both sides to cultivate a good understanding, that may hereafter be so useful to both; towards which a fair foundation is already laid in our minds, by the well founded popular opinion entertained here of Spanish integrity and honor. I hope my presumption in hinting this will be pardoned. If in any thing on this side the globe I can render either service or pleasure to your Royal Highness, your commands will make me happy. With the utmost esteem and veneration, I have the honor to be your Serene Highness's most obedient and most humble servant.

"Common Sense"

To Charles Lee. Philadelphia, 19 Feb., 1776.

I REJOICE that you are going to Canada. I hope the gout will not have the courage to follow you into that severe climate. I believe you will have the number of men you wish for. I am told there will be two thousand more, but there are always deficiencies.

The bearer, Mr. Paine, has requested a line of introduction to you, which I give the more willingly, as I know his sentiments are not very different from yours. He is the reputed, and, I think, the real author of *Common Sense*, a pamphlet that has made great impression here. I do not enlarge, both because he waits, and because I hope for the pleasure of conferring with you face to face in Canada. I will only add, that we are assured here on the part of France, that the troops sent to the West Indies have no inimical views to us or our cause. It is thought they intend a war without a previous declaration. God prosper all your undertakings, and return you with health, honor, and happiness.

Trade War

To Lord Howe. Philadelphia, July 20th, 1776.

I RECEIVED safe, the letters your Lordship so kindly forwarded to me, and beg you to accept my thanks.

The official despatches, to which you refer me, contain nothing more than what we had seen in the act of Parliament, viz. offers of pardon upon submission, which I am sorry to find, as it must give your Lordship pain to be sent so far on so hopeless a business.

Directing pardons to be offered the colonies, who are the very parties injured, expresses indeed that opinion of our ignorance, baseness, and insensibility, which your uninformed and proud nation has long been pleased to entertain of us; but it can have no other effect than that of increasing our resentment. It is impossible we should think of submission to a government, that has with the most wanton barbarity and cruelty burnt our defenceless towns in the midst of winter, excited the savages to massacre our farmers, and our slaves to murder their masters, and is even now bringing foreign mercenaries to deluge our settlements with blood. These atrocious injuries have extinguished every remaining spark of affection for that parent country we once held so dear; but, were it possible for *us* to forget and forgive them, it is not possible for *you* (I mean the British nation) to forgive the people you have so heavily injured. You can never confide again in those as fellow subjects, and permit them to enjoy equal freedom, to whom you know you have given such just cause of lasting enmity. And this must impel you, were we again under your government, to endeavour the breaking our spirit by the severest tyranny, and obstructing, by every means in your power, our growing strength and prosperity.

But your Lordship mentions "the King's paternal solicitude for promoting the establishment of lasting *peace* and union with the colonies." If by peace is here meant a peace to be entered into between Britain and America, as distinct states now at war, and his Majesty has given your Lordship powers

to treat with us of such a peace, I may venture to say, though without
authority, that I think a treaty for that purpose not yet quite impracticable,
before we enter into foreign alliances. But I am persuaded you have no
such powers. Your nation, though, by punishing those American governors,
who have created and fomented the discord, rebuilding our burnt towns,
and repairing as far as possible the mischiefs done us, might yet recover a
great share of our regard, and the greatest part of our growing commerce,
with all the advantage of that additional strength to be derived from a
friendship with us; but I know too well her abounding pride and deficient
wisdom, to believe she will ever take such salutary measures. Her fondness
for conquest, as a warlike nation, her lust of dominion, as an ambitious one,
and her thirst for a gainful monopoly, as a commercial one (none of them
legitimate causes of war) will all join to hide from her eyes every view
of her true interests, and continually goad her on in those ruinous distant
expeditions, so destructive both of lives and treasure, that must prove as
pernicious to her in the end, as the crusades formerly were to most of the
nations of Europe.

I have not the vanity, my Lord, to think of intimidating by thus predicting
the effects of this war; for I know it will in England have the fate of all
my former predictions, not to be believed till the event shall verify it.

Long did I endeavour, with unfeigned and unwearied zeal, to preserve
from breaking that fine and noble China vase, the British empire; for I
knew, that, being once broken, the separate parts could not retain even
their share of the strength or value that existed in the whole, and that a perfect reunion of those parts could scarce ever be hoped for. Your Lordship
may possibly remember the tears of joy that wet my cheek, when, at your
good sister's in London, you once gave me expectations that a reconciliation
might soon take place. I had the misfortune to find those expectations disappointed, and to be treated as the cause of the mischief I was laboring
to prevent. My consolation under that groundless and malevolent treatment was, that I retained the friendship of many wise and good men in that
country, and, among the rest, some share in the regard of Lord Howe.

The well-founded esteem, and, permit me to say, affection, which I shall
always have for your Lordship, makes it painful to me to see you engaged
in conducting a war, the great ground of which, as expressed in your letter,
is "the necessity of preventing the American trade from passing into foreign
channels." To me it seems, that neither the obtaining or retaining of any
trade, how valuable soever, is an object for which men may justly spill
each other's blood; that the true and sure means of extending and securing
commerce is the goodness and cheapness of commodities; and that the
profit of no trade can ever be equal to the expense of compelling it, and of
holding it, by fleets and armies.

I consider this war against . . . therefore, as both unjust and unwise; and
I am persuaded, that cool, compassionate posterity will condemn to infamy
those who advised it; and that even success will not save from some degree
of dishonor those, who voluntarily engaged to conduct it. I know your great

motive in coming hither was the hope of being instrumental in a reconciliation; and I believe, when you find *that* impossible on any terms given you to propose, you will relinquish so odious a command, and return to a more honorable private station.

With the greatest and most sincere respect, I have the honor to be, my Lord, your Lordship's most obedient humble servant.

"Gray Hair, Fur Cap"

To Mrs. Mary Hewson. Paris, 12 January, 1777.

FIGURE TO yourself an old man, with gray hair appearing under a martin fur cap, among the powdered heads of Paris. It is this odd figure that salutes you, with handfulls of blessings on you and your dear little ones.

On my arrival here, Mademoiselle Biheron gave me great pleasure in the perusal of a letter from you to her. It acquainted me that you and yours were well in August last. I have with me here my young grandson, Benjamin Franklin Bache, a special good boy. I shall give him a little French language and address, and then send him over to pay his respects to Miss Hewson. My love to all that love you, particularly to dear Dolly.

Temple, who attends me here, presents his respects. I must contrive to get you to America. I want all my friends out of that wicked country. I have just seen in the paper seven paragraphs about me, of which six were lies.

To Mrs. Mary Hewson. Paris, 26 January, 1777.

WHAT HAS become of my and your dear Dolly? Have you parted? for you mention nothing of her. I know your friendship continues; but perhaps she is with one of her brothers. How do they all do?

I have not yet received a line from my dear old friend, your mother. Pray tell me where she is, and how it is with her. Jonathan, who is now at Nantes, told me that she had a lodging in Northumberland Court. I doubt her being comfortably accommodated there. Is Miss Barwell a little more at rest, or as busy as ever? Is she well? And how fares it with our good friends of the Henckell family?

But, principally, I want to know how it is with you. I hear you have not quite settled yet with those people. I hope, however, that you have a sufficient income, and live at your ease, and that your money is safe out of the funds. Does my godson remember any thing of his Doctor papa? I suppose not. Kiss the dear little fellow for me; not forgetting the others. I long to see them and you. What became of the lottery ticket I left with your good mother, which was to produce the diamond ear-rings for you? Did you get them? If not, Fortune has wronged you, for you *ought* to have had them.

"Wickedest War"

To Joseph Priestley. Paris, 27 January, 1777.

I REJOICE to hear of your continual progress in those useful discoveries; I find that you have set all the philosophers of Europe at work upon *fixed air;* and it is with great pleasure I observe how high you stand in their opinion; for I enjoy my friends' fame as my own.

The hint you gave me jocularly, that you did not quite despair of the *philosopher's stone,* draws from me a request, that, when you have found it, you will take care to lose it again; for I believe in my conscience, that mankind are wicked enough to continue slaughtering one another as long as they can find money to pay the butchers. But, of all the wars in my time, this on the part of England appears to me the wickedest; having no cause but malice against liberty, and the jealousy of commerce. And I think the crime seems likely to meet with its proper punishment; a total loss of her own liberty, and the destruction of her own commerce.

I suppose you would like to know something of the state of affairs in America. In all probability we shall be much stronger the next campaign than we were in the last; better armed, better disciplined, and with more ammunition. When I was at the camp before Boston, the army had not five rounds of powder a man. This was kept a secret even from our people. The world wondered that we so seldom fired a cannon; we could not afford it; but we now make powder in plenty.

To me it seems, as it has always done, that this war must end in our favor, and in ruin of Britain, if she does not speedily put an end to it. An English gentleman here the other day, in company with some French, remarked, that it was folly in France not to make war immediately; *And in England,* replied one of them, *not to make peace.*

Do not believe the reports you hear of our internal divisions. We are, I believe, as much united as any people ever were, and as firmly.

Tory Friends

To Mrs. Thompson, at Lisle. Paris, 8 Feb., 1777.

You ARE too early, *hussy,* as well as too saucy, in calling me *rebel;* you should wait for the event, which will determine whether it is a *rebellion* or only a *revolution.* Here the ladies are more civil; they call us *les insurgens,* a character that usually pleases them; and methinks all other women who smart, or have smarted, under the tyranny of a bad husband, ought to be fixed in *revolution* principles, and act accordingly.

On my way to Canada last spring, I saw dear Mrs. Barrow at New York.

Mr. Barrow had been from her two or three months to keep Governor Tryon and other Tories company on board the Asia, one of the King's ships which lay in the harbour; and in all that time that naughty man had not ventured once on shore to see her. Our troops were then pouring into the town, and she was packing up to leave it, fearing, as she had a large house, they would incommode her by quartering officers in it. As she appeared in great perplexity, scarce knowing where to go, I persuaded her to stay; and I went to the general officers then commanding there, and recommended her to their protection; which they promised and performed. On my return from Canada, where I was a piece of a governor (and I think a very good one) for a fortnight, and might have been so till this time if your wicked army, enemies to all good government, had not come and driven me out, I found her still in quiet possession of her house. I inquired how our people had behaved to her. She spoke in high terms of the respectful attention they had paid her, and the quiet and security they had procured her. I said I was glad of it; and that, if they had used her ill, I would have turned Tory. Then said she, with that pleasing gayety so natural to her, *I wish they had*. For you must know she is a *Toryess* as well as you, and can as flippantly call *rebel*. I drank tea with her; we talked affectionately of you and our other friends the Wilkeses, of whom she had received no late intelligence. What became of her since, I have not heard. The street she lived in was some months after chiefly burnt down; but, as the town was then, and ever since has been, in possession of the King's troops, I have had no opportunity of knowing whether she suffered any loss in the conflagration. I hope she did not, as, if she did, I should wish I had not persuaded her to stay there.

I am glad to learn from you, that that unhappy, though deserving family, the W——s, are getting into some business, that may afford them subsistence. I pray, that God will bless them, and that they may see happier days. Mr. Cheap's and Dr. H——'s good fortunes please me. Pray learn, if you have not already learnt, like me, to be pleased with other people's pleasures, and happy with their happiness, when none occur of your own; and then perhaps you will not so soon be weary of the place you chance to be in, and so fond of rambling to get rid of your *ennui*. I fancy you have hit upon the right reason of your being weary of St. Omer's, viz. that you are out of temper, which is the effect of full living and idleness. A month in Bridewell, beating hemp, upon bread and water, would give you health and spirits, and subsequent cheerfulness and contentment with every other situation. I prescribe that regimen for you, my dear, in pure good will, without a fee. And let me tell you, if you do not get into temper, neither Brussels nor Lisle will suit you. I know nothing of the price of living in either of those places; but I am sure a single woman, as you are, might with economy upon two hundred pounds a year maintain herself comfortably anywhere, and me into the bargain. Do not invite me in earnest, however, to come and live with you; for, being posted here, I ought not to comply, and I am not sure I should be able to refuse.

Present my respects to Mrs. Payne and Mrs. Heathcot; for, though I have not the honor of knowing them, yet, as you say they are friends to the American cause, I am sure they must be women of good understanding. I know you wish you could see me; but, as you cannot, I will describe myself to you. Figure me in your mind as jolly as formerly, and as strong and hearty, only a few years older; very plainly dressed, wearing my thin gray straight hair, that peeps out under my only *coiffure*, a fine fur cap, which comes down my forehead almost to my spectacles. Think how this must appear among the powdered heads of Paris! I wish every lady and gentleman in France would only be so obliging as to follow my fashion, comb their own heads as I do mine, dismiss their *friseurs*, and pay me half the money they paid to them. You see, the gentry might well afford this, and I could then enlist these *friseurs*, who are at least one hundred thousand, and with the money I would maintain them, make a visit with them to England, and dress the heads of your ministers and privy counsellors; which I conceive at present to be *un peu dérangés*. Adieu, madcap; and believe me ever, your affectionate friend and humble servant.

P.S. Don't be proud of this long letter. A fit of the gout, which has confined me five days, and made me refuse to see company, has given me a little time to trifle; otherwise it would have been very short, visitors and business would have interrupted; and perhaps, with Mrs. Barrow, you wish they had.

On Alliances

To Arthur Lee. Passy, 21 March, 1777.

WE HAVE received your favors from Vitoria and Burgos. The Congress, sitting at Baltimore, despatched a packet to us the 9th of January, containing an account of the success at Trenton, and subsequent events to that date, as far as they had come to knowledge. The vessel was obliged to run up a little river in Virginia to avoid some men-of-war, and was detained there seventeen days, or we should have had these advices sooner. We learn however through England, where they have news from New York to the 4th of February, that in Lord Cornwallis's retreat to New Brunswick two regiments of his rear guard were cut to pieces; that, General Washington having got round him to Newark and Elizabethtown, he had retired to Amboy in his way to New York; that General Howe had called in the garrisons of Fort Lee and Fort Constitution, which were now possessed by our people; that, on the New York side, Forts Washington and Independence were retaken by our troops, and that the British forces at Rhode Island were recalled for the defence of New York.

The Committee in their letters mention the intention of Congress to send ministers to the courts of Vienna, Tuscany, Holland, and Prussia. They also send us a fresh commission, containing your name instead of Mr. Jefferson's, with this additional clause, "and also to enter into, and agree upon a treaty with His Most Christian Majesty, or such other person or persons as shall be by him authorized for that purpose, for assistance in carrying on the present war between Great Britain and these United States." The same clause is in a particular commission they have sent me, to treat with the court of Spain, similar to our common commission to the court of France; and I am accordingly directed to go to Spain; but, as I know that choice was made merely on the supposition of my being a little known there to the great personage for whom you have my letter (a circumstance of little importance), and I am really unable through age to bear the fatigue and inconveniences of such a journey, I must excuse myself to Congress, and join with Mr. Deane in requesting you to proceed in the business on the former footing, till you can receive a particular commission from Congress, which will no doubt be sent as soon as the circumstances are known.

We know of no plans or instructions to Mr. Deane but those you have with you. By the packet, indeed, we have some fresh instructions, which relate to your mission, viz. that, in case France and Spain will enter into the war, the United States will assist the former in the conquest of the British sugar islands, and the latter in the conquest of Portugal, promising the assistance of six frigates manned, of not less than twenty-four guns each, and provisions equal to two millions of dollars; America desiring only for her share, what Britain holds on the continent; but you shall by the first safe opportunity have the instructions at length. I believe we must send a courier.

If we can, we are ordered to borrow two millions of pounds on interest. Judge then what a piece of service you will do, if you can obtain a considerable subsidy, or even a loan without interest.

We are also ordered to build six ships of war. It is a pleasure to find the things ordered, which we were doing without orders.

We are also to acquaint the several courts with the determination of America to maintain at all events our independence. You will see, by the date of the resolution relating to Portugal, as well as by the above, that the Congress were stout in the midst of their difficulties. It would be well to sound the court of Spain on the subject of permitting our armed ships to bring prizes into her ports, and there dispose of them. If it can be done openly, in what manner can we be accommodated with the use of their ports, or under what restrictions?

. . . While we are asking aid, it is necessary to gratify the desires, and in some sort comply with the humors, of those we apply to. Our business now is to carry our point. But I have never yet changed the opinion I gave in Congress, that a virgin State should preserve the virgin character, and not go about suitoring for alliances, but wait with decent dignity for the applications of others. I was overruled; perhaps for the best.

Letters to Strangers

To M. Lith. Passy, 6 April, 1777.

I HAVE just been honored with a letter from you, dated the 26th past, in which you express yourself as astonished, and appear to be angry, that you have no answer to a letter you wrote me on the 11th of December, which you are sure was delivered to me.

In exculpation of myself, I assure you that I never received any letter from you of that date. And indeed, being then but four days landed at Nantes, I think you could scarce have heard so soon of my being in Europe.

But I received one from you of the 8th of January, which I own I did not answer. It may displease you, if I give you the reason; but, as it may be of use to you in your future correspondences, I will hazard that for a gentleman to whom I feel myself obliged, as an American, on account of his good will to our cause.

Whoever writes to a stranger should observe three points. 1. That what he proposes be practicable. 2. His propositions should be made in explicit terms, so as to be easily understood. 3. What he desires should be in itself reasonable. Hereby he will give a favorable impression of his understanding, and create a desire of further acquaintance. Now it happened that you were negligent in *all* these points; for, first, you desired to have means procured for you of taking a voyage to America *"avec sureté";* which is not possible, as the dangers of the sea subsist always, and at present there is the additional danger of being taken by the English. Then you desire that this may be *"sans trop grandes dépenses,"* which is not intelligible enough to be answered, because, not knowing your ability of bearing expenses, one cannot judge what may be *trop grandes.* Lastly, you desire letters of address to the Congress and to General Washington; which it is not reasonable to ask of one who knows no more of you, than that your name is Lith, and that you live at Bayreuth.

In your last you also express yourself in vague terms, when you desire to be informed whether you may expect *"d'être reçu d'une manière convenable"* in our troops. As it is impossible to know what your ideas are of the *manière convenable*, how can one answer this? And then you demand, whether I will support you by my authority in giving you letters of recommendation. I doubt not your being a man of merit; and, knowing it yourself, you may forget that it is not known to everybody; but reflect a moment, Sir, and you will be convinced, that, if I were to practise giving letters of recommendation to persons of whose character I knew no more than I do of yours, my recommendations would soon be of no authority at all.

I thank you, however, for your kind desire of being serviceable to my countrymen; and I wish in return, that I could be of service to you in the scheme you have formed of going to America. But numbers of experienced officers here have offered to go over and join our army, and I could give them no encouragement, because I have no orders for that purpose, and I know it is extremely difficult to place them when they arrive there. I cannot but think, therefore, that it is best for you not to make so long, so expensive, and so hazardous a voyage, but to take the advice of your friends, and "*stay in Franconia.*" I have the honor to be, Sir, &c.

"On Our Side"

To Samuel Cooper. Paris, 1 May, 1777.

I THANK YOU for your kind congratulations on my safe arrival here, and for your good wishes. I am, as you supposed, treated with great civility and respect by all orders of people; but it gives me still greater satisfaction to find, that our being here is of some use to our country. . . .

All Europe is on our side of the question, as far as applause and good wishes can carry them. Those who live under arbitrary power do nevertheless approve of liberty, and wish for it; they almost despair of recovering it in Europe; they read the translations of our separate colony constitutions with rapture; and there are such numbers everywhere, who talk of removing to America, with their families and fortunes, as soon as peace and our independence shall be established, that it is generally believed we shall have a prodigious addition of strength, wealth, and arts, from the emigrations of Europe; and it is thought, that, to lessen or prevent such emigrations, the tyrannies established there must relax, and allow more liberty to their people. Hence it is a common observation here, that our cause is *the cause of all mankind*, and that we are fighting for their liberty in defending our own. It is a glorious task assigned us by Providence; which has, I trust, given us spirit and virtue equal to it, and will at last crown it with success.

On Recommendations

To a friend. Passy. [Date unknown.]

PERMIT me to mention to you, that, in my opinion, the natural complaisance of this country often carries people too far in the article of *recommendations*. You give them with too much facility to persons of whose real characters you know nothing, and sometimes at the request of others of whom you know as little. Frequently, if a man has no useful talents, is good for nothing and burdensome to his relations, or is indiscreet, profligate, and extravagant, they are glad to get rid of him by sending him to the other end of the world; and for that purpose scruple not to recommend him to those they wish should recommend him to others, as "*un bon sujet, plein de mérite,*" &c. &c. In consequence of my crediting such recommendations, my own are out of credit, and I cannot advise anybody to have the least dependence on them. If, after knowing this, you persist in desiring my recommendation for this person, who is known neither to *me* nor to *you*, I will give it, though, as I said before, I ought to refuse it.

These applications are my perpetual torment.

You can have no conception how I am harassed. All my friends are sought out and teazed to teaze me. Great officers of all ranks, in all departments; ladies, great and small, besides professed solicitors, worry me from morning to night. The noise of every coach now that enters my court terrifies me. I am afraid to accept an invitation to dine abroad, being almost sure of meeting with some officer or officer's friend, who, as soon as I am put in good humor by a glass or two of champaigne, begins his attack upon me. Luckily I do not often in my sleep dream of these vexatious situations, or I should be afraid of what are now my only hours of comfort. If, therefore, you have the least remaining kindness for me, if you would not help to drive me out of France, for God's sake, my dear friend, let this your twenty-third application be your last.

"*Model of a Letter of Recommendation of a person you are
unacquainted with.*

"Paris, 2 April, 1777.

"SIR,

"The bearer of this, who is going to America, presses me to give him a letter of recommendation, though I know nothing of him, not even his name. This may seem extraordinary, but I assure you it is not uncommon here. Sometimes, indeed, one unknown person brings another equally unknown, to recommend him; and sometimes they recommend one another! As to this gentleman, I must refer you to himself for his character and merits, with which he is certainly better acquainted than I can possibly be. I recommend him, however, to those civilities, which every stranger, of whom one knows no harm, has a right to; and I request you will do him all the good offices, and show him all the favor, that, on further acquaintance, you shall find him to deserve. I have the honor to be, &c."

On Controversy

To a friend. Passy, 14 October, 1777.

I HAVE never entered into any controversy in defence of my philosophical opinions; I leave them to take their chance in the world. If they are *right*, truth and experience will support them; if *wrong*, they ought to be refuted and rejected. Disputes are apt to sour one's temper, and disturb one's quiet. I have no private interest in the reception of my inventions by the world, having never made, nor proposed to make, the least profit by any of them.

The King's changing his *pointed* conductors for *blunt* ones is, therefore, a matter of small importance to me. If I had a wish about it, it would be that he had rejected them altogether as ineffectual. For it is only since he thought himself and family safe from the thunder of Heaven, that he dared to use his own thunder in destroying his innocent subjects. I am, Sir, yours, &c.

Peace Proposal

To Charles de Weissenstein. Passy, July 1, 1778.

I HAVE received your letter, dated Brussels, the 16th past. My vanity might possibly be flattered by your expressions of compliment to my understanding, if your *proposals* did not more clearly manifest a mean opinion of it.

You conjure me, in the name of the omniscient and just God, before whom I must appear, and by my hopes of future fame, to consider if some expedient cannot be found to put a stop to the desolation of America, and prevent the miseries of a general war. As I am conscious of having taken every step in my power to prevent the breach, and no one to widen it, I can appear cheerfully before that God, fearing nothing from his justice in this particular, though I have much occasion for his mercy in many others. . . .

Our expectations of the future grandeur of America are not so magnificent, and therefore not so vain or visionary, as you represent them to be. The body of our people are not merchants, but humble husbandmen, who delight in the cultivation of their lands, which, from their fertility and the variety of our climates, are capable of furnishing all the necessaries and conveniences of life without external commerce; and we have too much land to have the least temptation to extend our territory by conquest from peaceable neighbours, as well as too much justice to think of it. Our militia, you find by experience, are sufficient to defend our lands from invasion; and the commerce with us will be defended by all the nations who find an advantage in it. We, therefore, have not the occasion you imagine, of fleets or standing armies, but may leave those expensive machines to be maintained for the pomp of princes, and the wealth of ancient states. We propose, if possible, to live in peace with all mankind; and after you have been convinced, to your cost, that there is nothing to be got by attacking us, we have reason to hope, that no other power will judge it prudent to quarrel with us, lest they divert us from our own quiet industry, and turn us into corsairs preying upon theirs. The weight therefore of an independent empire, which you seem certain of our inability to bear, will not be so great as you imagine. The expense of our civil government we have always borne, and can easily bear, because it is small. A virtuous and laborious people may be cheaply governed. Determining, as we do, to have no offices of profit, nor any sinecures or useless appointments, so common in ancient or corrupted states, we can govern ourselves a year, for the sum you pay in a single department, or for what one jobbing contractor, by the favor of a minister, can cheat you out of in a single article.

You think we flatter ourselves, and are deceived into an opinion that England *must* acknowledge our independency. We, on the other hand, think you flatter yourselves in imagining such an acknowledgment a vast boon, which we strongly desire, and which you may gain some great advantage by granting or withholding. We have never asked it of you; we only tell you, that you can have no treaty with us but as an independent state; and you may please yourselves and your children with the rattle of your right to govern us, as long as you have done with that of your King's being King of France, without giving us the least concern, if you do not attempt to exercise it. That this pretended right is indisputable, as you say, we utterly deny. Your Parliament never had a right to govern us, and your King has forfeited it by his bloody tyranny. But I thank you for letting me know a little of your mind, that, even if the Parliament should acknowledge our independency, the act would not be binding to posterity, and that your nation would resume and prosecute the claim as soon as they found it convenient from the influence of your passions, and your present malice against us. We suspected before, that you would not be actually bound by your conciliatory acts, longer than till they had served their purpose of inducing us to disband our forces; but we were not certain, that you were knaves by principle, and that we ought not to have the least confidence in your offers, promises, or treaties, though confirmed by Parliament.

I now indeed recollect my being informed, long since, when in England, that a certain very great personage, then young, studied much a certain book, called "Arcana Imperii." I had the curiosity to procure the book and read it. There are sensible and good things in it, but some bad ones; for, if I remember rightly, a particular King is applauded for his politically exciting a rebellion among his subjects, at a time when they had not strength to support it, that he might, in subduing them, take away their privileges, which were troublesome to him; and a question is formally stated and discussed, *Whether a prince, who, to appease a revolt, makes promises of indemnity to the revolters, is obliged to fulfil those promises.* Honest and good men would say, Ay; but this politician says, as you say, No. And he gives this pretty reason, that, though it was right to make the promises, because otherwise the revolt would not be suppressed, yet it would be wrong to keep them, because revolters ought to be punished to deter from future revolts.

If these are the principles of your nation, no confidence can be placed in you; it is in vain to treat with you; and the wars can only end in being reduced to an utter inability of continuing them.

One main drift of your letter seems to be, to impress me with an idea of your own impartiality, by just censures of your ministers and measures, and to draw from me propositions of peace, or approbations of those you have enclosed to me, which you intimate may by your means be conveyed to the King directly, without the intervention of those ministers. You would have me give them to, or drop them for, a stranger, whom I may find next Monday in the church of Notre Dame, to be known by a rose in his hat. You yourself, Sir, are quite unknown to me; you have not trusted me with your true name. Our taking the least step towards a treaty with England through you, might, if you are an enemy, be made use of to ruin us with our new and good friends. I may be indiscreet enough in many things; but certainly, if I were disposed to make propositions (which I cannot do, having none committed to me to make), I should never think of delivering them to the Lord knows who, to be carried to the Lord knows where, to serve no one knows what purposes. Being at this time one of the most remarkable figures in Paris, even my appearance in the church of Notre Dame, where I cannot have any conceivable business, and especially being seen to leave or drop any letter to any person there, would be a matter of some speculation, and might, from the suspicions it must naturally give, have very mischievous consequences to our credit here. . . .

. . . Your true way to obtain peace, if your ministers desire it, is, to propose openly to the Congress fair and equal terms, and you may possibly come sooner to such a resolution, when you find, that personal flatteries, general cajolings, and panegyrics on our *virtue* and *wisdom* are not likely to have the effect you seem to expect; the persuading us to act basely and foolishly, in betraying our country and posterity into the hands of our most bitter enemies, giving up or selling our arms and warlike stores, dismissing our ships of war and troops, and putting those enemies in possession of our forts and ports.

This proposition of delivering ourselves, bound and gagged, ready for hanging, without even a right to complain, and without a friend to be found afterwards among all mankind, you would have us embrace upon the faith of an act of Parliament! Good God! an act of your Parliament! This demonstrates that you do not yet know us, and that you fancy we do not know you; but it is not merely this flimsy faith, that we are to act upon; you offer us *hope*, the hope of PLACES, PENSIONS, and PEERAGES. These, judging from yourselves, you think are motives irresistible. This offer to corrupt us, Sir, is with me your credential, and convinces me that you are not a private volunteer in your application. It bears the stamp of British court character. It is even the signature of your King. But think for a moment in what light it must be viewed in America. By PLACES, you mean places among us, for you take care by a special article to secure your own to yourselves. We must then pay the salaries in order to enrich ourselves with these places. But you will give us PENSIONS, probably to be paid too out of your expected American revenue, and which none of us can accept without deserving, and perhaps obtaining, a SUS-*pension*. PEERAGES! alas! Sir, our long observation of the vast servile majority of your peers, voting constantly for every measure proposed by a minister, however weak or wicked, leaves us small respect for that title. We consider it as a sort of *tar-and-feather* honor, or a mixture of foulness and folly, which every man among us, who should accept it from your King, would be obliged to renounce, or exchange for that conferred by the mobs of their own country, or wear it with everlasting infamy. I am, Sir, your humble servant.

Small Vanities

To Mrs. Sarah Bache. Passy, 3 June, 1779.

THE clay medallion of me you say you gave to Mr. Hopkinson was the first of the kind made in France. A variety of others have been made since of different sizes; some to be set in the lids of snuffboxes, and some so small as to be worn in rings; and the numbers sold are incredible. These, with the pictures, busts, and prints (of which copies upon copies are spread everywhere), have made your father's face as well known as that of the moon, so that he durst not do any thing that would oblige him to run away, as his phiz would discover him wherever he should venture to show it. It is said by learned etymologists, that the name *doll*, for the images children play with, is derived from the word IDOL. From the number of *dolls* now made of him, he may be truly said, *in that sense*, to be *i-doll-ized* in this country.

I think you did right to stay out of town till the summer was over, for the sake of your child's health. I hope you will get out again this summer, during the hot months; for I begin to love the dear little creature from your description of her.

I was charmed with the account you gave me of your industry, the tablecloths of your own spinning, &c.; but the latter part of the paragraph, that you had sent for linen from France because weaving and flax were grown dear, alas, that dissolved the charm; and your sending for long black pins, and lace, and *feathers!* disgusted me as much as if you had put salt into my strawberries. The spinning, I see, is laid aside, and you are to be dressed for the ball! You seem not to know, my dear daughter, that, of all the dear things in this world, idleness is the dearest, except mischief. . . .

When I began to read your account of the high prices of goods, "a pair of gloves seven dollars, a yard of common gauze twenty-four dollars, and that it now required a fortune to maintain a family in a very plain way," I expected you would conclude with telling me, that everybody as well as yourself was grown frugal and industrious; and I could scarce believe my eyes in reading forward, that "there never was so much pleasure and dressing going on"; and that you yourself wanted black pins and feathers from France to appear, I suppose, in the mode! This leads me to imagine, that perhaps it is not so much that the goods are grown dear, as that the money is grown cheap, as every thing else will do when excessively plenty; and that people are still as easy nearly in their circumstances, as when a pair of gloves might be had for half a crown. The war indeed may in some degree raise the prices of goods, and the high taxes which are necessary to support the war may make our frugality necessary; and, as I am always preaching that doctrine, I cannot in conscience or in decency encourage the contrary, by my example, in furnishing my children with foolish modes and luxuries. I therefore send all the articles you desire, that are useful and necessary, and omit the rest; for, as you say you should "have great pride in wearing any thing I send, and showing it as your father's taste," I must avoid giving you an opportunity of doing that with either lace or feathers. If you wear your cambric ruffles as I do, and take care not to mend the holes, they will come in time to be lace; and feathers, my dear girl, may be had in America from every cock's tail.

If you happen again to see General Washington, assure him of my very great and sincere respect, and tell him, that all the old Generals here amuse themselves in studying the accounts of his operations, and approve highly of his conduct.

Sword of Honor

To the Marquis de Lafayette. Passy, 24 August, 1779.

THE CONGRESS, sensible of your merit towards the United States, but unable adequately to reward it, determined to present you with a sword, as a small mark of their grateful acknowledgment. They directed it to be ornamented with suitable devices. Some of the principal actions of the war, in which you distinguished yourself by your bravery and conduct, are therefore represented upon it. These, with a few emblematic figures, all admirably well executed, make its principal value. By the help of the exquisite artists France affords, I find it easy to express every thing but the sense we have of your worth and our obligations to you. For this, figures and even words are found insufficient. I therefore only add, that with the most perfect esteem and respect, I have the honor to be, &c.

P.S. My grandson goes to Havre with the sword, and will have the honor of presenting it to you.

Progress of the War

To John Jay, President of Congress. Passy, 4 October, 1779.

THE extravagant luxury of our country, in the midst of all its distresses, is to me amazing. When the difficulties are so great to find remittances to pay for the arms and ammunition necessary for our defence, I am astonished and vexed to find upon inquiry, that much the greatest part of the Congress interest bills come to pay for tea, and a great part of the remainder is ordered to be laid out in gewgaws and superfluities. It makes me grudge the trouble of examining, and entering, and accepting them, which indeed takes a great deal of time.

To a friend in America. Passy, 25 October, 1779.

THE account you have had of the vogue I am in here has some truth in it. Perhaps few strangers in France have had the good fortune to be so universally popular; but the story you allude to, mentioning "mechanic rust," is totally without foundation. But one is not to expect being always in fashion. I hope, however, to preserve, while I stay, the regard you mention of the French ladies; for their society and conversation, when I have time to enjoy them, are extremely agreeable.

The enemy have been very near you indeed. When only at the distance of a mile, you must have been much alarmed. We have given them a little taste of this disturbance upon their own coasts this summer; and, though we have burnt none of their towns, we have occasioned a good deal of terror and bustle in many of them, as they imagined our Commodore Jones had four thousand troops with him for descents.

I am glad to learn that my dear sister continued in good health, and good spirits, and that she had learnt not to be afraid of her friend, fresh air. With the tenderest affection, &c.

To Samuel Cooper. Passy, 27 October, 1779.

IT IS a long time since I have had the pleasure of hearing from you. The intelligence you were used to favor me with was often useful to our affairs. I hope I have not lost your friendship, together with your correspondence. Our excellent Mr. Winthrop, I see, is gone. He was one of those old friends, for the sake of whose society I wished to return and spend the small remnant of my days in New England. A few more such deaths will make me a stranger in my own country. The loss of friends is the tax a man pays for living long himself. I find it a heavy one.

You will see by the newspapers that we have given some disturbance to the British coasts this year. One little privateer out of Dunkirk, the *Black Prince*, with a Congress commission, and a few Americans mixed with the Irish and English smugglers, went round their Islands and took thirty-seven prizes in less than three months. The little squadron of Commodore Jones, under the same commission and colors, has alarmed those coasts exceedingly, occasioned a good deal of internal expense, done great damage to their trade, and taken two frigates, with four hundred prisoners. He is now with his principal prizes in Holland, where he is pretty well received, but must quit that neutral country as soon as his damages are repaired. The English watch with a superior force his coming out, but we hope he will manage so as to escape their vigilance. Few actions at sea have demonstrated such steady, cool, determined bravery, as that of Jones in taking the *Serapis*.

There has been much rumor this summer throughout Europe, of an approaching peace, through the mediation of Russia and Holland; but it is understood to arise from the invention of stockjobbers and others interested in propagating such opinions. England seems not to be yet sufficiently humbled, to acknowledge the independence of the American States, or to treat with them on that footing; and our friends will not make a peace on any other. So we shall probably see another campaign.

By the invoices I have seen and heard of, sent hither with Congress interest bills of exchange to purchase the goods, it should seem that there is not so great a want of necessaries as of superfluities among our people. It is difficult to conceive that your distresses can be great, when one sees that much the greatest part of that money is lavished in modes, and gewgaws, and tea! It is impossible for us to become wiser, when by simple economy, and avoiding unnecessary expenses, we might more than defray the charge of the war. We export solid provision of all kinds, which is necessary for the sustenance of man, and we import fashions, luxuries, and trifles. Such trade may enrich the traders, but never the country.

The good will of all Europe to our cause as being the cause of liberty, which is the cause of mankind, still continues, as does the universal wish to see the English pride humiliated, and their power curtailed. Those circumstances are encouraging, and give hopes of a happy issue. Which may God grant, and that you, my friend, may live long a blessing to your country.

The Price of a Whistle

To Madame Brillon. Passy, 10 November, 1779.

I AM charmed with your description of Paradise, and with your plan of living there; and I approve much of your conclusion, that, in the mean time, we should draw all the good we can from this world. In my opinion, we might all draw more good from it than we do, and suffer less evil, if we would take care not to give too much for *whistles*. For to me it seems, that most of the unhappy people we meet with, are become so by neglect of that caution.

You ask what I mean? You love stories, and will excuse my telling one of myself.

When I was a child of seven years old, my friends, on a holiday, filled my pockets with coppers. I went directly to a shop where they sold toys for children; and, being charmed with the sound of a *whistle*, that I met by the way in the hands of another boy, I voluntarily offered and gave all my money for one. I then came home, and went whistling all over the house, much pleased with my *whistle*, but disturbing all the family. My brothers, and sisters, and cousins, understanding the bargain I had made, told me I had given four times as much for it as it was worth; put me in mind what good things I might have bought with the rest of the money; and laughed at me so much for my folly, that I cried with vexation; and the reflection gave me more chagrin than the *whistle* gave me pleasure.

This however was afterwards of use to me, the impression continuing on my mind; so that often, when I was tempted to buy some unnecessary thing, I said to myself, *Don't give too much for the whistle;* and I saved my money.

As I grew up, came into the world, and observed the actions of men, I thought I met with many, very many, who *gave too much for the whistle*.

When I saw one too ambitious of court favor, sacrificing his time in attendance on levees, his repose, his liberty, his virtue, and perhaps his friends, to attain it, I have said to myself, *This man gives too much for his whistle*.

When I saw another fond of popularity, constantly employing himself in political bustles, neglecting his own affairs, and ruining them by that neglect, *He pays, indeed,* said I, *too much for his whistle*.

If I knew a miser, who gave up every kind of comfortable living, all the pleasure of doing good to others, all the esteem of his fellow-citizens, and the joys of benevolent friendship, for the sake of accumulating wealth, *Poor man,* said I, *you pay too much for your whistle*.

When I met with a man of pleasure, sacrificing every laudable improvement of the mind, or of his fortune, to mere corporeal sensations, and ruining his health in their pursuit, *Mistaken man,* said I, *you are providing pain for yourself, instead of pleasure; you give too much for your whistle*.

If I see one fond of appearance, or fine clothes, fine houses, fine furniture, fine equipages, all above his fortune, for which he contracts debts, and ends his career in a prison, *Alas!* say I, *he has paid dear, very dear, for his whistle*.

When I see a beautiful, sweet-tempered girl married to an ill-natured brute of a husband, *What a pity,* say I, *that she should pay so much for a whistle!*

In short, I conceive that great part of the miseries of mankind are brought upon them by the false estimates they have made of the value of things, and by their *giving too much for their whistles*.

Yet I ought to have charity for these unhappy people, when I consider, that, with all this wisdom of which I am boasting, there are certain things in the world so tempting, for example, the apples of King John, which happily are not to be bought; for if they were put to sale by auction, I might very easily be led to ruin myself in the purchase, and find that I had once more given too much for the *whistle*.

War Time Resentment

To David Hartley. Passy, 2 Feb., 1780.

I HAVE long postponed answering your letter of the 29th of June. A principal point in it, on which you seemed to desire my opinion, was the conduct you thought America ought to hold, in case her allies should, from motives of ambition or resentment of former injuries, desire her to continue the war, beyond what should be reasonable and consistent with her particular interests. As often as I took up your letter in order to answer it, this suggestion displeased me, and I laid it down again. I saw no occasion for discussing such a question at present, nor any good end it could serve to discuss it before the case should happen; and I saw inconveniences in discussing it. I wish, therefore, you had not mentioned it. For the rest, I am as much for peace as ever I was, and as heartily desirous of seeing the war ended, as I was to prevent its beginning; of which your ministers know I gave a strong proof before I left England, when, in order to an accommodation, I offered at my own risk, without orders for so doing, and without knowing whether I should be owned in doing it, to pay the whole damage of destroying the tea at Boston, provided the acts made against that province were repealed. This offer was refused. I still think it would have been wise to have accepted it. If the Congress have therefore intrusted to others, rather than to me, the negotiations for peace, when such shall be set on foot, as has been reported, it is perhaps because they may have heard of a very singular opinion of mine, that there hardly ever existed such a thing as a bad peace, or a good war, and that I might therefore easily be induced to make improper concessions. But at the same time they and you may be assured, that I should think the destruction of our whole country, and the extirpation of our whole people, preferable to the infamy of abandoning our allies.

As neither you nor I are at present authorized to treat of peace, it seems to little purpose to make or consider propositions relating to it. I have had so many such put into my hands, that I am tired of them. I will, however, give your proposal of a ten years' truce this answer, that, though I think a solid peace made at once a much better thing, yet, if the truce is practicable and the peace not, I should be for agreeing to it. At least I see at present no sufficient reasons for refusing it, provided our allies approve of it. But this is merely a private opinion of mine, which perhaps may be changed by reasons, that at present do not offer themselves. This, however, I am clear in, that withdrawing your troops will be best for you, if you wish a cordial reconciliation, and that the truce should produce a peace. . . .

You may have heard, that accounts upon oath have been taken in America, by order of Congress, of the British barbarities committed there. It is expected of me to make a schoolbook of them, and to have thirty-five prints designed here by good artists, and engraved, each expressing one or more of the different horrid facts, to be inserted in the book, in order to impress the minds of children and posterity with a deep sense of your bloody and insatiable malice and wickedness. Every kindness I hear of, done by an Englishman to an American prisoner, makes me resolve not to proceed in the work, hoping a reconciliation may yet take place. But every fresh instance of your devilism weakens that resolution, and makes me abominate the thought of a reunion with such a people. You, my friend, have often persuaded me, and I believed it, that the war was not theirs, nor approved by them. But their suffering it so long to continue, and the wretched rulers to remain who carry it on, makes me think you have too good an opinion of them.

Progress of Science

To Joseph Priestley. Passy, 8 Feb., 1780.

YOUR kind letter of September 27th came to hand but very lately, the bearer having stayed long in Holland. I always rejoice to hear of your being still employed in experimental researches into nature, and of the success you meet with. The rapid progress *true* science now makes, occasions my regretting sometimes that I was born so soon. It is impossible to imagine the height to which may be carried, in a thousand years, the power of man over matter. We may perhaps learn to deprive large masses of their gravity, and give them absolute levity, for the sake of easy transport. Agriculture may diminish its labor and double its produce; all diseases may by sure means be prevented or cured, not excepting even that of old age, and our lives lengthened at pleasure even beyond the antediluvian standard. O that moral science were in as fair a way of improvement, that men would cease to be wolves to one another, and that human beings would at length learn what they now improperly call humanity!

. . . All human situations have their inconveniences; we *feel* those that we find in the present, and we neither *feel* nor *see* those that exist in another. Hence we make frequent and troublesome changes without amendment, and often for the worse.

In my youth, I was passenger in a little sloop, descending the river Delaware. There being no wind, we were obliged, when the ebb was spent, to cast anchor, and wait for the next. The heat of the sun on the vessel was excessive, the company strangers to me, and not very agreeable. Near the river side I saw what I took to be a pleasant green meadow, in the middle of which was a large shady tree, where it struck my fancy I could sit and read (having a book in my pocket), and pass the time agreeably till the tide turned. I therefore prevailed with the captain to put me ashore. Being landed, I found the greatest part of my meadow was really a marsh, in crossing which, to come at my tree, I was up to my knees in mire; and I had not placed myself under its shade five minutes, before the mosquitoes in swarms found me out, attacked my legs, hands, and face, and made my reading and my rest impossible; so that I returned to the beach, and called for the boat to come and take me on board again, where I was obliged to bear the heat I had strove to quit, and also the laugh of the company. Similar cases in the affairs of life have since frequently fallen under my observation.

Father of His Country

To George Washington. Passy, 5 March, 1780.

I HAVE received but lately the letter your Excellency did me the honor of writing to me in recommendation of the Marquis de Lafayette. His modesty detained it long in his own hands. We became acquainted, however, from the time of his arrival at Paris; and his zeal for the honor of our country, his activity in our affairs here, and his firm attachment to our cause and to you, impressed me with the same regard and esteem for him that your Excellency's letter would have done, had it been immediately delivered to me.

Should peace arrive after another campaign or two, and afford us a little leisure, I should be happy to see your Excellency in Europe, and to accompany you, if my age and strength would permit, in visiting some of its ancient and most famous kingdoms. You would, on this side of the sea, enjoy the great reputation you have acquired, pure and free from those little shades that the jealousy and envy of a man's countrymen and contemporaries are ever endeavouring to cast over living merit. Here you would know, and enjoy, what posterity will say of Washington. For a thousand leagues have nearly the same effect with a thousand years. The feeble voice of those grovelling passions cannot extend so far either in time or distance. At present I enjoy that pleasure for you; as I frequently hear the old generals of this martial country, who study the maps of America, and mark upon them all your operations, speak with sincere approbation and great applause of your conduct; and join in giving you the character of one of the greatest captains of the age.

I must soon quit this scene, but you may live to see our country flourish, as it will amazingly and rapidly after the war is over; like a field of young Indian corn, which long fair weather and sunshine had enfeebled and discolored, and which in that weak state, by a thunder gust of violent wind, hail, and rain, seemed to be threatened with absolute destruction; yet the storm being past, it recovers fresh verdure, shoots up with double vigor, and delights the eye, not of its owner only, but of every observing traveller.

The best wishes that can be formed for your health, honor, and happiness, ever attend you from yours, &c.

French Popularity

To John Jay. Passy, 13 June, 1780.

MRS. JAY does me much honor in desiring to have one of the prints, that have been made here of her countryman. I send what is said to be the best of five or six engraved by different hands, from different paintings. The verses at the bottom are truly extravagant. But you must know, that the desire of pleasing, by a perpetual rise of compliments in this polite nation, has so used up all the common expressions of approbation, that they are become flat and insipid, and to use them almost implies censure. Hence music, that formerly might be sufficiently praised when it was called *bonne*, to go a little farther they call it *excellente*, then *superbe, magnifique, exquise, céleste*, all which being in their turns worn out, there only remains *divine*; and, when that is grown as insignificant as its predecessors, I think they must return to common speech and common sense; as, from vying with one another in fine and costly paintings on their coaches, since I first knew the country, not being able to go farther in that way, they have returned lately to plain carriages, painted without arms or figures, in one uniform color.

Dialogue Between Franklin and the Gout

Midnight, 22 October, 1780.

FRANKLIN. Eh! Oh! Eh! What have I done to merit these cruel sufferings?

GOUT. Many things; you have ate and drank too freely, and too much indulged those legs of yours in their indolence.

FRANKLIN. Who is it that accuses me?

GOUT. It is I, even I, the Gout.

FRANKLIN. What! my enemy in person?

GOUT. No, not your enemy.

FRANKLIN. I repeat it; my enemy; for you would not only torment my body to death, but ruin my good name; you reproach me as a glutton and a tippler; now all the world, that knows me, will allow that I am neither the one nor the other.

GOUT. The world may think as it pleases; it is always very complaisant to itself, and sometimes to its friends; but I very well know that the quantity of meat and drink proper for a man, who takes a reasonable degree of exercise, would be too much for another, who never takes any.

FRANKLIN. I take—Eh! Oh!—as much exercise—Eh!—as I can, Madam Gout. You know my sedentary state, and on that account, it would seem, Madam Gout, as if you might spare me a little, seeing it is not altogether my own fault.

GOUT. Not a jot; your rhetoric and your politeness are thrown away; your apology avails nothing. If your situation in life is a sedentary one, your amusements, your recreations, at least, should be active. You ought to walk or ride; or, if the weather prevents that, play at billiards. But let us examine your course of life. While the mornings are long, and you have leisure to go abroad, what do you do? Why, instead of gaining an appetite for breakfast, by salutary exercise, you amuse yourself with books, pamphlets, or newspapers, which commonly are not worth the reading. Yet you eat an inordinate breakfast, four dishes of tea, with cream, and one or two buttered toasts, with slices of hung beef, which I fancy are not things the most easily digested. Immediately afterward you sit down to write at your desk, or converse with persons who apply to you on business. Thus the time passes till one, without any kind of bodily exercise. But all this I could pardon, in regard, as you say, to your sedentary condition. But what is your practice after dinner? Walking in the beautiful gardens of those friends, with whom you have dined, would be the choice of men of sense; yours is to be fixed down to chess, where you are found engaged for two or three hours! This is your perpetual recreation, which is the least eligible of any for a sedentary man, because, instead of accelerating the motion of the fluids, the rigid attention it requires helps to retard the circulation and obstruct internal secretions. Wrapt in the speculations of this wretched game, you destroy your constitution. What can be expected from such a course of living, but a body replete with stagnant humors, ready to fall a prey to all kinds of dangerous maladies, if I, the Gout, did not occasionally bring you relief by agitating those humors, and so purifying or dissipating them? If it was in some nook or alley in Paris, deprived of walks, that you played awhile at chess after dinner, this might be excusable; but the same taste prevails with you in Passy, Auteuil, Montmartre, or Sanoy, places where there are the finest gardens and walks, a pure air, beautiful women, and most agreeable and instructive conversation; all which you might enjoy by frequenting the walks. But these are rejected for this abominable game of chess. Fie, then, Mr. Franklin! But amidst my instructions, I had almost forgot to administer my wholesome corrections; so take that twinge,—and that.

FRANKLIN. Oh! Eh! Oh! Ohhh! As much instruction as you please, Madam Gout, and as many reproaches; but pray, Madam, a truce with your corrections!

GOUT. No, Sir, no,—I will not abate a particle of what is so much for your good,—therefore——

FRANKLIN. Oh! Ehhh!—It is not fair to say I take no exercise, when I do very often, going out to dine and returning in my carriage.

GOUT. That, of all imaginable exercises, is the most slight and insignificant, if you allude to the motion of a carriage suspended on springs. By observing the degree of heat obtained by different kinds of motion, we may form an estimate of the quantity of exercise given by each. Thus, for example, if you turn out to walk in winter with cold feet, in an hour's time you will be in a glow all over; ride on horseback, the same effect will scarcely be perceived by four hours' round trotting; but if you loll in a carriage, such as you have mentioned, you may travel all day, and gladly enter the last inn to warm your feet by a fire. Flatter yourself then no longer, that half an hour's airing in your carriage deserves the name of exercise. Providence has appointed few to roll in carriages, while he has given to all a pair of legs, which are machines infinitely more commodious and serviceable. Be grateful, then, and make a proper use of yours. Would you know how they forward the circulation of your fluids, in the very action of transporting you from place to place; observe when you walk, that all your weight is alternately thrown from one leg to the other; this occasions a great pressure on the vessels of the foot, and repels their contents; when relieved, by the weight being thrown on the other foot, the vessels of the first are allowed to replenish, and, by a return of this weight, this repulsion again succeeds; thus accelerating the circulation of the blood. The heat produced in any given time, depends on the degree of this acceleration; the fluids are shaken, the humors attenuated, the secretions facilitated, and all goes well; the cheeks are ruddy, and health is established. Behold your fair friend at Auteuil, a lady who received from bounteous nature more really useful science, than half a dozen such pretenders to philosophy as you have been able to extract from all your books. When she honors you with a visit, it is on foot. She walks all hours of the day, and leaves indolence, and its concomitant maladies, to be endured by her horses. In this see at once the preservative of her health and personal charms. But when you go to Auteuil, you must have your carriage, though it is no further from Passy to Auteuil than from Auteuil to Passy.

FRANKLIN. Your reasonings grow very tiresome.

GOUT. I stand corrected. I will be silent and continue my office; take that, and that.

FRANKLIN. Oh! Ohh! Talk on, I pray you!

GOUT. No, no; I have a good number of twinges for you to-night, and you may be sure of some more to-morrow.

FRANKLIN. What, with such a fever! I shall go distracted. Oh! Eh! Can no one bear it for me?

GOUT. Ask that of your horses; they have served you faithfully.

FRANKLIN. How can you so cruelly sport with my torments?

GOUT. Sport! I am very serious. I have here a list of offences against your own health distinctly written, and can justify every stroke inflicted on you.

FRANKLIN. Read it then.

GOUT. It is too long a detail; but I will briefly mention some particulars.

FRANKLIN. Proceed. I am all attention.

GOUT. Do you remember how often you have promised yourself, the following morning, a walk in the grove of Boulogne, in the garden de la Muette, or in your own garden, and have violated your promise, alleging, at one time, it was too cold, at another too warm, too windy, too moist, or what else you pleased; when in truth it was too nothing, but your insuperable love of ease?

FRANKLIN. That I confess may have happened occasionally, probably ten times in a year.

GOUT. Your confession is very far short of the truth; the gross amount is one hundred and ninety-nine times.

FRANKLIN. Is it possible?

GOUT. So possible, that it is fact; you may rely on the accuracy of my statement. You know Mr. Brillon's gardens, and what fine walks they contain; you know the handsome flight of an hundred steps, which lead from the terrace above to the lawn below. You have been in the practice of visiting this amiable family twice a week, after dinner, and it is a maxim of your own, that "a man may take as much exercise in walking a mile, up and down stairs, as in ten on level ground." What an opportunity was here for you to have had exercise in both these ways! Did you embrace it, and how often?

FRANKLIN.   I cannot immediately answer that question.

GOUT.   I will do it for you; not once.

FRANKLIN.   Not once?

GOUT.   Even so. During the summer you went there at six o'clock. You found the charming lady, with her lovely children and friends, eager to walk with you, and entertain you with their agreeable conversation; and what has been your choice? Why to sit on the terrace, satisfying yourself with the fine prospect, and passing your eye over the beauties of the garden below, without taking one step to descend and walk about in them. On the contrary, you call for tea and the chess-board; and lo! you are occupied in your seat till nine o'clock, and that besides two hours' play after dinner; and then, instead of walking home, which would have bestirred you a little, you step into your carriage. How absurd to suppose that all this carelessness can be reconcilable with health, without my interposition!

FRANKLIN.   I am convinced now of the justness of Poor Richard's remark, that "Our debts and our sins are always greater than we think for."

GOUT.   So it is. You philosophers are sages in your maxims, and fools in your conduct.

FRANKLIN.   But do you charge among my crimes, that I return in a carriage from Mr. Brillon's?

GOUT.   Certainly; for, having been seated all the while, you cannot object the fatigue of the day, and cannot want therefore the relief of a carriage.

FRANKLIN.   What then would you have me do with my carriage?

GOUT.   Burn it if you choose; you would at least get heat out of it once in this way; or, if you dislike that proposal, here's another for you; observe the poor peasants, who work in the vineyards and grounds about the villages of Passy, Auteuil, Chaillot, &c.; you may find every day, among these deserving creatures, four or five old men and women, bent and perhaps crippled by weight of years, and too long and too great labor. After a most fatiguing day, these people have to trudge a mile or two to their smoky huts. Order your coachman to set them down. This is an act that will be good for your soul; and, at the same time, after your visit to the Brillons, if you return on foot, that will be good for your body.

FRANKLIN.   Ah! how tiresome you are!

GOUT.   Well, then, to my office; it should not be forgotten that I am your physician. There.

FRANKLIN.   Ohhh! what a devil of a physician!

GOUT.   How ungrateful you are to say so! Is it not I who, in the character of your physician, have saved you from the palsy, dropsy, and apoplexy? one or other of which would have done for you long ago, but for me.

FRANKLIN. I submit, and thank you for the past, but entreat the discontinuance of your visits for the future; for, in my mind, one had better die than be cured so dolefully. Permit me just to hint, that I have also not been unfriendly to *you*. I never feed physician or quack of any kind, to enter the list against you; if then you do not leave me to my repose, it may be said you are ungrateful too.

GOUT. I can scarcely acknowledge that as any objection. As to quacks, I despise them; they may kill you indeed, but cannot injure me. And, as to regular physicians, they are at last convinced, that the gout, in such a subject as you are, is no disease, but a remedy; and wherefore cure a remedy?—but to our business,—there.

FRANKLIN. Oh! Oh!—for Heaven's sake leave me; and I promise faithfully never more to play at chess, but to take exercise daily, and live temperately.

GOUT. I know you too well. You promise fair; but, after a few months of good health, you will return to your old habits; your fine promises will be forgotten like the forms of the last year's clouds. Let us then finish the account, and I will go. But I leave you with an assurance of visiting you again at a proper time and place; for my object is your good, and you are sensible now that I am your *real friend*.

An Economical Project for Diminishing the Cost of Light

To the Authors of the Journal of Paris.

MESSIEURS,

You often entertain us with accounts of new discoveries. Permit me to communicate to the public, through your paper, one that has lately been made by myself, and which I conceive may be of great utility.

I was the other evening in a grand company, where the new lamp of Messrs. Quinquet and Lange was introduced; and much admired for its splendor; but a general inquiry was made, whether the oil it consumed was not in proportion to the light it afforded, in which case there would be no saving in the use of it. No one present could satisfy us in that point, which all agreed ought to be known, it being a very desirable thing to lessen, if possible, the expense of lighting our apartments, when every other article of family expense was so much augmented.

I was pleased to see this general concern for economy, for I love economy exceedingly.

I went home, and to bed, three or four hours after midnight, with my head full of the subject. An accidental sudden noise waked me about six in the morning, when I was surprised to find my room filled with light; and

I imagined at first, that a number of those lamps had been brought into it; but, rubbing my eyes, I perceived the light came in at the windows. I got up and looked out to see what might be the occasion of it, when I saw the sun just rising above the horizon, from whence he poured his rays plentifully into my chamber, my domestic having negligently omitted, the preceding evening, to close the shutters.

I looked at my watch, which goes very well, and found that it was but six o'clock; and still thinking it something extraordinary that the sun should rise so early, I looked into the almanac, where I found it to be the hour given for his rising on that day. I looked forward, too, and found he was to rise still earlier every day till towards the end of June; and that at no time in the year he retarded his rising so long as till eight o'clock. Your readers, who with me have never seen any signs of sunshine before noon, and seldom regard the astronomical part of the almanac, will be as much astonished as I was, when they hear of his rising so early; and especially when I assure them, *that he gives light as soon as he rises.* I am convinced of this. I am certain of my fact. One cannot be more certain of any fact. I saw it with my own eyes. And, having repeated this observation the three following mornings, I found always precisely the same result.

Yet it so happens, that when I speak of this discovery to others, I can easily perceive by their countenances, though they forbear expressing it in words, that they do not quite believe me. One, indeed, who is a learned natural philosopher, has assured me that I must certainly be mistaken as to the circumstance of the light coming into my room; for it being well known, as he says, that there could be no light abroad at that hour, it follows that none could enter from without; and that of consequence, my windows being accidentally left open, instead of letting in the light, had only served to let out the darkness; and he used many ingenious arguments to show me how I might, by that means, have been deceived. I owned that he puzzled me a little, but he did not satisfy me; and the subsequent observations I made, as above mentioned, confirmed me in my first opinion.

This event has given rise in my mind to several serious and important reflections. I considered that, if I had not been awakened so early in the morning, I should have slept six hours longer by the light of the sun, and in exchange have lived six hours the following night by candle-light; and, the latter being a much more expensive light than the former, my love of economy induced me to muster up what little arithmetic I was master of, and to make some calculations, which I shall give you, after observing that utility is, in my opinion, the test of value in matters of invention, and that a discovery which can be applied to no use, or is not good for something, is good for nothing.

I took for the basis of my calculation the supposition that there are one hundred thousand families in Paris, and that these families consume in the night half a pound of bougies, or candles, per hour. I think this is a moderate allowance, taking one family with another; for though I believe some consume less, I know that many consume a great deal more. Then estimating

seven hours per day as the medium quantity between the time of the sun's
rising and ours, he rising during the six following months from six to eight
hours before noon, and there being seven hours of course per night in which
we burn candles, the account will stand thus;—

In the six months between the 20th of March and the 20th of September,
there are

Nights	183
Hours of each night in which we burn candles . . .	7

Multiplication gives for the total number of hours . . . 1,281

These 1,281 hours multiplied by 100,000, the number of inhabitants, give 128,100,000

One hundred twenty-eight millions and one hundred thousand
hours, spent at Paris by candle-light, which, at half a pound
of wax and tallow per hour, gives the weight of . . 64,050,000

Sixty-four millions and fifty thousand of pounds, which,
estimating the whole at the medium price of thirty sols the
pound, makes the sum of ninety-six millions and seventy-five
thousand livres tournois 96,075,000

An immense sum! that the city of Paris might save every year, by the
economy of using sunshine instead of candles.

If it should be said, that people are apt to be obstinately attached to old
customs, and that it will be difficult to induce them to rise before noon,
consequently my discovery can be of little use; I answer, *Nil desperandum*.
I believe all who have common sense, as soon as they have learnt from this
paper that it is daylight when the sun rises, will contrive to rise with him;
and, to compel the rest, I would propose the following regulations;

First.   Let a tax be laid of a louis per window, on every window that is
provided with shutters to keep out the light of the sun.

Second.   Let the same salutary operation of police be made use of, to prevent our burning candles, that inclined us last winter to be more economical
in burning wood; that is, let guards be placed in the shops of the wax and
tallow chandlers, and no family be permitted to be supplied with more than
one pound of candles per week.

Third.   Let guards also be posted to stop all the coaches, &c. that would
pass the streets after sun-set, except those of physicians, surgeons, and mid-
wives.

Fourth.   Every morning as soon as the sun rises, let all the bells in every
church be set ringing; and if that is not sufficient, let cannon be fired in every
street, to wake the sluggards effectually, and make them open their eyes to
see their true interest.

All the difficulty will be in the first two or three days; after which the
reformation will be as natural and easy as the present irregularity; for, *ce
n'est que le premier pas qui coûte*. Oblige a man to rise at four in the morning, and it is more than probable he will go willingly to bed at eight in the

evening; and, having had eight hours sleep, he will rise more willingly at four in the morning following. But this sum of ninety-six millions and seventy-five thousand livres is not the whole of what may be saved by my economical project. You may observe, that I have calculated upon only one half of the year, and much may be saved in the other, though the days are shorter. Besides, the immense stock of wax and tallow left unconsumed during the summer, will probably make candles much cheaper for the ensuing winter, and continue them cheaper as long as the proposed reformation shall be supported.

For the great benefit of this discovery, thus freely communicated and bestowed by me on the public, I demand neither place, pension, exclusive privilege, nor any other reward whatever. I expect only to have the honor of it. And yet I know there are little, envious minds, who will, as usual, deny me this, and say, that my invention was known to the ancients, and perhaps they may bring passages out of the old books in proof of it. I will not dispute with these people, that the ancients knew not the sun would rise at certain hours; they possibly had, as we have, almanacs that predicted it; but it does not follow thence, that they knew *he gave light as soon as he rose*. This is what I claim as my discovery. If the ancients knew it, it might have been long since forgotten; for it certainly was unknown to the moderns, at least to the Parisians, which to prove, I need use but one plain simple argument. They are as well instructed, judicious, and prudent a people as exist anywhere in the world, all professing, like myself, to be lovers of economy; and, from the many heavy taxes required from them by the necessities of the state, have surely an abundant reason to be economical. I say it is impossible that so sensible a people, under such circumstances, should have lived so long by the smoky, unwholesome, and enormously expensive light of candles, if they had really known, that they might have had as much pure light of the sun for nothing. I am, &c.   A Subscriber.

Russian Plan

To the President of Congress. Passy, 9 August, 1780.

The great public event in Europe of this year is the proposal, by Russia, of an armed neutrality for protecting the liberty of commerce. The proposition is accepted now by most of the maritime powers. As it is likely to become the law of nations, *that free ships should make free goods*, I wish the Congress to consider, whether it may not be proper to give orders to their cruisers not to molest foreign ships, but conform to the spirit of that treaty of neutrality.

Religious Tests

To Richard Price. Passy, 9 Oct., 1780.

I AM fully of your opinion respecting religious tests; but, though the people of Massachusetts have not in their new constitution kept quite clear of them, yet, if we consider what that people were one hundred years ago, we must allow they have gone great lengths in liberality of sentiment on religious subjects; and we may hope for greater degrees of perfection, when their constitution, some years hence, shall be revised. If Christian preachers had continued to teach as Christ and his Apostles did, without salaries, and as the Quakers now do, I imagine tests would never have existed; for I think they were invented, not so much to secure religion itself, as the emoluments of it. When a religion is good, I conceive that it will support itself; and, when it cannot support itself, and God does not take care to support it, so that its professors are obliged to call for the help of the civil power, it is a sign, I apprehend, of its being a bad one. But I shall be out of my depth, if I wade any deeper in theology, and I will not trouble you with politics, nor with news which are almost as uncertain; but conclude with a heartfelt wish to embrace you once more, and enjoy your sweet society in peace, among our honest, worthy, ingenious friends at the *London.*

A Fable

To a friend. Passy.

YOUR comparison of the *keystone of an arch* is very pretty, tending to make me content with my situation. But I suppose you have heard our story of the *harrow;* if not, here it is. A farmer, in our country, sent two of his servants to borrow one of a neighbour, ordering them to bring it between them on their shoulders. When they came to look at it, one of them, who had much wit and cunning, said; "What could our master mean by sending only two men to bring this harrow? No two men upon earth are strong enough to carry it." "Poh!" said the other, who was vain of his strength, "what do you talk of two men? One man may carry it. Help it upon my shoulders and see." As he proceeded with it, the wag kept exclaiming, "Zounds, how strong you are! I could not have thought it. Why, you are a Samson! There is not such another man in America. What amazing strength God has given you! But you will kill yourself! Pray put it down and rest a little, or let me bear a part of the weight." "No, no," said he, being more encouraged by the compliments, than oppressed by the burden; "you shall see I can carry it quite home." And so he did. In this particular I am afraid my part of the imitation will fall short of the original.

Peace-making

To John Adams. Passy, 12 October, 1781.

I HAVE never known a peace made, even the most advantageous, that was not censured as inadequate, and the makers condemned as injudicious or corrupt. "BLESSED *are the peace-makers*" is, I suppose, to be understood in the other world; for in this they are frequently *cursed*. Being as yet rather too much attached to this world, I had therefore no ambition to be concerned in fabricating this peace, and know not how I came to be put into the commission. I esteem it, however, as an honor to be joined with you in so important a business; and, if the execution of it shall happen in my time, which I hardly expect, I shall endeavour to assist in discharging the duty according to the best of my judgment.

I have heard nothing of Mr. Jefferson. I imagine the story of his being taken prisoner is not true. From his original unwillingness to leave America, when I was sent hither, I think his coming doubtful, unless he had been made acquainted with and consented to the appointment.

Prisoner of War

To Edmund Burke. Passy, 15 October, 1781.

I RECEIVED but a few days since your very friendly letter of August last, on the subject of General Burgoyne.

Since the foolish part of mankind will make wars from time to time with each other, not having sense enough otherwise to settle their differences, it certainly becomes the wiser part, who cannot prevent those wars, to alleviate as much as possible the calamities attending them. Mr. Burke always stood high in my esteem; but his affectionate concern for his friend renders him still more amiable, and makes the honor he does me of admitting me of the number still more precious.

I do not think the Congress have any wish to persecute General Burgoyne. I never heard, till I received your letter, that they had recalled him; if they have made such a resolution, it must be, I suppose, a conditional one, to take place in case their offer of exchanging him for Mr. Laurens should not be accepted; a resolution intended merely to enforce that offer.

I have just received an authentic copy of the resolve containing that offer; and authorizing me to make it. As I have no communication with your ministers, I send it enclosed to you. If you can find any means of negotiating this business, I am sure the restoring of another worthy man to his family and friends will be an addition to your pleasure.

Peace Rumors

To David Hartley. Passy, 15 Jan., 1782.

I received a few days since your favor of the 2d instant, in which you tell me, that Mr. Alexander had informed you, "America was disposed to enter into a separate treaty with Great Britain." I am persuaded, that your strong desire for peace has misled you, and occasioned your greatly misunderstanding Mr. Alexander; as I think it scarce possible, he should have asserted a thing *so utterly void of foundation.* I remember that you have, as you say, often urged this on former occasions, and that it always gave me more disgust than my friendship for you permitted me to express. But, since you have now gone so far as to carry such a proposition to Lord North, as arising from us, it is necessary that I should be explicit with you, and tell you plainly, that I never had such an idea; and I believe there is not a man in America, a few *English Tories* excepted, that would not spurn at the thought of deserting a noble and generous friend, for the sake of a truce with an unjust and cruel enemy.

I have again read over your Conciliatory Bill, with the manuscript propositions that accompany it, and am concerned to find, that one cannot give vent to a simple wish for peace, a mere sentiment of humanity, without having it interpreted as *a disposition to submit to any base conditions* that may be offered us, rather than continue the war; for on no other supposition could you propose to us a truce of ten years, during which we are to engage not to assist France, while you continue the war with her. A truce, too, wherein nothing is to be mentioned that may weaken your pretensions to dominion over us, which you may therefore resume at the end of the term, or at pleasure; when we should have so covered ourselves with infamy, by our treachery to our first friend, as that no other nation can ever after be disposed to assist us, however cruelly you might think fit to treat us. Believe me, my dear friend, America has too much understanding, and is too sensible of the value of the world's good opinion, to forfeit it all by such perfidy. The Congress will never instruct their Commissioners to obtain a peace on such ignominious terms; and though there can be but few things in which I should venture to disobey their orders, yet, if it were possible for them to give me such an order as this, I should certainly refuse to act; I should instantly renounce their commission, and banish myself for ever from so infamous a country.

We are a little ambitious too of your esteem; and, as I think we have acquired some share of it by our manner of making war with you, I trust we shall not hazard the loss of it by consenting meanly to a dishonorable peace.

Lord North was wise in demanding of you some authorized acknowledgment of the proposition from authorized persons. He justly thought it too improbable to be relied on, so as to lay it before the Privy Council. You can now inform him, that the whole has been a mistake, and that no such proposition as that of a separate peace has been, is, or is ever likely to be made by me; and I believe by no other authorized person whatever in behalf of America. You may further, if you please, inform his Lordship, that Mr. Adams, Mr. Laurens, Mr. Jay, and myself, have long since been empowered, by a special commission, to treat of peace whenever a negotiation shall be opened for that purpose; but it must always be understood, that this is to be in conjunction with our allies, conformably to the solemn treaties made with them.

You have, my dear friend, a strong desire to promote peace, and it is a most laudable and virtuous desire. Permit me then to wish, that you would, in order to succeed as a mediator, avoid such invidious expressions as may have an effect in preventing your purpose. You tell me, that no stipulation for our independence must be in the treaty, because you "verily believe, so deep is the jealousy between England and France, that England would fight for a straw, to the last man and the last shilling, rather than be *dictated to* by France." And again, that "the nation would proceed to every extremity, rather than be brought to a formal recognition of independence at the *haughty command* of France." My dear Sir, if every proposition of terms for peace, that may be made by one of the parties at war, is to be called and considered by the other as *dictating*, and a *haughty command*, and for that reason rejected, with a resolution of fighting to the last man rather than agree to it, you see that in such case no treaty of peace is possible.

In fact, we began the war for independence on your government, which we found tyrannical, and this before France had any thing to do with our affairs; the article in our treaty, whereby the "two parties engage, that neither of them shall conclude either truce or peace with Great Britain, without the formal consent of the other first obtained; and mutually engage, not to lay down their arms until the independence of the United States shall have been formally or *tacitly* assured, by the treaty or treaties, that shall terminate the war," was an article inserted at our instance, being in our favor. And you see, by the article itself, that your great difficulty may be easily got over, as a formal acknowledgment of our independence is not made necessary. But we hope by God's help to enjoy it; and I suppose we shall fight for it as long as we are able.

I do not make any remarks upon the other propositions, because I think, that, unless they were made by authority, the discussion of them is unnecessary, and may be inconvenient. The supposition of our being disposed to make a separate peace I could not be silent upon, as it materially affected our reputation and its essential interests. If I have been a little warm on that offensive point, reflect on your repeatedly urging it and endeavour to excuse me. Whatever may be the fate of our poor countries, let you and me die as we have lived, in peace with each other.

To David Hartley. Passy, 16 Feb., 1782.

MY DEAR FRIEND, the true pains you are taking to restore peace, whatever may be the success, entitle you to the esteem of all good men. If your ministers really desire peace methinks they would do well to empower some person to make propositions for that purpose. One or other of the parties at war must take the first step. To do this belongs properly to the wisest. America being a novice in such affairs, has no pretence to that character; and indeed after the answer given by Lord Stormont (when we proposed to him something relative to the mutual treatment of prisoners with humanity), that "*the King's ministers receive no applications from rebels, unless when they come to implore his Majesty's clemency*," it cannot be expected, that we should hazard the exposing ourselves again to such insolence. All I can say further at present is, that in my opinion your enemies do not aim at your destruction, and that if you propose a treaty you will find them reasonable in their demands, provided that on your side they meet with the same good dispositions. But do not dream of dividing us; you will certainly never be able to effect it.

Victory

To George Washington. Passy, 2 April, 1782.

I RECEIVED duly the honor of your letter, accompanying the capitulation of General Cornwallis. All the world agree, that no expedition was ever better planned or better executed; it has made a great addition to the military reputation you had already acquired, and brightens the glory that surrounds your name, and that must accompany it to our latest posterity. No news could possibly make me more happy. The infant Hercules has now strangled the two serpents* that attacked him in his cradle, and I trust his future history will be answerable. . . .

The English seem not to know either how to continue the war, or to make peace with us. Instead of entering into a regular treaty for putting an end to a contest they are tired of, they have voted in Parliament, that the recovery of America by force is impracticable, that an offensive war against us ought not to be continued, and that whoever advises it shall be deemed an enemy to his country.

To George Washington. Passy, 8 April, 1782.

I HAVE HERETOFORE congratulated your Excellency on your victories over our enemy's generals; I can now do the same on your having overthrown

*Burgoyne and Cornwallis, with their armies.

their politicians. Your late successes have so strengthened the hands of opposition in Parliament, that they are become the majority, and have compelled the King to dismiss all his old ministers and their adherents. The unclean spirits he was possessed with are now cast out of him; but it is imagined, that, as soon as he has obtained a peace, they will return with others worse than themselves, *and the last state of that man*, as the Scripture says, *shall be worse than the first*.

Men and Devils

To Joseph Priestley. Passy, 7 June, 1782.

I HAVE always great pleasure in hearing from you, in learning that you are well, and that you continue your experiments. I should rejoice much, if I could once more recover the leisure to search with you into the works of nature; I mean the *inanimate*, not the *animate* or moral part of them; the more I discovered of the former, the more I admired them; the more I know of the latter, the more I am disgusted with them. Men I find to be a sort of beings very badly constructed, as they are generally more easily provoked than reconciled, more disposed to do mischief to each other than to make reparation, much more easily deceived than undeceived, and having more pride and even pleasure in killing than in begetting one another; for without a blush they assemble in great armies at noonday to destroy, and when they have killed as many as they can, they exaggerate the number to augment the fancied glory; but they creep into corners, or cover themselves with the darkness of night, when they mean to beget, as being ashamed of a virtuous action. A virtuous action it would be, and a vicious one the killing of them, if the species were really worth producing or preserving; but of this I begin to doubt.

I know you have no such doubts, because, in your zeal for their welfare, you are taking a great deal of pains to save their souls. Perhaps as you grow older, you may look upon this as a hopeless project, or an idle amusement, repent of having murdered in mephitic air so many honest, harmless mice, and wish, that, to prevent mischief, you had used boys and girls instead of them. In what light we are viewed by superior beings, may be gathered from a piece of late West India news, which possibly has not yet reached you. A young angel of distinction being sent down to this world on some business, for the first time, had an old courier-spirit assigned him as a guide. They arrived over the seas of Martinico, in the middle of the long day of obstinate fight between the fleets of Rodney and De Grasse. When, through the clouds of smoke, he saw the fire of the guns, the decks covered with mangled limbs, and bodies dead or dying; the ships sinking, burning, or blown into the air; and the quantity of pain, misery, and destruction, the crews yet alive were thus with so much eagerness dealing round to one another; he turned angrily to his guide, and said, "You blundering blockhead, you are ignorant of your business; you undertook to conduct me to the earth, and you have brought me into hell!" "No, Sir," says the guide, "I have made no mistake; this is really the earth, and these are men. Devils never treat one another in this cruel manner; they have more sense, and more of what men (vainly) call humanity."

But to be serious, my dear old friend, I love you as much as ever, and I love all the honest souls that meet at the London Coffee-House. I only wonder how it happened, that they and my other friends in England came to be such good creatures in the midst of so perverse a generation. I long to see them and you once more, and I labor for peace with more earnestness, that I may again be happy in your sweet society.

Power of the Press

To Richard Price. Passy, 13 June, 1782.

THE ANCIENT Roman and Greek orators could only speak to the number of citizens capable of being assembled within the reach of their voice. Their writings had little effect, because the bulk of the people could not read. Now by the press we can speak to nations; and good books and well written pamphlets have great and general influence. The facility, with which the same truths may be repeatedly enforced by placing them daily in different lights in newspapers, which are everywhere read, gives a great chance of establishing them. And we now find, that it is not only right to strike while the iron is hot, but that it may be very practicable to heat it by continually striking.

Journal of the Negotiations for Peace with Great Britain, from March 21 to July 1, 1782

Passy, 9 May, 1782.

As SINCE the change of the ministry in England some serious professions have been made of their dispositions to peace, and of their readiness to enter into a general treaty for that purpose; and as the concerns and claims of five nations are to be discussed in that treaty, which must therefore be interesting to the present age and to posterity, I am inclined to keep a journal of the proceedings as far as they come to my knowledge; and, to make it more complete, I will first endeavour to recollect what has already past. Great affairs sometimes take their rise from small circumstances. My good friend and neighbour Madame Brillon, being at Nice all last winter for her health, with her very amiable family, wrote to me, that she had met with some English gentry there, whose acquaintance proved agreeable. Among them she named Lord Cholmondely, who she said had promised to call, in his return to England, and drink tea with us at Passy. He left Nice sooner than she supposed, and came to Paris long before her. On the 21st March I received the following note.

"Lord Cholmondely's compliments to Dr. Franklin; he sets out for London to-morrow evening, and should be glad to see him for five minutes before he went. Lord Cholmondely will call upon him at any time in the morning he shall please to appoint.

"*Thursday evening. Hôtel de Chartres.*"

I wrote for answer, that I should be at home all the next morning, and glad to see his Lordship, if he did me the honor of calling on me. He came accordingly. I had before no personal knowledge of this nobleman. We talked of our friends whom he left at Nice, then of affairs in England, and the late resolutions of the Commons on Mr. Conway's motion. He told me, that he knew Lord Shelburne had a great regard for me, that he was sure his Lordship would be pleased to hear from me, and that if I would write a line he should have a pleasure in carrying it. On which I wrote the following.

To Lord Shelburne. Passy, 22 March, 1782.

"MY LORD,

"Lord Cholmondely having kindly offered to take a letter from me to your Lordship, I embrace the opportunity of assuring the continuance of my ancient respect for your talents and virtues, and of congratulating you on the returning good disposition of your country in favor of America, which appears in the late resolutions of the Commons. I am persuaded it will have good effects. I hope it will tend to produce a *general peace*, which I am sure your Lordship, with all good men, desires, which I wish to see before I die, and to which I shall, with infinite pleasure, contribute every thing in my power.

"Your friends, the Abbé Morellet and Madame Helvétius, are well. You have made the latter very happy by your present of gooseberry bushes, which arrived in five days, and in excellent order. With great and sincere esteem, I have the honor to be, &c. &c.

"B. FRANKLIN."

Soon after this we heard from England, that a total change had taken place in the ministry, and that Lord Shelburne had come in as Secretary of State. But I thought no more of my letter, till an old friend and near neighbour of mine many years in London appeared at Passy, and introduced a Mr. Oswald, who, he said, had a great desire to see me; and Mr. Oswald, after some little conversation, gave me the following letters from Lord Shelburne and Mr. Laurens.

From Lord Shelburne to B. Franklin. London, 6 April, 1782.

"DEAR SIR,

"I have been favored with your letter and am much obliged by your remembrance. I find myself returned nearly to the same situation, which you remember me to have occupied nineteen years ago; and I should be very glad to talk to you as I did then, and afterwards, in 1767, upon the means of promoting the happiness of mankind, a subject much more agreeable to my nature, than the best concerted plans for spreading misery and devastation. I have had a high opinion of the compass of your mind, and of your foresight. I have often been beholden to both, and shall be glad to be so again, as far as is compatible with your situation. Your letter, discovering the same disposition, has made me send to you Mr. Oswald. I have had a longer acquaintance with him, than even I have had the pleasure to have with you. I believe him an honest man, and, after consulting some of our common friends, I have thought him the fittest for the purpose. He is a pacifical man, and conversant in those negotiations, which are most interesting to mankind. This has made me prefer him to any of our speculative friends, or to any person of higher rank. He is fully apprized of my mind, and you may give full credit to every thing he assures you of. At the same time, if any other channel occurs to you, I am ready to embrace it. I wish to retain the same simplicity and good faith, which subsisted between us in transactions of less importance. I have the honor to be, &c.

"SHELBURNE."

From Henry Laurens to B. Franklin. London, 7 April, 1782.

"DEAR SIR,

"Richard Oswald, Esquire, who will do me the honor of delivering this, is a gentleman of the strictest candor and integrity. I dare give such assurances from an experience little short of thirty years, and to add, you will be perfectly safe in conversing freely with him on the business he will introduce, a business, which Mr. Oswald has disinterestedly engaged in, from motives of benevolence; and from the choice of the man a persuasion follows, that the electors mean to be in earnest.

"Some people in this country, who have too long indulged themselves in abusing every thing American, have been pleased to circulate an opinion, that Dr. Franklin is a very cunning man; in answer to which, I have remarked to Mr. Oswald, 'Dr. Franklin knows very well how to manage a cunning man; but, when the Doctor converses or treats with a man of candor, there is no man more candid than himself.' I do not know whether you will ultimately agree on political sketches; but I am sure, as gentlemen, you will part very well pleased with each other. Should you, Sir, think proper to communicate to me your sentiments and advice on our affairs, the more amply the more acceptable, and probably the more serviceable; Mr. Oswald will take charge of your despatches, and afford a secure means of conveyance.

"To this gentleman I refer you for general information of a journey, which I am immediately to make, partly in his company, to Ostend, to file off for the Hague. I feel a willingness, infirm as I am, to attempt doing as much good as can be expected from such a prisoner upon parole. As General Burgoyne is certainly exchanged (a circumstance, by the by, which possibly might have embarrassed us, had your late propositions been accepted), may I presume at my return to offer another lieutenant-general, now in England, a prisoner upon parole, in exchange; or what shall I offer in exchange for myself, a thing in my own estimation of no great value? I have the honor to be, with great respect, and, permit me to add, great reverence, Sir, &c.

"HENRY LAURENS."

I entered into conversation with Mr. Oswald. He was represented in the letter as fully apprized of Lord Shelburne's mind, and I was desirous of knowing it. All I could learn was, that the new ministry sincerely wished for a peace; that they considered the object of the war, to France and America, as obtained; that, if the independence of the United States was agreed to, there was no other point in dispute, and therefore nothing to hinder a pacification; that they were ready to treat of *peace*, but he intimated, that, if France should insist upon terms too humiliating to England, they could still continue the war, having yet great strength and many resources left. I let him know, that America would not treat but in concert with France, and that, my colleagues not being here, I could do nothing of importance in the affair; but that, if he pleased, I would present him to M. de Vergennes, Secretary of State for Foreign Affairs. He consenting, I wrote and sent the following letter.

To Count de Vergennes. Passy, 16 April, 1782.

"SIR,

"An English nobleman, Lord Cholmondely, lately returning from Italy, called upon me here, at the time when we received the news of the first resolutions of the House of Commons relating to America. In conversation he said, that he knew his friend, Lord Shelburne, had a great regard for me, that it would be pleasing to him to hear of my welfare, and receive a line from me, of which he, Lord Cholmondely, should like to be the bearer, adding, if there should be a change of ministry, he believed Lord Shelburne would be employed. I thereupon wrote a few lines, of which I enclose a copy. This day I received an answer, which I also enclose, together with another letter from Mr. Laurens. They both, as your Excellency will see, recommend the bearer, Mr. Oswald, as a very honest, sensible man. I have had a little conversation with him. He tells me, that there has been a desire of making a separate peace with America, and continuing the war with

France and Spain, but that now all wise people give up that idea as impracticable; and it is his private opinion, that the ministry do sincerely desire a *general peace*, and that they will readily come into it, provided France does not insist upon conditions too humiliating for England, in which case she will make great and violent efforts, rather than submit to them, and that much is still in her power, &c.

"I told the gentleman, that I could not enter into particulars with him, but in concert with the ministers of this court. And I proposed introducing him to your Excellency, after communicating to you the letters he brought me, in case you should think fit to see him, with which he appeared to be pleased. I intend waiting on you to-morrow, when you will please to acquaint me with your intentions, and favor me with your counsels. He had heard nothing of Forth's mission, and the old ministry had not acquainted the new with that transaction. Mr. Laurens came over with him in the same vessel, and went from Ostend to Holland. With great respect, I am, &c.

"B. Franklin."

The next day, being at court with the foreign ministers, as usual on Tuesdays, I saw M. de Vergennes, who acquainted me, that he had caused the letters to be translated, had considered the contents, and should like to see Mr. Oswald. We agreed that the interview should be on Wednesday at ten o'clock. Immediately on my return home, I wrote to Mr. Oswald, acquainting him with what had passed at Versailles, and proposing that he should be with me at half past eight the next morning, in order to proceed thither. I received from him the following answer.

Paris, 17 April.

"Sir,

"I have the honor of yours by the bearer, and shall be sure to wait on you to-morrow, at half past eight, and am, with much respect, &c.

"Richard Oswald."

He came accordingly, and we arrived at Versailles punctually. M. de Vergennes received him with much civility. Mr. Oswald not being ready in speaking French, M. de Rayneval interpreted. Mr. Oswald at first thought of sending an express, with the account of the conversation, which continued near an hour, and was offered a passport, but finally concluded to go himself; and I wrote the next day the letter following.

To Lord Shelburne. Passy, 18 April, 1782.

"My Lord,

"I have received the letter your Lordship did me the honor of writing to me on the 6th instant. I congratulate you on your new appointment to the honorable and important office you formerly filled so worthily, which must be so far pleasing to you, as it affords you more opportunities of doing good, and of serving your country essentially in its great concerns.

"I have conversed a good deal with Mr. Oswald, and am much pleased with him. He appears to me a wise and honest man. I acquainted him, that I was commissioned, with others, to treat of and conclude a peace. That full powers were given us for that purpose, and that the Congress promised in good faith to ratify, confirm, and cause to be faithfully observed, the treaty we should make; but that we would not treat separately from France, and I proposed introducing him to the Count de Vergennes, to whom I communicated your Lordship's letter containing Mr. Oswald's character, as a foundation for the interviews. He will acquaint you, that the assurance he gave of His Britannic Majesty's good dispositions towards peace was well received, and assurances returned of the same good dispositions in His Most Christian Majesty.

"With regard to circumstances relative to a treaty, M. de Vergennes observed, that the King's engagements were such, that he could not treat without the concurrence of his allies; that the treaty should, therefore, be for a general, not a partial peace; that, if the parties were disposed to finish the war speedily by themselves, it would perhaps be best to treat at Paris, as an ambassador from Spain was already there, and the Commissioners from America might easily and soon be assembled there. Or, if they chose to make use of the proposed mediation, they might treat at Vienna; but that the King was so truly willing to put a speedy end to the war, that he would agree to any place the King of England should think proper.

"I leave the rest of the conversation to be related to your Lordship by Mr. Oswald . . . With great and sincere respect, I have the honor to be, my Lord, &c.

"B. FRANKLIN."

. . . On our return from Versailles, Mr. Oswald took occasion to impress me with ideas, that the present weakness of the government of England, with regard to continuing the war, was owing chiefly to the division of sentiments about it; that, in case France should make demands too humiliating for England to submit to, the spirit of the nation would be roused, unanimity would prevail, and resources would not be wanting. He said, there was no want of money in the nation; that the chief difficulty lay in the finding out new taxes to raise it; and, perhaps, that difficulty might be avoided by shutting up the Exchequer, stopping the payment of the interest of the public funds, and applying that money to the support of the war. I made no reply to this; for I did not desire to discourage their stopping payment, which I considered as cutting the throat of the public credit, and a means of adding fresh exasperation against them with the neighbouring nations. Such menaces were besides an encouragement with me, remembering the adage, that *they who threaten are afraid*.

. . . On Tuesday I was at Court, as usual on that day. The next morning I wrote the following letter to Mr. Adams.

To John Adams. Passy, 8 May, 1782.

"SIR,

"Mr. Oswald, whom I mentioned in a former letter, which I find you have received, is returned, and brought me another letter from Lord Shelburne. . . . It says, Mr. Oswald is instructed to communicate to me his Lordship's thoughts. He is, however, very sparing of such communication. All I have got from him is, that the ministry have in contemplation the allowing independence to America, on condition of Britain being put again into the state she was left in by the peace of 1763, which I suppose means being put again in the possession of the islands, which France has taken from her. This seems to me a proposition of selling to us a thing, that was already our own, and making France pay the price they are pleased to ask for it.

"Mr. Grenville, who is sent by Mr. Fox, is expected here daily. Mr. Oswald tells me, that Mr. Laurens will soon be here also. Yours of the 2d instant is just come to hand. I shall write to you on this affair hereafter, by the court couriers; for I am certain, that your letters to me are opened at the post-office, either here or in Holland, and I suppose that mine to you are treated in the same manner. I enclose the cover of your last, that you may see the seal. With great respect, I am, Sir, &c.

"B. FRANKLIN."

I had but just sent away this letter, when Mr. Oswald came in, bringing with him Mr. Grenville, who was just arrived. He gave me the following letter from Mr. Secretary Fox.

From Charles J. Fox to B. Franklin. St. James's, 1 May, 1782.

"SIR,

"Though Mr. Oswald will, no doubt, have informed you of the nature of Mr. Grenville's commission, yet I cannot refrain from making use of the opportunity, that his going offers me, to assure you of the esteem and respect, which I have borne to your character, and to beg you to believe, that no change in my situation has made any in those ardent wishes for reconciliation, which I have invariably felt from the very beginning of this unhappy contest.

"Mr. Grenville is fully acquainted with my sentiments upon this subject, and with the sanguine hopes, which I have conceived, that those with whom we are contending are too reasonable to continue a contest which has no longer any object, either real or even imaginary. I know your liberality of mind too well to be afraid, lest any prejudices against Mr. Grenville's *name* may prevent you from esteeming those excellent qualities of heart and head, which belong to him, or from giving the fullest credit to the sincerity of his wishes for peace, in which no man in either country goes beyond him. I am, with great truth and regard, &c.

"C. J. Fox."

I imagined the gentleman had been at Versailles, as I supposed Mr. Grenville would first have waited on M. de Vergennes before he called on me. But finding, in conversation, that he had not, and that he expected me to introduce him, I immediately wrote to that minister, acquainting him, that Mr. Grenville was arrived, and desired to know when his Excellency would think fit to receive him, and I sent an express with my letter.

I then entered into conversation with him on the subject of his mission, Mr. Fox having referred me to him, as being fully acquainted with his sentiments. He said, that peace was really wished for by everybody, if it could be obtained on reasonable terms; and, as the idea of subjugating America was given up, and both France and America had thereby obtained what they had in view originally, it was hoped, that there now remained no obstacle to a pacification. That England was willing to treat of a general peace with all the powers at war against her, and that the treaty should be at Paris. . . .

The coming and going of these gentlemen were observed, and made much talk at Paris; and the Marquis de Lafayette, having learned something of their business from the minister, discoursed with me about it. Agreeably to the resolutions of Congress, directing me to confer with him, and take his assistance in our affairs, I communicated to him what had passed. He told me, that, during the treaty at Paris for the last peace, the Duke de Nivernais had been sent to reside in London, that this court might, through him, state what was from time to time transacted in the light they thought best, to prevent misrepresentations and misunderstandings. That such an employ would be extremely agreeable to him on many accounts; that as he was now an American citizen, spoke both languages, and was well acquainted with our interests, he believed he might be useful in it; and that, as peace was likely from appearances to take place, his return to America was perhaps not so immediately necessary. I liked the idea, and encouraged his proposing it to the ministry. He then wished I would make him acquainted with Messrs. Oswald and Grenville, and for that end proposed meeting them at breakfast with me, which I promised to contrive if I could, and endeavour to engage them for Saturday.

Friday morning, the 10th of May, I went to Paris, and visited Mr. Oswald. I found him in the same friendly dispositions, and very desirous of good, and seeing an end put to this ruinous war. But I got no further sight as to the sentiments of Lord Shelburne respecting the terms. I told him, the Marquis de Lafayette would breakfast with me to-morrow, and as he, Mr. Oswald, might have some curiosity to see a person who had in this war rendered himself so remarkable, I proposed his doing me the same honor. He agreed to it cheerfully.

The Monday following, I called to visit Mr. Grenville. I found with him Mr. Oswald, who told me he was just about returning to London. . . .

Since his departure Mr. Grenville has made me a visit; and entered into conversation with me, exactly of the same tenor with letters I formerly received from Mr. Hartley, stating suppositions that France might insist on points totally different from what had been the object of our alliance, and that, in such case, he should imagine we were not at all bound to continue the war to obtain such points for her, &c. I thought I could not give him a better answer to this kind of discourse, than what I had given in two letters to Mr. Hartley, and, therefore, calling for those letters, I read them to him. He smiled, and would have turned the conversation; but I gave a little more of my sentiments on the general subject of benefits, obligation, and gratitude. I said, I thought people had often imperfect notions of their duty on those points, and that a state of obligation was to many so uneasy a state, that they became ingenious in finding out reasons and arguments to prove that they had been laid under no obligation at all, or that they had discharged it, and they too easily satisfied themselves with such arguments.

To explain clearly my ideas on the subject, I stated a case. A, a stranger to B, sees him about to be imprisoned for a debt by a merciless creditor; he lends him the sum necessary to preserve his liberty. B then becomes the debtor of A, and, after some time, repays the money. Has he then discharged the obligation? No. He has discharged the money debt, but the obligation remains, and he is a debtor for the kindness of A, in lending him the sum so seasonably. If B should afterwards find A in the same circumstances, that he, B, had been in when A lent him the money, he may then discharge this obligation or debt of kindness *in part,* by lending him an equal sum. *In part,* I said, and not *wholly,* because, when A lent B the money, there had been no prior benefit received to induce him to it. And, therefore, if A should a second time need the same assistance, I thought B, if in his power, was in duty bound to afford it to him.

Mr. Grenville conceived that it was carrying gratitude very far, to apply this doctrine to our situation in respect to France, who was really the party served and obliged by our separation from England, as it lessened the power of her rival and relatively increased her own.

I told him, I was so strongly impressed with the kind assistance afforded us by France in our distress, and the generous and noble manner in which it was granted, without exacting or stipulating for a single privilege, or particular advantage to herself in our commerce, or otherwise, that I could never suffer myself to think of such reasonings for lessening the obligation; and I hoped, and, indeed, did not doubt, but my countrymen were all of the same sentiments.

Thus he gained nothing of the point he came to push; we parted, however, in good humor. His conversation is always polite, and his manner pleasing. As he expressed a strong desire to discourse with me on the means of a reconciliation with America, I promised to consider the subject, and appointed Saturday the first day of June, for our conversation, when he proposed to call on me. . . .

Mr. Jay had written to me, from time to time, of the unaccountable delays he had met with since his residence at the court of Spain, and that he was now no nearer in the business he had been charged with, than when he first arrived. Upon the first coming of Mr. Oswald, and the apparent prospect of a treaty, I wrote to press his coming hither, and, being a little out of humor with that court, I said, they have taken four years to consider whether they should treat with us, give them forty, and let us mind our own business; and I sent the letter under cover to a person at Madrid, who I hoped would open and read it.

It seems to me, that we have, in most instances, hurt our credit and importance, by sending all over Europe, begging alliances, and soliciting declarations of our independence. The nations, perhaps, from thence seemed to think, that our independence is something they have to sell, and that we do not offer enough for it. Mr. Adams has succeeded in Holland, owing to their war with England, and a good deal to the late votes in the Commons towards a reconciliation; but the ministers of the other powers refused, as I hear, to return his visits, because our independence was not yet acknowledged by their courts. I had heard here, by good luck, that the same resolution was taken by several of them not to return the visits I should make them (as they supposed) when I was first received here as minister plenipotentiary, and disappointed their project by visiting none of them. In my private opinion, the first civility is due from the old resident to the stranger and new comer. My opinion indeed is good for nothing against custom, which I should have obeyed, but for the circumstances, that rendered it more prudent to avoid disputes and affronts, though at the hazard of being thought rude or singular.

While I am writing, something ridiculous enough on this head has happened to me. The Count du Nord, who is son of the Empress of Russia, arriving at Paris, ordered, it seems, cards of visit to be sent to all the foreign ministers. One of them, on which was written, "*Le Comte du Nord et le Prince Bariatinski,*" was brought to me. It was on Monday evening last. Being at court the next day, I inquired of an old minister, my friend, what was the etiquette, and whether the Count received visits. The answer was, "*Non; on se fait écrire; voilà tout.*" This is done by passing the door, and ordering your name to be written on the porter's book. Accordingly, on Wednesday I passed the house of Prince Bariatinski, ambassador of Russia, where the Count lodged, and left my name on the list of each. I thought no more of the matter; but this day, May the 24th, comes the servant who brought the card, in great affliction, saying he was like to be ruined by his mistake in bringing the card here, and wishing to obtain from me some paper, of I know not what kind, for I did not see him.

In the afternoon came my friend, M. Le Roy, who is also a friend of the Prince's, telling me how much he, the Prince, was concerned at the accident, that both himself and the Count had great personal regard for me and my character, but that, our independence not yet being acknowledged by the court of Russia, it was impossible for him to permit himself to make me a visit as minister. I told M. Le Roy it was not my custom to seek such honors, though I was very sensible of them when conferred upon me; that I should not have voluntarily intruded a visit, and that, in this case, I had only done what I was informed the etiquette required of me; but if it would be attended with any inconvenience to Prince Bariatinski, whom I much esteemed and respected, I thought the remedy was easy; he had only to erase my name out of his book of visits received, and I would burn their card.

All the northern princes are not ashamed of a little civility committed towards an American. The King of Denmark, travelling in England under an assumed name, sent me a card, expressing in strong terms his esteem for me, and inviting me to dinner with him at St. James's. And the ambassador from the King of Sweden lately asked me, whether I had powers to make a treaty of commerce with their kingdom, for, he said, his master was desirous of such a treaty with the United States, had directed him to ask me the question, and had charged him to tell me, that it would flatter him greatly to make it with a person whose character he so much esteemed, &c. Such compliments might make me a little proud, if we Americans were not naturally as much so already as the porter, who, being told he had with his burden jostled the great Czar, Peter, then in London, walking the street; "*Poh!*" says he, "*we are all Czars here.*"

. . . May 26th, I received the following from Mr. Hartley.

From David Hartley to B. Franklin. London, 13 May, 1782.

"My dear Friend,

"I wrote you a long letter dated May 1st, by Mr. Laurens, who left London on Saturday last, but I will add a few lines now by a conveyance, which I believe will overtake him, just to tell you two or three things, which I believe I omitted in my last.

. . . "I do not believe that there is any difference of sentiment between you and me, *personally*, in our own minds upon independence, &c. &c. But we belong to different communities, and the right of judgment, and of consent and dissent, is vested in the community. Divide independence into six millions of shares, and you should have been heartily *welcome* to *my* share from the beginning of the war. Divide Canada into six millions of shares, I could find a better method of disposing of *my* share, than by offering it to France to abandon America. Divide the Rock of Gibraltar into six millions of pieces, I can only answer for one portion. Let Reason and Justice decide in any such case, as universal umpires between contending parties, and those, who wish well to the permanent peace of mankind, will not refuse to give and to receive equal justice.

"I agree with you, that the equitable and the philosophical principles of politics can alone form a solid foundation of permanent peace; and the contraries to them, though highly patronized by nations themselves, and their ministers, are no better than vulgar errors; but nations are slow to convictions from the personal arguments of individuals. They are 'jealous in honor, seeking the *bubble reputation* even in the cannon's mouth.' But until a confirmed millennium, founded upon wiser principles, shall be generally established, the *reputation* of nations is not merely a *bubble*. It forms their real security.

"To apply all this, in one word, let all nations agree, with one accord, to beat their swords into ploughshares, and their spears into pruning hooks, or give me wooden walls to Great Britain! I have nothing further to add. My reason for writing this was just to communicate to you in what position I had delivered over my conferences and arguments with the late ministry into the hands of the present. And I will conclude with your own words, may God send us all more wisdom. I am ever, most affectionately, yours, &c.

"D. HARTLEY."

. . . On Tuesday I dined at Versailles with some friends, so was not at home when the Marquis de Lafayette called to acquaint me, that M. de Vergennes informed him, that the full power received by Mr. Grenville from London, and communicated by him, related to France only. The Marquis left for me this information, which I could not understand.

M. de Vergennes said he should see Mr. Grenville on Thursday, and would speak his mind to him on the subject very plainly. "They want," said he, "to treat with us for you, but this the King will not agree to. He thinks it not consistent with the dignity of your state. You will treat for yourselves; and every one of the powers at war with England will make its own treaty. All that is necessary for our common security is, that the treaties go hand in hand, and are signed all on the same day."

Prince Bariatinski, the Russian ambassador, was particularly civil to me this day at court, apologized for what passed relating to the visit, expressed himself extremely sensible of my friendship in covering the affair, which might have occasioned him very disagreeable consequences, &c. The Count du Nord came to M. de Vergennes, while we were drinking coffee, after dinner. He appears lively and active, with a sensible, spirited countenance. There was an opera that night for his entertainment. The house being richly finished with abundance of carving and gilding, well illuminated with wax tapers, and the company all superbly dressed, many of the men in cloth of tissue, and the ladies sparkling with diamonds, formed altogether the most splendid spectacle my eyes ever beheld. . . .

Saturday, June 5th.

MR. GRENVILLE came, according to appointment. Our conversation began by my acquainting him, that I had seen the Count de Vergennes, and had perused the copy left with him of the power to treat. That, after what he, Mr. Grenville, told me of its being to treat with France *and her allies*, I was a little surprised to find in it no mention of the allies, and that it was only to treat with the King of France and his ministers; that, at Versailles, there was some suspicion of its being intended to occasion delay; the professed desire of a speedy peace being, perhaps, abated in the British court since its late successes; but that I imagined the words relating to the allies might have been accidentally omitted in transcribing, or that, perhaps, he had a special power to treat with us distinct from the other.

He answered, that the copy was right, and that he had no such power in form, but that his instructions were full to that purpose, and that he was sure the ministers had no desire of delay, nor any of excluding us from the treaty, since the greatest part of those instructions related to treating with me. . . . Mr. Grenville then spoke much of the high opinion the present ministry had of me, and their great esteem for me, their desire of a perfect reconciliation between the two countries, and the firm and general belief in England, that no man was so capable as myself of proposing the proper means of bringing about such a reconciliation; adding that, if the old ministers had formerly been too little attentive to my counsels, the present were very differently disposed, and he hoped that in treating with them, I would totally forget their predecessors.

The time has been when such flattering language, as from great men, might have made me vainer, and had more effect on my conduct, than it can at present, when I find myself so near the end of life as to esteem lightly all personal interests and concerns, except that of maintaining to the last, and leaving behind me the tolerably good character I have hitherto supported.

On Monday the 3d, Mr. Oswald came according to appointment. He told me, he had seen and had conversations with Lord Shelburne, Lord Rockingham, and Mr. Fox. That their desire of peace continued uniformly the same, though he thought some of them were a little too much elated with the late victory in the West Indies; and when, observing his coolness, they asked him, if he did not think it a very good thing; "yes," said he, "if you do not rate it too high." He went on with the utmost frankness to tell me, that the peace was absolutely necessary for them. That the nation had been foolishly involved in four wars, and could no longer raise money to carry them on, so that if they continued, it would be absolutely necessary for them to stop payment of the interest money on the funds, which would ruin their future credit. He spoke of stopping on all sums above one thousand pounds, and continuing to pay on those below, because the great sums belonged to the rich, who could better bear the delay of their interest, and the smaller sums to poorer persons, who would be more hurt, and make more clamor, and that the rich might be quieted by promising them interest upon their interest. All this looked as if the matter had been seriously thought on.

Mr. Oswald has an air of great simplicity and honesty, yet I could hardly take this to be merely a weak confession of their deplorable state, and thought it might be rather intended as a kind of intimidation, by showing us that they had still all that resource in their power, which he said would furnish five millions a year. But, he added, our enemies may now do what they please with us; *they have the ball at their foot*, was his expression, and we hope they will show their moderation and magnanimity. He then repeatedly mentioned the great esteem the ministers had for me, that they, with all the considerate people of England, looked to, and depended on me for the means of extricating the nation from its present desperate situation; and that, perhaps, no single man had ever in his hands an opportunity of doing so much good as I had at this present time, with much more to that purpose.

June 15th.

Mr. Oswald came out to breakfast with me. We afterwards took a walk in the garden, when he told me, that Mr. Grenville's courier returned last night. That he had received by him a letter from Mrs. Oswald, but not a line from the ministry, nor had he heard a word from them since his arrival, nor had he heard of any news brought by the courier. That he should have gone to see Mr. Grenville this morning, but he had omitted it, that gentleman being subject to morning headaches, which prevented his rising so early. I said, I supposed he would go to Versailles, and call on me on his return. We had but little farther discourse, having no new subject.

Monday, the 17th.

I find myself in some perplexity with regard to these two negotiators. Mr. Oswald appears to have been the choice of Lord Shelburne, Mr. Grenville that of Mr. Secretary Fox. Lord Shelburne is said to have lately acquired much of the King's confidence. Mr. Fox calls himself the minister of the people, and it is certain that his popularity is lately much increased. Lord Shelburne seems to wish to have the management of the treaty; Mr. Fox seems to think it in his department. I hear that the understanding between these ministers is not quite perfect. Mr. Grenville is clever, and seems to feel reason as readily as Mr. Oswald, though not so ready to own it. Mr. Oswald appears quite plain and sincere; I sometimes a little doubt Mr. Grenville. Mr. Oswald, an old man, seems now to have no desire but that of being useful in doing good. Mr. Grenville, a young man, naturally desirous of acquiring reputation, seems to aim at that of being an able negotiator.

Monday, the 24th.

Wrote a note of excuse to Mr. Oswald, promising to see him on Wednesday, and went with Mr. Jay to Versailles. . . . I wrote the following letters to Mr. Secretary Livingston and Mr. Morris.

To Robert R. Livingston. Passy, 25 June, 1782.

"Sir,

"I have received your respective letters of January 26th and February 13th. . . .

"By the newspapers I have sent, you will see, that the general disposition of the British nation towards us had been changed. Two persons have been sent here by the new ministers, to propose treating for peace. They had at first some hopes of getting the belligerent powers to treat separately, one after another; but, finding that impracticable, they have, after several messengers sent to and fro, come to a resolution of treating with all together for a general peace, and have agreed, that the place shall be Paris. Mr. Grenville is now here with full powers for that purpose (if they can be reckoned full with regard to America, till a certain act is completed for enabling his Majesty to treat, &c., which has gone through the Commons, and has been once read in the House of Lords). I keep a very particular journal of what passes every day in the affair, which is transcribing, to be sent to you. I shall, therefore, need to say no more about it in this letter, except, that though I still think they were sincere at first in their desire of peace, yet, since their success in the West Indies, I imagine, that I see marks of their desiring rather to draw the negotiations into length, that they may take the chance of what the campaign shall produce in their favor; and, as there are so many interests to adjust, it will be prudent for us to suppose, that even another campaign may pass before all can be agreed. Something, too, may happen to break off the negotiations, and we should be prepared for the worst. . . ."

To Robert Morris. Passy, 25 June, 1782.

"Sir,

"For what relates to war and peace, I must refer you to Mr. Livingston, to whom I write fully. I will only say, that, though the English a few months since seemed desirous of peace, I suspect they now intend to draw out the negotiation into length, till they can see what this campaign will produce. I hope our people will not be deceived by fair words, but be on their guard, ready against every attempt that our insidious enemies may make upon us. I am, &c.

"B. Franklin."

To Samuel Cooper. Passy, 28 June, 1782.

"Sir,

"Our public affairs are in a good situation here. England, having tried in vain to make a separate peace with each of the powers she is at war with, has at length agreed to treat for a general peace with them all together; and at Paris. If we all continue firm in the resolution not to separate, we shall command the terms. I have no doubt of this steadiness here; and though we are told, that endeavours are making on your side the water to induce America to a reunion, on the terms now granting to Ireland, and that powers are sent to General Carleton for that purpose, I am persuaded the danger of this project will appear so evident, that, if offered, it will be immediately rejected. We have no safety but in our independence; with that we shall be respected, and soon become great and happy. Without it, we shall be despised, lose all our friends, and then either be cruelly oppressed by the King, who hates, and is incapable of forgiving us, or, having all that nation's enemies for ours, shall sink with it. I am ever, my dear friend, yours most affectionately,

"B. Franklin."

Saturday, June 29th.

We went together to the Spanish ambassador's, who received us with great civility and politeness. He spoke with Mr. Jay on the subject of the treaty they were to make together, and mentioned in general, as a principle, that the two powers should consider each other's conveniency, and accommodate and compensate each other as well as they could. That an exact compensation might, perhaps, not be possible, but should be approached as nearly as the nature of things would admit. "Thus," says he, "if there is a certain thing which would be convenient to each of us, but more convenient to one than to the other, it should be given to the one to whom it would be most convenient, and compensation made by giving another thing to the other, for the same reason." I suppose he had in view something relating to boundaries or territories, because, he added, we will sit down together with maps in our hands, and, by that means, shall see our way more clearly. . . .

The Killing of Indians

To James Hutton. Passy, 7 July, 1782.

A letter written by you to M. Bertin, *Ministre d'Etat*, containing an account of the abominable murders committed by some of the frontier people on the poor Moravian Indians, has given me infinite pain and vexation. The dispensations of Providence in this world puzzle my weak reason; I cannot comprehend why cruel men should have been permitted thus to destroy their fellow creatures. Some of the Indians may be supposed to have committed sins, but one cannot think the little children had committed any worthy of death. Why has a single man in England, who happens to love blood and to hate Americans, been permitted to gratify that bad temper by hiring German murderers, and, joining them with his own, to destroy in a continued course of bloody years near one hundred thousand human creatures, many of them possessed of useful talents, virtues, and abilities, to which he has no pretension? It is he who has furnished the savages with hatchets and scalping knives, and engages them to fall upon our defenceless farmers, and murder them with their wives and children, paying for their scalps, of which the account kept in America already amounts, as I have heard, to near *two thousand!*

Perhaps the people of the frontiers, exasperated by the cruelties of the

Indians, have been induced to kill all Indians that fall into their hands without distinction; so that even these horrid murders of our poor Moravians may be laid to his charge. And yet this man lives, enjoys all the good things this world can afford, and is surrounded by flatterers, who keep even his conscience quiet by telling him he is the best of Princes! I wonder at this, but I cannot therefore part with the comfortable belief of a Divine Providence; and the more I see the impossibility, from the number and extent of his crimes, of giving equivalent punishment to a wicked man in this life, the more I am convinced of a future state, in which all that here appears to be wrong shall be set right, all that is crooked made straight. In this faith let you and me, my dear friend, comfort outselves; it is the only comfort, in the present dark scene of things, that is allowed us.

On Boundaries

To Robert R. Livingston. Passy, 12 August, 1782.

THE SECOND CHANGES in the ministry of England have occasioned, or have afforded, pretences for various delays in the negotiation for peace. Mr. Grenville had two successive imperfect commissions. He was at length recalled, and Mr. Fitzherbert is now arrived to replace him, with a commission in due form to treat with France, Spain, and Holland. Mr. Oswald, who is here, is informed by a letter from the new Secretary of State, that a commission, empowering him to treat with the Commissioners of Congress, will pass the seals, and be sent him in a few days; till he arrives, this court will not proceed in its own negotiation. I send the *Enabling Act*, as it is called. Mr. Jay will acquaint you with what passes between him and the Spanish ambassador, respecting the proposed treaty with Spain. I will only mention, that my conjecture of that court's design to coop us up within the Allegany Mountains is now manifested. I hope Congress will insist on the Mississippi as the boundary, and the free navigation of the river, from which they could entirely exclude us.

Property Claims

To Richard Oswald. Passy, 26 November, 1782.

You may well remember, that in the beginning of our conferences, before the other Commissioners arrived, on your mentioning to me a retribution for the Royalists, whose estates had been confiscated, I acquainted you that nothing of that kind could be stipulated by us, the confiscation being made by virtue of laws of particular States, which the Congress had no power to contravene or dispense with, and therefore could give us no such authority in our commission. And I gave it as my opinion and advice, honestly and cordially, that, if a reconciliation was intended, no mention should be made in our negotiations of those people; for, they having done infinite mischief to our properties, by wantonly burning and destroying farm houses, villages, towns, if compensation for their losses were insisted on, we should certainly exhibit again an account of all the ravages they had committed, which would necessarily recall to view scenes of barbarity, that must inflame, instead of conciliating, and tend to perpetuate an enmity that we all profess a desire of extinguishing. Understanding, however, from you, that this was a point your ministry had at heart, I wrote concerning it to Congress, and I have lately received the following resolution, viz.

"By the United States in Congress assembled.

"September 10th, 1782.

"*Resolved*, That the Secretary for Foreign Affairs be, and he is hereby, directed to obtain, as speedily as possible, authentic returns of the slaves and other property, which have been carried off or destroyed in the course of the war by the enemy, and to transmit the same to the ministers plenipotentiary for negotiating peace.

"*Resolved*, That, in the mean time, the Secretary for Foreign Affairs inform the said ministers, that many thousands of slaves, and other property, to a very great amount, have been carried off, or destroyed, by the enemy; and that, in the opinion of Congress, the great loss of property, which the citizens of the United States have sustained by the enemy, will be considered by the several States as an insuperable bar to their making restitution or indemnification to the former owners of property, which has been, or may be forfeited to, or confiscated by, any of the States."

. . . The present British ministers, when they reflect a little, will certainly be too equitable to suppose, that their nation has a right to make an unjust war (which they have always allowed this against us to be), and do all sorts of unnecessary mischief, unjustifiable by the practice of any individual people, which those they make war with are to suffer without claiming any satisfaction; but that, if Britons, or their adherents, are in return deprived of any property, it is to be restored to them, or they are to be indemnified. The British troops can never excuse their barbarities. They were unprovoked. The Loyalists may say in excuse of theirs, that they were exasperated by the loss of their estates, and it was revenge. They have then had their revenge. *Is it right they should have both?*

Some of those people may have merit in their regard for Britain, and espoused her cause from affection; these it may become you to reward. But there are many of them who were waverers, and were only determined to engage in it by some occasional circumstance or appearances; these have not much of either merit or demerit; and there are others, who have abundance of demerit respecting your country, having by their falsehoods and misrepresentations brought on and encouraged the continuance of the war; these, instead of being recompensed, should be punished.

It is usual among Christian people at war to profess always a desire of peace; but, if the ministers of one of the parties choose to insist particularly on a certain article, which they have known the others are not and cannot be empowered to agree to, what credit can they expect should be given to such professions?

Your ministers require, that we should receive again into our bosom those who have been our bitterest enemies, and restore their properties who have destroyed ours, and this, while the wounds they have given us are still bleeding! It is many years since your nation expelled the Stuarts and their adherents, and confiscated their estates. Much of your resentment against them may by this time be abated; yet, if we should propose it, and insist on it as an article of our treaty with you, that that family should be recalled and the forfeited estates of its friends restored, would you think us serious in our professions of earnestly desiring peace?

Problems of Peace

To Mrs. Mary Hewson. Passy, 27 Jan., 1783.

AT LENGTH we are in peace, God be praised, and long, very long, may it continue. All wars are follies, very expensive, and very mischievous ones. When will mankind be convinced of this, and agree to settle their differences by arbitration? Were they to do it, even by the cast of a die, it would be better than by fighting and destroying each other.

Spring is coming on, when travelling will be delightful. Can you not, when you see your children all at school, make a little party, and take a trip hither? I have now a large house, delightfully situated, in which I could accommodate you and two or three friends, and I am but half an hour's drive from Paris.

To Robert R. Livingston. Passy, 15 April, 1783.

YOU COMPLAIN sometimes of not hearing from us. It is now near three months since any of us have heard from America. I think our last letters came with General de Rochambeau. There is now a project under consideration for establishing monthly packet boats between France and New York, which I hope will be carried into execution; our correspondence then may be more regular and frequent. . . .

A multitude of people are continually applying to me personally, and by letters, for information respecting the means of transporting themselves, families, and fortunes to America. I give no encouragement to any of the King's subjects, as I think it would not be right in me to do it without their sovereign's approbation; and, indeed, few offer from France but persons of irregular conduct and desperate circumstances, whom we had better be without; but I think there will be great emigrations from England, Ireland, and Germany. There is a great contest among the ports, which of them shall be of those to be declared *free* for the *American trade*. Many applications are made to me to interest myself in the behalf of all of them; but having no instructions on that head, and thinking it a matter more properly belonging to the consul, I have done nothing in it.

Literate America

To David Hartley. Passy, 6 Sept., 1783.

ENCLOSED is my letter to Mr. Fox. I beg you would assure him, that my expressions of esteem for him are not mere professions. I really think him a *great* man, and I should not think so, if I did not believe he was at bottom, and would prove himself a *good* one. Guard him against mistaken notions of the American people. You have deceived yourselves too long with vain expectations of reaping advantage from our little discontents. We are more thoroughly an enlightened people, with respect to our political interests, than perhaps any other under heaven. Every man among us reads, and is so easy in his circumstances as to have leisure for conversations of improvement, and for acquiring information. Our domestic misunderstandings, when we have them, are of small extent, though monstrously magnified by your microscopic newspapers. He who judges from them, that we are on the point of falling into anarchy, or returning to the obedience of Britain, is like one who, being shown some spots in the sun, should fancy, that the whole disk would soon be overspread with them, and that there would be an end of daylight. The great body of intelligence among our people, surrounds and overpowers our petty dissensions, as the sun's great mass of fire diminishes and destroys his spots. Do not, therefore, any longer delay the evacuation of New York, in the vain hope of a new revolution in your favor, if such a hope has indeed had any effect in occasioning the delay. It is now nine months since the evacuations were promised. You expect with reason, that the people of New York should do your merchants justice in the payment of their old debts; consider the injustice you do them in keeping them so long out of their habitations, and out of their business, by which they might have been enabled to make payment.

There is no truth more clear to me than this, that the great interest of our two countries is a thorough reconciliation. Restraints on the freedom of commerce and intercourse between us, can afford no advantage equivalent to the mischief they will do, by keeping up ill humor, and promoting a total alienation. Let you and me, my dear friend, do our best towards advancing and securing that reconciliation. We can do nothing, that will in a dying hour afford us more solid satisfaction.

I wish you a prosperous journey, and a happy sight of your friends.

To Mrs. Mary Hewson. Passy, 7 Sept., 1783.

WITH REGARD to the future establishment of your children, which you say you want to consult me about, I am still of opinion, that America will afford you more chances of doing it well than England. All the means of good education are plenty there, the general manners are simple and pure, temptations to vice and folly fewer, the profits of industry in business as great and sure as in England; and there is one advantage more, which your command of money will give you there, I mean the laying out a part of your fortune in new land, now to be had extremely cheap; but which must be increased immensely in value, before your children come of age, by the rapid population of the country. If you should arrive there while I live, you know you may depend on every assistance in my power to afford you, and I think my children will have a pleasure too in serving their father's friend. I do not offer it as a motive, that you will be much esteemed and respected there; for that you are, and must be, everywhere; but give me leave to flatter myself, that my being made happier in my last years by your neighbourhood and society may be some inducement to you.

Hand of Providence

To Josiah Quincy. Passy, 11 Sept., 1783.

. . . CONSIDERING all our mistakes and mismanagements, it is wonderful we have finished our affairs so well, and so soon. Indeed, I am wrong in using that expression, "*we* have finished our affairs so well." Our blunders have been many, and they serve to manifest the hand of Providence more clearly in our favor; so that we may much more properly say, "These are *thy* doings, O Lord, and they are marvellous in our eyes."

. . . The definitive treaty was signed the 3d instant. We are now friends with England and with all mankind. May we never see another war, for in my opinion *there never was a good war, or a bad peace.*

Man's Business

To Thomas Brand Hollis. Passy, 5 Oct., 1783.

I RECEIVED but lately (though sent in June) your most valuable present of the "Memoirs of Thomas Hollis," who was truly, as you describe him in your letter, "a good citizen of the world, and a faithful friend of America." America, too, is extremely sensible of his benevolence and great beneficence towards her, and will ever revere his memory. These volumes are a proof of what I have sometimes had occasion to say, in encouraging people to undertake difficult public services, that it is prodigious the quantity of good that may be done by one man, *if he will make a business of it.*

National Friendships

To David Hartley. Passy, 16 October, 1783.

WHAT would you think of a proposition, if I should make it, of a compact between England, France, and America? America would be as happy as the Sabine girls, if she could be the means of uniting in perpetual peace her father and her husband. What repeated follies are those repeated wars! You do not want to conquer and govern one another. Why then should you be continually employed in injuring and destroying one another? How many excellent things might have been done to promote the internal welfare of each country; what bridges, roads, canals, and other useful public works and institutions, tending to the common felicity, might have been made and established with the money and men foolishly spent during the last seven centuries by our mad wars in doing one another mischief! You are near neighbours, and each have very respectable qualities. Learn to be quiet and to respect each other's rights. You are all Christians. One is *The Most Christian King*, and the other *Defender of the Faith*. Manifest the propriety of these titles by your future conduct. "By this," says Christ, "shall all men know that ye are my disciples, if ye love one another." "Seek peace, and ensue it."

To the President of Congress. Passy, 25 December, 1783

WITH RESPECT to the British court, we should, I think, be constantly upon our guard, and impress strongly upon our minds, that, though it has made peace with us, it is not in truth reconciled either to us, or to its loss of us, but still flatters itself with hopes, that some change in the affairs of Europe, or some disunion among ourselves, may afford them an opportunity of recovering their dominion, punishing those who have most offended, and securing our future dependence. It is easy to see by the general turn of the ministerial newspapers (light things, indeed, as straws and feathers, but like them they show which way the wind blows), and by the malignant improvement their ministers make, in all the foreign courts, of every little accident or dissension among us, the riot of a few soldiers at Philadelphia, the resolves of some town meetings, the reluctance to pay taxes, &c., all which are exaggerated, to represent our government as so many anarchies, of which the people themselves are weary, and the Congress as having lost its influence, being no longer respected; I say it is easy to see from this conduct, that they bear us no good will, and that they wish the reality of what they are pleased to imagine. They have, too, a numerous royal progeny to provide for, some of whom are educated in the military line. In these circumstances we cannot be too careful to preserve the friendships we have acquired abroad, and the union we have established at home, to secure our credit by a punctual discharge of our obligations of every kind, and our reputation by the wisdom of our councils; since we know not how soon we may have a fresh occasion for friends, for credit, and for reputation.

The extravagant misrepresentations of our political state in foreign countries, made it appear necessary to give them better information, which I thought could not be more effectually and authentically done, than by publishing a translation into French, now the most general language in Europe, of the book of Constitutions, which had been printed by order of Congress. This I accordingly got well done, and presented two copies, handsomely bound, to every foreign minister here, the one for himself, the other more elegant for his Sovereign. It has been well taken, and has afforded matter of surprise to many, who had conceived mean ideas of the state of civilization in America, and could not have expected so much political knowledge and sagacity had existed in our wilderness. And from all parts I have the satisfaction to hear, that our constitutions in general are much admired. I am persuaded, that this step will not only tend to promote the emigration to our country of substantial people from all parts of Europe, by the numerous copies I shall disperse, but will facilitate our future treaties with foreign courts, who could not before know what kind of government and people they had to treat with. As, in doing this, I have endeavoured to further the apparent views of Congress in the first publication, I hope it may be approved, and the expense allowed. I send herewith one of the copies.

On Taxes

To Robert Morris. Passy, 25 December, 1783.

THE REMISSNESS of our people in paying taxes is highly blamable; the unwillingness to pay them is still more so. I see, in some resolutions of town meetings, a remonstrance against giving Congress the power to take, as they call it, the people's money out of their pockets, though only to pay the interest and principal of debts duly contracted. They seem to mistake the point. Money, justly due from the people, is their creditors' money, and no longer the money of the people, who, if they withhold it, should be compelled to pay by some law.

All property, indeed, except the savage's temporary cabin, his bow, his matchcoat, and other little acquisitions, absolutely necessary for his subsistence, seems to me to be the creature of public convention. Hence the public has the right of regulating descents, and all other conveyances of property, and even of limiting the quantity and the uses of it. All the property that is necessary to a man, for the conservation of the individual and the propagation of the species, is his natural right, which none can justly deprive him of; but all property superfluous to such purposes is the property of the public, who, by their laws, have created it, and who may therefore by other laws dispose of it, whenever the welfare of the public shall demand such disposition. He that does not like civil society on these terms, let him retire and live among savages. He can have no right to the benefits of society, who will not pay his club towards the support of it.

I am sorry for the public's sake, that you are about to quit your office, but on personal considerations I shall congratulate you; for I cannot conceive of a more happy man, than he, who having been long loaded with public cares, finds himself relieved from them, and enjoying repose in the bosom of his friends and family.

Use of Enemies

To John Jay. Passy, 6 Jan., 1784.

. . . I HAVE, as you observe, some enemies in England, but they are my enemies as an *American;* I have also two or three in America, who are my enemies as a *minister;* but I thank God there are not in the whole world any who are my enemies as a *man;* for by His grace, through a long life, I have been enabled so to conduct myself, that there does not exist a human being who can justly say, "Ben. Franklin has wronged me." This, my friend, is in old age a comfortable reflection. You too have, or may have, your enemies; but let not that render you unhappy. If you make a right use of them, they will do you more good than harm. They point out to us our faults; they put us upon our guard, and help us to live more correctly.

Hereditary Honors

To Mrs. Sarah Bache. Passy, 26 Jan., 1784.

YOUR CARE in sending me the newspapers is very agreeable to me. I received by Captain Barney those relating to the *Cincinnati.* My opinion of the institution cannot be of much importance; I only wonder that, when the united wisdom of our nation had, in the articles of confederation, manifested their dislike of establishing ranks of nobility, by authority either of the Congress or of any particular State, a number of private persons should think proper to distinguish themselves and their posterity, from their fellow citizens, and form an order of *hereditary knights,* in direct opposition to the solemnly declared sense of their country! I imagine it must be likewise contrary to the good sense of most of those drawn into it by the persuasion of its projectors, who have been too much struck with the ribands and crosses they have seen hanging to the buttonholes of foreign officers. And I suppose those, who disapprove of it, have not hitherto given it much opposition,

rom a principle somewhat like that of your good mother, relating to punc-
ilious persons, who are always exacting little observances of respect; "that,
f *people can be pleased with small matters, it is a pity but they should have
hem."*

In this view, perhaps, I should not myself, if my advice had been asked,
lave objected to their wearing their riband and badge themselves according
o their fancy, though I certainly should to the entailing it as an honor on
heir posterity. For honor, worthily obtained (as that for example of our
fficers), is in its nature a *personal* thing, and incommunicable to any but
hose who had some share in obtaining it. Thus among the Chinese, the most
incient, and from long experience the wisest of nations, honor does not
descend, but *ascends.* If a man from his learning, his wisdom, or his valor, is
promoted by the Emperor to the rank of Mandarin, his parents are immediately entitled to all the same ceremonies of respect from the people, that
ire established as due to the Mandarin himself; on the supposition that it
must have been owing to the education, instruction, and good example afforded him by his parents, that he was rendered capable of serving the
public.

This *ascending* honor is therefore useful to the state, as it encourages parents to give their children a good and virtuous education. But the *descending
honor,* to a posterity who could have no share in obtaining it, is not only
groundless and absurd, but often hurtful to that posterity, since it is apt to
make them proud, disdaining to be employed in useful arts, and thence
falling into poverty, and all the meannesses, servility, and wretchedness
attending it; which is the present case with much of what is called the
noblesse in Europe. Or if, to keep up the dignity of the family, estates are
entailed entire on the eldest male heir, another pest to industry and improvement of the country is introduced, which will be followed by all the odious
mixture of pride, and beggary, and idleness, that have half depopulated and
decultivated Spain; occasioning continual extinction of families by the discouragements of marriage, and neglect in the improvement of estates.

I wish, therefore, that the Cincinnati, if they must go on with their project, would direct the badges of their order to be worn by their fathers and
mothers, instead of handing them down to their children. It would be a
good precedent, and might have good effects. It would also be a kind of
obedience to the fourth commandment, in which God enjoins us to *honor*
our father and mother, but has nowhere directed us to honor our children.
And certainly no mode of honoring those immediate authors of our being
can be more effectual, than that of doing praiseworthy actions, which reflect
honor on those who gave us our education; or more becoming, than that of
manifesting, by some public expression or token, that it is to their instruction
and example we ascribe the merit of those actions.

But the absurdity of *descending honors* is not a mere matter of philosophical opinion; it is capable of mathematical demonstration. A man's son,
for instance, is but half of his family, the other half belonging to the family
of his wife. His son, too, marrying into another family, his share in the

grandson is but a fourth; in the great grandson, by the same process, it is but an eighth; in the next generation a sixteenth; the next a thirty-second; the next a sixty-fourth; the next an hundred and twenty-eighth; the next a two hundred and fifty-sixth; and the next a five hundred and twelfth; thus in nine generations, which will not require more than three hundred years (no very great antiquity for a family), our present Chevalier of the Order of Cincinnatus's share in the then existing knight, will be but a five hundred and twelfth part; which, allowing the present certain fidelity of American wives to be insured down through all those nine generations, is so small a consideration, that methinks no reasonable man would hazard for the sake of it the disagreeable consequences of the jealousy, envy, and ill will of his countrymen.

Let us go back with our calculation from this young noble, the five hundred and twelfth part of the present knight, through his nine generations, till we return to the year of the institution. He must have had a father and mother, they are two; each of them had a father and mother, they are four. Those of the next preceding generation will be eight, the next sixteen, the next thirty-two, the next sixty-four, the next one hundred and twenty-eight, the next two hundred and fifty-six, and the ninth in this retrocession five hundred and twelve, who must be now existing, and all contribute their proportion of this future *Chevalier de Cincinnatus*. These, with the rest, make together as follows;

$$
\begin{array}{r}
2 \\
4 \\
8 \\
16 \\
32 \\
64 \\
128 \\
256 \\
512 \\
\hline
\end{array}
$$

Total   1022

One thousand and twenty-two men and women, contributors to the formation of one knight. And, if we are to have a thousand of these future knights, there must be now and hereafter existing one million and twenty-two thousand fathers and mothers, who are to contribute to their production, unless a part of the number are employed in making more knights than one. Let us strike off then the twenty-two thousand, on the supposition of this double employ, and then consider whether, after a reasonable estimation of the number of rogues, and fools, and scoundrels, and prostitutes, that are mixed with, and help to make up necessarily their million of predecessors, posterity will have much reason to boast of the noble blood of the then existing set of Chevaliers of Cincinnatus. The future genealogists, too, of these Chevaliers, in proving the lineal descent of their honor through so many generations (even supposing honor capable in its nature of descending), will only prove the small share of this honor, which can be justly claimed by any one of them; since the above simple process in arithmetic makes it quite plain and clear, that, in proportion as the antiquity of the family shall augment, the right to the honor of the ancestor will diminish; and a few generations more would reduce it to something so small as to be very near an absolute nullity. I hope, therefore, that the Order will drop this part of their project, and content themselves, as the Knights of the Garter, Bath, Thistle, St. Louis, and other Orders of Europe do, with a life enjoyment of their little badge and riband, and let the distinction die with those who have merited it. This I imagine will give no offence. For my own part, I shall think it a convenience, when I go into a company where there may be faces unknown to me, if I discover, by this badge, the persons who merit some particular expression of my respect; and it will save modest virtue the trouble of calling for our regard, by awkward roundabout intimations of having been heretofore employed as officers in the Continental service.

The gentleman, who made the voyage to France to provide the ribands and medals, has executed his commission. To me they seem tolerably done; but all such things are criticized. Some find fault with the Latin, as wanting classical elegance and correctness; and, since our nine universities were not able to furnish better Latin, it was a pity, they say, that the mottos had not been in English. Others object to the title, as not properly assumable by any but General Washington, and a few others, who served without pay. Others object to the *bald eagle* as looking too much like a *dindon*, or turkey. For my own part, I wish the bald eagle had not been chosen as the representative of our country; he is a bird of bad moral character; he does not get his living honestly; you may have seen him perched on some dead tree, where, too lazy to fish for himself, he watches the labor of the fishing-hawk; and, when that diligent bird has at length taken a fish, and is bearing it to his nest for the support of his mate and young ones, the bald eagle pursues him, and takes it from him. With all this injustice he is never in good case; but, like those among men who live by sharping and robbing, he is generally poor, and often very lousy. Besides, he is a rank coward; the little *kingbird*, not bigger than a sparrow, attacks him boldly and drives him out of the district. He is therefore by no means a proper emblem for the brave and honest Cincinnati of America, who have driven all the *kingbirds* from our country; though exactly fit for that order of knights, which the French call *Chevaliers d'Industrie.*

I am, on this account, not displeased that the figure is not known as a bald eagle, but looks more like a turkey. For in truth, the turkey is in comparison a much more respectable bird, and withal a true original native of America. Eagles have been found in all countries, but the turkey was peculiar to ours; the first of the species seen in Europe, being brought to France by the Jesuits from Canada, and served up at the wedding table of Charles the Ninth. He is, besides (though a little vain and silly, it is true, but not the worse emblem for that) a bird of courage, and would not hesitate to attack a grenadier of the British guards, who should presume to invade his farmyard with a *red* coat on.

Political Disorders

To William Strahan. Passy, 16 Feb., 1784.

YOUR ARGUMENTS, persuading me to come once more to England, are very powerful. To be sure, I long to see again my friends there, whom I love abundantly; but there are difficulties and objections of several kinds, which at present I do not see how to get over.

I lament with you the political disorders England at present labors under. Your papers are full of strange accounts of anarchy and confusion in America, of which we know nothing, while your own affairs are really in a deplorable situation. In my humble opinion, the root of the evil lies not so much in too long, or too unequally chosen Parliaments, as in the enormous salaries, emoluments and patronage of your great offices; and that you will never be at rest till they are all abolished, and every place of honor made at the same time, instead of a place of profit, a place of expense and burden.

Good Advice

To Samuel Mather. Passy, 12 May, 1784.

I RECEIVED your kind letter, with your excellent advice to the people of the United States, which I read with great pleasure, and hope it will be duly regarded. Such writings, though they may be lightly passed over by many readers, yet, if they make a deep impression on one active mind in a hundred, the effects may be considerable. Permit me to mention one little instance, which, though it relates to myself, will not be quite uninteresting to you. When I was a boy, I met with a book, entitled *"Essays to do Good,"* which I think was written by your father.* It had been so little regarded by a former possessor, that several leaves of it were torn out; but the remainder gave me such a turn of thinking, as to have an influence on my conduct through life; for I have always set a greater value on the character of a *doer of good*, than on any other kind of reputation; and if I have been, as you seem to think, a useful citizen, the public owes the advantage of it to that book.

You mention your being in your seventy-eighth year; I am in my seventy-ninth; we are grown old together. It is now more than sixty years since I left Boston, but I remember well both your father and grandfather, having heard them both in the pulpit, and seen them in their houses. The last time

* Cotton Mather.

made. Some of those who grow rich will be prudent, live within bounds, and preserve what they have gained for their posterity; others, fond of showing their wealth, will be extravagant and ruin themselves. Laws cannot prevent this; and perhaps it is not always an evil to the public. A shilling spent idly by a fool, may be picked up by a wiser person, who knows better what to do with it. It is therefore not lost. A vain, silly fellow builds a fine house, furnishes it richly, lives in it expensively, and in a few years ruins himself; but the masons, carpenters, smiths, and other honest tradesmen have been by his employ assisted in maintaining and raising their families; the farmer has been paid for his labor, and encouraged, and the estate is now in better hands. In some cases, indeed, certain modes of luxury may be a public evil, in the same manner as it is a private one. If there be a nation, for instance, that exports its beef and linen, to pay for the importation of claret and porter, while a great part of its people live upon potatoes, and wear no shirts, wherein does it differ from the sot, who lets his family starve, and sells his clothes to buy drink? Our American commerce is, I confess, a little in this way. We sell our victuals to the Islands for rum and sugar; the substantial necessaries of life for superfluities. But we have plenty, and live well nevertheless, though, by being soberer, we might be richer. . . .

It has been computed by some political arithmetician, that, if every man and woman would work for four hours each day on something useful, that labor would produce sufficient to procure all the necessaries and comforts of life, want and misery would be banished out of the world, and the rest of the twenty-four hours might be leisure and pleasure.

How America Won

To William Strahan. Passy, 19 August, 1784.

. . . You fairly acknowledge, that the late war terminated quite contrary to expectation. Your expectation was ill founded; for you would not believe your old friend, who told you repeatedly, that by those measures England would lose her colonies, as Epictetus warned in vain his master that he would break his leg. You believed rather the tales you heard of our poltroonery and impotence of body and mind. Do you not remember the story you told me of the Scotch sergeant, who met with a party of forty American soldiers, and, though alone, disarmed them all, and brought them in prisoners? A story almost as improbable as that of the Irishman, who pretended to have alone taken and brought in five of the enemy by *surrounding* them. And yet, my friend, sensible and judicious as you are, but partaking of the general infatuation, you seemed to believe it.

The word *general* puts me in mind of a general, your General Clarke, who had the folly to say in my hearing at Sir John Pringle's, that, with a thousand British grenadiers, he would undertake to go from one end of America to the other, and geld all the males, partly by force and partly by a little coaxing. It is plain he took us for a species of animals very little superior to brutes. The Parliament too believed the stories of another foolish general, I forget his name, that the Yankeys never *felt bold*. Yankey was understood to be a sort of Yahoo, and the Parliament did not think the petitions of such creatures were fit to be received and read in so wise an assembly. What was the consequence of this monstrous pride and insolence? You first sent small armies to subdue us, believing them more than sufficient, but soon found yourselves obliged to send greater; these, whenever they ventured to penetrate our country beyond the protection of their ships, were either repulsed and obliged to scamper out, or were surrounded, beaten, and taken prisoners. An American planter, who had never seen Europe, was chosen by us to command our troops, and continued during the whole war. This man sent home to you, one after another, five of your best generals baffled, their heads bare of laurels, disgraced even in the opinion of their employers.

Your contempt of our understandings, in comparison with your own, appeared to be not much better founded than that of our courage, if we may judge by this circumstance, that, in whatever court of Europe a Yankey negotiator appeared, the wise British minister was routed, put in a passion, picked a quarrel with your friends, and was sent home with a flea in his ear.

But after all, my dear friend, do not imagine that I am vain enough to ascribe our success to any superiority in any of those points. I am too well acquainted with all the springs and levers of our machine, not to see, that our human means were unequal to our undertaking, and that if it had not been for the justice of our cause, and the consequent interposition of Providence, in which we had faith, we must have been ruined. If I had ever before been an atheist, I should now have been convinced of the being and government of a Deity! It is he who abases the proud and favors the humble. May we never forget his goodness to us, and may our future conduct manifest our gratitude.

The Forgotten People

To Benjamin Vaughan. Passy, 21 April, 1785.

WE see much in parliamentary proceedings, and in papers and pamphlets, of the injury the concessions to Ireland will do to the *manufacturers* of England, while the *people* of England seem to be forgotten, as if quite out of the question. If the Irish can manufacture cottons, and stuffs, and silks, and linens, and cutlery, and toys, and books, &c. &c. &c., so as to sell them cheaper in England than the *manufacturers* of England sell them, is not this good for the *people* of England, who are not manufacturers? And will not even the manufacturers themselves share the benefit? Since if cottons are cheaper, all the other manufacturers who wear cottons will save in that article; and so of the rest. If books can be had much cheaper from Ireland (which I believe, for I bought Blackstone there for twenty-four shillings, when it was sold in England at four guineas), is not this an advantage, not to English booksellers, indeed, but to English readers, and to learning?

The Damned Onions

To Jonathan Williams. Passy, 19 May, 1785.

THE conversations you mention respecting America are suitable. Those people speak what they wish; but she was certainly never in a more happy situation. They are angry with us, and speak all manner of evil of us; but we flourish, notwithstanding. They put me in mind of a violent High Church factor, resident in Boston, when I was a boy. He had bought upon speculation a Connecticut cargo of onions, which he flattered himself he might sell again to great profit, but the price fell, and they lay upon hand. He was heartily vexed with his bargain, especially when he observed they began to *grow* in the store he had filled with them. He showed them one day to a friend. "Here they are," said he, "and they are *growing* too! I damn them every day; but I think they are like the Presbyterians; the more I curse them, the more they grow."

Trust in God

To George Whatley. Passy, 23 May, 1785.

. . . I HAVE some reason to wish, that, in a future state, I may not only be *as well as I was*, but a little better. And I hope it; for I, too, with your poet, *trust in God*. And when I observe, that there is great frugality, as well as wisdom, in his works, since he has been evidently sparing both of labor and materials; for by the various wonderful inventions of propagation, he has provided for the continual peopling his world with plants and animals, without being at the trouble of repeated new creations; and by the natural reduction of compound substances to their original elements, capable of being employed in new compositions, he has prevented the necessity of creating new matter; so that the earth, water, air, and perhaps fire, which being compounded form wood, do, when the wood is dissolved, return, and again become air, earth, fire, and water; I say, that, when I see nothing annihilated, and not even a drop of water wasted, I cannot suspect the annihilation of souls, or believe, that he will suffer the daily waste of millions of minds ready made that now exist, and put himself to the continual trouble of making new ones. Thus finding myself to exist in the world, I believe I shall, in some shape or other, always exist; and, with all the inconveniences human life is liable to, I shall not object to a new edition of mine; hoping, however, that the *errata* of the last may be corrected.

The Porcelain Vase

To Francis Maseres. Passy, 26 June, 1785.

I AGREE with you perfectly in the opinion, that, though the contest has been hurtful to both our countries, yet the event, a separation, is better even for yours than success. The reducing and keeping us in subjection by an armed force would have cost you more than the dominion could be worth, and our slavery would have brought on yours. The ancient system of the British empire was a happy one, by which the colonies were allowed to govern and tax themselves. Had it been wisely continued, it is hard to imagine the degree of power and importance in the world that empire might have arrived at. All the means of growing greatness, extent of territory, agriculture, commerce, arts, population, were within its own limits, and therefore at its command.

I used to consider that system as a large and beautiful porcelain vase; I lamented the measures that I saw likely to break it, and strove to prevent them; because, once broken, I saw no probability of its being ever repaired. My endeavours did not succeed; we are broken, and the parts must now do as well as they can for themselves. We may still do well, though separated. I have great hopes of our side, and good wishes for yours. The anarchy and confusion you mention, as supposed to prevail among us, exist only in your newspapers. I have authentic accounts, which assure me, that no people were ever better governed, or more content with their respective constitutions and governments, than the present Thirteen States of America.

A little reflection may convince any reasonable man, that a government wherein the administrators are chosen annually by the free voice of the governed, and may also be recalled at any time if their conduct displeases their constituents, cannot be a tyrannical one, as your Loyalists represent it; who at the same time inconsistently desire to return and live under it. And, among an intelligent, enlightened people, as ours is, there must always be too numerous and too strong a party for supporting good government and the laws, to suffer what is called anarchy. This better account of our situation must be pleasing to your humanity, and therefore I give it you.

But we differ a little in our sentiments respecting the Loyalists (as they call themselves), and the conduct of America towards them, which, you think, "seems actuated by a spirit of revenge; and that it would have been more agreeable to policy, as well as justice, to have restored their estates upon their taking the oaths of allegiance to the new governments." That there should still be some resentment against them in the breasts of those, who have had their houses, farms, and towns so lately destroyed, and relations scalped under the conduct of these royalists, is not wonderful; though I believe the opposition given by many to their reëstablishing among us is owing to a firm persuasion, that there could be no reliance on their oaths;

and that the effect of receiving those people again would be an introduction of that very anarchy and confusion they falsely reproach us with. Even the example you propose, of the English Commonwealth's restoring the estates of the royalists after their being subdued, seems rather to countenance and encourage our acting differently, as probably if the power, which always accompanies property, had not been restored to the royalists, if their estates had remained confiscated, and their persons had been banished, they could not have so much contributed to the restoration of kingly power, and the new government of the republic might have been more durable.

The majority of examples in your history are on the other side of the question. All the estates in England and south of Scotland, and most of those possessed by the descendants of the English in Ireland, are held from ancient confiscations made of the estates of Caledonians and Britons, the original possessors in your island, or the native Irish, in the last century only. It is but a few months since, that your Parliament has, in a few instances, given up confiscations incurred by a rebellion suppressed forty years ago. The war against us was begun by a general act of Parliament, declaring all our estates confiscated; and probably one great motive to the loyalty of the royalists was the hope of sharing in these confiscations. They have played a deep game, staking their estates against ours; and they have been unsuccessful. But it is a surer game, since they had promises to rely on from your government, of indemnification in case of loss; and I see your Parliament is about to fulfil those promises. To this I have no objection, because, though still our enemies, they are men; they are in necessity; and I think even a hired assassin has a right to his pay from his employer. It seems too more reasonable, that the expense of paying these should fall upon the government who encouraged the mischief done, rather than upon us who suffered it; the confiscated estates making amends but for a very small part of that mischief. It is not, therefore, clear, that our retaining them is chargeable with injustice.

I have hinted above, that the name *loyalist* was improperly assumed by these people. *Royalists* they may perhaps be called. But the true *loyalists* were the people of America, against whom they acted. No people were ever known more truly loyal, and universally so, to their sovereigns. The Protestant succession in the House of Hanover was their idol. Not a Jacobite was to be found from one end of the Colonies to the other. They were affectionate to the people of England, zealous and forward to assist in her wars, by voluntary contributions of men and money, even beyond their proportion. The King and Parliament had frequently acknowledged this by public messages, resolutions, and reimbursements. But they were equally fond of what they esteemed their rights; and, if they resisted when those were attacked, it was a resistance in favor of a British constitution, which every Englishman might share in enjoying, who should come to live among them; it was resisting arbitrary impositions, that were contrary to common right and to their fundamental constitutions, and to constant ancient usage. It was indeed a resistance in favor of the liberties of England, which might have been endangered by success in the attempt against ours; and therefore a great man in your Parliament* did not scruple to declare, he *rejoiced that America had resisted.*

Journey Home

To Mrs. Mecom. St. Germain, 13 July, 1785.

I LEFT Passy yesterday afternoon, and am here on my way to Havre de Grace, a seaport, in order to embark for America. I make use of one of the King's litters, carried by mules, which walk steadily and easily, so that I bear the motion very well. I am to be taken on board a Philadelphia ship on the coast of England (Captain Truxtun) the beginning of next month.

Extracts from a Private Journal.

HAVING STAYED in France about eight years and a half, I took leave of the court and my friends, and set out on my return home July 12th, 1785, leaving Passy with my two grandsons at four P.M.; arrived about eight o'clock at St. Germain. M. de Chaumont, with his daughter Sophia, accompanied us to Nanterre. M. Le Veillard will continue with us to Havre. We met at St. Germain the Miss Alexanders, with Mrs. Williams, our cousin, who had provided a lodging for me at M. Benoît's. I found that the motion of the litter, lent me by the Duke de Coigny, did not much incommode me. It was one of the Queen's, carried by two very large mules, the muleteer riding another; M. Le Veillard and my children in a carriage. We drank tea at M. Benoît's, and went early to bed.

Wednesday, July 13th.—Breakfast with our friends; take leave and continue our journey; dine at a good inn at Meulon, and get to Mantes in the evening. A messenger from the Cardinal de la Rochefoucauld meets us there, with an invitation to us to stop at his house at Gaillon the next day; acquainting us at the same time, that he would take no excuse; for, being all-powerful in his archbishopric, he would stop us nolens volens at his habitation, and not permit us to lodge anywhere else. We consented. Lodged at Mantes. Found myself very little fatigued with the day's journey, the mules going only foot pace.

July 14th.—Proceed early, and breakfast at Vernon. Received a visit there from Vicomte de Tilly and his Comtesse. Arrive at the Cardinal's without dining, about six in the afternoon. It is a superb ancient château, built about three hundred and fifty years since; but in fine preservation, on an elevated situation, with an extensive and beautiful view over a well cultivated country. The Cardinal is Archbishop of Rouen. A long gallery contains the pictures of all his predecessors. The chapel is elegant in the old style, with well-painted glass windows. The terrace magnificent. We supped early. The entertainment was kind and cheerful. We were allowed to go early to bed,

William Pitt.

on account of our intention to depart early in the morning. The Cardinal pressed us to pass another day with him, offering to amuse us with hunting in his park; but the necessity we are under of being in time at Havre, would not permit. So we took leave and retired to rest. The Cardinal is much respected and beloved by the people of this country, bearing in all respects an excellent character.

July 15th.—Set out about five in the morning; travelled till ten, then stopped to breakfast, and remained in the inn during the heat of the day. We had heard at the Cardinal's that our friend Mr. Holker, of Rouen, had been out that day as far as Port St. Antoine to meet us, expecting us there from a letter of M. de Chaumont's. Here came to us one of his servants, who was sent to inquire if any accident had happened to us on the road, and was ordered to proceed till he got intelligence. He went directly back, and we proceeded. We passed a chain of chalk mountains, very high, with strata of flints. The quantity that appears to have been washed away on one side of these mountains, leaving precipices of three hundred feet high, gives an idea of extreme antiquity. It seems as if done by the beating of the sea. We got to Rouen about five; were most affectionately received by Mr. and Mrs. Holker. A great company of genteel people at supper, which was our dinner. The chief President of the Parliament and his lady invited us to dine the next day; but being preëngaged with Mr. Holker, we compounded for drinking tea. We lodge all at Mr. Holker's.

July 16th.—A deputation from the Academy of Rouen came with their compliments, which were delivered in form, and a present for me by one of the directors; being a magical square, which, I think he said, expressed my name. I have perused it since, but I do not comprehend it. The Duke de Chabot's son, lately married to a Montmorency, and colonel of a regiment now at Rouen, was present at the ceremony, being just come in to visit me. I forgot to mention that I saw with pleasure in the Cardinal's cabinet, a portrait of this young man's grandmother, Madame la Duchesse d'Enville, who had always been our friend, and treated us with great civilities at Paris; a lady of uncommon intelligence and merit.

I received here also a present of books, 3 vols. 4to., from Dr. ——, with a very polite letter, which I answered.

We had a great company at dinner, and at six went in a chair to the President's, where were assembled some gentlemen of the robe. We drank tea there, awkwardly made, for want of practice, very little being drunk in France. I went to bed early; but my company supped with a large invited party, and were entertained with excellent singing.

July 17th.—Set out early. Mr. Holker accompanied us some miles, when we took an affectionate leave of each other. Dine at Yvetot, a large town, and arrive at Bolbec; being the longest day's journey we have yet made. It is a market town of considerable business, and seems thriving. The people well clad, and appear better fed than those of the wine countries. A linen printer here offered to remove to America, but I did not encourage him.

July 18th.—Left Bolbec about ten o'clock, and arrived at Havre at five P.M., having stopped on the road at a miserable inn to bait. We were very kindly received by M. and Mde. Ruellan. The governor makes us a visit, and some other gentlemen.

July 19th.—We receive visits in form from the intendant, the governor or commandant, the officers of the regiment of Poitou and Picardy, the corps of engineers, and M. Limosin.

M. Limosin proposes several vessels; all very dear. We wait for the packet from Southampton. Dine at M. Ruellan's, where we lodge. Receive the affiliation of the lodge at Rouen.

July 20th.—Return the visits. Receive one from the corps de marine, and one from the corps d'artillerie. M. Houdon arrives and brings me letters. Dine at M. Limosin's. Present M. and Mde. Le Mesurier and their sister, agreeable people of Alderney (Aurigny). Kindly entertained by M. Limosin and his daughter. Return the last visits.

The packet-boat arrives, and, the captain (Jennings) calling at our lodging, we agreed with him to carry us and the baggage we have here for ten guineas, to land us at Cowes. We are to depart to-morrow evening.

July 21st.—We had another visit from M. de Villeneuve, the commandant, inviting us to dine with him to-morrow; but, intending to go off this evening, we could not accept that honor.

Dine with our friendly host and hostess. Mde. Feinés, Mde. de Clerval, and two other ladies visit M. Le Veillard with several gentlemen.

In the evening, when we thought we were on the point of departing, the captain of the packet comes and acquaints us that the wind is right against us, and blows so hard that it is impossible to get out, and we give up the project till to-morrow.

July 22d.—Breakfast and take leave of some friends, and go on board the packet at half after ten. Wind not very fair.

July 23d.—Buffet all night against the north-west wind, which was full in our teeth. This continued till two o'clock to-day, then came fair, and we stand on our course. At seven P.M. we discover land, the Isle of Wight.

July 24th.—We had a fair wind all night, and this morning at seven o'clock, being off Cowes, the captain represented to me the difficulty of getting in there against the flood, and proposed that we should rather run up to Southampton, which we did, and landed there between eight and nine. Met my son, who had arrived from London the evening before, with Mr. Williams and Mr. J. Alexander. Wrote a letter to the Bishop of St. Asaph, acquainting him with my arrival, and he came with his lady and daughter, Miss Kitty, after dinner to see us; they talk of staying here as long as we do. Our meeting was very affectionate. I write letters to London, viz. to Messrs. W. J. M. and Co., to acquaint them with our arrival, and desire to know when the ship will sail, to Mr. Williams. These letters went by post before we knew of his being here. Wrote also to Mr. B. Vaughan.

July 25th.—The Bishop and family lodging in the same inn, the Star, we all breakfast and dine together. I went at noon to bathe in Martin's salt-water hot-bath, and, floating on my back, fell asleep, and slept near an hour by my watch, without sinking or turning! A thing I never did before, and should hardly have thought possible. Water is the easiest bed that can be. Read over the writings of conveyance, &c., of my son's lands in New Jersey and New York to my grandson. Write to M. Ruellan, M. Limosin, M. Holker, and M. Grand. Southampton is a very neat, pretty place. The two French gentlemen, our friends, much pleased with it. The Bishop gives me a book in 4to., written by Dean Paley, and the family dine with us. Sundry friends came to see me from London; by one I receive a present of my friend Dr. Fothergill's works, from Dr. Lettsom, and a book on finance from Mr. Gale. Mr. Williams tells me the ship had fallen down to Gravesend the 22d, so that she might be in the Downs the 24th, and possibly here to-morrow; that is on the Mother Bank, which we can see hence. Mr. Williams brought a letter from Mr. Nepean, secretary to Lord Townshend, addressed to Mr. Vaughan, expressing that orders would be sent to the custom-house at Cowes not to trouble our baggage, &c. It is still here on board the packet that brought it over. Mr. Alexander takes leave for London; write by him to Mr. Jackson, Dr. Jeffries, Dr. Lettsom, and my son-in-law Bache, the latter to be sent by the packet.

July 26th.—Deeds signed between W. Franklin and W. T. Franklin.

Mr. Williams having brought sundry necessaries for me, goes down with them to Cowes, to be ready for embarking. Captain Jennings carries down our baggage that he brought from Havre. My dear friend, M. Le Veillard, takes leave to go with him. Mr. Vaughan arrives from London to see me.

July 27th.—Give a power to my son to recover what may be due to me from the British Government. Hear from J. Williams that the ship is come.

We all dine once more with the Bishop and family, who kindly accept our invitation to go on board with us. We go down in a shallop to the ship. The captain entertains us at supper. The company stay all night.

July 28th.—When I waked in the morning, found the company gone, and the ship under sail.

Tuesday, September 13th.—The wind springing fair last evening, after a calm, we found ourselves this morning at sunrising abreast of the light-house, and between Capes May and Henlopen. We sail into the bay very pleasantly; water smooth, air cool, day fair and fine.

We passed Newcastle about sunset, and went on near to Red Bank before the tide and wind failed, then came to an anchor.

Wednesday, September 14th.—With the flood in the morning came a light breeze, which brought us above Gloucester Point, in full view of dear Philadelphia! when we again cast anchor, to wait for the health officer, who, having made his visit and finding no sickness, gave us leave to land.

My son-in-law came with a boat for us; we landed at Market Street wharf, where we were received by a crowd of people with huzzas, and accompanied with acclamations quite to my door. Found my family well.

God be praised and thanked for all his mercies!

Pleasures of Philadelphia

To Mrs. Mary Hewson. Philadelphia, 6 May, 1786.

I HAVE FOUND my family here in health, good circumstances, and well respected by their fellow citizens. The companions of my youth are indeed almost all departed, but I find an agreeable society among their children and grandchildren. I have public business enough to preserve me from *ennui*, and private amusement besides in conversation, books, my garden, and *cribbage*. Considering our well-furnished, plentiful market as the best of gardens, I am turning mine, in the midst of which my house stands, into grass plots and gravel walks, with trees and flowering shrubs. Cards we sometimes play here, in long winter evenings; but it is as they play at chess, not for money, but for honor, or the pleasure of beating one another. This will not be quite a novelty to you, as you may remember we played together in that manner during the winter at Passy. I have indeed now and then a little compunction in reflecting that I spend time so idly; but another reflection comes to relieve me, whispering, *"You know that the soul is immortal; why then should you be such a niggard of a little time, when you have a whole eternity before you?"* So, being easily convinced, and, like other reasonable creatures, satisfied with a small reason, when it is in favor of doing what I have a mind to, I shuffle the cards again, and begin another game.

As to public amusements, we have neither plays nor operas, but we had yesterday a kind of oratorio, as you will see by the enclosed paper; and we have assemblies, balls, and concerts, besides little parties at one another's houses, in which there is sometimes dancing, and frequently good music; so that we jog on in life as pleasantly as you do in England; anywhere but in London, for there you have plays performed by good actors. That, however, is, I think, the only advantage London has over Philadelphia.

Bad Spelling

To Mrs. Jane Mecom. Philadelphia, 4 July, 1786.

You need not be concerned, in writing to me, about your bad spelling; for, in my opinion, as our alphabet now stands, the bad spelling, or what is called so, is generally the best, as conforming to the sound of the letters and of the words. To give you an instance. A gentleman received a letter, in which were these words,—*Not finding Brown at hom, I delivered your meseg to his yf.* The gentleman finding it bad spelling, and therefore not very intelligible, called his lady to help him read it. Between them they picked out the meaning of all but the *yf*, which they could not understand. The lady proposed calling her chambermaid, because Betty, says she, has the best knack at reading bad spelling of any one I know. Betty came, and was surprised, that neither Sir nor Madam could tell what *yf* was. "Why," says she, "*yf* spells *wife;* what else can it spell?" And, indeed, it is a much better, as well as shorter method of spelling *wife*, than *doubleyou, i, ef, e*, which in reality spell *doubleyifey*.

There is much rejoicing in town to-day, it being the anniversary of the Declaration of Independence, which we signed this day ten years, and thereby hazarded lives and fortunes. God was pleased to put a favorable end to the contest much sooner than we had reason to expect. His name be praised.

On Religion

To Thomas Paine [date uncertain].

I HAVE READ your manuscript with some attention. By the argument it contains against a particular Providence, though you allow a general Providence, you strike at the foundations of all religion. For without the belief of a Providence, that takes cognizance of, guards, and guides, and may favor particular persons, there is no motive to worship a Deity, to fear his displeasure, or to pray for his protection. I will not enter into any discussion of your principles, though you seem to desire it. At present, I shall only give you my opinion, that, though your reasonings are subtile, and may prevail with some readers, you will not succeed so as to change the general sentiments of mankind on that subject, and the consequence of printing this piece will be, a great deal of odium drawn upon yourself, mischief to you, and no benefit to others. He that spits against the wind, spits in his own face.

But, were you to succeed, do you imagine any good would be done by it? You yourself may find it easy to live a virtuous life, without the assistance afforded by religion; you having a clear perception of the advantages of virtue, and the disadvantages of vice, and possessing a strength of resolution sufficient to enable you to resist common temptations. But think how great a portion of mankind consists of weak and ignorant men and women, and of inexperienced, inconsiderate youth of both sexes, who have need of the motives of religion to restrain them from vice, to support their virtue, and retain them in the practice of it till it becomes *habitual*, which is the great point for its security. And perhaps you are indebted to her originally, that is, to your religious education, for the habits of virtue upon which you now justly value yourself. You might easily display your excellent talents of reasoning upon a less hazardous subject, and thereby obtain a rank with our most distinguished authors. For among us it is not necessary, as among the Hottentots, that a youth, to be raised into the company of men, should prove his manhood by beating his mother.

I would advise you, therefore, not to attempt unchaining the tiger, but to burn this piece before it is seen by any other person; whereby you will save yourself a great deal of mortification by the enemies it may raise against you, and perhaps a good deal of regret and repentance. If men are so wicked *with religion*, what would they be *if without it?*

B. FRANKLIN.

Hang the Rogue

To M. Le Veillard. Philadelphia, 15 April, 1787.

You were right in conjecturing that I wrote the remarks on the "Thoughts concerning Executive Justice." I have no copy of those remarks at hand, and forget how the saying was introduced that it was better 1000 guilty persons should escape than one innocent suffer. Your criticisms thereon appear to be just, and I imagine you may have misapprehended my intention in mentioning it. I always thought, with you, that the prejudice in Europe which supposes a family dishonored by the punishment of one of its members, was very absurd, it being, on the contrary, my opinion that a rogue hanged out of a family does it more honor than ten that live in it.

The Convention Dines

To Thomas Jordan, London. Philadelphia, 18 May, 1787.

I RECEIVED your very kind letter of February 27th, together with the cask of porter you have been so good as to send me. We have here at present what the French call *une assemblée des notables*, a convention composed of some of the principal people from the several States of our confederation. They did me the honor of dining with me last Wednesday, when the cask was broached, and its contents met with the most cordial reception and universal approbation. In short, the company agreed unanimously, that it was the best porter they had ever tasted. Accept my thanks, a poor return, but all I can make at present.

I am glad to hear, that Mr. Fitzmaurice is married, and has an amiable lady and children. It is a better plan than that he once proposed, of getting Mrs. Wright to make him a wax-work wife to sit at the head of his table. For after all, wedlock is the natural state of man. A bachelor is not a complete human being. He is like the odd half of a pair of scissors, which has not yet found its fellow, and therefore is not even half so useful as they might be together.

I hardly know which to admire most; the wonderful discoveries made by Herschel, or the indefatigable ingenuity by which he has been enabled to make them. Let us hope, my friend, that, when free from these bodily embarrassments, we may roam together through some of the systems he has explored, conducted by some of our old companions already acquainted with them.

Arithmetic of War

To Mrs. Jane Mecom. Philadelphia, 20 Sept., 1787.

I AGREE with you perfectly in your disapprobation of war. Abstracted from the inhumanity of it, I think it wrong in point of human prudence; for, whatever advantage one nation would obtain from another, whether it be part of their territory, the liberty of commerce with them, free passage on their rivers, &c., &c., it would be much cheaper to purchase such advantage with ready money than to pay the expense of acquiring it by war. An army is a devouring monster, and, when you have raised it, you have, in order to subsist it, not only the fair charges of pay, clothing, provisions, arms, and ammunition, with numberless other contingent and just charges to answer and satisfy, but you have all the additional knavish charges of the numerous tribe of contractors to defray, with those of every other dealer who furnishes the articles wanted for your army, and takes advantage of that want to demand exorbitant prices. It seems to me, that, if statesmen had a little more arithmetic, or were more accustomed to calculation, wars would be much less frequent. I am confident, that Canada might have been purchased from France for a tenth part of the money England spent in the conquest of it. And, if, instead of fighting with us for the power of taxing us, she had kept us in good humor by allowing us to dispose of our own money, and now and then giving us a little of hers, by way of donation to colleges, or hospitals, or for cutting canals, or fortifying ports, she might have easily drawn from us much more by our occasional voluntary grants and contributions, than ever she could by taxes. Sensible people will give a bucket or two of water to a dry pump, that they may afterwards get from it all they have occasion for. Her ministry were deficient in that little point of common sense. And so they spent one hundred millions of her money, and after all lost what they contended for.

I lament the loss your town has suffered this year by fire. I sometimes think men do not act like reasonable creatures, when they build for themselves combustible dwellings, in which they are every day obliged to use fire. In my new buildings, I have taken a few precautions, not generally used; to wit, none of the wooden work of one room communicates with the wooden work of any other room; and all the floors, and even the steps of the stairs, are plastered close to the boards, besides the plastering on the laths under the joists. There are also trap-doors to go out upon the roofs, that one may go out and wet the shingles in case of a neighbouring fire. But, indeed, I think the staircases should be stone, and the floors tiled as in Paris, and the roofs either tiled or slated.

Speech in the Federal Convention on Motion for Opening the Convention with Prayer

MR. PRESIDENT,

The small progress we have made, after four or five weeks' close attendance and continual reasonings with each other, our different sentiments on almost every question, several of the last producing as many *Noes* as *Ayes*, is, methinks, a melancholy proof of the imperfection of the human understanding. We indeed seem to *feel* our own want of political wisdom, since we have been running all about in search of it. We have gone back to ancient history for models of government, and examined the different forms of those republics, which, having been originally formed with the seeds of their own dissolution, now no longer exist; and we have viewed modern states all round Europe, but find none of their constitutions suitable to our circumstances.

In this situation of this assembly, groping, as it were, in the dark to find political truth, and scarce able to distinguish it when presented to us, how has it happened, Sir, that we have not hitherto once thought of humbly applying to the Father of Lights to illuminate our understandings? In the beginning of the contest with Britain, when we were sensible of danger, we had daily prayers in this room for the divine protection. Our prayers, Sir, were heard;—and they were graciously answered. All of us, who were engaged in the struggle, must have observed frequent instances of a superintending Providence in our favor. To that kind Providence we owe this happy opportunity of consulting in peace on the means of establishing our future national felicity. And have we now forgotten that powerful Friend? or do we imagine we no longer need its assistance? I have lived, Sir, a long time; and the longer I live, the more convincing proofs I see of this truth, *that* GOD *governs in the affairs of men.* And, if a sparrow cannot fall to the ground without his notice, is it probable that an empire can rise without his aid? We have been assured, Sir, in the Sacred Writings, that "except the Lord build the house, they labor in vain that build it." I firmly believe this; and I also believe, that, without his concurring aid, we shall succeed in this political building no better than the builders of Babel; we shall be divided by our little, partial, local interests, our projects will be confounded, and we ourselves shall become a reproach and a by-word down to future ages. And, what is worse, mankind may hereafter, from this unfortunate instance, despair of establishing government by human wisdom, and leave it to chance, war, and conquest.

I therefore beg leave to move,

That henceforth prayers, imploring the assistance of Heaven and its blessing on our deliberations, be held in this assembly every morning before we proceed to business; and that one or more of the clergy of this city be requested to officiate in that service.

Speech in the Convention, at the Conclusion of Its Deliberations

MR. PRESIDENT,

I confess, that I do not entirely approve of this Constitution at present; but, Sir, I am not sure I shall never approve it; for, having lived long, I have experienced many instances of being obliged, by better information or fuller consideration, to change opinions even on important subjects, which I once thought right, but found to be otherwise. It is therefore that, the older I grow, the more apt I am to doubt my own judgment of others. Most men, indeed, as well as most sects in religion, think themselves in possession of all truth, and that wherever others differ from them, it is so far error. Steele, a Protestant, in a dedication, tells the Pope, that the only difference between our two churches in their opinions of the certainty of their doctrine, is, the Romish Church is *infallible*, and the Church of England is *never in the wrong*. But, though many private persons think almost as highly of their own infallibility as of that of their sect, few express it so naturally as a certain French lady, who, in a little dispute with her sister, said, "But I meet with nobody but myself that is *always* in the right." "*Je ne trouve que moi qui aie toujours raison.*"

In these sentiments, Sir, I agree to this Constitution, with all its faults,—if they are such; because I think a general government necessary for us, and there is no *form* of government but what may be a blessing to the people, if well administered; and I believe, further, that this is likely to be well administered for a course of years, and can only end in despotism, as other forms have done before it, when the people shall become so corrupted as to need despotic government, being incapable of any other. I doubt, too, whether any other convention we can obtain, may be able to make a better constitution; for, when you assemble a number of men, to have the advantage of their joint wisdom, you inevitably assemble with those men all their prejudices, their passions, their errors of opinion, their local interests, and their selfish views. From such an assembly can a *perfect* production be expected? It therefore astonishes me, Sir, to find this system approaching so near to perfection as it does; and I think it will astonish our enemies, who are waiting with confidence to hear, that our counsels are confounded like those of the builders of Babel, and that our States are on the point of separation, only to meet hereafter for the purpose of cutting one another's throats. Thus I consent, Sir, to this Constitution, because I expect no better, and because I am not sure that it is not the best. The opinions I have had of its *errors* I sacrifice to the public good. I have never whispered a syllable of them abroad. Within these walls they were born, and here they shall die. If every one of us, in returning to our constituents, were to report the objections he has had to it, and endeavour to gain partisans in support of them, we might prevent its being generally received, and thereby lose all the salutary effects and great advantages resulting naturally in our favor among foreign nations, as well as among ourselves, from our real or apparent unanimity. Much of the strength and efficiency of any government, in procuring and securing happiness to the people, depends on *opinion*, on the general opinion of the goodness of that government, as well as of the wisdom and integrity of its governors. I hope, therefore, for our own sakes, as a part of the people, and for the sake of our posterity, that we shall act heartily and unanimously in recommending this Constitution, wherever our influence may extend, and turn our future thoughts and endeavours to the means of having it *well administered*.

On the whole, Sir, I cannot help expressing a wish, that every member of the convention who may still have objections to it, would with me on this occasion doubt a little of his own infallibility, and, to make *manifest* our *unanimity*, put his name to this instrument.

In Praise of Daughters

To Mather Byles, a Clergyman of Boston. Philadelphia, 1 Jan., 1788.

It GIVES me much pleasure to understand, that my points have been of service in the protection of you and yours. I wish for your sake, that electricity had really proved what it was at first supposed to be, a cure for the palsy. It is, however, happy for you, that, when old age and that malady have concurred to enfeeble you, and to disable you for writing, you have a daughter at hand to nurse you with filial attention, and to be your secretary, of which I see she is very capable, by the elegance and correctness of her writing in the letter I am now answering. I too have a daughter, who lives with me and is the comfort of my declining years, while my son is estranged from me by the part he took in the late war, and keeps aloof, residing in England, whose cause he *espoused;* whereby the old proverb is exemplified;

My son is my son till he gets him a wife;
But my daughter's my daughter all the days of her life.

I remember you had a little collection of curiosities. Please to honor with a place in it the enclosed medal, which I got struck in Paris. The thought was much approved by the connoisseurs there, and the engraving well executed.

Boston Remembered

To John Lathrop, a Clergyman of Boston. Philadelphia, 31 May, 1788.

It WOULD certainly, as you observe, be a very great pleasure to me, if I could once again visit my native town, and walk over the grounds I used to frequent when a boy, and where I enjoyed many of the innocent pleasures of youth, which would be so brought to my remembrance, and where I might find some of my old acquaintance to converse with. But when I consider how well I am situated here, with every thing about me, that I can call either necessary or convenient; the fatigues and bad accommodations to be met with and suffered in a land journey, and the unpleasantness of sea voyages, to one, who, although he has crossed the Atlantic eight times, and made many smaller trips, does not recollect his having ever been at sea without taking a firm resolution never to go to sea again; and that, if I were arrived in Boston, I should see but little of it, as I could neither bear walking nor riding in a carriage over its pebbled streets; and, above all, that I should find very few indeed of my old friends living, it being now sixty-five years since I left it to settle here;—all this considered, I say, it seems probable, though not certain, that I shall hardly again visit that beloved place. But I enjoy the company and conversation of its inhabitants, when any of them are so good as to visit me; for, besides their general good sense, which I value, the Boston manner, turn of phrase, and even tone of voice, and accent in pronunciation, all please, and seem to refresh and revive me.

I have been long impressed with the same sentiments you so well express, of the growing felicity of mankind, from the improvements in philosophy, morals, politics, and even the conveniences of common living, and the invention and acquisition of new and useful utensils and instruments; so that I have sometimes almost wished it had been my destiny to be born two or three centuries hence. For invention and improvement are prolific, and beget more of their kind. The present progress is rapid. Many of great importance, now unthought of, will before that period be produced; and then I might not only enjoy their advantages, but have my curiosity gratified in knowing what they are to be. I see a little absurdity in what I have just written, but it is to a friend, who will wink and let it pass, while I mention one reason more for such a wish, which is, that, if the art of physic shall be improved in proportion to other arts, we may then be able to avoid diseases, and live as long as the patriarchs in Genesis; to which I suppose we should have little objection.

I am glad my dear sister has so good and kind a neighbour. I sometimes suspect she may be backward in acquainting me with circumstances in which I might be more useful to her. If any such should occur to your observation, your mentioning them to me will be a favor I shall be thankful for.

The New Constitution

To M. Dupont de Nemours. Philadelphia, 9 June, 1788.

. . . IT WOULD take at least a year to convince thirteen States, that the Constitutions they have practised ever since the Revolution, without observing any imperfections in them so great as to be worth the trouble of amendment, are nevertheless so ill formed as to be unfit for continuation, or to be parts of a federal government. And, when they should be so convinced, it would probably take some years more to make the corrections.

But we must not expect, that a new government may be formed, as a game of chess may be played, by a skilful hand, without a fault. The players of our game are so many, their ideas so different, their prejudices so strong and so various, and their particular interests, independent of the general, seeming so opposite, that not a move can be made that is not contested; the numerous objections confound the understanding; the wisest must agree to some unreasonable things, that reasonable ones of more consequence may be obtained; and thus chance has its share in many of the determinations, so that the play is more like *tric-trac* with a box of dice.

To the Duke de la Rochefoucauld. Philadelphia, 22 Oct., 1788.

OUR public affairs begin to wear a more quiet aspect. The disputes about the faults of the new constitution are subsided. The first Congress will probably mend the principal ones, and future Congresses the rest. That which you mentioned did not pass unnoticed in the Convention. Many, if I remember right, were for making the President incapable of being chosen after the first four years; but the majority were for leaving the electors free to choose whom they pleased; and it was alleged, that such incapacity might tend to make the President less attentive to the duties of his office, and to the interests of the people, than he would be if a second choice depended on their good opinion of him. We are *making experiments* in politics; what knowledge we shall gain by them will be more certain, though perhaps we may hazard too much in *that* mode of acquiring it.

Memories of Paris

To Madame Lavoisier. Philadelphia, 23 Oct., 1788.

IT IS TRUE, as you observe, that I enjoy here every thing that a reasonable mind can desire, a sufficiency of income, a comfortable habitation of my own building, having all the conveniences I could imagine; a dutiful and affectionate daughter to nurse and take care of me, a number of promising grandchildren, some old friends still remaining to converse with, and more respect, distinction, and public honors than I can possibly merit. These are the blessings of God, and depend on his continued goodness; yet all do not make me forget Paris, and the nine years' happiness I enjoyed there, in the sweet society of a people whose conversation is instructive, whose manners are highly pleasing, and who, above all the nations of the world, have, in the greatest perfection, the art of making themselves beloved by strangers. And now, even in my sleep, I find, that the scenes of all my pleasant dreams are laid in that city, or in its neighbourhood.

Who Wins a War?

To John Ingenhousz. Philadelphia, 24 Oct., 1788.

I GRIEVE at the wars Europe is engaged in, and wish they were ended; for I fear even the victors will be losers.

We have no philosophical news here at present, except that a boat moved by a steam engine rows itself against tide in our river, and it is apprehended the construction may be so simplified and improved as to become generally useful.

To M. Le Veillard. Philadelphia, 24 Oct., 1788.

OUR affairs mend daily and are getting into good order very fast. Never was any measure so thoroughly discussed as our proposed new constitution. Many objections were made to it in the public papers, and answers to these objections. Much party heat there was, and some violent personal abuse. I kept out of the dispute, and wrote only one little paper on the occasion, which I enclose. You seem to me to be too apprehensive about our President's being perpetual. Neither he nor we have any such intention. What danger there may be of such an event, we are all aware of, and shall take care effectually to prevent it. The choice is from four years to four years, the appointments will be small; thus we may change our President if we don't like his conduct, and he will have less inducement to struggle for a new election. As to the two Chambers, I am of your opinion, that one alone would be better; but, my dear friend, nothing in human affairs and schemes is perfect, and perhaps that is the case of our opinions.

It must have been a terrible tempest that devastated such an extent of country. I have sometimes thought it might be well to establish an office of insurance for farms against the damage that may occur to them from storms, blight, insects, &c. A small sum paid by a number would repair such losses and prevent much poverty and distress.

Our adventurous merchants are hitherto successful in the East India trade. Perhaps it would be better for us if we used none of the commodities of those countries, but since we do use them, it is an advantage, that we have them cheaper than when they came through Britain. As to the other merchandise she formerly supplied us with, our demand is daily diminishing. Our people are more and more sensible of the mischievous consequences of drinking rum; the leaders of several religious sects have warned their people against it, and the consumption has, this last year, been less by one-third. This will affect her islands. And the restraints she has laid on our trade have contributed to raise a spirit of industry in families, who now manufacture more than ever for themselves, that must lessen greatly the importation.

Embrace for me *bien tendrement* your good dame and children.

I regret the immense quantity of misery brought upon mankind by this Turkish war; and I am afraid the King of Sweden may burn his fingers by attacking Russia. When will princes learn arithmetic enough to calculate, if they want pieces of one another's territory, how much cheaper it would be to buy them, than to make war for them, even though they were to give a hundred years' purchase? But, if glory cannot be valued, and therefore the wars for it cannot be subject to arithmetical calculation so as to show their advantage or disadvantage, at least wars for trade, which have gain for their object, may be proper subjects for such computation; and a trading nation, as well as a single trader, ought to calculate the probabilities of profit and loss, before engaging in any considerable adventure. This however nations seldom do, and we have had frequent instances of their spending more money in wars for acquiring or securing branches of commerce, than a hundred years' profit or the full enjoyment of them can compensate.

Remember me affectionately to good Dr. Price, and to the honest heretic, Dr. Priestley. I do not call him *honest* by way of distinction; for I think all the heretics I have known have been virtuous men. They have the virtue of fortitude, or they would not venture to own their heresy; and they cannot afford to be deficient in any of the other virtues, as that would give advantage to their many enemies; and they have not, like orthodox sinners, such a number of friends to excuse or justify them. Do not, however, mistake me. It is not to my good friend's heresy that I impute his honesty. On the contrary, it is his honesty that has brought upon him the character of heretic.

Imaginary Evils

To Mrs. Jane Mecom. Philadelphia, 26 Nov., 1788.

I AM SORRY you should suffer so much uneasiness with tears and apprehensions about my health. There are in life real evils enough, and it is a folly to afflict ourselves with imaginary ones; and it is time enough when the real ones arrive. I see by the papers that to-morrow is your thanksgiving day. The flour will arrive too late for your plum puddings, for I find it went from hence but a few days since. I hope, however, it will be with you before the winter shuts up your harbour.

I never see any Boston newspapers. You mention there being often something in them to do me honor. I am obliged to them. On the other hand, some of our papers here are endeavouring to disgrace me. I take no notice. My friends defend me. I have long been accustomed to receive more blame, as well as more praise, than I have deserved. It is the lot of every public man, and I leave one account to balance the other.

As you observe, there was no swearing in the story of the poker, when I told it. The late new dresser of it was, probably, the same, or perhaps akin to him, who, in relating a dispute that happened between Queen Anne and the Archbishop of Canterbury, concerning a vacant mitre, which the Queen was for bestowing on a person the Archbishop thought unworthy, made both the Queen and the Archbishop swear three or four thumping oaths in every sentence of the discussion, and the Archbishop at last gained his point. One present at this tale, being surprised, said, "But did the Queen and the Archbishop swear so at one another?" "O no, no," says the relator; "that is only *my way* of telling the story."

For Liberty

To John Wright, London. Philadelphia, 4 Nov., 1789.

I WISH success to your endeavours for obtaining an abolition of the Slave Trade. The epistle from your Yearly Meeting, for the year 1758, was not the *first sowing* of the good seed you mention; for I find by an old pamphlet in my possession, that George Keith, near a hundred years since, wrote a paper against the practice, said to be "given forth by the appointment of the meeting held by him, at Philip James's house, in the city of Philadelphia, about the year 1693"; wherein a strict charge was given to Friends, "that they should set their negroes at liberty, after some reasonable time of service, &c. &c." And about the year 1728, or 1729, I myself printed a book for Ralph Sandyford, another of your Friends in this city, against keeping negroes in slavery; two editions of which he distributed gratis. And about the year 1736, I printed another book on the same subject for Benjamin Lay, who also professed being one of your Friends, and he distributed the books chiefly among them. By these instances it appears, that the seed was indeed sown in the good ground of your profession, though much earlier than the time you mention, and its springing up to effect at last, though so late, is some confirmation of Lord Bacon's observation, that *a good motion never dies;* and it may encourage us in making such, though hopeless of their taking immediate effect.

To David Hartley. Philadelphia, 4 Dec., 1789.

THE convulsions in France are attended with some disagreeable circumstances; but if by the struggle she obtains and secures for the nation its future liberty, and a good constitution, a few years' enjoyment of those blessings will amply repay all the damages their acquisition may have occasioned. God grant, that not only the love of liberty, but a thorough knowledge of the rights of man, may pervade all the nations of the earth, so that a philosopher may set his foot anywhere on its surface, and say, "This is my country."

The English Language

To Noah Webster. Philadelphia, 26 Dec., 1789.

I RECEIVED some time since your "Dissertations on the English Language." The book was not accompanied by any letter or message, informing me to whom I am obliged for it, but I suppose it is to yourself. It is an excellent work, and will be greatly useful in turning the thoughts of our countrymen to correct writing. Please to accept my thanks for the great honor you have done me in its dedication. I ought to have made this acknowledgment sooner, but much indisposition prevented me.

I cannot but applaud your zeal for preserving the purity of our language, both in its expressions and pronunciation, and in correcting the popular errors several of our States are continually falling into with respect to both. Give me leave to mention some of them, though possibly they may have already occurred to you. I wish, however, in some future publication of yours, you would set a discountenancing mark upon them. The first I remember is the word *improved*. When I left New England, in the year 1723, this word had never been used among us, as far as I know, but in the sense of *ameliorated* or made better, except once in a very old book of Dr. Mather's, entitled "Remarkable Providences." As that eminent man wrote a very obscure hand, I remember that when I read that word in his book, used instead of the word *imployed*, I conjectured it was an error of the printer, who had mistaken a too short *l* in the writing for an *r*, and a *y* with too short a tail for a *v*; whereby *imployed* was converted into *improved*.

But when I returned to Boston, in 1733, I found this change had obtained favor, and was then become common; for I met with it often in perusing the newspapers, where it frequently made an appearance rather ridiculous. Such, for instance, as the advertisement of a country-house to be sold, which had been many years *improved* as a tavern; and, in the character of a deceased country gentleman, that he had been for more than thirty years *improved* as a justice of the peace. This use of the word *improved* is peculiar to New England, and not to be met with among any other speakers of English, either on this or the other side of the water.

During my late absence in France, I find that several other new words have been introduced into our parliamentary language; for example, I find a verb formed from the substantive *notice*; *I should not have* NOTICED *this, were it not that the gentleman*, &c. Also another verb from the substantive *advocate*; *The gentleman who* ADVOCATES *or has* ADVOCATED *that motion*, &c. Another from the substantive *progress*, the most awkward and abominable of the three; *The committee, having* PROGRESSED, *resolved to adjourn.* The word *opposed*, though not a new word, I find used in a new manner, as, *The gentlemen who are* OPPOSED *to this measure; to which I have also myself always been* OPPOSED. If you should happen to be of my opinion with respect to these innovations, you will use your authority in reprobating them. . . .

This leads me to mention an old error in our mode of printing. We are sensible, that, when a question is met with in reading, there is a proper variation to be used in the management of the voice. We have therefore a point called an interrogation, affixed to the question in order to distinguish it. But this is absurdly placed at its end; so that the reader does not discover it, till he finds he has wrongly modulated his voice, and is therefore obliged to begin again the sentence. To prevent this, the Spanish printers, more sensibly, place an interrogation at the beginning as well as at the end of a question. We have another error of the same kind in printing plays, where something often occurs that is marked as spoken *aside*. But the word *aside* is placed at the end of the speech, when it ought to precede it, as a direction to the reader, that he may govern his voice accordingly. The practice of our ladies in meeting five or six together to form a little busy party, where each is employed in some useful work while one reads to them, is so commendable in itself, that it deserves the attention of authors and printers to make it as pleasing as possible, both to the reader and hearers.

After these general observations, permit me to make one that I imagine may regard your interest. It is that *your Spelling Book* is miserably printed here, so as in many places to be scarcely legible, and on wretched paper. If this is not attended to, and the new one lately advertised as coming out should be preferable in these respects, it may hurt the future sale of yours.

On Christianity

To Ezra Stiles. Philadelphia, 9 March, 1790.

I RECEIVED your kind letter of January 28th, and am glad you have at length received the portrait of Governor Yale from his family, and deposited it in the College Library. He was a great and good man, and had the merit of doing infinite service to your country by his munificence to that institution. The honor you propose doing me by placing mine in the same room with his, is much too great for my deserts; but you always had a partiality for me, and to that it must be ascribed. I am however too much obliged to Yale College, the first learned society that took notice of me and adorned me with its honors, to refuse a request that comes from it through so esteemed a friend. . . .

You desire to know something of my religion. It is the first time I have been questioned upon it. But I cannot take your curiosity amiss, and shall endeavour in a few words to gratify it. Here is my creed. I believe in one God, the creator of the universe. That he governs it by his Providence. That he ought to be worshipped. That the most acceptable service we render to him is doing good to his other children. That the soul of man is immortal, and will be treated with justice in another life respecting its conduct in this. These I take to be the fundamental points in all sound religion, and I regard them as you do in whatever sect I meet with them.

As to Jesus of Nazareth, my opinion of whom you particularly desire, I think his system of morals and his religion, as he left them to us, the best the world ever saw or is like to see; but I apprehend it has received various corrupting changes, and I have, with most of the present Dissenters in England, some doubts as to his Divinity; though it is a question I do not dogmatize upon, having never studied it, and think it needless to busy myself with it now, when I expect soon an opportunity of knowing the truth with less trouble. I see no harm, however, in its being believed, if that belief has the good consequence, as probably it has, of making his doctrines more respected and more observed; especially as I do not perceive, that the Supreme takes it amiss, by distinguishing the unbelievers in his government of the world with any peculiar marks of his displeasure.

I shall only add, respecting myself, that, having experienced the goodness of that Being in conducting me prosperously through a long life, I have no doubt of its continuance in the next, though without the smallest conceit of meriting such goodness.

Clear Memory

*To Thomas Jefferson. Philadelphia, 8 April, 1790.**

I RECEIVED your letter of the 31st of last past, relating to encroachments made on the eastern limits of the United States by settlers under the British government, pretending that it is the *western,* and not the *eastern* river of the Bay of Passamaquoddy which was designated by the name of St. Croix, in the treaty of peace with that nation; and requesting of me to communicate any facts which my memory or papers may enable me to recollect, and which may indicate the true river, which the commissioners on both sides had in their view, to establish as the boundary between the two nations.

Your letter found me under a severe fit of my malady, which prevented my answering it sooner, or attending, indeed, to any kind of business. I now can assure you, that I am perfectly clear in the remembrance that the map we used in tracing the boundary, was brought to the treaty by the commissioners from England, and that it was the same that was published by Mitchell above twenty years before. Having a copy of that map by me in loose sheets, I send you that sheet which contains the Bay of Passamaquoddy, where you will see that part of the boundary traced. I remember, too, that in that part of the boundary we relied much on the opinion of Mr. Adams, who had been concerned in some former disputes concerning those territories. I think, therefore, that you may obtain still further light from him.

That the map we used was Mitchell's map, Congress were acquainted at the time, by a letter to their Secretary for Foreign Affairs, which I suppose may be found upon their files.

*Written nine days before Franklin's death, at the age of eighty-four.

FRANKLIN'S LAST WILL
AND TESTAMENT

I, BENJAMIN FRANKLIN, of Philadelphia, printer, late Minister Plenipotentiary from the United States of America to the Court of France, now President of the State of Pennsylvania, do make and declare my last will and testament as follows.

To my son, *William Franklin*, late Governor of the Jerseys, I give and devise all the lands I hold or have a right to, in the Province of Nova Scotia, to hold to him, his heirs and assigns for ever. I also give to him all my books and papers, which he has in his possession, and all debts standing against him on my account books, willing that no payment for, nor restitution of, the same be required of him by my executors. The part he acted against me in the late war, which is of public notoriety, will account for my leaving him no more of an estate he endeavoured to deprive me of. . . .

Having since my return from France demolished the three houses in Market Street, between Third and Fourth Streets, fronting my dwelling house, and erected two new and larger ones on the ground, and having also erected another house on the lot which formerly was the passage to my dwelling, and also a printing office between my dwelling and the front houses; now I do give and devise my said dwelling house, wherein I now live, my said three new houses, my printing office and the lots of ground thereto belonging; also my small lot and house in Sixth Street, which I bought of the widow Henmarsh; also my pasture ground which I have in Hickory Lane, with the buildings thereon; also my house and lot on the north side of Market Street, now occupied by Mary Jacobs, together with two houses and lots behind the same, and fronting on Pewter-Platter Alley; also my lot of ground in Arch Street, opposite the church burying ground, with the buildings thereon erected; also all my silver plate, pictures, and household goods, of every kind, now in my said dwelling house, to my daughter, *Sarah Bache,* and to her husband, *Richard Bache,* to hold to them for and during their natural lives, and the life of the longest liver of them. . . .

All the lands near the Ohio, and the lots near the centre of Philadelphia, which I lately purchased of the State, I give to my son-in-law, Richard Bache, his heirs and assigns for ever; I also give him the bond I have against him, of two thousand one hundred and seventy-two pounds, five shillings, together with the interest that shall or may accrue thereon, and direct the same to be delivered up to him by my executors, cancelled, requesting that, in consideration thereof, he would immediately after my decease manumit and set free his negro man Bob. . . .

The King of France's picture, set with four hundred and eight diamonds, I give to my daughter, *Sarah Bache,* requesting, however, that she would not form any of those diamonds into ornaments either for herself or daughters, and thereby introduce or countenance the expensive, vain, and useless fashion of wearing jewels in this country; and those immediately connected with the picture may be preserved with the same.

I give and devise to my dear sister, *Jane Mecom,* a house and lot I have in Unity Street, Boston, now or late under the care of Mr. Jonathan Williams, to her and to her heirs and assigns for ever. I also give her the yearly sum of fifty pounds sterling, during life, to commence at my death, and to be paid to her annually out of the interests or dividends arising on twelve shares, which I have since my arrival at Philadelphia purchased in the Bank of North America. . . .

The philosophical instruments I have in Philadelphia I give to my ingenious friend, Francis Hopkinson. . . .

I give to my grandson, Benjamin Franklin Bache, all the types and printing materials, which I now have in Philadelphia, with the complete letter foundry, which in the whole, I suppose to be worth near one thousand pounds. . . .

With regard to my books, those I had in France and those I left in Philadelphia, being now assembled together here, and a catalogue made of them, it is my intention to dispose of the same as follows. My "History of the Academy of Sciences," in sixty or seventy volumes quarto, I give to the Philosophical Society of Philadelphia, of which I have the honor to be President. My collection in folio of *Les Arts et les Métiers,* I give to the American Philosophical Society, established in New England, of which I am a member. My quarto edition of the same, *Arts et Métiers,* I give to the Library Company of Philadelphia. Such and so many of my books, as I shall mark on the said catalogue with the name of my grandson, *Benjamin Franklin Bache,* I do hereby give to him; and such and so many of my books, as I shall mark on the said catalogue with the name of my grandson, *William Bache,* I do hereby give to him; and such as shall be marked with the name of *Jonathan Williams,* I hereby give to my cousin of that name. The residue and remainder of all my books, manuscripts, and papers, I do give to my grandson *William Temple Franklin.* My share in the Library Company of Philadelphia, I give to my grandson, *Benjamin Franklin Bache,* confiding that he will permit his brothers and sisters to share in the use of it.

I was born in Boston, New England, and owe my first instructions in literature to the free grammar-schools established there. I therefore give one hundred pounds sterling to my executors, to be by them, the survivors or survivor of them, paid over to the managers or directors of the free schools in my native town of Boston, to be by them, or by those person or persons, who shall have the superintendence and management of the said schools, put out to interest, and so continued at interest for ever, which interest annually shall be laid out in silver medals, and given as honorary rewards annually by the directors of the said free schools belonging to the said town, in such manner as to the discretion of the selectmen of the said town shall seem meet.

Out of the salary that may remain due to me as President of the State, I do give the sum of two thousand pounds to my executors, to be by them, the survivors or survivor of them, paid over to such person or persons as the legislature of this State by an act of Assembly shall appoint to receive the same in trust, to be employed for making the river Schuylkill navigable. . . .

I would have my body buried with as little expense or ceremony as may be. I revoke all former wills by me made, declaring this only to be my last.

In witness thereof, I have hereunto set my hand and seal, this [SEAL.] seventeenth day of July, in the year of our Lord one thousand seven hundred and eighty-eight.

B. FRANKLIN.

CODICIL

I, Benjamin Franklin, in the foregoing or annexed last will and testament named, having further considered the same, do think proper to make and publish the following codicil or addition thereto.

It having long been a fixed political opinion of mine, that in a democratical state, there ought to be no offices of profit for the reasons I had given in an article of my drawing in our Constitution, it was my intention when I accepted the office of President, to devote the appointed salary to some public uses. Accordingly, I had already before I made my will in July last, given large sums of it to colleges, schools, building of churches, &c.; and in that will I bequeathed two thousand pounds more to the State for the purpose of making the Schuylkill navigable. But, understanding since, that such a sum will do but little towards accomplishing such a work, and that the project is not likely to be undertaken for many years to come, and having entertained another idea, that I hope may be more extensively useful, I do hereby revoke and annul that bequest, and direct that the certificates I have for what remains due to me of that salary be sold, towards raising the sum of two thousand pounds sterling, to be disposed of as I am now about to order. . . .

I was born in Boston, New England, and owe my first instructions in literature to the free grammar-schools established there. I have, therefore, already considered these schools in my will. But I am also under obligations to the State of Massachusetts for having, unasked, appointed me formerly their agent in England, with a handsome salary, which continued some years; and, although I accidentally lost in their service, by transmitting Governor

Hutchinson's letters, much more than the amount of what they gave me, I do not think that ought in the least to diminish my gratitude.

I have considered, that, among artisans, good apprentices are most likely to make good citizens, and, having myself been bred to a manual art, printing, in my native town, and afterwards assisted to set up my business in Philadelphia by kind loans of money from two friends there, which was the foundation of my fortune, and of all the utility in life that may be ascribed to me, I wish to be useful even after my death, if possible, in forming and advancing other young men, that may be serviceable to their country in both those towns. To this end, I devote two thousand pounds sterling, of which I give one thousand thereof to the inhabitants of the town of Boston, in Massachusetts, and the other thousand to the inhabitants of the city of Philadelphia, in trust, to and for the uses, intents, and purposes hereinafter mentioned and declared.

The said sum of one thousand pounds sterling, if accepted by the inhabitants of the town of Boston, shall be managed under the direction of the selectmen, united with the ministers of the oldest Episcopalian, Congregational, and Presbyterian churches in that town, who are to let out the sum upon interest, at five per cent per annum, to such young married artificers, under the age of twenty-five years, as have served an apprenticeship in the said town, and faithfully fulfilled the duties required in their indentures, so as to obtain a good moral character from at least two respectable citizens, who are willing to become their sureties, in a bond with the applicants, for the repayment of the moneys so lent, with interest, according to the terms hereinafter prescribed; all which bonds are to be taken for Spanish milled dollars, or the value thereof in current gold coin; and the managers shall keep a bound book or books, wherein shall be entered the names of those who shall apply for and receive the benefits of this institution, and of their sureties, together with the sums lent, the dates, and other necessary and proper records respecting the business and concerns of this institution. And, as these loans are intended to assist young married artificers in setting up their business, they are to be proportioned by the discretion of the managers, so as not to exceed sixty pounds sterling to one person, nor to be less than fifteen pounds; and, if the number of appliers so entitled should be so large as that the sum will not suffice to afford to each as much as might otherwise not be improper, the proportion to each shall be diminished so as to afford to every one some assistance. These aids may, therefore, be small at first, but, as the capital increases by the accumulated interest, they will be more ample. And, in order to serve as many as possible in their turn, as well as to make the repayment of the principal borrowed more easy, each borrower shall be obliged to pay, with the yearly interest, one-tenth part of the principal, which sums of principal and interest, so paid in, shall be again let out to fresh borrowers.

And, as it is presumed that there will always be found in Boston virtuous and benevolent citizens, willing to bestow a part of their time in doing good to the rising generation, by superintending and managing this institution gratis, it is hoped, that no part of the money will at any time be dead, or be diverted to other purposes, but be continually augmenting by the interest; in which case there may, in time, be more than the occasions in Boston shall require, and then some may be spared to the neighbouring or other towns in the said State of Massachusetts, who may desire to have it; such towns engaging to pay punctually the interest and the portions of the principal, annually, to the inhabitants of the town of Boston.

If this plan is executed, and succeeds as projected without interruption for one hundred years, the sum will then be one hundred and thirty-one thousand pounds; of which I would have the managers of the donation to the town of Boston then lay out, at their discretion, one hundred thousand pounds in public works, which may be judged of most general utility to the inhabitants, such as fortifications, bridges, aqueducts, public buildings, baths, pavements, or whatever may make living in the town more convenient to its people, and render it more agreeable to strangers resorting thither for health or a temporary residence. The remaining thirty-one thousand pounds I would have continued to be let out on interest, in the manner above directed, for another hundred years, as I hope it will have been found that the institution has had a good effect on the conduct of youth, and been of service to many worthy characters and useful citizens. . . .

All the directions herein given, respecting the disposition and management of the donation to the inhabitants of Boston, I would have observed respecting that to the inhabitants of Philadelphia, only, as Philadelphia is incorporated, I request the corporation of that city to undertake the management agreeably to the said directions; and I do hereby vest them with full and ample powers for that purpose. And, having considered that the covering a ground plat with buildings and pavements, which carry off most of the rain and prevent its soaking into the earth and renewing and purifying the springs, whence the water of the wells must gradually grow worse, and in time be unfit for use, as I find has happened in all old cities, I recommend that at the end of the first hundred years, if not done before, the corporation of the city employ a part of the hundred thousand pounds in bringing, by pipes, the water of Wissahickon Creek into the town, so as to supply the inhabitants, which I apprehend may be done without great difficulty, the level of the creek being much above that of the city, and may be made higher by a dam. I also recommend making the Schuylkill completely navigable. . . .

Considering the accidents to which all human affairs and projects are subject in such a length of time, I have, perhaps, too much flattered myself with a vain fancy, that these dispositions, if carried into execution, will be continued without interruption and have the effects proposed. I hope, however, that if the inhabitants of the two cities should not think fit to undertake the execution, they will, at least, accept the offer of these donations as a mark of my good will, a token of my gratitude, and a testimony of my earnest desire to be useful to them after my departure. . . .

My fine crabtree walking stick, with a gold head curiously wrought in the form of the cap of liberty, I give to my friend, and the friend of mankind, *General Washington*. If it were a sceptre he has merited it; and would become it. It was a present to me from that excellent woman Madame de Forbach, the Dowager Duchess of Deux-Ponts, connected with some verses which should go with it.

I give my gold watch to my son-in-law, Richard Bache, and also the gold watch chain of the thirteen United States, which I have not yet worn. My time-piece, that stands in my library, I give to my grandson, William Temple Franklin. I give him also my Chinese gong. To my dear old friend, Mrs. Mary Hewson, I give one of my silver tankards marked for her use during her life, and after her decease I give it to her daughter Eliza. I give to her son, William Hewson, who is my godson, my new quarto Bible, Oxford edition, to be for his family Bible, and also the botanic description of the plants in the Emperor's garden at Vienna, in folio, with colored cuts.

And to her son, Thomas Hewson, I give a set of Spectators, Tatlers, and Guardians handsomely bound.

There is an error in my will, where the bond of William Temple Franklin is mentioned as being four thousand pounds sterling, whereas it is but for three thousand five hundred pounds.

I give to my executors, to be divided equally among those that act, the sum of sixty pounds sterling, as some compensation for their trouble in the execution of my will; and I request my friend, Mr. Duffield, to accept moreover my French wayweiser, a piece of clockwork in brass, to be fixed to the wheel of any carriage; and that my friend, *Mr. Hill*, may also accept my silver cream-pot, formerly given to me by the good Doctor Fothergill, with the motto, *Keep bright the chain*. My reflecting telescope, made by Short, which was formerly Mr. Canton's, I give to my friend, *Mr. David Rittenhouse*, for the use of his observatory.

My picture, drawn by Martin, in 1767, I give to the Supreme Executive Council of Pennsylvania, if they shall be pleased to do me the honor of accepting it, and placing it in their chamber. . . .

And lastly, it is my desire that this, my present codicil, be annexed to, and considered as part of, my last will and testament to all intents and purposes.

In witness whereof, I have hereunto set my hand and seal this [SEAL.]   twenty-third day of June, Anno Domini one thousand seven hundred and eighty-nine.

B. FRANKLIN.

EPITAPH*

_____

The Body
of
Benjamin Franklin
Printer
(Like the cover of an old book
Its contents torn out
And stript of its lettering and gilding)
Lies here, food for worms.
But the work shall not be lost
For it will (as he believed) appear once more
In a new and more elegant edition
Revised and corrected
by
The Author.

*Written in 1728, when Franklin was twenty-three years old.

SELECTIONS FROM POOR RICHARD'S ALMANAC

Preface, *1733*.

COURTEOUS READER, I might in this place attempt to gain thy favour by declaring that I write Almanacks with no other view than that of the publick good, but in this I should not be sincere; and men are now a-days too wise to be deceiv'd by pretences, how specious soever. The plain truth of the matter is, I am excessive poor, and my wife, good woman, is, I tell her, excessive proud; she cannot bear, she says, to sit spinning in her shift of tow, while I do nothing but gaze at the stars; and has threatned more than once to burn all my books and rattling-traps (as she calls my instruments), if I do not make some profitable use of them for the good of my family. The printer has offer'd me some considerable share of the profits, and I have thus began to comply with my dame's desire. . . .

On this account . . . the buyer of my Almanack may consider himself not only as purchasing an useful utensil, but as performing an act of charity to his poor

Friend and servant,

R. SAUNDERS.

JANUARY.

> Old batchelor would have a wife that's wise,
> Fair, rich, and young, a maiden for his bed;
> Not proud, nor churlish, but of faultless size,
> A country housewife in the city bred.
> He's a nice fool, and long in vain hath staid;
> He should bespeak her, there's none ready made.

Never spare the parson's wine, nor the baker's pudding.

> Visits should be short, like a winter's day,
> Lest you're too troublesome, hasten away.

A house without woman and firelight, is like a body without soul or sprite.

Kings and bears often worry their keepers.

FEBRUARY.

Each age of men new fashions doth invent;
    Things which are old, young men do not esteem:
What pleas'd our fathers, doth not us content;
    What flourished then, we out of fashion deem:
        And that's the reason, as I understand,
        Why Prodigus did sell his father's land.

Light purse, heavy heart.

He 's a fool that makes his doctor his heir.

MARCH.

My love and I for kisses play'd,
    She would keep stakes, I was content,
But when I won, she would be paid,
    This made me ask her what she meant:
        Quoth she, since you are in this wrangling vein
        Here take your kisses, give me mine again.

APRIL.

Kind Katherine to her husband kiss'd these words,
    "Mine own sweet Will, how dearly I love thee!"
If true (quoth Will) the world no such affords.
    And that its true I durst his warrant be:
        For ne'er heard I of woman good or ill,
        But always loved best, her own sweet Will.

Great talkers, little doers.

A rich rogue is like a fat hog, who never does good till as dead as a log.

MAY.

Fools make feasts, and wise men eat them.

The poor have little, beggars none; the rich too much, enough, not one.

Eat to live, and not live to eat.

JUNE.

After three days men grow weary of a wench, a guest, and weather rainy.

To lengthen thy life, lessen thy meals.

The proof of gold is fire; the proof of woman, gold; the proof of man, a woman.

JULY.

Many estates are spent in the getting,
Since women for tea forsook spinning and knitting.

He that lieth down with dogs, shall rise up with fleas.

Tongue double, brings trouble.

AUGUST.

Take counsel in wine, but resolve afterwards in water.

He that drinks fast, pays slow.

Great famine when wolves eat wolves.

SEPTEMBER.

Men and melons are hard to know.

He's the best physician that knows the worthlessness of the most medicines.

A fine genius in his own country, is like gold in the mine.

There is no little enemy.

The heart of the fool is in his mouth, but the mouth of the wise man is in his heart.

OCTOBER.

Time was my spouse and I could not agree,
Striving about superiority:
The text which saith that man and wife are one,
Was the chief argument we stood upon:
She held, they both one woman should become;
I held they should be man, and both but one.
Thus we contended daily, but the strife
Could not be ended, till both were one wife.

Doors and walls are fool's paper.

Anoint a villain and he'll stab you, stab him, and he'll anoint you.

He has lost his boots, but sav'd his spurs.

NOVEMBER.

My neighbour H——y by his pleasing tongue,
Hath won a girl that's rich, wise, fair, and young;
The match (he saith) is half concluded, he
Indeed is wondrous willing; but not she,
And reason good, for he has run thro' all
Almost the story of the prodigal;
Yet swears he never with the hogs did dine;
That's true, for none would trust him with their swine.

Snowy winter, a plentiful harvest.

Nothing more like a fool, than a drunken man.

DECEMBER.

She that will eat her breakfast in her bed,
And spend the morn in dressing of her head,
And sit at dinner like a maiden bride,
And talk of nothing all day but of pride;
God in his mercy may do much to save her,
But what a case is he in that shall have her.

God works wonders now and then;
Behold! a lawyer, an honest man.

He that lives carnally, won't live eternally.

Innocence is its own defence.

Time eateth all things, could old poets say,
The times are chang'd, our times *drink* all away.

THE BENEFIT OF GOING TO LAW.

Two beggars travelling along,
  One blind, the other lame.
Pick'd up an oyster on the way,
  To which they both laid claim:
The matter rose so high, that they
  Resolv'd to go to law,
As often richer fools have done,
  Who quarrel for a straw.
A lawyer took it straight in hand,
  Who knew his business was
To mind nor one nor t'other side,
  But make the best o' th' cause,
As always in the law 's the case;
  So he his judgment gave,
And lawyer-like he thus resolv'd
  What each of them should have;
    Blind plaintif, lame defendant, share
    The friendly law 's impartial care,
    A shell for him, a shell for thee,
    The middle is the *lawyer's fee.*

Preface, 1734.

Courteous Reader. Your kind and charitable assistance last year, in purchasing so large an impression of my Almanacks, has made my circumstances much more easy in the world, and requires my grateful acknowledgement. My wife has been enabled to get a pot of her own, and is no longer obliged to borrow one from a neighbour; nor have we ever since been without something of our own to put in it. She has also got a pair of shoes, two new shifts, and a new warm petticoat; and for my part I have bought a second-hand coat, so good that I am not now ashamed to go to town or be seen there. These things have render'd her temper so much more pacifick than it us'd to be, that I may say, I have slept more and more quietly within this last year, than in the three foregoing years put together. Accept my hearty thanks therefor, and my sincere wishes for your health and prosperity. . . .

I am,

Courteous and kind reader,

Your poor friend and servant,

R. SAUNDERS.

October 30, 1733.

> From a cross neighbour, and a sullen wife,
> A pointless needle, and a broken knife;
> From suretyship, and from an empty purse,
> A smoaky chimney, and jolting horse;
> From a dull razor, and an aking head;
> From a bad conscience, and a buggy bed,
> A blow upon the elbow and the knee;
> From each of these, good L—d, deliver me.

Many dishes, many diseases.
Many medicines, few cures.

Where carcasses are, eagles will gather,
And where good laws are, much people flock thither.

Would you live with ease, do what you ought, and not what you please.

Better slip with foot than tongue.

Blame-all and praise-all are two block heads.

Be temperate in wine, in eating, girls, and sloth, or the gout will seize you and plague you both.

Take this remark from Richard, poor and lame,
Whate'er 's begun in anger, ends in shame.

What one relishes, nourishes.

No man e'er was glorious, who was not laborious.

If you ride a horse, sit close and tight,
If you ride a man, sit easy and light.

A new truth is a truth, an old error is an error,
Tho' Clodpate won't allow either.

Hope of gain lessens pain.

> Wedlock, as old men note, hath likened been,
> Unto a public crowd or common rout;
> Where those that are without would fain get in,
> And those that are within, would fain get out.

> Grief often treads upon the heels of pleasure,
> Marry'd in haste, we oft repent at leisure;
> Some by experience find these words missplaced,
> Marry'd at leisure, they repent in haste.

Do good to thy friend to keep him, to thy enemy to gain him.

Teach your child to hold his tongue, he 'll learn fast enough to speak.

Bucephalus, the horse of Alexander, hath as lasting fame as his master.

He that cannot obey, cannot command.

An innocent plowman is more worthy than a vicious prince.

He that is rich need not live sparingly, and he that can live sparingly need not be rich.

An egg to-day is better than a hen to-morrow.

Necessity has no law; I know some attorneys of the same.

The thrifty maxim of the wary Dutch, is to save all the money they can touch.

A learned blockhead is a greater blockhead than an ignorant one.

Marry your son when you will, but your daughter when you can.

Avarice and happiness never saw each other, how then should they become acquainted.

> By Mrs. Bridget Saunders, my Dutchess, in answer
> to the December verses of last year.

> He that for the sake of drink neglects his trade,
> And spends each night in taverns till 't is late,
> And rises when the sun is four hours high,
> And ne'er regards his starving family,
> God in his mercy may do much to save him,
> But, woe to the poor wife, whose lot it is to have him.

Is 't not enough plagues, wars, and famine, rise to lash our crimes, but must our wives be wise?

> Reader, farewell! all happiness attend thee;
> May each new-year better and richer find thee.

POOR RICHARD FOR 1735.

> Bad commentators spoil the best of books,
> So God sends meat (they say) the devil cooks.

Approve not of him who commends all you say.

By diligence and patience, the mouse bit in two the cable.

Look before, or you'll find yourself behind.

He that goes far to marry, will either deceive or be deceived.

The family of fools is ancient.

Necessity never made a good bargain.

Keep thy shop, and thy shop will keep thee.

The king's cheese is half wasted in parings; but no matter, 't is made of the peoples milk.

On Louis the XIV. of France

> Louis ('t is true, I own to you)
> Paid learned men for writing,
> And valiant men for fighting;
> Himself could neither write nor fight,
> Nor make his people happy;
> Yet fools will prate, and call him great,
> Shame on their noddles sappy.

Of learned fools, I have seen ten times ten; of unlearned wise men, I have seen a hundred.

Three may keep a secret, if two of them are dead.

Sloth and silence are a fool's virtues.

A man is never so ridiculous by those qualities that are his own, as by those that he affects to have.

Deny self for self's sake.

> Little half wits are wondrous pert, we find,
> Scoffing and jeering on whole womankind,
> All false, all whores, all this, and that, and t' other,
> Not one exception left, ev'n for their mother.
> But men of wisdom and experience know,
> That there 's no greater happiness below,
> Than a good wife affords; and such there 's many,
> For every man has one the best of any.

Early to bed and early to rise, makes a man healthy, wealthy, and wise.

To be humble to superiors is duty, to equals courtesy, to inferiors nobleness.

Here comes the orator, with his flood of words, and his drop of reason.

Sal laughs at every thing you say. Why? Because she has fine teeth.

An old young man will be a young old man.

Are you angry that others disappoint you? remember you cannot depend upon yourself.

POOR RICHARD FOR 1736.

Fish and visitors smell in three days.

Diligence is the mother of good luck.

Wealth is not his that has it, but his that enjoys it.

Here comes Courage! that seized the lion absent, and ran away from the present mouse.

He that can have patience can have what he will.

Now I have a sheep and a cow, every body bids me good-morrow.

God helps them that help themselves.

The absent are never without fault, nor the present without excuse.

The rotten apple spoils his companion.

He that speaks much, is much mistaken.

Creditors have better memories than debtors.

Forewarn'd, forearm'd.

> Whymsical *Will* once fancy'd he was ill,
> The Doctor call'd, who thus examin'd *Will;*
> *How is your appetite?* O, as to that
> I eat quite heartily, you see I 'm fat;
> *How is your sleep anights?* 'T is sound and good;
> I eat, drink, sleep, as well as e'er I cou'd.
> *Will,* says the doctor, clapping on his hat,
> I 'll give you something shall remove all that.

Poverty, poetry, and new titles of honour, make men ridiculous.

He that scatters thorns, let him not go barefoot.

God heals and the doctor takes the fee.

I saw few die of hunger, of eating—100,000.

> He that would live in peace and at ease,
> Must not speak all he knows, nor judge all he sees.
> Adieu.

In my last year's Almanack, I mentioned that the visible Eclipses of this year, 1736, portended some great and surprising events relating to these NORTHERN COLONIES, *of which I proposed this year to speak at large. But as those events are not to happen immediately this year, I chuse rather, upon second thought, to defer farther mention of them, till the publication of my Almanack for that year in which they are to happen. However, that the reader may not be entirely disappointed, here follow, for his present amusement, a few*

ENIGMATICAL PROPHECIES,

Which they that do not understand, cannot well explain.

1. Before the middle of this year, a wind at N. East will arise, during which the *water of the sea* and rivers will be in such a manner raised, that great part of the towns of *Boston, Newport, New-York, Philadelphia,* the low lands of *Maryland* and *Virginia,* and the town of *Charleston* in *South Carolina* will be *under water.* Happy will it be for the sugar and salt, standing in the cellars of those places, if there be tight roofs and ceilings overhead; otherwise without being a Conjurer, a man may easily foretell that such commodities will receive damage.

2. About the middle of the year, great number of vessels fully laden, will be taken out of the ports aforesaid, by a power with which we are not now at war, and whose forces shall not be descried or seen, either coming or going. But in the end this may not be disadvantageous to those places.

3. However, not long after, a visible Army of 20,000 *Musketeers* will land, some in Virginia and Maryland, and some in the lower counties on both sides of Delaware, who will over-run the country, and sorely annoy the inhabitants: But the air in this climate will agree with them so ill towards winter, that they will die in the beginning of cold weather like rotten sheep, and by Christmas the inhabitants will get the better of them.

Note,—*In my next Almanack these Enigmatical Prophecies will be explained.*

POOR RICHARD FOR 1737.

HINTS TO THOSE THAT WOULD BE RICH.

The use of money is all the advantage there is in having money.

For 6£ a year you may have use of 100£, if you are a man of known prudence and honesty.

He that spends a groat a-day idly, spends idly above 6£ a year, which is the price of using 100£.

He that wastes idly a groat's worth of his time per day, one day with another, wastes the privilege of using 100£ each day.

He that idly loses 5s. worth of time, loses 5s., and might as prudently throw 5s. into the river.

He that loses 5s. not only loses that sum, but all the other advantage that might be made by turning it in dealing, which, by the time a young man becomes old, amounts to a comfortable bag of money.

Again, He that sells upon credit, asks a price for what he sells equivalent to the principal and interest of his money for the time he is like to be kept out of it;—therefore,

He that buys upon credit pays interest for what he buys,

And he that pays ready money, might let that money out to use; so that

He that possesses any thing he has bought, pays interest for the use of it.

Consider then, when you are tempted to buy any unnecessary household stuff, or any superfluous thing, whether you will be willing to pay *interest, and interest upon interest* for it as long as you live, and more if it grows worse by using.

Yet, in buying goods, 't is best to pay ready money, because,

He that sells upon credit, expects to lose 5 *per cent,* by bad debts; therefore he charges on all he sells upon credit, an advance that shall make up that deficiency.

Those who pay for what they buy upon credit, pay their share of this advance.

He that pays ready money, escapes, or may escape, that charge.

A penny saved is two pence clear. A pin a-day is a groat a-year. Save and have.

Every little makes a mickle.

A traveller should have a hog's nose, deer's legs, and an ass's back.

At the working man's house hunger looks in, but dares not enter.

The worst wheel of the cart makes the most noise.

> To-morrow you 'll reform, you always cry;
> In what far country does this morrow lie,
> That 't is so mighty long ere it arrive?
> Beyond the *Indies* does this morrow live?
> 'T is so far-fetched, this morrow, that I fear
> 'T will be both very old, and very dear.
> To-morrow I 'll reform, the fool does say;
> To-day itself 's too late;—the *wise* did yesterday.

Let the letter stay for the post, and not the post for the letter.

Three good meals a day is bad living.

If you'd have a servant that you like, serve yourself.

He that pursues two hares at once, does not catch one and lets t' other go.

> Women are books, and men the readers be,
> Who sometimes in those books erratas see;
> Yet oft the reader 's raptured with each line,
> Fair print and paper, fraught with sense divine;
> Tho' some, neglectful, seldom care to read,
> And faithful wives no more than bibles heed.
> Are women books? says Hodge, then would mine were
> An Almanack, to change her every year.

The noblest question in the world is, *What good may I do in it?*

In my last I published some *Enigmatical Prophecies*, which I did not expect any one would take for serious predictions. The explanation I promised follows, *viz:*

1. The water of the sea and rivers is raised in vapours by the sun, is form'd into clouds in the air, and thence descends in rain. Now when there is rain overhead (which frequently happens when the wind is at N.E.) the cities and places on the earth below, are certainly *under water*.

2. The power with which *we were not then at war*, but which, it was said, would take many full laden vessels out of our ports before the end of the year, is the WIND, whose forces also *are not descried either coming or going*.

3. The army which it was said would *land* in *Virginia, Maryland,* and the *lower counties* on *Delaware*, were not *Musketeers*, with guns on their shoulders as some expected; but their namesakes, in pronunciation, tho' truly spelt *Moschitos*, arm'd only with a sharp sting. Every one knows they are fish before they fly, being bred in the water; and therefore may properly be said *to land* before they become generally troublesome.

POOR RICHARD FOR 1738.

Preface by Mistress Saunders.

DEAR READERS, My good man set out last week for Potowmack, to visit an old stargazer of his acquaintance, and to see about a little place for us to settle and end our days on. He left a copy of his Almanack seal'd up, and bid me send it to the press. I suspected something, and therefor, as soon as he was gone, I open'd it, to see if he had not been flinging some of his old skitts at me. Just as I thought, so it was. And truly (for want of something else to say, I suppose,) he had put into his preface, that his wife Bridget was this, and that, and t' other. What a pease-cods! cannot I have a little fault or two, but all the country must see it in print! They have already been told, at one time that I am proud, another time that I am loud, and that I have got a new petticoat, and abundance of that kind of stuff; and now forsooth! all the world must know, that *poor Dick's* wife has lately taken a fancy to drink a little tea now and then. A mighty matter truly, to make a song of! 'T is true I had a little tea of a present from the Printer last year; and what, must a-body throw it away? In short, I thought the preface was not worth a-printing, and so I fairly scratch'd it all out, and I believe you 'll like our Almanack never the worse for it.

Upon looking over the months, I see he has put in abundance of foul weather this year; and therefor I have scattered here and there, where I could find room, some *fair, pleasant, sunshiny,* &c., for the good women to dry their clothes in. If it does not come to pass according to my desire, I have shown my goodwill, however; and I hope they 'll take it in good part.

I had a design to make some other corrections; and particularly to change

some of the verses that I don't very well like; but I have just now unluckily broke my spectacles; which obliges me to give it you as it is, and conclude
Your loving friend,
                              BRIDGET SAUNDERS.

You will excuse me, dear readers, that I afford you no eclipses of the moon this year. The truth is, I do not find they do you any good.

When there is one you are apt in observing it to expose yourselves too much and too long to the night air, whereby great numbers of you catch cold. Which was the case last year, to my very great concern. However, if you will promise to take more care of yourselves, you shall have a fine one to stare at the year after next.

There are three faithful friends—an old wife, an old dog, and ready money.

Who has deceiv'd thee so oft as thyself?

> In Christendom we all are *christians* now,
> And thus I answer, if you ask me how;
> Where with *Christ's rules* our lives will not comply,
> We bend it like a rule of lead, say I;
> Making it thus comply with what we be,
> And only thus our lives with th' rule agree.
> But from our fathers we 've the name perchance,
> So as our king is called the king of France.

Read much, but not too many books.

Write with the learned, pronounce with the vulgar.

Fly pleasures, and they'll follow you.

The Old Gentry.

> That all from Adam first begun,
>   Since none but *Whiston* doubts,
> And that his son, and his son's son
>   Were ploughmen, clowns and louts;
> Here lies the only difference now,
>   Some shot off late, some soon;
> Your sires i' th' morning left the plow,
>   And ours i' th' afternoon.

Cæsar did not merit the triumphal car more than he that conquers himself.

If you would not be forgotten, as soon as you are dead and rotten, either write things worth reading, or do things worth the writing.

Sell not virtue to purchase wealth, nor liberty to purchase power.

The ancients tell us what is best; but we must learn of the moderns what is fittest.

Since I cannot govern my own tongue tho' within my own teeth, how can I hope to govern the tongues of others?

If you do what you should not, you must hear what you would not.

As we must account for every idle word, so we must for every idle silence.

Time is an herb that cures all diseases.

Drive thy business;—let not that drive thee.

There is much difference between imitating a good man, and counterfeiting him.

> The wise man says, *it is a wise man's part*
> *To keep his tongue close prisoner in his heart.*
> If he then be a fool whose thought denies
> *There is a God*, how desp'rately unwise,
> How much more fool is he, whose language shall
> Proclaim in public, *there 's no God at all:*
> What then are they, nay fools in what degree,
> Whose actions shall maintain 't?—*Such fools are we.*

Wink at small faults—remember thou hast great ones.

Eat to please thyself, but dress to please others.

POOR RICHARD FOR 1739.

> *Giles Jolt*, as sleeping in his cart he lay,
> Some pilfering villains stole his team away;
> Giles wakes and cries,—What 's here? a dickens, what?
> Why, how now?—Am I Giles? or am I not?
> If he, I 've lost six geldings, to my smart;
> If not, odds buddikins, I 've found a cart.

> When death puts out our flame, the snuff will tell
> If we are wax, or tallow by the smell.

At a great penny worth, pause a while.

As to his wife, *John* minds St. Paul, he 's one that hath a wife, and is as if he 'd none.

Historians relate, not so much what is done, as what they would have believed.

He that falls in love with himself, will have no rivals.

Blessed is he that expects nothing, for he shall never be disappointed.

> What legions of fables and whimsical tales
> Pass current for gospel where priestcraft prevails!
> Our ancestors were thus most strangely deceiv'd,
> What stories and nonsense for truth they believ'd.
> But we their wise sons, who these fables reject,
> Ev'n truth now-a-days, are too apt to suspect;
> From believing too much, the right faith we let fall;
> So now we believe,—'troth,—nothing at all.

Proclaim not all thou knowest, all thou owest, all thou hast, nor all thou can'st.

Let our fathers and grandfathers be valued for *their* goodness, ourselves for our own.

Industry need not wish.

Sin is not hurtful because it is forbidden, but it is forbidden because it is hurtful.

Nor is a duty beneficial because it is commanded, but it is commanded because it is beneficial.

A cure for poetry.—Seven wealthy towns contend for Homer dead,
Thro' which the living Homer beg'd his bread.

POOR RICHARD FOR 1740.

OF THE ECLIPSES FOR 1740.

There will be six Eclipses this year, &c. &c. &c. Some of these Eclipses foreshow great grief and many tears among the soft sex this year; whether for the breaking of their crockery ware, the loss of their loves, or in repentance for their sins, I shall not say: tho' I must own I think there will be a great deal of the latter in the case.—War we shall hear but too much of (for all christians have not yet learn'd to *love one another*), and, I doubt, of some ineffectual treaties of peace. I pray Heav'n defend these Colonies from every enemy; and give them bread enough, peace enough, money enough, and plenty of good cyder.

To bear other people's afflictions, every one has courage and enough to spare.

An empty bag cannot stand upright.

What is a Butterfly?—at best he 's but a catterpillar drest.—The gaudy Fop 's his picture just.

Man's tongue is soft, and bone doth lack;
Yet a stroke therewith may break a man's back.

The poor have little,—beggars none;
The rich too much—enough not one.

There are lazy minds as well as lazy bodies.

Who says Jack is not generous?—he is always fond of giving, and cares not for receiving,—what?—why, *advice*.

Those who in quarrels interpose,
Must often wipe a bloody nose.

When you speak to a man, look on his eyes; when he speaks to thee, look on his mouth.

Observe all men; thyself most.

Thou hadst better eat salt with the philosophers of Greece, *than sugar with the courtiers* of Italy.

Marry above thy match, and thou 'lt get a master.

Fear to do ill, and you need fear nought else.

Employ thy time well, if thou meanest to gain leisure.

A flatterer never seems absurd:
The flatter'd always takes his word.

Lend money to an enemy, and thou 'lt gain him; to a friend, and thou 'lt lose him.

POOR RICHARD FOR 1741.

Learn of the skilful: He that teaches himself, hath a fool for his master.

No wood without bark.

Don't overload gratitude; if you do, she 'll kick.

Be always ashamed to catch thyself idle.

Where yet was ever found the mother,
Who 'd change her booby for another?

At 20 years of age the will reigns; at 30 the wit; at 40 the judgment.

Christianity commands us to pass by injuries; policy, to let them pass by us.

Nature expects mankind should share
The duties of the publick care.

If evils come not, then our fears are vain;
And if they do, fear but augments the pain.

Let no pleasure tempt thee, no profit allure thee, no ambition corrupt thee, no example sway thee, no persuasion move thee, to do any thing which thou knowest to be evil; so shalt thou always live jollily: for a good conscience is a continual Christmas. Adieu.

POOR RICHARD FOR 1742.

He that hath a Trade, hath an Estate.

Have you somewhat to do to-morrow; do it to-day.

No workman without tools,
Nor Lawyer without Fools,
Can live by their Rules.

As honest *Hodge* the Farmer sow'd his Field,
Chear'd with the Hope of future Gain 't would yield,
Two upstart Jacks in Office, proud and vain,
Come riding by, and thus insult the Swain:
You drudge and sweat, and labour here, Old Boy,
But we the Fruit of your hard Toil enjoy.
Belike you may, *quoth Hodge, and but your Due,*
For, Gentlemen, 't is HEMP I 'm sowing now.

Visit your Aunt, but not every Day; and call at your Brother's, but not every night.

Bis dat, qui cito dat.*

Money and good Manners make the Gentleman.

Ill Customs & bad Advice are seldom forgotten.

When Knaves fall out, honest Men get their goods: When Priests dispute, we come at the Truth.

One good Husband is worth two good Wives; for the scarcer things are the more they 're valued.

The Busy-Man's Picture.

BUSINESS, thou Plague and Pleasure of my Life,
Thou charming Mistress, thou vexatious Wife;
Thou Enemy, thou Friend, to Joy, to Grief,
Thou bring'st me all, and bring'st me no Relief,
Thou bitter, sweet, thou pleasing, teazing Thing,
Thou Bee, that with thy Honey wears a Sting;
Some Respite, prithee do, yet do not give,
I cannot with thee, nor without thee, live.

The Reverse.

Studious of Ease, and fond of humble Things,
Below the Smiles, below the Frowns of Kings:
Thanks to my Stars, I prize the Sweets of Life,
No sleepless Nights I count, no Days of Strife.
I rest, I wake, I drink, I sometimes love,
I read, I write, I settle, or I rove;
Content to live, content to die unknown,
Lord of myself, accountable to none.

He that riseth late, must trot all day, and shall scarce overtake his business at night.

He that speaks ill of the Mare, will buy her.

You will be careful, if you are wise; How you touch men's Religion, or Credit, or Eyes.

*He who gives promptly, gives twice as much.

Heb Ddnw heb ddim, a Dnw, a digon.*

They who have nothing to trouble them, will be troubled at nothing.

On him true HAPPINESS shall wait
Who shunning noisy Pomp and State
Those *little* Blessings of the *Great*
       Consults the Golden Mean.
In prosp'rous Gales with Care he steers,
Nor adverse Winds, dejected, fears,
In ev'ry Turn of Fortune bears
       A Face and Mind serene.

Against Diseases here, the strongest Fence,
Is the defensive Virtue, Abstinence.

If thou dost ill, the joy fades, not the pains;
If well, the pain doth fade, the joy remains.

Celia's rich Side-board seldom sees the Light,
Clean is her Kitchen, and her Spits are bright;
Her Knives and Spoons, all rang'd in even Rows,
No Hands molest, nor Fingers discompose:
A curious Jack, hung up to please the Eye,
Forever still, whose Flyers never fly;
Her Plates unsully'd shining on the Shelf;
For *Celia* dresses nothing, *but herself.*

To err is human, to repent divine; to persist devilish.

Money & Man a mutual Friendship show:
Man makes false Money, Money makes Man so.

Among the Divines there has been much Debate,
Concerning the World in its ancient Estate;
Some say 't was once good, but now is grown bad,
Some say 't is reform'd of the Faults it once had:
I say 't is the best World, this that we now live in,
Either to lend, or to spend, or to give in;
But to borrow, to beg, or to get a Man's own,
It is the worst World that ever was known.

Here comes Glib-Tongue: who can out-flatter a Dedication; and lie, like te▶
Epitaphs.

With the old Almanack and the old Year,
Leave thy old Vices, tho' ever so dear.

*Without God without ought, God and enough.

POOR RICHARD FOR 1743.

Men differ daily, about things which are subject to Sense, is it likely then they should agree about things invisible?

The World is full of fools and faint hearts; and yet every one has courage enough to bear the misfortunes, and wisdom enough to manage the Affairs of his neighbour.

Content and Riches seldom meet together,
Riches take thou, contentment I had rather.

The church, the state, and the poor, are 3 daughters which we should maintain, but not portion off.

Cold & cunning come from the north:
but cunning sans wisdom is nothing worth.

On buying a BIBLE.

'T is but a Folly to rejoice, or boast,
How small a Price thy well bought Purchase cost,
Until thy Death, thou shalt not fully know
Whether it was a Pennyworth or no;
And, at that time, believe me 't will appear
Extreamly cheap, or else extreamly dear.

A year of Wonders now behold!
Britons despising *Gallic* Gold!
A Year that stops the *Spanish* Plunders!
A Year that they must be Refunders!
A Year that sets our Troops a marching!
A Year secures our Ships from Searching!
A Year that Charity's extended!
A Year that *Whig* and *Tory 's* blended!
Amazing Year! that we 're defended!

Hear what Jack Spaniard says,
Con todo el Munda Guerra
Y Paz con Ingalatierra.*

If you 'd have it done, Go: If not, send.

Many a long dispute among Divines may be thus abridg'd, It is so: It is not so, It is so; It is not so.

Experience keeps a dear school, yet Fools will learn in no other.

How many observe Christ's Birth-day! How few his Precepts! O! 't is easier to keep Holidays than Commandments.

*With all the world at war, there is peace in England.

Once on a Time it by Chance came to pass,
That a Man and his Son were leading an Ass.
Cries a Passenger, Neighbour, you 're shrewdly put to 't,
To lead an Ass empty, and trudge it on foot.
Nay, quoth the old Fellow, if Folk do so mind us
I 'll e'en climb the Ass, and Boy mount behind us:
But as they jogg'd on they were laugh't and hiss'd,
What, two booby Lubbers on one sorry Beast!
This is such a Figure as never was known;
'T is a Sign that the Ass is none of your own.
Then down gets the Boy, and walks by the Side,
Till another cries, What, you old Fool must you ride?
When you see the poor Child that 's weakly and young
Forc'd thro' thick and thin to trudge it along,
Then down gets the Father, and up gets the Son;
If this cannot please them we ne'er shall have done.
They had not gone far, but a Woman cries out,
O you young graceless Imp, you 'll be hang'd, no doubt!
Must you ride an Ass, and your Father that 's grey
E'en foot it, and pick out the best of his Way?
So now to please all they but one Trick lack,
And that was to carry the Ass a pick pack:
But when that was try'd, it appear'd such a Jest,
It occasioned more Laughter by half than the rest.
Thus he who 'd please all, and their God liking gain,
Shows a deal Good Nature, but labours in vain.

POOR RICHARD FOR 1744.

Who is strong? He that can conquer his bad Habits.

Who is rich? He that rejoices in his Portion.

Without Repentance none to Heav'n can go,
Yet what Repentance is few seem to know:
'T is not to cry out *Mercy*, or to sit
And droop, or to confess that thou hast fail'd;
'T is to bewail the Sins thou didst commit,
And not commit those Sins thou hast bewail'd.
He that *bewails*, and not *forsakes* them too,
Confesses rather what he *means to do*.

If you 'd lose a troublesome Visitor, lend him money.

Tart Words make no Friends: spoonful of honey will catch more flies than Gallon of Vinegar.

Make haste slowly.

Keep thou from the Opportunity, and God will keep thee from the Sin.

As Pride increases, Fortune declines

All other Goods by Fortune's Hand are giv'n,
A WIFE is the peculiar gift of Heav'n.
Vain Fortune's Favours, never at a Stay,
Like empty Shadows, pass, and glide away;
One solid Comfort, our eternal Wife,
Abundantly supplies us all our Life:
This Blessing lasts (if those that try say true)
As long as Heart can wish—and longer too.

Epitaph on a Scolding Wife by her Husband. Here my poor Bridget's Corps doth lie, she is at rest,—and so am I.

POOR RICHARD FOR 1745.

Beware of little Expences, a small leak will sink a great ship.

Wars bring scars.

A light purse is a heavy curse.

It 's common for Men to give pretended Reasons instead of one real one.

He 's a Fool that cannot conceal his Wisdom.

Great spenders are bad lenders.

All blood is alike ancient.

No gains without pains.

POOR RICHARD FOR 1746.

When the well 's dry, we know the worth of water.

He that whines for Glass without G
Take away L and that's he.

A good Wife & Health, is a Man's best Wealth.

A quarrelsome Man has no good Neighbours.

Wide will wear, but narrow will tear.

Silks and sattins put out the kitchen fire.

A Plowman on his Legs is higher than a Gentleman on his Knees.

The generous Mind least regards Money and yet most feels the Want of it.

Dost thou love Life? Then do not squander Time; for that 's the Stuff Life is made of.

Good Sense is a Thing all need, few have, and none think they want.

What 's proper is becoming: See the Blacksmith with his white Silk Apron!

Do me the favour to deny me at once.

Mad Kings and mad Bulls are not to be held by treaties and packthread.

A true great Man will neither trample on a Worm nor sneak to an Emperor.

POOR RICHARD FOR 1747.

Strive to be the greatest Man in your Country, and you may be disappointed; Strive to be the best and you may succeed: He may well win the race that runs by himself.

None know the unfortunate, and the fortunate do not know themselves.

There 's a time to Wink as well as to see.

Honest Tom! you may trust him with a house full of untold Milstones.

There is no Man so bad but he secretly respects the Good.

Pride and the Gout are seldom cur'd throughout.

We are not so sensible of the greatest Health as of the least Sickness.

A good Example is the best Sermon.

He that won't be counsell'd, can't be help'd.

Craft must be at charge for clothes, but Truth can go naked.

Write Injuries in Dust, Benefits in Marble.

What is Serving God? 'T is doing Good to Man.

POOR RICHARD FOR 1748.

Don't after foreign Food and Clothing roam,
But learn to eat and wear what 's rais'd at Home.
Kind Nature suits each Clime with what it wants,
Sufficient to subsist th' Inhabitants.
Observing this, we less impair our Health,
And by this Rule we more increase our Wealth:
Our Minds a great Advantage also gain,
And more sedate and uncorrupt remain.
To lead a virtuous Life, my Friends,
And get to Heaven in Season,
You 've just so much more Need of Faith,
As you have less of Reason.

Knaves & Nettles are akin; stroak 'em kindly, yet they 'll sting.

Life with Fools consists in Drinking; With the wise Man, Living 's Thinking.

> To Friend, Lawyer, Docter, tell plain your whole Case;
> Nor think on Bad Matters to put a good Face:
> How can they advise, if they see but a Part?
> 'T is very ill driving black Hogs in the dark.

Suspicion may be no fault, but showing it may be a great one.

He that 's secure is not safe.

The second Vice is Lying; the first is running in Debt.

The Muses love the Morning.

If Jack 's in love, he 's no Judge of Jill's Beauty.

Most fools think they are only ignorant.

Pardoning the Bad, is injuring the Good.

He is not well bred, that cannot bear Ill-Breeding in others.

In Christmas feasting pray take care;
Let not your table be a Snare;
But with the Poor God's Bounty share.
Adieu, my Friends, till the next year.

POOR RICHARD FOR 1749.

Many Foxes grow grey, but few grow good.

If Passion drives, let Reason hold the Reins.

Neither trust, nor contend, nor lay wagers, nor lend;
And you 'll have peace to your Lives end.

Drink does not drown Care, but waters it, and makes it grow faster.

Who dainties love, shall Beggars prove.

Different Sects like different clocks, may be all near the matter, tho' they don't quite agree.

> Honour the softer Sex; with courteous Style,
> And Gentleness of Manners, win their Smile;
> Nor shun their virtuous Converse; but when Age
> And Circumstance consent, thy Faith engage
> To some discreet, well-natur'd, chearful Fair,
> One not too stately for the Household Care,
> One form'd in Person and in Mind to please,
> To season Life, and all its Labours ease.

If your head is wax, don't walk in the Sun.

Pretty & Witty will wound if they hit ye.

Having been poor is no shame, but being ashamed of it, is.

'T is a laudable Ambition, that aims at being better than his Neighbours.

The wise Man draws more Advantage from his Enemies, than the Fool from his Friends.

All would live long, but none would be old.

9 Men in 10 are suicides.

Doing an Injury puts you below your Enemy; Revenging one makes you but even with him; Forgiving it sets you above him.

POOR RICHARD FOR 1750.

Hunger is the best Pickle.

He is a Governor that governs his Passions, and he a Servant that serves them.

Pay what you owe, and what you 're worth you 'll know.

Sorrow is good for nothing but Sin.

Many a Man thinks he is buying Pleasure, when he is really selling himself a Slave to it.

'T is hard (but glorious) to be poor and honest: An empty Sack can hardly stand upright; but if it does, 't is a stout one!

He that spills the Rum loses that only; He that drinks it, often loses both that and himself.

Little Strokes, Fell great Oaks.

Genius without Education is like Silver in the Mine.

Many would live by their Wits, but break for want of stock.

Poor Plain dealing! dead without Issue.

You can bear your own Faults, and why not a Fault in your Wife.

Tho' Modesty is a Virtue, Bashfulness is a Vice.

Hide not your Talents, they for Use were made. What 's a Sun-Dial in the Shade?

What signifies knowing the Names, if you know not the Natures of Things.

Tim was so learned, that he could name a Horse in nine Languages. So ignorant, that he bought a Cow to ride on.

The Golden Age never was the present Age.

'T is a Shame that your Family is an Honour to you!
You ought to be an Honour to your Family.

Glass, China, and Reputation, are easily crack'd, and never well mended.

POOR RICHARD FOR 1751.

Pray don't burn my House to roast your Eggs.

Some Worth it argues, a Friend's Worth to know; Virtue to own the Virtue of a Foe.

Prosperity discovers Vice, Adversity Virtue.

> Affect not that vain Levity of Thought,
> Which sets Religion, Virtue, all at nought.
> For true Religion like the Sun's blest Beam,
> Darts thro' the conscious Mind a heav'nly Gleam,
> Irradiates all the Soul, no Care allows,
> Calms the best Heart, and smooths the easy Brows.
> Yet think it not enough what 's right to know,
> But let your Practice that right Knowledge show.
> To *Christians* bad rude *Indians* we prefer;
> 'T is better not to know, than knowing err.

Most People return small Favours, acknowledge middling ones, and repay great ones with Ingratitude.

> What will not *Lux'ry* taste? Earth, Sea, and Air,
> Are daily ransack'd for the Bill of Fare.
> Blood stuff'd in Guts is *British* Christian's Food,
> And *France* robs Marshes of the croaking Brood;
> But he had sure a Palate cover'd o'er
> With Brass or Steel, that on the rocky Shore,
> First broke the oozy Oister's pearly Coat,
> And risk'd the living Morsel down his Throat.

Friendship increases by visiting Friends, but by visiting seldom.

If your Riches are yours, why don't you take them with you to t' other World?

'T is great Confidence in a Friend to tell him your Faults, greater to tell him his.

Great Estates may venture more; Little Boats must keep near Shore.

POOR RICHARD FOR 1752.

Kings have long Arms, but misfortune longer: Let none think themselves out of her Reach.

For want of a Nail the Shoe is lost; for want of a Shoe the Horse is lost; for want of a Horse the Rider is lost.

Mankind are very odd Creatures: One Half censure what they practise, the other half practise what they censure; the rest always say and do as they ought.

An undutiful Daughter, will prove an unmanageable Wife.

Old Boys have their Playthings as well as young Ones; the Difference is only in the Price.

Success has ruin'd many a Man.

POOR RICHARD FOR 1753.

Philosophy as well as Foppery often changes Fashion.

A great Talker may be no Fool, but he is one that relies on him.

When Reason preaches, if you don't hear her she 'll box your ears.

The Good-Will of the Govern'd will be starved, if not fed by the good Deeds of the Governors.

Paintings and Fightings are best seen at a distance.

If you would reap Praise you must sow the Seeds, gentle Words and useful Deeds.

Ignorance leads Men into a party, and Shame keeps them from getting out again.

Haste makes Waste.

Many have quarrel'd about Religion, that never practised it.

Sudden Pow'r is apt to be insolent, Sudden Liberty saucy; that behaves best which has grown gradually.

He that is of Opinion Money will do every Thing may well be suspected of doing every Thing for Money.

God, Parents, and Instructors, can never be requited.

HOW TO SECURE HOUSES, &C. FROM LIGHTNING

It has pleased God in his Goodness to Mankind, at length to discover to t'em the Means of securing their Habitations and other Buildings from

Mischief by thunder and Lightning. The Method is this: Provide a small Iron Rod (it may be of the Rod-iron used by the Nailors) but of such a length, that one End being three or four Feet in the moist Ground, the other may be six or eight Feet above the highest Part of the Building. To the upper end of the Rod fasten about a Foot of Brass Wire, the size of a common Knitting-needle, sharpened to a fine Point; the Rod may be secured to the House by a few small Staples. If the House or Barn, be long, there may be a Rod and Point at each End, and a middling Wire along the Ridge from one to the other. A house thus furnished will not be damaged by Lightning, it being attracted by the Points, and passing thro' the Metal into the Ground without hurting anything. Vessels also, having a sharp pointed Rod fix'd on the Top of their Masts, with a Wire from the Foot of the Rod reaching down, round one of the Shrouds, to the Water, will not be hurt by Lightning.

POOR RICHARD FOR 1754.

The First Degree of Folly, is to conceit one's self wise; the second to profess it; the third to despise Counsel.

Take heed of the Vinegar of sweet Wine, and the Anger of Good-nature.

The Bell calls others to Church, but itself never minds the Sermon.

Cut the Wings of your Hens and Hopes, lest they lead you a weary Dance after them.

In Rivers and bad Governments, the lightest Things swim at top.

The Cat in Gloves catches no Mice.

If you 'd know the Value of Money, go and borrow some.

The Horse thinks one thing, and he that saddles him another.

Love your Neighbour; yet don't pull down your Hedge.

Some make Conscience of wearing a Hat in the Church, who make none of robbing the Altar.

Friendship cannot live with Ceremony, nor without Civility.

Praise little, dispraise less.

The learned Fool writes his Nonsense in better Language than the unlearned; but still 't is Nonsense.

A Child thinks 20 Shillings and 20 Years can scarce ever be spent.

Don't think so much of your own Cunning, as to forget other Men's: A Cunning Man is overmatched by a cunning Man and a Half.

Willows are weak, but they bind the Faggot.

You may give a Man an Office, but you cannot give him Discretion.

Little Rogues easily become great Ones.

Many Princes sin with David, but few repent with him.

POOR RICHARD FOR 1755.

Where there is Hunger, Law is not regarded; and where Law is not regarded, there will be Hunger.

Two dry Sticks will burn a green One.

The honest Man takes Pains, and then enjoys Pleasures; the knave takes Pleasure, and then suffers Pains.

Think of three Things, whence you came, where you are going, and to whom you must account.

There was never a good knife made of bad Steel.

Who is wise? He that learns from every One.
Who is powerful? He that governs his Passions.
Who is rich? He that is content.
Who is that? Nobody.

The Master's Eye will do more Work than both his Hands.

When you taste Honey, remember Gall.

Being ignorant is not so much a Shame, as being unwilling to learn.

POOR RICHARD FOR 1756.

A Change of Fortune hurts a wise Man no more than a Change of the Moon.

Love your Enemies, for they tell you your Faults.

The Wit of Conversation consists more in finding it in others, than shewing a great deal yourself. He who goes out of your Company pleased with his own Facetiousness and Ingenuity, will the sooner come into it again. Most men had rather *please* than *admire* you, and seek less to be *instructed* and *diverted*, than *approved* and *applauded*, and it is certainly the most delicate Sort of Pleasure, to *please another*.

But that sort of *Wit*, which employs itself insolently in Criticizing and Censuring the Words and Sentiments of others in Conversation, is absolute *Folly;* for it answers none of the Ends of Conversation. He who uses it neither *improves others*, is *improved* himself, or pleases any one.

Be civil to all; sociable to many; familiar with few; Friend to one; enemy to none.

Vain-glory flowereth, but beareth no Fruit.

Laws too gentle are seldom obeyed; too severe, seldom executed.

Trouble springs from Idleness; Toil from Ease.

Love and be loved.

A wise Man will desire no more than what he may get justly, use soberly, distribute chearfully and leave contentedly.

It is observable that God has often called Men to Places of Dignity and Honour, when they have been busy in the honest Employment of their Vocation. *Saul* was seeking his Father's Asses, and *David* keeping his Father's Sheep, when called to the kingdom. The Shepherds were feeding their Flocks, when they had their glorious Revelation. God called the four Apostles from their Fishery, and *Matthew* from the Receipt of Custom; *Amos* from among the Horsemen of *Tekoah*, *Moses* from keeping *Jethro's* Sheep, *Gideon* from the Threshing Floor, etc. God never encourages Idleness, and despises not Persons in the meanest Employments.

Laziness travels so slowly that Poverty soon overtakes him.

Sampson with his strong Body, had a weak Head, or he would not have laid it in a Harlot's lap.

POOR RICHARD FOR 1757.

He that would rise at Court, must begin by creeping.

Many a Man's own Tongue gives Evidence against his Understanding.

Nothing dries sooner than a Tear.

ON THE FREEDOM OF THE PRESS.

> While free from Force the Press remains,
> Virtue and Freedom chear our Plains,
> And Learning Largesses bestows,
> And keeps unlicens'd open House.
> We to the Nation's publick Mart
> Our Works of Wit, and Schemes of Art,
> And philosophic Goods, this Way,
> Like Water carriage, cheap convey.
> This Tree which Knowledge so affords,
> Inquisitors with flaming Swords
> From Lay-Approach with Zeal defend,
> Lest their own Paradise should end. . . .
>
> This Nurse of Arts, and Freedom's Fence,
> To chain, is Treason against Sense:
> And Liberty, thy thousand Tongues
> None silence who design no Wrongs;
> For those who use the Gag's Restraint,
> First Rob, before they stop Complaint.

Singularity in the right, hath ruined many: Happy those who are convinced of the general Opinion.

POOR RICHARD FOR 1758.

Fools need Advice most, but wise Men only are the better for it.

Half the Truth is often a great Lie.

The Morning Daylight appears plainer when you put out your Candle.

In a corrupt Age, the putting the World in order would breed Confusion; then e'en mind your own Business.

To serve the Publick faithfully, and at the same time please it entirely is impracticable.

Proud Modern Learning despises the antient: School-men are now laught at by school-boys.

Men often mistake themselves, seldom forget themselves.

Rob not God, nor the Poor, lest thou ruin thyself; The Eagle snatcht a Coal from the Altar, but it fired her Nest.

With bounteous cheer
Conclude the Year.

JEFFERSON ON FRANKLIN

_____

To Robert Walsh, Monticello. December 4, 1818.

DEAR SIR,—Yours of November the 8th has been some time received; but it is in my power to give little satisfaction as to its inquiries. Dr. Franklin had many political enemies, as every character must, which, with decision enough to have opinions, has energy and talent to give them effect on the feelings of the adversary opinion. These enmities were chiefly in Pennsylvania and Massachusetts. In the former, they were merely of the proprietary party. In the latter, they did not commence till the Revolution, and then sprung chiefly from personal animosities, which spreading by little and little, became at length of some extent. Dr. Lee was his principal calumniator, a man of much malignity, who, besides enlisting his whole family in the same hostility, was enabled, as the agent of Massachusetts with the British government, to infuse it into that State with considerable effect. Mr. Izard, the Doctor's enemy also, but from a pecuniary transaction, never countenanced these charges against him. Mr. Jay Silas Deane, Mr. Laurens, his colleagues also, ever maintained towards him unlimited confidence and respect. That he would have waived the formal recognition of our independence, I never heard on any authority worthy notice. As to the fisheries, England was urgent to retain them exclusively, France neutral, and I believe, that had they been ultimately made a *sine qua non*, our commissioners (Mr. Adams excepted) would have relinquished them, rather than have broken off the treaty. To Mr. Adams' perseverance alone, on that point, I have always understood we were indebted for their reservation. As to the charge of subservience to France, besides the evidence of his friendly colleagues before named, two years of my own service with him at Paris, daily visits, and the most friendly and confidential conversation, convince me it had not a shadow of foundation. He possessed the confidence of that government in the highest degree, insomuch, that it may truly be said, that they were more under his influence, than he under theirs. The fact is, that his temper was so amiable and conciliatory, his conduct so rational, never urging impossibilities, or even things unreasonably inconvenient to them, in short, so moderate and attentive to their difficulties, as well as our own, that what his enemies called subserviency, I saw was only that reasonable disposition, which, sensible that advantages are not all to be on one side, yielding what is just and liberal, is the more certain of obtaining liberality and justice. Mutual confidence produces, of course, mutual influence, and this was all which subsisted between Dr. Franklin and the government of France.

I state a few anecdotes of Dr. Franklin, within my own knowledge, too much in detail for the scale of Delaplaine's work:

Our revolutionary process, as is well known, commenced by petitions, memorials, remonstrances, etc., from the old Congress. These were followed by a non-importation agreement, as a pacific instrument of coercion. While that was before us, and sundry exceptions, as of arms, ammunition, etc., were moved from different quarters of the house, I was sitting by Dr. Franklin and observed to him that I thought we should except books; that we ought not to exclude science, even coming from an enemy. He thought so too, and I proposed the exception, which was agreed to. Soon after it occurred that medicine should be excepted, and I suggested that also to the Doctor. "As to that," said he, "I will tell you a story. When I was in London, in such a year, there was a weekly club of physicians, of which Sir John Pringle was president, and I was invited by my friend Dr. Fothergill to attend when convenient. Their rule was to propose a thesis one week and discuss it the next. I happened there when the question to be considered was whether physicians had, on the whole, done most good or harm? The young members, particularly, having discussed it very learnedly and eloquently till the subject was exhausted, one of them observed to Sir John Pringle, that although it was not usual for the President to take part in a debate, yet they were desirous to know his opinion on the question. He said they must first tell him whether, under the appellation of physicians, they meant to include *old women*, if they did he thought they had done more good than harm, otherwise more harm than good." . . .

When Dr. Franklin went to France, on his revolutionary mission, his eminence as a philosopher, his venerable appearance, and the cause on which he was sent, rendered him extremely popular. For all ranks and conditions of men there, entered warmly into the American interest. He was, therefore, feasted and invited into all the court parties. At these he sometimes met the old Duchess of Bourbon, who, being a chess player of about his force, they very generally played together. Happening once to put her king into prize, the Doctor took it. "Ah," said she, "we do not take kings so." "We do in America," said the Doctor.

At one of these parties the Emperor Joseph III, then at Paris, incog., under the title of Count Falkenstein, was overlooking the game in silence, while the company was engaged in animated conversations on the American question. "How happens it M. le Comte," said the Duchess, "that while we all feel so much interest in the cause of the Americans, you say nothing for them?" "I am a king by trade," said he.

When the Declaration of Independence was under the consideration of Congress, there were two or three unlucky expressions in it which gave offence to some members. The words "Scotch and other foreign auxiliaries" excited the ire of a gentleman or two of that country. Severe strictures on the conduct of the British king, in negotiating our repeated repeals of the law which permitted the importation of slaves, were disapproved by some Southern gentlemen, whose reflections were not yet matured to the full abhorrence of that traffic. Although the offensive expressions were immediately yielded these gentlemen continued their depredations on other parts of the instrument. I was sitting by Dr. Franklin, who perceived that I was not insensible to these mutilations. "I have made it a rule," said he, "whenever in my power, to avoid becoming the draughtsman of papers to be reviewed by a public body. I took my lesson from an incident which I will relate to you. When I was a journeyman printer, one of my companions, an apprentice hatter, having served out his time, was about to open shop for himself. His first concern was to have a handsome signboard, with a proper inscription. He composed it in these words, 'John Thompson, *Hatter*, *makes* and *sells hats* for ready money,' with a figure of a hat subjoined; but he thought he would submit it to his friends for their amendments. The first he showed it to thought the word '*Hatter*' tautologous, because followed by the words 'makes hats,' which show he was a hatter. It was struck out. The next observed that the word '*makes*' might as well be omitted, because his customers would not care who made the hats. If good and to their mind, they would buy, by whomsoever made. He struck it out. A third said he thought the words '*for ready money*' were useless, as it was not the custom of the place to sell on credit. Every one who purchased expected to pay. They were parted with, and the inscription now stood, 'John Thompson sells hats.' '*Sells hats!*' says his next friend. 'Why nobody will expect you to give them away, what then is the use of that word?' It was stricken out, and '*hats*' followed it, the rather as there was one painted on the board. So the inscription was reduced ultimately to 'John Thompson' with the figure of a hat subjoined."

The Doctor and Silas Deane were in conversation one day at Passy, on the numerous errors in the Abbé's *Histoire des deux Indes*, when he happened to step in. After the usual salutations, Silas Deane said to him, "The Doctor and myself, Abbé, were just speaking of the errors of fact into which you have been led in your history." "Oh, no Sir," said the Abbé, "that is impossible. I took the greatest care not to insert a single fact, for which I had not the most unquestionable authority." "Why," says Deane, "there is the story of Polly Baker, and the eloquent apology you have put into her mouth, when brought before a court of Massachusetts to suffer punishment under a law which you cite, for having had a bastard. I know there never was such a law in Massachusetts." "Be assured," said the Abbé, "you are mistaken, and that that is a true story. I do not immediately recollect indeed the particular information on which I quote it; but I am certain that I had for it unquestionable authority." Doctor Franklin, who had been for some time shaking with unrestrained laughter at the Abbé's confidence in his authority for that tale, said, "I will tell you, Abbé, the origin of that story. When I was a printer and editor of a newspaper, we were sometimes slack of news, and to amuse our customers, I used to fill up our vacant columns with anecdotes and fables, and fancies of my own, and this of Polly Baker is a story of my making, on one of these occasions." The Abbé, without the least disconcert, exclaimed with a laugh, "Oh, very well, Doctor, I had rather relate your stories than other men's truths."